CORPORATE SOCIAL RESPONSIBILITY AND CANADA'S ROLE IN AFRICA'S EXTRACTIVE SECTORS

Africa's natural resource sectors are experiencing unprecedented levels of foreign investment and production. Hailed as a means of reducing poverty and reliance on foreign aid, the role of foreign corporations in Africa's extractive sector is not well understood, and important questions remain about the impact of such activities on people and on the environment.

With reference to global governance initiatives aimed at promoting ethical business practices, this volume offers a timely examination of Canada-Africa relations and natural resource governance. Few Canadians realize how significant a role their country plays in investing in Africa's natural resource sector. The editors and contributors consider the interplay between public opinion, corporate social responsibility, and debates about the extraction and trade of Africa's natural resources.

NATHAN ANDREWS is an assistant professor in the Department of Global and International Studies at the University of Northern British Columbia.

J. ANDREW GRANT is an associate professor in the Department of Political Studies at Queen's University.

Corporate Social Responsibility and Canada's Role in Africa's Extractive Sectors

EDITED BY NATHAN ANDREWS
AND J. ANDREW GRANT

UNIVERSITY OF TORONTO PRESS
Toronto Buffalo London

ISBN 978-1-4875-0308-6 (cloth)   ISBN 978-1-4875-1704-5 (EPUB)
ISBN 978-1-4875-2245-2 (paper)   ISBN 978-1-4875-1703-8 (PDF)

Library and Archives Canada Cataloguing in Publication

Title: Corporate social responsibility and Canada's role in Africa's extractive
    sectors / edited by Nathan Andrews and J. Andrew Grant.
Names: Andrews, Nathan, editor. | Grant, J. Andrew, 1974– editor.
Description: Includes bibliographical references and index.
Identifiers: Canadiana 20190151986 | ISBN 9781487522452 (paper) |
    ISBN 9781487503086 (cloth)
Subjects: LCSH: Social responsibility of business – Africa. | LCSH:
    Natural resources – Africa. | LCSH: Canada – Foreign economic
    relations – Africa. | LCSH: Africa – Foreign economic relations –
    Canada.
Classification: LCC HD60.5.A35 C67 2020 | DDC 658.4/08096–dc23

This book has been published with the help of a grant from the Federation
for the Humanities and Social Sciences, through the Awards to Scholarly
Publications Program, using funds provided by the Social Sciences and
Humanities Research Council of Canada.

University of Toronto Press acknowledges the financial assistance to its
publishing program of the Canada Council for the Arts and the Ontario Arts
Council, an agency of the Government of Ontario.

Canada Council   Conseil des Arts
for the Arts   du Canada

Funded by the   Financé par le
Government   gouvernement
of Canada   du Canada

ONTARIO ARTS COUNCIL
CONSEIL DES ARTS DE L'ONTARIO
an Ontario government agency
un organisme du gouvernement de l'Ontario

MIX
Paper from
responsible sources
FSC® C016245

For

Vera, Jaden, and Jeremy
Elizabeth, Audrey, and Chloe

Contents

Section IV – Concluding Remarks: Reflections on Corporate Social Responsibility, Legitimacy, and Development

Foreword

In May 2016 a workshop on corporate social responsibility (CSR), governance frameworks, and human security was convened at Queen's University, with the aim of examining Canada's role in the development of Africa's natural resource sectors. A working group of senior and junior academics (mainly political scientists) and some field practitioners gathered to share research results and ideas, stimulate or provoke discussion within the group and, it was hoped, identify knowledge deficiencies and research gaps relating to the understanding of some of the complex resource development dynamics that exist in the different cultural and political environments of Africa. Part of this discussion focused on the nature of the relationships and interactions among the various key actors: extractive companies, local communities, civil society groups, local and national host governments, multilateral institutions, and companies' home governments. Another part of the discussion reviewed the emergence of important international multistakeholder initiatives and their effectiveness. The question underlying much of the discussion then – and now in this book – is how best to describe and conceptualize the involvement and effect of Canadian companies and the Canadian government in this evolving governance and development dynamic at national and subnational levels across Africa.

The Importance of the Canadian Dimension of CSR, Governance, and Human Security

Natural resource development has been a foundational element of Canada's own political history, its institutional development, governance structures, and economic and social development and growth. Canada has been home to and/or a participant in a number of significant domestic and international initiatives related to the extractive sector, and has given rise to institutions and organizations directly involved in monitoring, tracking, researching, creating, and implementing oversight mechanisms and tools for activity in that sector, including:

- multistakeholder dialogues, such as the Whitehorse Mining Initiative, the Global Mining Initiative, the Kimberley Process, the National Roundtables on CSR and the Canadian Extractive Industry in Developing Countries, and the Devonshire Initiative;
- research initiatives and special projects, such as the International Development Research Centre, the North-South Institute, the Mining, Minerals and Sustainable Development project, the Intergovernmental Forum on Mining, Minerals, Metals and Sustainable Development, the Canadian International Resources and Development Institute, and the African Minerals Development Centre;
- international development assistance, such as the Canadian International Development Agency's[1] on-and-off mining sector assistance programs, a number of which have been quite substantive;
- various policy, legal, and bilateral or multilateral oversight initiatives specifically related to corruption, responsible business conduct, revenue transparency, supply chain certification programs, and human rights, which have been sponsored, implemented, or supported by Canadian organizations, companies, and the federal government;[2] and
- the emergence of a community of activist and advocacy civil society groups, including faith-based organizations and academic groups, which have been critical of extractive activities, and especially Canadian mining companies operating abroad.

As of September 2018 the Toronto Stock Exchange and its associated Venture Exchange listed close to twelve hundred mineral exploration and mining companies – approximately half of the world's publicly listed total. Based on the most recent data available from Natural Resources Canada,[3] 651 Canadian-based companies were present or active in 101 foreign countries in 2016. Canadian mining assets abroad totalled an estimated $164 billion in value, 17.5 per cent of which related to assets located in African countries.

The largest international industry association of small and large mining companies, the Prospectors & Developers Association of Canada (PDAC), with headquarters in Toronto, has a membership of over eight thousand corporate and individual members from around the world. The PDAC has created and promotes its own CSR framework called *e3 Plus*.[4] The Mining Association of Canada (MAC), Canada's peak umbrella organization representing large and mid-tier producing companies with operating mines in Canada, currently has forty-four full-time members, about half of which also have operating mines outside Canada. MAC has pioneered the development of a self-assessment and third-party verification framework, *Toward Sustainable Mining* (TSM), focused on promoting the continuous improvement of the social and environmental performance of member companies.[5] Some of its members have applied TSM to their foreign operations, and five other country mining associations – in Finland, Botswana, Argentina, Spain, and the Philippines – have adopted and adapted TSM for their own use.

For its part, Canada's federal government has created two oversight units. Canada's National Contact Point for the Organisation for Economic Co-operation and Development Guidelines for Multinational Enterprises (2000–present)[6] operates within the government, while the first of its kind, the Office of the Extractive Sector Corporate Social Responsibility Counsellor (2010–18),[7] operated at arm's length, both working with reference to recognized international codes of conduct and norms and under specific government policy directives.[8] Since the closure of the latter body in May 2018, the government has been in the process of establishing a new unit, the Canadian Ombudsperson for Responsible Enterprise.[9]

Despite this extensive engagement and involvement of various Canadian actors, a key multifaceted question persists: to what extent have these various policy initiatives, CSR commitments, research and monitoring efforts, and oversight mechanisms helped shape policy, governance, and operating environments both at home and in those African countries with a significant Canadian business or diplomatic presence? Further, to what extent have they increased possibilities for extractive activities that result in demonstrable and sustained positive development outcomes for host countries and communities, while also securing the well-being and safety of host communities? These important questions remain central to the contributions in this volume.

The Contribution of the Book

The chapters in this volume reflect the revisions, modifications, updates, and, in a few cases, new contributions of scholars who participated in the 2016 workshop. The editors have detailed some of the important concepts and concerns that underlie much of the discussion, summarizing the content of the various contributions (see Chapter 1), and have drawn out the critical findings and future research focuses or targets that emerged from the workshop discussions and research (see Chapter 12).

As one who has worked in various ways and for over forty years to understand and deal, oftentimes in the field, with many of the issues the authors in this book raise, I am fully aware of the technical, cultural, and geopolitical constraints and challenges that extractive companies, governments, local communities, civil society groups, and multilateral institutions face – individually or together – in their efforts to *ensure* that mineral exploration and extraction are undertaken in ways and by means that will:

- minimize the potential risks of social and environmental harms to host countries and communities;
- responsibly address host government and community concerns, priorities, and aspirations;
- serve to strengthen – not weaken – local, regional, and national communities, economies, and institutions as an intrinsic part of the resource development process;
- enable more equitable benefit sharing, and result in the realization of net positive outcomes for the country, affected communities, and project developers; and
- allow mine developers and communities to define *together* acceptable and constructive ways of working collaboratively.

Can mineral resource development play a positive role in the realization of a country's chosen development paradigm and meet the expectations of key stakeholders, given their differing perspectives and priorities? Extractive activity can be viewed in so many different ways: as a source of tax revenues or national income, as an opportunity for local employment or business development, as a potential or actual threat to the sustainability of traditional livelihoods and values of affected communities, as a wealth-generating business activity that profits offshore owners, or as a way to serve the material needs of domestic and international economies and lifestyles now dependent on the continuing availability of minerals and metals to sustain them. Can these views, which appear to be disparate or at odds with one another, be reconciled or balanced within a country to enable resource development to be carried out in socially and environmentally respectful and responsible ways that equitably benefit all key actors?

There are differing opinions as to what may be possible, and what the constraints, obstacles, and opportunities may be. They are well reflected in the wider academic discourse, not just in this volume.[10] There is a general recognition that the prospects for putting in place conditions, policies, practices, and attitudes that will allow mining to become a true partner in national and local development are an ongoing challenge. Much progress has been made over the past decades in improving community engagement, social investment processes, impact mitigation and management practices, and social and environmental performance within the extractive sector. At many sites, however, there remains a disparity between the claims by operating companies of "success" in community relations and how successful relationships are understood by affected communities. This perceptual paradox is not always apparent, and might be the greatest existential divide that needs to be bridged to enable truly respectful relationships to emerge and participatory decision making to occur.

A part of the academic community has a very different interpretation of what is happening on the ground, taking a more binary approach, arguing that "responsible" mining is not at all possible to achieve within existing "neoliberal" economic policies and development frameworks, and questioning the legitimacy and purpose of private and public sector CSR efforts and policy initiatives, and of extractive activities in general. These differences in understanding and approach to the issues are also reflected in the chapters in this book.

Whatever one's perspective – whether as a politician, government official, affected community member or local entrepreneur, academic or researcher, civil society activist or rights advocate, exploration geologist or senior manager of an oil, gas, or mining company – the search for and extraction of mineral resources has become part of many national development realities, and the issues posed and challenges faced as described in many of the chapters in this book have become critical elements of both domestic and international discussions regarding the "developmental" value of extractive activities.

Some of what you read in this book will be controversial, if not disturbing. You will find contradictory statements and information about the same policies or companies across chapters. You will come across allegations and assertions that are disconcerting or even questionable relating to certain policy or international governance initiatives, to the motivations and behaviour of different government and private sector actors, to the effectiveness or ineffectiveness or positive or negative impacts of CSR policies and programs. You will also find analyses and explanations that clarify complex situations, elucidate unfamiliar con- cepts, and stimulate new thinking.

However you may feel about the completeness or accuracy of the various contributions, the discussions and analyses in this book under- score the *importance* and *seriousness* of the issues raised. In particular, the chapters underscore the politically sensitive, ideologically divisive, and contextually relevant nature of the discussions around Canada's role in Africa on the one hand, and the developmental impetus of Africa's resource sectors on the other.

Here are a few additional thoughts that came out of my reading of the book that may be worth considering as you turn the pages:

- the importance of understanding historical and social context, as well as the local institutional dynamics and complex interactions that take place between parties and how these factors and conditions limit or enable the implementation of good governance or CSR practices in any given country;
- the need to understand the difference between an enterprise's failing to deliver on promises or commitments made to an affected community versus a company's inability to understand how a community perceives the value of its social investment efforts and what these differences mean for ensuring community participation, beneficiation, and security;
- ambiguities in the identification of extractive companies as "Canadian," for which a variety of criteria can be applied: companies listed on the Toronto stock exchange(s) can have multiple national identities or be legally registered offshore in, for example, the Cayman Islands or British Virgin Islands and therefore not recognized as Canadian by Canadian government tax or regulatory authorities;
- the increasing role and importance of what some scholars label "private authority," particularly the role of private enterprise in creating social and economic development opportunities where the public sector is absent, unwilling, or unable to fulfil such functions;
- the reality that the implementation of good practice or policies is uneven across jurisdictions and within both companies and countries;
- the ways in which private sector CSR initiatives and programs may hinder or even undermine the development or strengthening of democratic institutions at national and local levels, or foster the development of new dependencies in the absence of national government initiatives; and

- the value of adopting a multidisciplinary research approach involving collaboration with other social scientists or technical specialists, given the complex nature of extractive activity, its limitations and its possibilities.

Jeffrey Davidson
Extractive Sector CSR Counsellor
of the Government of Canada (2015–18)
November 2018

NOTES

1 More recently the International Development branch of the Department of Foreign Affairs, Trade and Development, now referred to as Global Affairs Canada.
2 Many of these are the focus of discussion in the book.
3 See Canada, Natural Resources Canada, "Canadian Mining Assets," Information Bulletin (Ottawa, February 2019), available online at https://www.nrcan.gc.ca/mining-materials/publications/19323
4 See Prospectors & Developers Association of Canada, "e3 Plus: A Framework for Responsible Exploration" (Toronto: PDAC, 2019), available online at https://www.pdac.ca/priorities/responsible-exploration/e3-plus
5 See Mining Association of Canada, "Towards Sustainable Mining" (Ottawa: MAC, 2019), available online at http://mining.ca/towards-sustainable-mining
6 See Canada, Global Affairs Canada, "Canada's National Contact Point for the Organisation for Economic Co-operation and Development Guidelines for Multinational Enterprises" (Ottawa, October 2018), available online at https://www.international.gc.ca/trade-agreements-accords-commerciaux/ncp-pcn/index.aspx?lang=eng
7 See Canada, Global Affairs Canada, "Office of the Extractive Sector Corporate Social Responsibility (CSR) Counsellor" (Ottawa, June 2018), available online at https://www.international.gc.ca/csr_counsellor-conseiller_rse/index.aspx?lang=eng
8 These include the OECD Guidelines for Multinational Enterprises, the Voluntary Principles on Security and Human Rights, the Global Reporting Initiative (linked to the United Nations Global Compact with business), the International Finance Corporation's Social and Environmental Performance Standards, the UN Guiding Principles on Business and Human Rights, and the OECD Due Diligence Guidance for Responsible Supply Chains of Minerals from Conflict-Affected and High-Risk Areas,

as well as the Canadian federal government's two extractive sector CSR strategies, "Building the Canadian Advantage" (2009) followed by "Doing Business the Canadian Way" (2014).

9 See Canada, "Advancing Canada's Approach on Responsible Business Conduct Abroad" (Ottawa, Janury 2018), available online at https://www.canada.ca/en/global-affairs/news/2018/01/advancing_canadasapproach onresponsiblebusinessconductabroad.html

10 See, for example, the thought-provoking collection of short essays gathered by the Africa-based non-governmental organization, Good Governance Africa, on natural resource development issues, and published in the January-March 2018 issue of its journal, *Africa in Fact*, available online at https://soundcloud.com/user-305848826/africa-in-fact-issue-44-podcast-natural-resources

Acknowledgments

We would like to thank Daniel Quinlan for his enthusiasm and tireless support throughout all aspects of the edited book project. Rebecca Wallace, Paula Butler, and University of Toronto Press staff were very generous with their time during the production process. We also thank freelance copy editor Barry Norris. Diane Davies, Maureen Bartram, David Haglund, and Zsuzsa Csergö at Queen's University provided timely institutional support during the early stages of the project. The Social Sciences and Humanities Research Council of Canada afforded vital financial support for the book project in three ways. First, the Banting Postdoctoral Fellowships program allowed us to collaborate on the project and work closely together at Queen's University. Second, the Connection Grant program funded a scholarly workshop at Queen's, which permitted the contributors to present their research and receive feedback on earlier versions of the chapters. Third, the Awards to Scholarly Publications Program defrayed some of the publication costs of the book. We thank our families for their patience and support while we worked on the project. We would also like to thank the anonymous referees for their helpful comments, which improved the manuscript, and our contributors for their time and effort during the many phases of the book project.

SECTION I

Introduction: Conceptual Approaches and Policy Implications

1 Africa-Canada Relations in Natural Resource Sectors: Approaches to (and Prospects for) Corporate Social Responsibility, Good Governance, and Human Security

NATHAN ANDREWS AND J. ANDREW GRANT

Introduction

Africa's natural resource sectors are witnessing unprecedented levels of foreign investment and production. Although such economic activity has been hailed as a means of reducing poverty levels and reliance on foreign aid, its attendant effect on the human security of local communities is often given but cursory considerations linked to promises of good governance, best practices, and corporate social responsibility (CSR) (see Alao 2008; Andrews 2019; du Preez 2015; Grant 2009; Grant et al. 2015a; Grant, Djomo, and Krause 2016; Hilson and Maconachie 2008). Recent global governance initiatives, such as the Voluntary Principles on Security and Human Rights (VPs), have sought to operationalize and develop these considerations to address grievances and prevent violent conflict from arising in areas of resource extraction. Global governance has gained primacy in the lexicon of natural resource sector discussions due to the growing role of non-state actors, including representatives of private authority – such as transnational corporations, as well as national and transnational security companies – in extracting natural resources across the continent of Africa.

Global governance is also in the ascendancy owing to the perceived reduction in the power of nation-states (occasional acts of resource nationalism notwithstanding), resulting in hybrid and collaborative governance arrangements (see Abrahamsen and Williams 2010; Cooper, English, and Thakur 2002; Hall and Biersteker 2002). Hybrid governance arrangements in natural resource sectors have also opened up participatory space for civil society in the form of transnational and local non-governmental organizations (NGOs), as well as transnational policy networks (Alorse, Compaoré, and Grant 2015; Grant et al. 2015b; Grant, Balraj, and Mavropoulos-Vagelis 2013; Teye 2013).

The Extractive Industries Transparency Initiative (EITI), for instance, is seen to represent a cooperative apparatus (states, firms, civil society) with the potential to advance the governance and management of natural resource benefits – albeit with mixed evidence at this point (see Aaronson 2011; Van Alstine and Andrews 2016; Andrews 2016b; Compaoré 2015; Rustad, Le Billon, and Lujala 2017; Sovacool et al. 2016; Sovacool and Andrews 2015).

Notwithstanding the many years of natural resource extraction in Africa, host communities often have little to show for it in terms of sustained economic development or improved livelihoods (Andrews 2013b, 2015; Campbell 2004; Collins, Grant, and Ackah-Baidoo 2019; Essah and Andrews 2016; Frynas 2005, 2008; Grant 2014b; Grant, Compaoré, and Mitchell 2015; Idemudia 2007, 2010, 2014; International Council on Mining and Metals 2006; Okpanachi and Andrews 2012; Osei-Kojo and Andrews 2018). Ranging from governance initiatives that promote broadly conceived ethical business practices, such as the United Nations Global Compact, to an important aspect of particular industries, such as the EITI and the Kimberley Process, to specific minerals and regions – for example, the Organisation for Economic Co-operation and Development (OECD) Due Diligence Guidance for Responsible Supply Chains of Minerals from Conflict-Affected and High-Risk Areas, or the International Conference on the Great Lakes Region Regional Certification Mechanism – a common thread is the aim to bring in multiple stakeholders in order to improve governance and foster economic growth. These initiatives also seek to engage different types of stakeholders, ranging from industry to government to civil society to local communities, as part of their overall efforts to develop holistic governance and encourage human security approaches to mining in conflict-prone environments (Campbell 2012; Dashwood 2007, 2012; Dashwood and Puplampu 2010, 2015; Hilson 2007, 2012). It is appropriate, therefore, to examine the role the private sector plays in the day-to-day lives of local communities, with the goal of identifying and recommending viable options for positive change (Andrews 2017, 2019).

The past two decades have witnessed an increased interest in Africa's natural resource sectors not only in Canadian public opinion, but also among Canadian firms (and transnational firms with Canadian offices and employees), investors, civil society organizations, and government agencies (Campbell 1999; Grant 2014a). The $6.7 million public-private partnership arrangement launched in 2011 by the erstwhile Canadian International Development Agency (CIDA) to help alleviate poverty in selected countries is a case in point. This has produced a marked change in Canadian policy towards Africa as new alignments, partnerships, and relationships have been established in the context of natural resource sector governance – for example, as evidenced by the Canadian International Resources and Development Institute, especially during the Conservative government's period in office from 2011 to 2015. In turn, such developments have been encouraged and criticized by Canadian stakeholders, opinion leaders, and observers alike (see Brown 2012; Butler 2015; Deneault and Sacher 2012; Engler 2015; Gordon 2010). Since the Liberal government took office, many of these same stakeholders have become impatient, calling on the government to implement campaign promises that would see Canada resuming its role as a global leader in natural resource governance. In a positive first step, after roughly a decade-long interval, Canada took on the chair of the VPs for the 2016–17 period.

Yet aside from a welcome set of preliminary accounts of the perceived benefits and drawbacks of this change in Canadian policy towards Africa, there is a dearth of in-depth, policy-relevant analyses of these developments in the scholarly literature – especially one that captures the multiple dimensions of this phenomenon. This book sets out to remedy this gap in the literature by bringing together accounts based on extensive field research and primary sources from a variety of leading senior scholars and experienced practitioners/development consultants (drawing upon an average of ten to twenty and more years of work on Africa's extractive sectors) as well as accomplished junior scholars (with published works based on fieldwork observations and interviews). The objective is to explore such related themes as the interplay between global governance frameworks and domestic legislation; Canadian public opinion on CSR and new trends in Africa-Canada relations in natural resource sectors; governance networks and public-private partnerships; the consistency of best practices and CSR efforts in relation to the VPs and maintaining a "social licence to operate"; and sustainable development and human security vis-à-vis the livelihood ramifications of resource extraction.

There is a welcome body of literature that engages with Canada's foreign policy and role in Africa (see, for instance, Akuffo 2012, 2013; Black 2015; Black and Hornsby 2016; Butler 2015; Engler 2015; Hornsby 2014; Medhora and Samy 2013). Canada also enjoys a reputation as a global leader in the extractive sectors in particular, and there is increased investment in Africa's natural resources by Canadian companies. Yet there is a dearth of academic publications that comprehensively examine the country's role in this important issue-area. At the theoretical level, Canada is often taken for granted as a "middle power" on the world stage in comparison with the United States, which many see as a leading major power – if not a superpower arguably in decline. In comparative terms, however, investments from these two North American countries in Africa's extractive sectors actually provide a stark contrast to their respective conventional images and positions in international affairs. This book therefore attempts to add more nuance and rigour to the discussion to illuminate the multiple dimensions of Canada's engagement with the continent, particularly illustrating how and why Canada is not merely a "middle power" when it comes to Africa's natural resource sectors.

It is worth noting that, by "Africa," we are primarily referring to sub-Saharan Africa. And by juxtaposing Canada (as a country) with Africa (as a continent), we neither seek to generalize either contexts nor take for granted the many specific themes and issue-areas with which the book does not engage. Rather, we seek to contribute to discourses that address the roles of Canadian firms, transnational mining firms, civil society, and government agencies in Africa's natural resource sectors, while illuminating the actions and inactions of these different actors on grassroots-related issues such as poverty, livelihoods, development, and human security (including human rights).

Understanding Canada's Foreign Policy and Presence in Africa

Canada is influential in world politics. As put forward by Nossal, Roussel, and Paquin (2015), successive Canadian governments have been preoccupied with peace, war, and the international order while equally being concerned about the "low politics" of economics, trade, the environment, and social affairs. These varied interests underscore the different perspectives and narratives that explain Canada's foreign policy. The two perspectives of interest to us border around notions of altruistic and egoistic behaviour on the international stage. Altruistic perspectives present a picture of Canada as partner, friend, and rescuer – one concerned about world peace and proactively engaging in humanitarian work abroad to promote peace. This perspective elevates Canada's moral identity abroad as "a non-imperialist, internationalist nation" – a narrative that relies predominantly on an idealized version of Canadian history both at home and in Africa (Hornsby 2014, 335; see also Akuffo 2012). The egoistic perspective, on the other hand, sees Canadian foreign policy as consciously driven by geostrategic and self-centred economic interests. Furthermore this rationalistic behaviour is seen to undergird much of Canada's engagement with Africa (see Akuffo 2013; Black and Hornsby 2016). The irony is not lost among observers who note that Canada is sensitive to – and still experiences the legacy of – its erstwhile status as a country that is home to a population of "hewers of wood and drawers of water." This characterization often overlooks the mercurial relationship between federal and provincial governments and First Nations, Inuit, and Métis in the context of natural resource governance in Canada.[1]

The egoistic perspective could be stretched further to discussions of Canada as an immoral (and even imperialist) actor. Proponents of this stance argue that the idea of "Canada as either a benevolent, neutral or subordinated international actor that does not put its own self-interests first is badly misleading" (Gordon 2010, 12). Although Canada might not be readily regarded as a superpower, Gordon believes that the country has power in its own right and uses it to participate actively in the global system of domination, in which the resources of poorer countries are exploited to the advantage of richer nations in the Global North. It is believed that Canadian foreign policy has been greatly driven by the quest to create enabling conditions for Canadian corporations to expand in the developing world. For instance, profits from Canadian investments in these areas increased from $3.7 billion in 1980 to about $23.6 billion in 2007 – an increase of 535 per cent (Gordon 2010, 11). Contemporary imperialism is therefore justified by racist crude formulations in which the people of the South are viewed "as inferior, helpless, irrational and potentially dangerous" (Gordon 2010, 47). This further justifies intervention of any kind, and thereby makes it the "white man's burden" to save the world's poor from their self-imposed predicament, perpetuating supposedly "altruistic" forms of global salvationism. Particularly in the case of Africa's mining sector, Butler (2015, 21–2) presents an unsettling perspective that conceptualizes "Canada as not only a 'white settler state' and a 'racial state' but also as a contemporary colonizer-nation." Yves Engler (2015) emphasizes Ottawa's explicit and implicit opposition to anticolonial struggles in Africa, including its contribution to violence in places such as Somalia, Rwanda, and the Democratic Republic of Congo (DRC).

This critical perspective seeks to expose Canada's false history as a non-colonizing state and debunk the global depiction of Canadians as moral giants characterized by innocence, fairness, tolerance, ethical standards, inclusivity, and humanitarianism. Butler (2015) therefore questions the narratives of Canadian mining industry professionals that present Canadians as "just rock-jocks," "doing good wherever we are," "quite sensitive people," and "environmentally responsible." To be sure, Deneault and Sacher (2012) cite Canadian companies such as IAMGOLD (in Mali), Prestea Resources Limited and Birim Goldfields (in Ghana), First Quantum Minerals (in the DRC), Diamond Works (in Sierra Leone), and Heritage Oil (in Angola) whose work has social and environmental ramifications that are not improving the lives and livelihoods of local communities. Although such perspectives that engage with colonialist practices of resource appropriation are often sidelined in the mainstream literature on Canada's foreign policy, we believe they need to be factored into the equation to get a nuanced picture of the different dimensions of the country's involvement in the global extractive industry – in Africa in particular.

Albeit problematic, binaries are quite rampant in scholarly and theoretical discussions (see Andrews 2013a). However, binaries in the form of the two contradictory or arbitrary narratives discussed above might limit our understanding of Canada's foreign policy. As such, there should be room for a possible "third way" that imagines the country as a middle power that can be both friend and foe. Although several contributors in this volume take a critical stance on Canada's role in Africa, others explore the possibility of working towards potentially promising engagements. As a result, the book aligns with a purposive middle-ground position that encourages a more context-specific and case-by-case reflection to arrive at a particular stance. This is not to presume neutrality or the absence of personal opinions; rather, our goal as editors is to encourage ongoing debates that proceed from both the progressive and policy-relevant chapters in this volume, instead of stifling them at the outset. Despite one's particular ontological, epistemological, or political position, most of us may agree on at least a couple of broad observations: 1) Canada has had – and will continue to have – a significant presence in Africa's natural resource sectors; and 2) Canada's presence has not often translated into demonstrable and sustained development outcomes for recipient countries and host communities. Ultimately these observations serve as good starting points of discussion for the different contributions to this volume.

In terms of actual presence, Canadian extractive companies are active in forty-three African countries, representing the largest component of foreign investment in the sector in comparison with investment from other countries around the world (see Engler 2015, 2016). As of March 2013, 189 companies listed on the Toronto Stock Exchange and its Venture Exchange had operations in the mining and hydrocarbon sectors in Africa (Bhushan 2014); we believe this number has not dramatically changed in recent years. Even for the mining sector alone, evidence from Natural Resources Canada shows an incremental increase in assets over the 2009–15 period. Table 1.1 includes assets in thirty-six different African countries, with data based on financial

Table 1.1.   Global Presence of Canadian Mining Companies, 2009–16

Region	2009	2012	2013	2014	2015	2016*
	($ billions)					
Africa	20.0	22.4	24.1	27.0	31.3	28.6
Americas (excluding Canada)	71.0	99.8	103.9	113.4	113.3	112.5
Asia	6.0	9.2	9.7	9.4	11.1	8.9
Europe	7.0	9.7	11.2	11.7	10.7	9.8
Oceania	5.0	5.5	4.3	4.9	4.3	4.1
Total	109.0	146.6	153.2	166.4	170.7	163.9

* Projected.
Source: Canada 2019a.

reports for public companies headquartered in Canada that are not under foreign control.

As the table shows, although Asia, Europe, and Oceania experienced a reduction in Canadian mining assets abroad over the 2009–15 period, Africa maintained significant growth of between 7 and 15 per cent annually. In 2013 the $2 billion growth from the previous year was attributable mainly to projects in Zambia, including the development of the Sentinel copper mine and expansion of the Kansanshi mine, the largest copper mine in Africa, by First Quantum Minerals. The growth in 2015 was attributable to developments in the DRC and Zambia. In the DRC, Ivanhoe Mines reassessed the value of its Kamoa copper project following its partial sale; in Zambia, First Quantum Minerals officially opened the Sentinel copper mine and continued to make investments at Kansanshi (Canada 2019a). Canadian energy (including oil and gas) assets are also quite substantial despite the fall in global oil and gas prices. As of 2015, Natural Resources Canada reports that these assets in total stood at $4.7 billion across Africa, compared with $2.8 billion in Asia and $8.4 billion in the Americas (Canada 2018b). Although it is notable that there was a projected change in Canadian assets in Africa for 2016, all regions experienced a decline in value in that particular year, as Table 1.1 shows.

Approaches to CSR, Good Governance, and Human Security

Corporate social responsibility is a topic that is heavily debated, with clear division on whether it should become a mandatory activity or remain discretionary (see, for example, Andrews 2016a, 2019; Banerjee 2007; Dashwood 2012; Frynas 2009; Idemudia 2014; Raman and

Lipschutz 2010; Sagebien and Lindsay 2011). Despite this debate, the concept has been taken up by Canadian extractive companies, most of which are spending millions of dollars on special initiatives, ranging from the construction of key infrastructure to monetary handouts in the form of scholarships to micro finance for alternative livelihood initiatives. Governments and civil society organizations make reference to CSR in the context of the extractive sectors. In a similar vein, governance – especially good governance – is often paired with CSR. Since CSR and governance risk are becoming "buzzwords" akin to globalization, it is important to flesh out the conceptual elements of these norms and related concepts, which appear throughout this volume. Here we examine both the notions of and actual mechanisms towards CSR, good governance, and human security.

Corporate Social Responsibility

Despite the long history of corporate philanthropy, CSR is best understood as a norm that emerged in the 1950s and continues to evolve in the 2010s. In its earliest incarnation, CSR sought to guide business stakeholders by infusing greater ethical, moral, and legal considerations into firms' day-to-day operations. These considerations first appeared in books (see, for example, Bowen 1953) aimed primarily at management-level decision makers in a wide variety of firms, and then later in the scholarly journals of business, management, and commerce that began to proliferate in the 1960s (see, for example, Carroll 1999; Votaw 1972). By the 1980s CSR began to be linked with firm performance. Specifically, the CSR literature began to suggest that a correlation existed between "better" performance on CSR indicators (e.g., behaving more "ethically") and business performance (e.g., profits). Although this correlation did not influence the behaviour of all firms, it did become an axiom in the wider environment in which firms operated – that of shareholders, consumers, governments, and civil society organizations. This axiom also contributed to the establishment of CSR as a tangible norm with local, regional, and global reach.

To be sure, CSR cannot be deemed a fully global norm. The vast majority of studies of CSR from the 1980s to early 2000s focused on how CSR norms influenced firm behaviour in countries or regions of the Global North such as the United States, the United Kingdom, and Japan, or North America, the European Union, and Scandinavia. The rise of state-owned enterprises in China and firms from former communist countries such as Russia in the 2000s represented alternative conceptions of CSR, wherein allusions to human rights are either muted or absent. Concomitantly the 2000s and 2010s witnessed the rise of governance initiatives, such as the UN Global Compact and the EITI, that seek to promote CSR on a global level. This period also saw the establishment and proliferation of CSR-related norm-reinforcing global campaigns directed by non-profits such as Publish What You Pay and Transparency International.

Global Affairs Canada's list of "Canada's comprehensive approach to supporting CSR" includes the 1998 Corruption of Foreign Public Officials Act, which makes it a criminal offence to bribe a foreign public official in the course of business (Canada 2019b). To help with company-community dialogue facilitation and conflict management, a National Contact Point for the OECD Guidelines for Multinational Enterprises (the dispute resolution mechanism on responsible business conduct) and an Office of the Extractive Sector CSR Counsellor were established in 2000 and 2010, respectively. As part of Canada's efforts to help foster and promote sustainable economic development and responsible business practices by Canadian extractive companies in host countries, the government unveiled a framework in 2009 titled "Building the Canadian Advantage: A CSR Strategy for the International Extractive Sector." The framework at the time was meant to be a one-stop policy document with pointers to capacity building, transparency, and disclosure initiatives, including CSR performance guidelines and principles. Although the 2009 strategy promoted general compliance with CSR guidelines and actually led to the establishment of the CSR counsellor's office in 2010, its overall enforcement capacity was limited. The 2014 CSR strategy, "Doing Business the Canadian Way: A Strategy to Advance Corporate Social Responsibility in Canada's Extractive Sector Abroad," therefore came to build on the 2009 policy instrument by placing more emphasis on enforcement mechanisms and the social concerns of host communities, among other things.

The contributions by Idemudia and colleagues and Johnston-Taylor (Chapters 2 and 3 in this volume) provide a more detailed account of the differences between the two national CSR strategies, including the challenge of framing development in the current document. But we can say that, despite the enduring challenges, the CSR counsellor's office, for instance, which was enabled by both the 2009 and 2014 CSR strategies, could be regarded as a peculiar and quite progressive step by Canada, especially compared to other global leaders in the extractive industry, such as Australia, the United States, and China. For example, the 2014 CSR strategy put in place better provisions to connect the work of the CSR counsellor with the National Contact Point for the OECD Guidelines (Canada 2018a). Nevertheless the CSR counsellor was replaced in 2018 by an independent, multisectoral Canadian Ombudsperson for Responsible Enterprise (CORE), heralded as "the first of its kind in the world" (Canada 2018c). If this ombudsperson role is practically endowed with the capacity and "genuine" independence needed proactively to seek and address cases involving Canadian extractive companies in Africa, some difference could be made in securing the well-being of host communities whose rights and livelihoods are often not given priority by either corporations or, sometimes, their own governments.

Good Governance

As is the case when seeking to understand a particular concept, it is useful to begin with its etymology. The Latin foundation of "governance" connotes the action of "steering." This is consistent with the way in which governance was previously applied to the execution of government policy. Governance, however, means much more than the mere activities of government. Governance is applied to decision-making processes of a wide variety of groups ranging from informal grassroots organizations to formal institutions (Jabeen 2007; Mayntz 2003; Schneider and Bauer 2007; Thauer 2014). When applying governance to CSR, one could readily envisage the norm (and its constituent norms) steering firm behaviour. To complete the definition, governance is usually conceived as a participatory form of decision making that incorporates – via a variety of mechanisms, both formal and informal – the views of stakeholder groups. Although "good governance" traditionally has been ascribed to government objectives, decision making, and behaviour (see, for example, Grindle 2004, 2007), it has also entered the lexicon of CSR and firms.

Promoting good governance is laudable, but such efforts risk the promulgation of "laundry lists" for governments and firms alike that serve not only as guidelines, but also as sets of boxes to be checked. Government scorecards for poverty reduction or literacy gains tend to downplay difficulties of measurement, retroactive baselines, and veritable achievement. Equivalent scorecards for extractive sector firms – the number of health clinics opened, schools built and staffed, scholarships awarded to students from local communities – risk moving the concept and constituent norms of CSR away from genuine ethical considerations and towards "cookie cutter good works" that can be tabulated and included in glossy annual reports (with photos of smiling recipients) for public consumption. These insights serve as a caution against empty generalizations concerning CSR and good governance, and highlight the complex dynamics at hand – which the contributors to this volume seek to illustrate.

In December 2014 the government of Canada also passed into law the Extractive Sector Transparency Measures Act (ESTMA), which came into force in June 2015 and forms part of the omnibus Bill C-43. Similar to provisions in the Dodd-Frank Act in the United States, this act – also informally known as a "publish-what-you-pay" law – requires public and private oil, gas, and mining companies to disclose payments made to governments both in Canada and abroad.[2] Despite this regulatory provision, there is evidence that Canada is "home to oil, gas, and mining companies that choose to register here in order to benefit from our permissive mining regulations and preferential tax structure" (Deneault and Sacher 2012, 1). It is also unclear why Canada remains only an EITI "supporting country," not a member. Regardless of domestic mechanisms such as ESTMA, Canada's non-member status tends to undermine the essence of global standards for transparency in the extractive industry. It also gives resource-rich African countries, some of which consider the initiative a double standard, a reason to avoid taking up membership. This has implications for Canadian extractive companies operating in Africa in terms of how payments are reported and the mechanisms that track these reports.

Despite the several Canadian CSR and other "good governance" arrangements (including CORE and ESTMA) noted above, the failure of Bill C-300 (a private member's bill) in the House of Commons in October 2010 only goes to support the perception that lawmakers themselves might not be interested in establishing strict ethical requirements for Canadian extractive companies abroad. This bill, if passed, would have instituted prescriptive and broader CSR guidelines that would have been binding on Canadian mining companies abroad. Its passage could have had a positive effect on corporate behaviour, as even the official government strategy, "Building the Canadian Advantage," was considered to have failed to impose human rights obligations on Canadian companies overseas (Deneault and Sacher 2012).[3] Rather, the bill's failure was regarded as a "win" for Canada's mining industry (see Dagenais 2010).

On the theme of good governance, it should be added that the Canadian government's efforts to promote CSR have also materialized at the bilateral level through the Foreign Investment Promotion and Protection Agreements (FIPPAs) and other free trade agreements signed since 2010. Yet FIPPAs have been criticized as not offering profitable trade outcomes but, rather, helping Canadian companies to sue African governments that attempt to pursue policies that do not align with these companies' profit-making objectives (see Engler 2015). The EITI and Canada's own domestic arrangements, such as ESTMA and the two CSR strategies, emerged in an era considered to be a "fourth generation" of mining codes in Africa, representing voluntary, regional, and global initiatives spearheaded by a multiplicity of actors in Africa and abroad (see Besada and Martin 2015). Yet the critiques against FIPPAs suggest a return to previous generations of governance, where a "do-as-you-please" approach was used to marginalize African governments and peoples (Campbell 2011). Regardless of the position one takes, this point shows that despite positive trends, nothing can be taken for granted.

Human Security

Beginning nearly three decades ago, the concept of human security quickly entered the lexicon of practitioners and academics alike, resulting in a flurry of activity around its definition. Although myriad definitions were produced, a common tenet that underpins and explains human security is its focus on the *individual*, rather than on the broader state or country. The concept has been expanded in some contexts and applied to wider communities, but this usually connotes a marginalized group or relatively small community – one that is being repressed or persecuted – such as a religious minority. This conceptual elasticity has been useful from an instrumentalist perspective and in its service as a conceptual shorthand. These characteristics, however, have led to critiques that human security is not only an amorphous concept, but also one exceedingly difficult to quantify or measure with precision (Paris 2001). Although such critiques have a great deal of validity, they do not outweigh the benefits of human security's conceptual flexibility, which calls attention, in a parsimonious manner, to security needs ranging from human rights to human development (Breslin and Christou 2015; Glasius 2008; Hampson et al. 2002; Mack 2012; Martin and Owen 2014; Tadjbakhsh and Chenoy 2007; UNDP 1994).

A brief reflection on human security mechanisms in the Canadian context is useful here. By assuming the chairperson position of the VPs for 2011–12 – which coincided with the publication of the first implementation guide, the Voluntary Principles on Security and Human Rights: Implementation Guidance Tools – the Canadian government began to take leadership on the topic of human security as applied to the extractive sectors. In 2016–17 Canada took on the chair role again, and put in place several mechanisms to streamline the VPs in its extractive sectors. For instance, as Charis Enns (Chapter 4 in this volume) points out, Canadian extractive companies requesting loans from Export Development Canada were required to showcase adherence to the VPs and other global CSR norms. Also, diplomatic support that Canadian extractive companies abroad could receive from trade commissioners is tied to their adherence to the government's CSR strategy and proactive implementation of the VPs. Inasmuch as the VPs and other global norms of CSR are still voluntary by design, these initiatives by both the Canadian government and Canadian companies operating abroad attest to some efforts towards the security and well-being of communities in which extraction takes place.

Scholars have argued that the multistakeholder nature of these initiatives tends to accord them legitimacy and overall authority (see Baumann-Pauly and Nolan 2016). As Enns shows (in Chapter 4), however, these notions of legitimacy do not align with contestations from both Canadian-based and local NGOs that feel marginalized and therefore question the initiatives' potential to advance human security and human rights in sites of resource extraction. This evidence makes us question the extent to which the activities of Canadian companies in conflict-prone or high-risk areas in East and Central Africa can further human security efforts. Nketti Johnston-Taylor continues this type of assessment (Chapter 3 in this volume) in her examination of the cases of Talisman Energy in Sudan, "illegal" exploitation of natural resources by eight Canadian companies in the DRC, and Barrick Gold's complicity in "irresponsible" behaviour in Tanzania, among others, which reflect the insufficient commitment towards human security and people's well-being (see also Butler 2015; Engler 2015). The contribution by Jason McSparren (Chapter 5 in this volume) sheds further light on malpractices, including allegations of human rights violations, by both IAMGOLD and SEMAFO in Burkina Faso and Kinross in Ghana.

In addition to assessing the extent to which global governance initiatives on natural resources can promote human security, the chapters in this collection reflect on how these regulatory regimes were established, and elucidate the constitutive norms that are being generated. The EITI, VPs, and other global governance initiatives examined in this book are particularly instructive on both fronts. The complex interface between human security – which places a moral and quasi-legal priority upon the individual ahead of state security – and the proliferation of the CSR norm provides an illustrative set of cases applicable in, and beyond, Africa's extractive sectors.

Scope and Overview of the Book

The book is thematically integrated, and the chapters are linked in four sections. The objective of the current chapter has been to introduce readers to Africa-Canada relations, with an emphasis on the dynamics of Canada's role in Africa's natural resource sectors. We also invite readers to consider approaches to – and prospects for – the various avenues for more innovative theorizing around CSR and good governance, as well as more creative forms of policy and practice that are being applied to extractive resource sectors in Africa. To this end, the chapter elucidates the volume's core analytical perspectives and concepts such as governance, norms, and human security. In the next section of the book, the constituent chapters address Canada's role in Africa's extractive sectors, while also focusing on aforementioned themes such as development, human security, global governance, and CSR.

In recent years there have been concerted debates about the need for Canadian extractive companies operating abroad to be socially responsible. This debate is partly due to the key role of extractive companies in the Canadian economy and the fact that negative social and environmental externalities are often associated with their operations abroad. Central to the debate is the role of the Canadian government and how Canadian extractive companies are institutionally enabled to be socially responsible. As a result the Canadian government has responded by devising national CSR strategies meant to provide guidance and support for Canadian companies to become socially responsible. Drawing on a critical reading of Canada's CSR strategies, Uwafiokun Idemudia, Nadège Compaoré, and Cynthia Kwakyewah (Chapter 2) critically examine the relationship between the Canadian government and CSR and the extent to which the CSR strategies facilitate or hinder efforts to promote sustainable development by Canadian extractive companies in local communities in Africa. The authors conclude by considering the theoretical and practical implications of the changing role of government in CSR in the extractive industries more broadly. Their chapter also presents an important juxtaposition to some prevailing notions that global governance and the growing influence of private authority necessarily implies the reduction in the power of the nation-state.

In Chapter 3, Nketti Johnston-Taylor further examines the expanding role of the Canadian government in CSR. Since Canada launched its first formal CSR policy in 2009, there has been considerable progress as the Canadian government has increased support for CSR initiatives. It has also established CSR guidelines and a formal remediation process based on the OECD Guidelines for Multinational Enterprises on responsible business conduct. Observers such as Campbell (1999), Gordon (2010), and Butler (2015) have reported, however, that Canadian mining companies have been the most significant group involved in issues of violence, environmental damage, and human rights abuses in mineral-rich Africa, thus questioning the role and effectiveness of Canada's CSR efforts. Johnston-Taylor explores this conundrum by critically evaluating Canada's approach to CSR and assessing the role of neoliberalism in constraining and undermining Canada's efforts. Her chapter, therefore, is tasked with four objectives. First, she outlines Canada's approach to CSR. Second, she explores the disparity between rhetoric and reality in Africa. Third, she examines the rationale behind the aforementioned disparity and, in so doing, assesses the role of neoliberal structures, processes, and powers in shaping Canadian companies' behaviour abroad. As part of her fourth objective, she closes by making recommendations on how to bridge the gap between rhetoric and reality.

Using the VPs as a multistakeholder initiative, Charis Enns (Chapter 4) presents an in-depth case in the Canadian context. She discusses how the VPs have been employed, advanced, and critiqued by various Canadian stakeholders, and how Canadian stakeholders participate in this multistakeholder initiative. She evaluates the legitimacy of the VPs as a multistakeholder initiative, supporting the analysis with examples from Canadian extractive company operations in sub-Saharan Africa. This evaluation provides a helpful framework that makes it possible to show specific areas where the initiative lacks legitimacy and, in so doing, the analysis makes it clear why some Canadian NGOs remain sceptical about the credibility and effectiveness of this particular multistakeholder initiative. The chapter is grounded in empirical data collected from desk research, as well as fieldwork such as site visits and interviews with Canadian extractive companies, industry associations, and civil society organizations between 2014 and 2015. Enns concludes by considering the practical and policy-oriented implications of the study.

Shedding more light on global-local linkages, Jason McSparren (Chapter 5) also engages with the VPs, but from a different perspective. In analysing the effect of the VPs on CSR, McSparren assesses policies of a sample of Canadian mining firms operating in Africa in accordance with the recommendations stated in the VPs. He also examines the implementation of the CSR policies within the "Protect, Respect, and Remedy" framework through an analysis of media reports on recent conflicts between corporations and local communities affected by mining operations in Africa. As noted earlier, the VPs are part of a broad international movement within the extractive sectors to instil new norms of operation geared towards sustainable development. They are meant to guide corporations in avoiding complicity in human rights abuses through due diligence and stakeholder engagement. McSparren finds that, across the study sample, CSR policies reflect certain aspects of the

VPs more frequently and with more emphasis than others. This leads to a provisional conclusion that there is a gradual shift occurring in the industry's approach to responsible corporate citizenship. In practice, however, it is important to recognize that the implementation of the VPs framework remains uneven across cases – evidence that lends support to Enns's evaluation in Chapter 4.

In Chapter 6, Timothy Adivilah Balag'kutu examines artisanal and small-scale mining (ASM), which represents an important aspect of Africa's natural resource sectors. Despite ASM's economic potential – in Ghana, for example, such mining contributes more than a third of total annual gold production – the sector poses serious human security threats to individuals and communities. ASM causes deforestation, mercury poisoning, and various kinds of pollution, and it inflicts physical harm and causes death, among other deleterious effects. As mostly informal and having a fluid labour force, however, ASM also presents a governance challenge. Mainstream governance focuses on revenue maximization and targets large-scale mining ventures, but these analyses miss an important part of the governance and human security nexus. To remedy this oversight, Balag'kutu explores the governance of ASM as a human security issue within a critical theory framework. Canada is a significant development partner in Africa's natural resource governance process; hence, an illustrative example that animates Balag'kutu's chapter is a detailed assessment of Canada's interests, objectives, and ultimate role in ASM governance challenges in the African context.

The third section examines complex relationships between norms and development on the one hand, and global governance initiatives and national governance strategies on the other. Specifically, these relationships are addressed in the context of how they fit with contemporary debates about the extraction and trade of natural resources. A major barrier to African countries' ability to experience greater socio-economic benefits from mineral resource extraction is the general paucity of "backward" and "forward" linkages with foreign-owned mines. This enclave nature of African mining has been recognized as problematic by numerous analysts since the publication of Greg Lanning's 1979 classic study, *Africa Undermined*. One aspect of "backward" linkages – "local procurement" or "local content" – has gained visibility in recent years as part of moves towards "new" forms of developmentalism (see, for example, Andrews and Nwapi 2018; Ovadia 2014), and has appeared on the program of major mining events such as the Prospectors & Developers Association of Canada (PDAC) annual convention in Toronto, Canada, and the Mining Indaba meetings in Cape Town, South Africa.

In Chapter 7, Paula Butler assesses the meaning of the above developments. Informed by post-colonial, critical political economy, and critical race theory, Butler investigates how a new field of ideas – such as local procurement – emerges, gains traction in the public domain, and effects or gives shape to new institutional practices and policies. Butler observes that the World Bank's 1992 policy document, *Strategy for African Mining*, set the stage for concentrated international neoliberal reform and governance of African mining. In this context the emergence of "local procurement" as a discursive field and field of intervention presents an important locus for theorizing new and continuing manifestations of neoliberal power in late capitalism. Butler also explores the Africa Mining Vision, as well as the following critical questions: What institutional strategies and interests have fostered the emergence of local procurement as a new "common sense" dimension of CSR? What institutions are involved (and why)? What are the characteristics of the dominant institutional discourse pertaining to local procurement as it has emerged since 2011? And, lastly, what alternate strategies, visions, or conceptual frameworks for mining (or development more generally) might be suppressed as local procurement gains prominence? These questions help to critically examine the mechanisms at play in this governing device called "local procurement."

In Chapter 8, Raynold Wonder Alorse asserts that there is no doubt that non-state actors, such as transnational corporations (TNCs), have become powerful socio-economic agents in global politics.[4] As a result of the growing influence of TNCs and reports of business complicity in human rights abuses, global governance initiatives such as the VPs and the UN Guiding Principles on Business and Human Rights have emerged to promote CSR in natural resource sectors. Drawing on recently conducted field research and insights from multistakeholder governance and institutional theories, Alorse focuses on understanding how institutional dynamics and state responses in South Africa and Ghana facilitate (or hinder) the promotion of CSR initiatives in each country's mineral sectors. Given the significant number of Canadian gold mining firms in both countries, Alorse also examines these firms' commitments to the UN Guiding Principles and VPs based on their *size* (large, mid-tier, junior). The author argues that, in order to understand how firms differ in their adoption of voluntary governance norms, it is imperative *first* to examine the domestic *institutional* dynamics of where these firms operate. In other words, firms do not operate in a vacuum. As such, a study focusing on their CSR commitments and practices requires a deep understanding of the institutional factors that might enable or constrain the agency of firms. Alorse also finds that the commitment to security and human rights norms and stakeholder approaches undertaken by Canadian TNCs is largely influenced by visibility and legitimacy.

David Orr offers additional insights into the case of South Africa in Chapter 9, identifying the corporate actor as the key variable of analysis and exploring how mining firms have responded to South Africa's complex network of CSR initiatives. Illustrating the country's unique conception of CSR, these corporate rationales are, among other factors, deeply grounded upon the need to redress the inequalities generated during apartheid, which, in turn, informs how mining firms perceive and frame their CSR contributions. Based on the results of in-person interviews with corporate stakeholders undertaken in South Africa in 2016, Orr explores how mining firms have responded to mining legislation, industry charters, and voluntary initiatives, and the effect these have had on both firms' CSR strategies and their engagement/identities with both state and non-state actors. Acknowledging the limitations of CSR for spurring development outcomes, Orr concludes that collaborative efforts between South African state legislation and corporate-led CSR provisions are not mutually exclusive endeavours for developing stronger CSR policies.

In Chapter 10, Shingirai Taodzera shifts the reader's attention to the oil and gas sector. The discoveries of new oil and gas deposits in East Africa over the past decade have given rise to interest in academic and policy circles regarding whether the region will avoid or experience the "resource curse" (Nwapi and Andrews 2017). Taodzera contributes to the growing literature on this subject by providing a critique of the resource curse metanarrative, employing the "political settlements" analytical framework and using Uganda as a case study. The author focuses analytical attention on the informal structures of power – or political settlements – that underlie societal, political, and economic institutions. In the case of Uganda, this includes the nature of President Yoweri Museveni's National Resistance Movement (NRM) regime and its relationship with other political actors – especially traditional kingdoms, which are a formidable political force in Uganda. Taodzera's central argument is that academic researchers and development practitioners ought to prioritize the need to boost their understanding of the nature of political settlements in Uganda in order to attain a comprehensive view of the political and economic outcomes from resource endowment. This would also help to determine the feasibility and effectiveness of policy prescriptions for managing the oil industry and its revenues. Ultimately, Taodzera assesses Uganda's prospects in terms of achieving positive developmental outcomes from resource wealth.

The book concludes, in the fourth section, with two chapters. In Chapter 11, Bonnie Campbell assesses the findings, arguments, and policy-oriented recommendations presented in the book, and revisits her own research on Africa's extractive resource sectors over the past fifteen years. This comparative analysis offers a compelling way to reflect upon the two main thematic aspects of the book in a manner that is integrated within the broader scholarly literature. To that end, Campbell assesses research on the reform of regulatory and legal frameworks for mining in a number of mineral-rich African countries, introduced to establish a more favourable environment for foreign investment, and elucidates the implications for social and economic development and the protection of the environment in the countries concerned.

Chapter 12 offers some final thoughts on the various contributions in the volume, including a reflection on the key themes of CSR, "good governance," and human security in the context of Africa-Canada relations. As many of the chapters explore, CSR strategies might be seen as an attempt to respond to the very real challenges concerning the legitimacy of the activities of companies, which, in turn, could be linked at a deeper structural level to the perpetuation of particular and often very asymmetrical structural relations of power between companies and communities and between companies and governments that go far beyond the control of any single enterprise. It follows that issues linking CSR, good governance, and human security need to be resituated within a much broader institutional and political perspective that takes account of the origins of these problems.

Some Concluding Reflections on Prospects for Africa-Canada Relations

During the 2016 workshop held at Queen's University, which served as the genesis of this book project, we had an interesting presentation from the Canadian government's then Extractive Sector CSR Counsellor. In the presentation, titled "Promoting Responsible Business Conduct in the Extractives – A Canadian Government Approach," Jeffrey Davidson explained both the challenges and prospects he faced in his daily role as a mediator between Canadian extractive companies and host governments or local communities. It was an insightful start to our workshop, as the mundane realities of the CSR counsellor's office cautiously guided the rest of discussions for the remaining day-and-a-half. One key takeaway was that the office appeared more proactive about in-person visits to local sites of extraction, investigating cases, and engaging with diverse stakeholders than was the case a few years ago.

Also, there seemed to be a few more resources committed to achieving the overall objectives of the office, despite the plethora of practical challenges identified and debated by both the counsellor and audience members. Perhaps these prevailing concerns identified during the workshop were consistent with the government's rationale to establish the CORE in 2018, especially considering its potential for greater independence, a multisectoral focus, and even possibly "teeth to bite." In reflecting on prospects for Africa-Canada relations in light of the extractive sector, these CSR-related institutional arrangements might be a good start for a relationship that historically has been lopsided, but they are certainly not *the* panacea.

A good amount of the critical scholarship on Canada's foreign policy came out during the period of the previous government under Stephen Harper from 2006 to 2015 (see, for example, Black 2009; Brown 2012; Butler 2015; Chapnick and Kukucha 2016; Deneault and Sacher 2012; Gordon 2010; Nossal and Sarson 2014; Schmitz 2014; Stoett and Kersten 2014). During the Harper era, several policy changes were made that influenced the country's role in the world at large and Africa in particular. While falling short in its international commitments (in areas such as aid and humanitarian assistance), the extractive industry was receiving a boost in investment. The strategy document "Building the Canadian Advantage" was unveiled as a comprehensive way to highlight the government's commitment to CSR. Chapters 2 and 3 in this book examine the origins, relevance, and implications of this CSR strategy document. But a careful reading of the document's title alone – and that of the 2014 strategy, "Doing Business the Canadian Way" – immediately denotes an emphasis on Canada's advantage (for example, its economic interests), not necessarily those of the communities abroad in which these activities might take place. In fall 2010, during the Conservative government's period in office, Bill C-300 – which would have provided stricter ethical requirements for Canadian extractive companies abroad – failed in the House of Commons. This failure, among other factors, made Canada gain the status as a haven for global mining corporations – including those with notorious reputations (see Deneault and Sacher 2012; Gordon 2010).

At this juncture, two questions emerge: To what extent does (and should) the Canadian government monitor, supervise, and enforce the various aspirational goals embedded in the term "corporate social responsibility"? And to what extent does the behaviour of Canadian mining companies affect or compromise the reputation of Canadian foreign policy? The various chapters in this volume engage with these important questions, some explicitly and others in a more implicit fashion. We can argue that the existence of the CORE partly answers the first question, as we believe that, although Bill C-300 failed to pass, at least this new institution signals the government's interest in monitoring and enforcing some of the goals embedded in notions around CSR. In a way, this endeavour addresses the second question, in the sense that, by the government's establishing the CORE and other normative mechanisms such as ESTMA, there seems to be a growing consensus that the activities of Canadian mining companies are closely tied to the global reputation of the Canadian state and its foreign policy.

With a change in government nearly four years ago and an election forthcoming towards the end of 2019, one can have a prospective look into whether or not the actions and inactions of the previous Harper Conservative government were any different than those under the Trudeau Liberal government. If early political statements were anything to go by, we might even postulate that there could be a marked difference in the two governments' approaches to foreign policy. It remains unclear, however, if this would present positive outcomes for countries that have experienced years of resource exploitation at the hands of Canadian companies. In light of Canada's taking on the chair of the VPs for 2016–17, we can anticipate some significant leadership in the areas of human rights, human security, and best practices in the extractive sector. It is noteworthy that Canada had previously served as the VPs chair in 2011–12, but that did not make a significantly positive difference in local sites where the VPs were being implemented. Although there is a gradual shift towards these norms in companies' operations, as noted in both Chapters 4 and 5 of this book, the implementation of the VPs framework remains uneven. This evidence casts doubts on Canada's leadership potential in this important area.

Additionally, future budgetary allocations for certain key aspects of Canada's international engagements have either been reduced or left unchanged from current and previous years – including priority areas such as humanitarian assistance, international security, and contributions to international organizations (see Table 1.2). The only areas projected to see increases over a two-year period were international development and efforts towards empowering women and girls; advancing democracy, human rights, and freedom; and promoting the rule of law. Perhaps the latter partly reflects the country's current active role in the VPs, but the fact is that these planned spending amounts do not necessarily provide an adequate prediction of Canada's leading role in global affairs, contrary to the political rhetoric surrounding the election that brought the Liberals into office in late 2015 and the fanfare surrounding the "feminist international assistance policy" announced in mid-2018.

Table 1.2. Planned Spending by Global Affairs Canada, by Category, Fiscal Years 2016/17 to 2018/19

Program Area	Planned Spending		
	2016–17	2017–18	2018–19
	($ millions)		
Integrated foreign affairs, trade, and development policy	82.4	80.5	80.3
International policy advice	45.3	44.4	44.4
Diplomacy, advocacy, and international agreements	957.8	953.4	953.1
Bilateral and regional diplomacy and advocacy	174.0	171.6	171.3
Summitry and multilateral diplomacy and advocacy	81.1	79.5	79.4
Assessed contributions to international organizations	667.6	667.6	667.6
International security and democratic development	237.9	238.8	161.6
International security and threat reduction	120.9	121.0	43.5
Advancing democracy, human rights, freedom, and the rule of law	117.0	117.7	118.0
International development	2,335.2	2,302.8	2,451.9
Food security	428.4	426.7	416.4
International humanitarian assistance	561.9	563.0	475.8
Humanitarian programming	430.4	431.2	355.1
Partners for humanitarian assistance	131.6	131.8	120.6

Source: Authors' compilation from Canada (2016).

Moreover, Canada is seen to be involved in formulating extractive industry legislation that favours the foreign operators instead of the local context within which such operations take place (Butler 2015; Campbell 1999, 2010; Deneault and Sacher 2012). If this practice persists, will there be real positive prospects for Africa-Canada relations? As discussed in several chapters in this volume, the development question cuts across global and local terrains. Yet assertive African countries have begun to envisage extractive industry legislation and mechanisms to support the retention of resource profits in-country, a trend that seems to suggest some good tidings for the future. If Canada is indeed interested in facilitating the development of these countries via investment in their extractive industries, then some support could be directed towards such efforts. But since the budget for international policy advice was not projected to increase substantially by 2019, as Table 1.2 shows, it is hard to discern if funds would be committed to that end. On the other hand, since these regulatory changes could "significantly affect the risk calculations of many extractive industry investors" (Roberts 2014, 9), they are quite unlikely to gain strong backing from industry. Admittedly it is "early days," but we have yet to see the difference that the new CORE is expected to make in specific locations of extraction in Africa.

There are no readily available data to shed light on the potential positive effect of the $6.7 million CIDA funding that enabled a partnership between Canadian companies and NGOs working on international development and poverty issues in Africa. We expect that once details of its impact are made public, both scholars and policy makers would be able to gauge the effectiveness of these increasingly popular multisectoral public-private partnerships. At least for now, one can expect that such partnerships would make a difference only when Africans themselves are involved in the negotiation and implementation of the projects they target. This idea aligns with Roberts's (2014) recommendation for ongoing public consultation and education about the benefits and rights to be expected in extractive industry activities. Furthermore, in an era when several Global South countries are offering a hand to African countries, often in exchange for access to one natural resource or another, options have expanded beyond the previous "North-South" mindset that governed both bilateral and multilateral activities. These concluding remarks – albeit preliminary by necessity – illuminate a few aspects of the many issues at play in the political economy of Africa's natural resource sectors and the role Canada currently plays or could play in the future. As such, we hope that they represent modest yet important theoretical, analytical, and practical signposts for how this relationship might be examined in both scholarly and policy circles.

NOTES

1 See, for example, Panagos and Grant (2013), Grant and colleagues (2014), and Grant (2014c).

2 For the complete wording of the Extractive Sector Transparency Measures Act, see www.parl.gc.ca/HousePublications/Publication.aspx?Language=E&Mode=1&DocId=6737565&File=464#27, accessed 8 June 2015.

3 This point recognizes that some firms might be registered at the provincial level and therefore subject to provincial regulations. Still, the federal government can play a leadership role in setting overarching standards that do more than is set out in ESTMA.

4 For an application of this assertion concerning the power and influence of African state and non-state actors in establishing and transforming transnational norms, see, for example, Grant (2018).

BIBLIOGRAPHY

Aaronson, Susan Ariel. 2011. "Limited Partnership: Business, Government, Civil Society, and the Public in the Extractive Industries Transparency Initiative (EITI)." *Public Administration and Development* 31 (1): 50–63. https://doi.org/10.1002/pad.588.

Abrahamsen, Rita, and Michael C. Williams, eds. 2010. *Security beyond the State: Private Security in International Politics.* Cambridge: Cambridge University Press.

Akuffo, Edward A. 2012. *Canadian Foreign Policy in Africa: Regional Approaches to Peace, Security, and Development.* Aldershot, UK: Ashgate.

Akuffo, Edward A. 2013. "Beyond Apartheid: Moral Identity, FIPAs, and NEPAD in Canada-South Africa Relations." *Commonwealth & Comparative Politics* 51 (2): 173–88. https://doi.org/10.1080/14662043.2013.774196.

Alao, Abiodun. 2008. *Natural Resources and Conflict in Africa: The Tragedy of Endowment.* Rochester, NY: University of Rochester Press.

Alorse, Raynold Wonder, W.R. Nadège Compaoré, and J. Andrew Grant. 2015. "Assessing the European Union's Engagement with Transnational Policy Networks on Conflict-Prone Natural Resources." *Contemporary Politics* 21 (3): 245–57. http://dx.doi.org/10.1080/13569775.2015.1061238.

Andrews, Nathan. 2013a. "Beyond the Ivory Tower: A Case for 'Praxeological Deconstructionism' as a 'Third Way' in IR Theorising." *Third World Quarterly* 34 (1): 59–76. https://doi.org/10.1080/01436597.2012.755011.

Andrews, Nathan. 2013b. "Community Expectations from Ghana's New Oil Find: Conceptualizing Corporate Social Responsibility as a Grassroots-Oriented Process." *Africa Today* 60 (1): 54–75. https://doi.org/10.2979/africatoday.60.1.55.

Andrews, Nathan. 2015. "Digging for Survival and/or Justice? The Drivers of Illegal Mining Activities in Western Ghana." *Africa Today* 62 (2): 3–24. https://doi.org/10.2979/africatoday.62.2.3.

Andrews, Nathan. 2016a. "Challenges of Corporate Social Responsibility (CSR) in Domestic Settings: An Exploration of Mining Regulation vis-à-vis

CSR in Ghana." *Resources Policy* 47: 9–17. https://doi.org/10.1016/j.resourpol.2015.11.001.

Andrews, Nathan. 2016b. "A Swiss-Army Knife? A Critical Assessment of the Extractive Industries Transparency Initiative (EITI) in Ghana." *Business and Society Review* 121 (1): 59–83. https://doi.org/10.1111/basr.12081.

Andrews, Nathan. 2017. "Normative Spaces and the UN Global Compact for Transnational Corporations: The Norm Diffusion Paradox." *Journal of International Relations and Development* (advance access version 16 May 2017), 1–30. https://doi.org/10.1057/s41268-017-0103-3.

Andrews, Nathan. 2019. *Gold Mining and Discourses of Corporate Social Responsibility in Ghana*. New York: Palgrave Macmillan.

Andrews, Nathan, and Chilenye Nwapi. 2018. "Bringing the State Back in Again? The Emerging Developmental State in Africa's Energy Sector." *Energy Research & Social Science* 41 (July): 48–58. https://doi.org/10.1016/j.erss.2018.04.004.

Banerjee, Subhabatra Bobby. 2007. *Corporate Social Responsibility: The Good, the Bad and the Ugly*. Northampton, MA: Edward Elgar.

Baumann-Pauly, Dorothée, and Justine Nolan. 2016. *Business and Human Rights: From Principles to Practice*. New York: Routledge.

Besada, Hany, and Philip Martin. 2015. "Mining Codes in Africa: Emergence of a 'Fourth' Generation?" *Cambridge Review of International Affairs* 28 (2): 263–82. https://doi.org/10.1080/09557571.2013.840823.

Bhushan, Aniket. 2014. "Canada and Africa's Natural Resources: Key Features 2013." Ottawa: North-South Institute. Available online at http://www.nsi-ins.ca/wp-content/uploads/2014/01/Report-Canada-and-Africa's-Natural-Resources.pdf, accessed 27 November 2018.

Black, David R. 2009. "Out of Africa? The Harper Government's New 'Tilt' in the Developing World." *Canadian Foreign Policy Journal* 15 (2): 41–56. https://doi.org/10.1080/11926422.2009.9673486.

Black, David R. 2015. *Canada and Africa in the New Millennium: The Politics of Consistent Inconsistency*. Waterloo, ON: Wilfrid Laurier University Press.

Black, David R., and David J. Hornsby. 2016. "Living Up to Expectations: Canada and South Africa in the Era of the Global Markets Action Plan." *Canadian Foreign Policy Journal* 22 (1): 12–25. https://doi.org/10.1080/11926422.2015.1129633.

Bowen, Howard R. 1953. *Social Responsibilities of the Businessman*. New York: Harper & Row.

Breslin, Shaun, and George Christou. 2015. "Has the Human Security Agenda Come of Age? Definitions, Discourses and Debates." *Contemporary Politics* 21 (1): 1–10. https://doi.org/10.1080/13569775.2014.993904.

Brown, Stephen, ed. 2012. *Struggling for Effectiveness: CIDA and Canadian Foreign Aid*. Montreal; Kingston, ON: McGill-Queen's University Press.

Butler, Paula. 2015. *Colonial Extractions: Race and Canadian Mining in Contemporary Africa.* Toronto: University of Toronto Press.

Campbell, Bonnie. 1999. *Canadian Mining Interests and Human Rights in Africa in the Context of Globalization.* Ottawa: International Centre for Human Rights & Democratic Development.

Campbell, Bonnie, ed. 2004. *Regulating Mining in Africa: For Whose Benefit?* Discussion Paper 26. Uppsala: Nordic Africa Institute.

Campbell, Bonnie. 2010. "Revisiting the Reform Process of African Mining Regimes." *Canadian Journal of Development Studies* 30 (1–2): 197–217. https://doi.org/10.1080/02255189.2010.9669288.

Campbell, Bonnie. 2011. "Canadian Mining in Africa. 'Do As You Please' Approach Comes at High Cost." *Canadian Dimension* 45 (1): 28–32.

Campbell, Bonnie. 2012. "Corporate Social Responsibility and Development in Africa: Redefining the Roles and Responsibilities of Public and Private Actors in the Mining Sector." *Resources Policy* 37 (2): 138–43. https://doi.org/10.1016/j.resourpol.2011.05.002.

Canada. 2016. Global Affairs Canada. "Report on Plans and Priorities 2016-17." Ottawa, 2016. Available online at https://international.gc.ca/gac-amc/assets/pdfs/publications/plans/rpp/RPP_2016_2017_ENG.pdf.

Canada. 2018a. Global Affairs Canada. "Canada's Enhanced Corporate Social Responsibility Strategy to Strengthen Canada's Extractive Sector Abroad." Ottawa, January. Available online at https://www.international.gc.ca/trade-agreements-accords-commerciaux/topics-domaines/other-autre/csr-strat-rse.aspx?lang=eng, accessed 10 January 2018.

Canada. 2018b. Natural Resources Canada. "Energy and the Economy." Ottawa, September. Available online at https://www.nrcan.gc.ca/energy/facts/energy-economy/20062, accessed 1 May 2018.

Canada. 2018c. Global Affairs Canada. "The Government of Canada Brings Leadership to Responsible Business Conduct Abroad." News Release, 17 January. Available online at https://www.canada.ca/en/global-affairs/news/2018/01/the_government_ofcanadabringsleadershiptoresponsible businesscond.html, accessed 26 November 2018.

Canada. 2019a. Natural Resources Canada. "Canadian Mining Assets." Information Bulletin. Ottawa, February. Available online at https://www.nrcan.gc.ca/mining-materials/publications/19323.

Canada. 2019b. Global Affairs Canada. "Responsible Business Conduct Abroad." Ottawa, March. Available online at https://www.international.gc.ca/trade-agreements-accords-commerciaux/topics-domaines/other-autre/csr-rse.aspx?lang=eng, accessed 20 March 2019.

Carroll, Archie B. 1999. "Corporate Social Responsibility: Evolution of a Definitional Construct." *Business and Society* 38 (3): 268–95. https://doi.org/10.1177%2F000765039903800303.

Chapnick, Adam, and Christopher J. Kukucha, eds. 2016. *The Harper Era in Canadian Foreign Policy: Parliament, Politics, and Canada's Global Posture.* Vancouver: UBC Press.

Collins, Andrea M., J. Andrew Grant, and Patricia Ackah-Baidoo. 2019. "The Glocal Dynamics of Land Reform in Natural Resource Sectors: Insights from Tanzania." *Land Use Policy* 81: 889–96. https://doi.org/10.1016/j.landusepol. 2017.05.027.

Compaoré, W.R. Nadège. 2015. "Re-politicizing State Sovereignty in Global Governance: The Political Economy of Transparency in the Oil Sectors of Gabon and Ghana." PhD diss., Queen's University.

Cooper, Andrew F., John English, and Ramesh Thakur, eds. 2002. *Enhancing Global Governance: Towards a New Diplomacy?* New York: United Nations University Press.

Dagenais, Pierre. 2010. "Canadian Mining Industry Wins with Bill C-300's Defeat." *Canadian Mining Journal*, 1 December. Available online at http://www.canadianminingjournal.com/features/canadian-mining-industry-wins-with-bill-c-300-s-defeat/1000395591/?er=NA, accessed 1 May 2018.

Dashwood, Hevina S. 2007. "Towards Sustainable Mining: The Corporate Role in the Construction of Global Standards." *Multinational Business Review* 15 (1): 47–65. https://doi.org/10.1108/1525383x200700003.

Dashwood, Hevina S. 2012. *The Rise of Global Corporate Social Responsibility: Mining and the Spread of Global Norms.* Cambridge: Cambridge University Press.

Dashwood, Hevina S., and Bill B. Puplampu. 2010. "Corporate Social Responsibility and Canadian Mining Companies in the Developing World: The Role of Organizational Leadership and Learning." *Canadian Journal of Development Studies* 30 (1–2): 175–96. https://doi.org/10.1080/02255189.201 0.9669287.

Dashwood, Hevina S., and Bill B. Puplampu. 2015. "Multi-Stakeholder Partnerships in Mining: From Engagement to Development in Ghana." In *New Approaches to the Governance of Natural Resources: Insights from Africa,* edited by J. Andrew Grant, W.R. Nadège Compaoré, and Matthew I. Mitchell, 131–53. London: Palgrave Macmillan.

Deneault, Alain, and William Sacher. 2012. *Imperial Canada Inc.: Legal Haven of Choice for the World's Mining Industry.* With Catherine Browne, Mathieu Denis, and Patrick Ducharme. Translated by Fred A. Reed and Robin Philpot. Vancouver: Talonbooks.

du Preez, Mari-Lise. 2015. "Interrogating the 'Good' in 'Good Governance': Rethinking Natural Resource Governance Theory and Practice in Africa." In *New Approaches to the Governance of Natural Resources: Insights from Africa,* edited by J. Andrew Grant, W.R. Nadège Compaoré, and Matthew I. Mitchell, 25–42. London: Palgrave Macmillan.

Engler, Yves. 2015. *Canada in Africa: 300 Years of Aid and Exploitation.* Vancouver: Fernwood Books.

Engler, Yves. 2016. "The Hypocrisy of Canadian Ownership in Africa." *Huffington Post*, 13 June. Available online at https://www.huffingtonpost.ca/ yves-engler/canada-african-mining_b_10382436.html, accessed 11 January 2018.

Essah, Marcellinus, and Nathan Andrews. 2016. "Linking or De-linking Sustainable Mining Practices and Corporate Social Responsibility? Insights from Ghana." *Resources Policy* 50: 75–85. https://doi.org/10.1016/j. resourpol.2016.08.008.

Frynas, Jedrzej G. 2005. "The False Developmental Promise of Corporate Social Responsibility: Evidence from Multinational Oil Companies." *International Affairs* 81 (3): 581–98. https://doi.org/10.1111/j.1468-2346.2005.00470.x.

Frynas, Jedrzej G. 2008. "Corporate Social Responsibility and International Development: Critical Assessment." *Corporate Governance* 16 (4): 274–81. https://doi.org/10.1111/j.1467-8683.2008.00691.x.

Frynas, Jedrzej G. 2009. *Beyond Corporate Social Responsibility: Oil Multinationals and Social Challenges.* Cambridge: Cambridge University Press.

Glasius, Marlies. 2008. "Human Security from Paradigm Shift to Operationalization: Job Description for a Human Security Worker." *Security Dialogue* 39 (1): 31–54. https://doi.org/10.1177/0967010607086822.

Gordon, Todd. 2010. *Imperialist Canada.* Winnipeg: Arbeiter Ring Publishing.

Grant, J. Andrew. 2009. *Digging Deep for Profits and Development? Reflections on Enhancing the Governance of Africa's Mining Sector.* Johannesburg: South African Institute of International Affairs.

Grant, J. Andrew. 2014a. *Canada's Long Legacy of Multilateral Sustainable Development.* Toronto: Canadian International Council.

Grant, J. Andrew. 2014b. "Cleaning up the Market: Governance Initiatives on Conflict-Prone Minerals." *BioRes: Analysis and News on Trade and Environment* 8 (8): 16–19. Available online at https://www.ictsd.org/ bridges-news/biores/news/cleaning-up-the-market-governance-initiatives-on-conflict-prone-minerals.

Grant, J. Andrew. 2014c. *Resources and Canada's First Nations.* Toronto: Canadian International Council.

Grant, J. Andrew. 2018. "Agential Constructivism and Change in World Politics." *International Studies Review* 20 (2): 255–63. https://doi.org/10.1093/isr/viy021.

Grant, J. Andrew, Dianne Balraj, and Georgia Mavropoulos-Vagelis. 2013. "Reflections on Network Governance in Africa's Forestry Sector." *Natural Resources Forum* 37 (4): 269–79. https://doi.org/10.1111/1477-8947.12028.

Grant, J. Andrew, W.R. Nadège Compaoré, and Matthew I. Mitchell, eds. 2015. *New Approaches to the Governance of Natural Resources: Insights from Africa.* London: Palgrave Macmillan.

Grant, J. Andrew, Adrien N. Djomo, and Maria G. Krause. 2016. "Afro-Optimism Reinvigorated? Reflections on the Glocal Networks of Sexual Identity, Health, and Natural Resources in Africa." *Global Change, Peace & Security* 28 (3): 317–28. https://doi.org/10.1080/14781158.2016.1193847.

Grant, J. Andrew, W.R. Nadège Compaoré, Matthew I. Mitchell, and Mats Ingulstad. 2015a. "'New' Approaches to the Governance of Africa's Natural Resources." In *New Approaches to the Governance of Natural Resources: Insights from Africa*, edited by J. Andrew Grant, W.R. Nadège Compaoré, and Matthew I. Mitchell, 3–24. London: Palgrave Macmillan.

Grant, J. Andrew, Dianne Balraj, Jeremy Davison, and Georgia Mavropoulos-Vagelis. 2015b. "Network Governance and the African Timber Organization: Prospects for Regional Forestry Governance in Africa." In *New Approaches to the Governance of Natural Resources: Insights from Africa*, edited by J. Andrew Grant, W.R. Nadège Compaoré, and Matthew I. Mitchell, 154–80. London: Palgrave Macmillan.

Grant, J. Andrew, Dimitrios Panagos, Michael Hughes, and Matthew I. Mitchell. 2014. "A Historical Institutionalist Understanding of Participatory Governance and Aboriginal Peoples: The Case of Policy Change in Ontario's Mining Sector." *Social Science Quarterly* 95 (4): 978–1000. https://doi.org/10.1111/ssqu.12115.

Grindle, Merilee S. 2004. "Good Enough Governance: Poverty Reduction and Reform in Developing Countries." *Governance* 17 (4): 525–48. https://doi.org/10.1111/j.0952-1895.2004.00256.x.

Grindle, Merilee S. 2007. "Good Enough Governance Revisited." *Development Policy Review* 25 (5): 553–74. https://doi.org/10.1111/j.1467-7679.2007.00385.x.

Hall, Rodney Bruce, and Thomas J. Biersteker, eds. 2002. *The Emergence of Private Authority in Global Governance*. Cambridge: Cambridge University Press.

Hampson, Fen Osler, Jean Daudelin, John B. Hay, Todd Martin, and Holly Reid. 2002. *Madness in the Multitude: Human Security and World Disorder*. Oxford: Oxford University Press.

Hilson, Gavin. 2007. "Championing the Rhetoric? 'Corporate Social Responsibility' in Ghana's Mining Sector." *Greener Management International* 53: 43–56.

Hilson, Gavin. 2012. "Corporate Social Responsibility in the Extractive Industries: Experiences from Developing Countries." *Resources Policy* 37 (2): 131–7. https://doi.org/10.1016/j.resourpol.2012.01.002.

Hilson, Gavin, and Roy Maconachie. 2008. "'Good Governance' and the Extractive Industries in Sub-Saharan Africa." *Mineral Processing and Extractive Metallurgy Review* 30 (1): 52–100. https://doi.org/10.1080/08827500802045511.

Hornsby, David J. 2014. "Changing Perception into Reality: Canada in Africa." *International Journal* 69 (3): 334–52. https://doi.org/10.1177/0020702014540867.

Idemudia, Uwafiokun. 2007. "Community Perceptions and Expectations: Reinventing the Wheels of Corporate Social Responsibility Practices in the Nigerian Oil Industry." *Business and Society Review* 112 (3): 369–405. https://doi.org/10.1111/j.1467-8594.2007.00301.x.

Idemudia, Uwafiokun. 2010. "Rethinking the Role of Corporate Social Responsibility in the Nigerian Oil Conflict: The Limits of CSR." *Journal of International Development* 22 (7): 833–45. https://doi.org/10.1002/jid.1644.

Idemudia, Uwafiokun. 2014. "Corporate Social Responsibility and Development in Africa: Issues and Possibilities." *Geography Compass* 8 (7): 421–35. https://doi.org/10.1111/gec3.12143.

International Council on Mining and Metals. 2006. *The Challenge of Mineral Wealth: Using Resource Endowments to Foster Sustainable Development*. The Analytical Framework: Main Report. London: ICMM.

Jabeen, Nasira. 2007. "Good or Good Enough Governance in South Asia: Constraints and Possibilities." Inaugural Address as Professor to the Prince Claus Chair in Development and Equity, 2006–7. Utrecht University, 2 April.

Mack, Andrew, ed. 2012. *Human Security Report 2012: Sexual Violence, Education, and War: Beyond the Mainstream Narrative*, Vancouver: Human Security Press.

Martin, Mary, and Taylor Owen, eds. 2014. *Routledge Handbook of Human Security*. New York: Routledge.

Mayntz, Renate. 2003. "New Challenges to Governance Theory." In *Governance as Social and Political Communication*, edited by Henrik P. Bang, 27–40. Manchester: Manchester University Press.

Medhora, Rohinton, and Yiagadeesen Samy, eds. 2013. *Canada and Africa: From Aid to Engagement – Looking Back, Looking Ahead (Canada Among Nations)*. Montreal; Kingston, ON: McGill-Queen's University Press.

Nossal, Kim Richard, and Leah Sarson. 2014. "About Face: Explaining Changes in Canada's China Policy, 2006–2012." *Canadian Foreign Policy Journal* 20 (2): 146–62. https://doi.org/10.1080/11926422.2014.934864.

Nossal, Kim Richard, Stéphane Roussel, and Stéphane Paquin. 2015. *The Politics of Canadian Foreign Policy*. 4th ed. Montreal; Kingston, ON: McGill-Queen's University Press.

Nwapi, Chilenye, and Nathan Andrews. 2017. "A New Developmental State in Africa: Evaluating Recent State Interventions vis-à-vis Resource Extraction in Kenya, Tanzania, and Rwanda." *McGill Journal of Sustainable Development Law* 13 (2): 223–67. Available online at https://www.mcgill.ca/mjsdl/files/mjsdl/4_nwapi_web.pdf.

Okpanachi, Eyene, and Nathan Andrews. 2012. "Preventing the Oil 'Resource Curse' in Ghana: Lessons from Nigeria." *World Futures* 68 (6): 430–50. https://doi.org/10.1080/02604027.2012.693854.

Osei-Kojo, Alex, and Nathan Andrews. 2018. "A Developmental Paradox? The 'Dark Forces' against Corporate Social Responsibility in Ghana's Extractive Industry." *Environment, Development and Sustainability* (advance access version 12 August 2018), 1–21. https://doi.org/10.1007/s10668-018-0233-9.

Ovadia, Jesse S. 2014. "Local Content and Natural Resource Governance: The Cases of Angola and Nigeria." *Extractive Industries and Society* 1 (2): 137–46. https://doi.org/10.1016/j.exis.2014.08.002.

Panagos, Dimitrios, and J. Andrew Grant. 2013. "Constitutional Change, Aboriginal Rights, and Mining Policy in Canada." *Commonwealth & Comparative Politics* 51 (4): 405–23. https://doi.org/10.1080/14662043.2013.838373.

Paris, Roland. 2001. "Human Security: Paradigm Shift or Hot Air?" *International Security* 26 (2): 87–102. https://doi.org/10.1162/016228801753191141.

Raman, K. Ravi, and Ronnie D. Lipschutz, eds. 2010. *Corporate Social Responsibility: Comparative Critiques*. London: Palgrave Macmillan.

Roberts, Chris. 2014. "Extractive Sector Regulations and Policy in Africa: Old Practices and New Models for Change." Ottawa: North-South Institute. Available online at http://www.nsi-ins.ca/wp-content/uploads/2014/01/Brief-Roberts-Extractive-Sector-Regulations.pdf, accessed 18 January 2017.

Rustad, Siri Aas, Philippe Le Billon, and Päivi Lujala. 2017. "Has the Extractive Industries Transparency Initiative Been a Success? Identifying and Evaluating EITI Goals." *Resources Policy* 51: 151–62. https://doi.org/10.1016/j.resourpol.2016.12.004.

Sagebien, Julia, and Nicole Marie Lindsay, eds. 2011. *Governance Ecosystems: CSR in the Latin American Mining Sector*. London: Palgrave Macmillan.

Schmitz, Gerald J. 2014. "The Harper Government and the De-democratization of Canadian Foreign Policy." *Canadian Foreign Policy Journal* 20 (2): 224–8. https://doi.org/10.1080/11926422.2014.934859.

Schneider, Volker, and Johannes M. Bauer. 2007. "Governance: Prospects of Complexity Theory in Revisiting System Theory." Paper presented at the Midwest Political Science Association conference, Chicago, 14 April.

Sovacool, Benjamin K., Götz Walter, Thijs Van de Graaf, and Nathan Andrews. 2016. "Energy Governance, Transnational Rules, and the Resource Curse: Exploring the Effectiveness of the Extractive Industries Transparency Initiative (EITI)." *World Development* 86: 179–92. https://doi.org/10.1016/j.worlddev.2016.01.021.

Sovacool, Benjamin K., and Nathan Andrews. 2015. "Does Transparency Matter? Evaluating the Governance Impacts of the Extractive Industries Transparency Initiative (EITI) in Azerbaijan and Liberia." *Resources Policy* 45: 183–92. https://doi.org/10.1016/j.resourpol.2015.04.003.

Stoett, Peter, and Mark Stefan Kersten. 2014. "Beyond Ideological Fixation: Ecology, Justice, and Canadian Foreign Policy under Harper." *Canadian Foreign Policy Journal* 20 (2): 229–32. https://doi.org/10.1080/11926422.2014.934857.

Tadjbakhsh, Shahrbanou, and Anuradha M. Chenoy. 2007. *Human Security: Concepts and Implications*. New York: Routledge.

Teye, Joseph K. 2013. "Analysing Forest Resource Governance in Africa: Proposition for an Integrated Policy Network Model." *Forest Policy and Economics* 26: 63–70. https://doi.org/10.1016/j.forpol.2012.08.012.

Thauer, Christian R. 2014. *The Managerial Sources of Corporate Social Responsibility: The Spread of Global Standards*. Cambridge: Cambridge University Press.

UNDP (United Nations Development Programme). 1994. *Human Development Report 1994*. New York: Oxford University Press.

Van Alstine, James, and Nathan Andrews. 2016. "Corporations, Civil Society and Disclosure: A Case Study of the EITI." In *Palgrave Handbook of the International Political Economy of Energy*, edited by Thijs Van de Graaf, Benjamin K. Sovacool, Arunabha Ghosh, Florian Kern, and Michael T. Klare, 95–114. London: Palgrave Macmillan.

Votaw, Dow. 1972. "Genius Becomes Rare: A Comment on the Doctrine of Social Responsibility Pt. I." *California Management Review* 15 (2): 25–31. https://doi.org/10.2307/41164415.

SECTION II

Canada in Africa: From the Global to the Local (and Back)

2 The Canadian Government and Corporate Social Responsibility: Implications for Sustainable Development in Africa

UWAFIOKUN IDEMUDIA, W.R. NADÈGE COMPAORÉ,

AND CYNTHIA KWAKYEWAH

Introduction

The role of government in corporate social responsibility (CSR) has received limited attention because analyses of government-CSR relationships are largely counterintuitive to many scholars and observers. This is because CSR is defined as actions that go beyond compliance (Gond, Kang, and Moon 2011). Thus, by definition, CSR precludes a role for government (Gjølberg 2010). Indeed, Vallentin and Murillo (2012) have noted that, in the few instances where CSR-government relationships have been examined in mainstream CSR debates, government tends to be reduced to a powerful force that determines the rules of the game, largely by delimiting what is located inside and outside the domain of CSR. Dentchev, Haezendonck, and van Balen (2015) point out, however, that governments are not just regulators or facilitators of CSR. Rather, "they are also key actors that strategically use CSR either for liberalizing specific aspects of social and political life or for enhancing indirect market and civil society pressure on corporations to behave in a socially responsible manner" (Gond, Kang, and Moon 2011, 642). This is particularly the case given the recent government approach to CSR, which seems to blur the boundaries of public and private governance of CSR (Crane 2010). Indeed the governing of CSR now often takes place within network spaces that require the use of "soft modes" of governing and other strategies associated with civil regulation, which tends to go beyond a traditional "command-and-control" strategy (Crane 2010; Vallentin 2015; Valletin and Murillo 2012). This hybrid form of governing CSR, according to Steurer (2010), now constitutes part of the new mode of societal governance. Lepoutre, Dentchev, and Heene (2007) suggest, however, that, while this network mode of governing is supposedly more flexible than traditional command-and-control regulatory strategies because it avoids the lengthy and difficult process of creating legislation and might be more inclusive and participatory, it also tends to generate substantive, strategic, and institutional uncertainties. Besides, network governance risks drawing attention away from the nature of social interests at play among key actors and, thus, inadvertently masking relations of powers among them (Grant, Balraj, and Mavropoulos-Vagelis 2013; Lascoumes and Les Galès 2007).

Nonetheless, Albareda and colleagues (2008) note that a critical literature review reveals two basic dimensions to the analysis of government and CSR. The first dimension generally emphasizes the need for government involvement in CSR. The focus in this aspect of the literature is on the drivers of government action in CSR. For example, Moon (2002, 2004) identifies three reasons for government involvement in CSR: 1) CSR can substitute for government efforts; 2) it can complement government efforts; and 3) it can legitimize government policies (see also Steurer 2010). The second dimension of the literature focuses either on the different roles governments can adopt in the promotion of CSR (see Fox, Ward, and Howard 2002) or on how governments have understood, designed, and implemented CSR public policy initiatives in order to promote CSR (see Albareda et al. 2008; Albareda, Lozano, and Ysa 2007) – Steurer (2010), for example, identifies five CSR policy instruments: legal, economic, informational, partnering, and hybrid.[1] The major theme to emerge from the foregoing discussion is that public policy has a considerable effect on CSR since governments are key drivers of CSR practices (Dentchev, Haezendonck, and van Balen 2015). The reason is that, if CSR is at the heart of managing the socio-environmental costs and benefits of business activities, then setting the boundaries on how these costs and benefits are managed is partly a question of business policy and partly a question of public governance (Fox, Ward, and Howard 2002; Ward 2004). Hence, from this perspective, the state is not only an important role-player in enforcing, facilitating, or motivating CSR; state institutions themselves also have much to learn from the principles and practices associated with CSR (Hamann 2006; Rasche et al. 2013). Yet analysis of the relationship between government and CSR remains largely embryonic (Dentchev, Haezendonck, and van Balen 2015; Gond, Kang, and Moon 2011; Vallentin 2015).

Against the above background, this chapter seeks to enhance our understanding of the relationship between government and CSR by addressing some specific gaps in the scholarly literature. The chapter is structured around two main themes. The first is a critical examination of the nature of Canada's national CSR strategy in terms of the assumptions that underpin that strategy, and how the federal government conceptualizes CSR and understands its role. Second, we assess the possible implications of Canada's CSR strategy for sustainable development in local African communities. The rest of the chapter is divided as follows. We first present the conceptual framework informing our discussion.[2] Next, guided by our conceptual framework, we offer an in-depth comparative analysis of Canada's 2009 and 2014 national CSR strategies. We conclude with an evaluation of the implications of Canada's strategy for sustainable development in local African communities.

The Conceptual Framework

In the extant literature, efforts to examine the relationship between CSR and government have either adopted a relational state model or comparative national case studies approach. For example, while Albareda and colleagues (2006) adopt a relational state framework to examine the role of the UK and Italian governments in CSR (see also Albareda et al. 2008; Albareda, Lozano, and Ysa 2007). Gond, Kang, and Moon (2011) use comparative national case studies to devise the different types of relationships between CSR and government. Hence, Vallentin (2015) and Vallentin and Murillo (2012) argue that institutional theory has emerged as the dominant perspective in analyses of government-CSR relationships, and that this approach has been particularly insightful, especially in providing a clear outline of the basic forms through which CSR has gradually become institutionalized. Vallentin and Murillo (2012, 36) suggest, however, that there is also a need to "find ways to question and problematize governmental discourse and practices that are often self-appraising and shrouded in win-win rhetoric, with a promise of value creation and other societal benefits." Ergo, they call for a "governmentality perspective" to government-CSR relationships. This approach would allow for the examination of how specific meanings are constructed through systems of representation or discourse, and how this discursive mode of governing via networks operates and carries political rationality. For example, we can understand how the Canadian government might deploy a strategy of accommodation by legitimation to address competing perspectives in the formulation of an appropriate public policy that can guide CSR activities of Canadian extractive companies. According to Hamann and Acutt (2003, 258–9), to accommodate is to "adapt to, or reconcile with changed circumstances, and the underlying motive for accommodation is to make small, feasible changes to how things are so that demands for more significant changes can be precluded." They note that, although accommodation occurs largely in explicit interactions between interests, for example, within multi-stakeholder dialogue, legitimation works at the level of influencing discourse. Legitimation functions to define the nature of the problem at hand, to identify which stakeholders are part of the solution, and to determine what the appropriate solution might be (Hamann and Acutt 2003).

At any rate, drawing on the analytics of governmentality, Vallentin and Murillo (2012, 827) state that "governmentality studies specialize in exploring the subtle and intricate liberal and indirect modes of governing which aim to shape the economic and social conduct of business, without shattering its formally distinct and autonomous character." From this perspective, governing "acts on the governed as a locus of action and freedom" (Dean 1999, 15). Hence, they argue that "an enabling government signifies an absence of force (regulation), but not the absence of power" (Vallentin and Murillo 2012, 827). This is because the absence of force – that is, hard regulation – does not necessarily amount to *self-limitation*; rather, it is an attempt at *self-extension* as governments use different disciplinary efforts to affect, direct, and provide guidance for business CSR initiatives (Vallentin and Murillo 2012). Furthermore, Vallentin (2015) identifies a three-part analytical framework – political rationalities, government programs, and government technologies – for analysing the CSR-government relationship. Political rationalities refer to the kind of political reasons that inform and guide government's role in CSR, and they can be specified and differentiated in terms of the languages within which government's object and objectives are construed and constructed. Government programs refer to programs, policies, strategies, and actions that seek to reconfigure specific locales and relations in ways that are believed to be desirable from government's perspective (Vallentin 2015; Vallentin and Murillo 2012). Finally, it is through government technologies – techniques, devices, systems, procedures, vocabularies, professional areas of expertise, and designs – that the political rationalities and programs of government get enacted (Vallentin 2015). Taken together, this three-part framework represents the translation of political rationality into social practice and, in effect, the three levels are closely intertwined (Vallentin 2015; Vallentin and Murillo 2012). We adopt this framework to examine the role of the Canadian government in CSR and its implications for sustainable development in local communities where Canadian mining companies operate.

Canadian Government CSR Strategies: From "Building the Canadian Advantage" to "Doing Business the Canadian Way"

Canada's first national CSR strategy, "Building the Canadian Advantage: A CSR Strategy for the International Extractive Sector," was launched in 2009. The second, revised strategy was released in 2014 to become "Doing Business the Canadian Way: A Strategy to Advance Corporate Social Responsibility in Canada's Extractive Sector Abroad." Both strategies seem to share a common core but with some differences, given the government's efforts to respond to criticisms of the 2009 version.

In June 2005, the Standing Committee on Foreign Affairs and Trade (SCFAIT) submitted a report to the Canadian government titled *Mining in Developing Countries and Corporate Social Responsibility*, in which it called for the government to do more to ensure that Canadian mining companies operating abroad conduct their business in a responsible manner and respect human rights (Canada 2005). In response, the government instituted a multistakeholder roundtable to discuss and provide recommendations on how it should respond. The report of the advisory group called for the government to create a mandatory CSR standard and a compliance review committee that would support and monitor companies to ensure they meet the mandatory CSR standard, as well as the appointment of an ombudsperson office to address complaints (Canada 2016; Sagebien et al. 2008). Yet, in its 2009 strategy, the Canadian government adopted an accommodating stance by creating the Office of the Extractive Sector CSR Counsellor, as opposed to an ombudsperson, whose role was merely to facilitate complaints, rather than arbitrate them as civil society groups demanded. Similarly, following the failure to secure a mandatory CSR standard in the first national CSR strategy, the corporate accountability movement mobilized support for Bill C-300, which was supposed to: 1) put in place minimum mandatory human rights, labour, and environmental standards; 2) create a complaint mechanism that would allow communities in developing countries that have been injured by Canadian companies to file complaints against them in Canada; and 3) create sanctions for companies that are non-compliant with those standards, including loss of government financial and political support (Moore 2012). By a narrow margin, the bill failed to pass.

In its revised national CSR strategy, the government avoided setting a mandatory CSR standard for Canadian extractive companies and failed to give more power to the CSR counsellor's office, but, in response to Bill C-300, adopted the potential withdrawal of government political and financial support for companies that failed to participate voluntarily in dialogue facilitated by the CSR counsellor's office. In both cases, the government's accommodating strategy was not to dismiss the concerns of the accountability movement, so as not to appear unresponsive, but to adopt a frame that allowed it to address some concerns in a manner that ultimately did not undermine its preference for voluntary obligations over mandatory ones. Indeed the trade minister at the time, Ed Fast, responded to the call for an ombudsperson by stating that "the use of voluntary initiatives, based on internationally recognized standards, can be effective in resolving issues of mutual concerns, and can advance public policy objectives in a more flexible, expeditious and less costly way than regulatory or legislative regimes" (Do 2014). Although the specific outcomes of this government strategy of accommodation and legitimation are not necessarily predetermined, it takes place within the context of unequal power relations between pro-market forces and the protectionist movement. For example, when "Building the Canadian Advantage" was under review, Engineers Without Borders, in its written submission to the federal government, argued that "reforming the office into an ombudsperson role, with powers of investigation and sanction, would help lower the potential for conflicts in resource-rich countries where Canadian companies operate. This, in turn, would help developing countries feel more confident in allowing Canadian-led natural resource projects to go forward" (Do 2014).

In contrast, the president of the Mining Association of Canada (MAC) said his organization favoured a two-step process that would start with the mandatory verification of complaints by the CSR counsellor's office, followed by a voluntary mediation through Canada's National Contact Point for the Organisation for Economic Co-operation and Development Guidelines for Multinational Enterprises (Do 2014). The enhanced national CSR strategy, however, seems to reflect the concerns of MAC more than the demands of local NGOs. This has significant implications for two reasons. First, although the outcome of the tension between pro-market and protectionist movements in CSR is not necessarily predetermined, it is clear that unequal power relations between the two camps have some effect on the content and nature of the national CSR strategy. Second, the Canadian case seems to provide empirical support for the assertion by Lascoumes and Les Galès (2007) that there is a need to pay attention to the interplay of social interest and unequal power relations in the network governance of business behaviour.

Defining CSR, the Problem, and Setting the Focus in the National Strategies: New Direction or Old Framework?

In "Doing Business the Canadian Way," CSR was redefined as "the voluntary activities undertaken by a company, over and above legal requirements, to operate in an economically, socially, and environmentally suitable manner" (Canada 2014, 3). Previously, in "Building the Canadian Advantage," CSR was conceptualized as "the voluntary activities undertaken by a company to operate in an economically, socially, and environmentally suitable manner" (Canada 2009). The significance of the change lies in the fact that, although the government previously appeared unwilling to set a minimum standard, the addition of "going over and above the law" now introduced a new minimum performance standard. Yet this new standard does not constrain corporate freedom or put extra demands on Canadian companies. It is thus consistent with a neoliberal and indirect way of governing that "acts on the governed as a locus of action and freedom" (Dean 1999, 15). However, "[t]he Government expects Canadian companies to integrate CSR throughout their management structures so that they operate abroad in an economic, social and environmentally sustainable manner. This means that companies should understand the impact of each of their functions on the surrounding economy, community and environment, and adjust their activities and operations to create value for themselves and for other stakeholders" (Canada 2014, 3). The implication of this change in the CSR definition is twofold. First, it suggests a realignment of the Canadian government's understanding of CSR with a more conventional notion of CSR as adopted by other government bodies such as the European Union. Hence, there is some evidence that institutional learning might be taking place. Second, the new definition seemed to signify a gradual move from the voluntary to the "enabling environment" perspective, as the government's expectation of CSR now included the need for corporations to understand their effect and to create value for local stakeholders.

Interestingly, in both CSR strategies, the Canadian government conceptualized CSR challenges as issues within the host countries and, in so doing, shifted responsibility away from Canadian extractive companies. The weak institutions and "governance gap" plaguing many developing countries are usually understood as "risks" that a company must manage through the application of management tools. For instance, the government stated that "many companies are looking to the Canadian government for guidance and support in managing the risks of operating in complex and challenging environments" (Canada 2009). Consequently, the first CSR strategy focused on building the capacity of host countries to reap the benefits of responsible resource management. Yet this one-sided characterization of corporate-community relations failed to capture the complexities of the issue – for example, its historical and cultural contexts. More important, it disregarded the ways in which corporations, directly and indirectly, contribute to undermining local institutions. Dashwood (2016) notes that the interactions between Canadian mining companies and community members have sometimes led to violent conflicts and corporate human rights abuses. Indeed, SCFAIT's Subcommittee on Human Rights and International Development heard evidence on the adverse effects of Canadian mining companies (Canada 2005). Perhaps due to this deficiency in the original conception of the problem, the enhanced national CSR strategy had to change from focusing on capacity building to conflict prevention; as evidenced by the following statement from Global Affairs Canada (Canada 2014, 9): "the Government is stepping up efforts to support engagement between companies and communities, including at the exploration stage. Meaningful and regular dialogue between companies and communities, local communities, civil society and host country governments ... can be of critical importance to addressing potential conflicts." In particular, the emphasis was being placed on the "prevention of disputes at their early detection" (11) and "understand[ing] local customs, culture and expectations" (3). It is important to recognize that the shift from an emphasis on capacity building to conflict prevention represented an attempt to redefine the nature of the governance gap that the Canadian national CSR strategy intended to address. The new focus on conflict prevention, however, is still consistent with the view that resource-extraction problems are not due to activities of Canadian extractive companies, but are non-technical risks that need to be managed for operations to continue. This is the case because both strategies are underpinned by the same political rationalities.

A Comparative Analysis of the Political Rationalities: Why the Canadian Government Cares about CSR

Gjølberg (2010) categorizes government perspectives on CSR along two central dimensions: the national-international dimension and the normative-instrumental dimension, which, when combined, produce four basic interpretations of CSR. Whereas the normative-instrumental dimension is concerned with the justification of CSR policy – e.g., relief of welfare expenses, the business case for CSR, the moral duty of businesses, the realization of international norms – the national-international dimension is concerned with the geographic focus of government CSR policy. These four basic interpretations of CSR, by extension, also form the political rationalities for governments' engagement with CSR, and they provide insight into why governments care about CSR.

An examination of the political rationalities of both of Canada's national CSR strategies reveal that they are largely driven by an economic policy rationalization – that is, they focus on economic growth and maintaining competitiveness in the global extractive industry (see Chapter 1, Table 1.2, in this volume). This is perhaps due to the fact that Canada can be seen as a competition state that seeks to equip its firms for competition abroad. Indeed Crouch (2010) notes that the competition tends to give free rein to market forces and transnational corporations to pursue some developmental goals in the context of profit maximization. Hence, support for CSR has been couched largely in the language of the business case – that is, the ability to create win-win outcomes and secure competitive advantage for Canadian companies. According to the government, "Canadian extractive sector activities abroad can result in a win-win outcome both for the Canadian economy and that of host countries" (Canada 2014). Similarly, the government stated that *"Building the Canadian Advantage* will improve the competitive advantage of Canadian international extractive sector companies by enhancing their ability to manage social and environmental risks. By doing so, companies can manage risks more efficiently and effectively, foster good relations with investment partners, employees, and surrounding communities; increase access to capital; and improve their reputation" (Canada 2009). Correspondingly, Gjølberg (2010) elucidates that a combination of instrumental justification and international focus results in an interpretation of CSR as a *competitive advantage of the nation,* whereby CSR becomes a vehicle to drive success and give domestic companies an edge in the global market. Within this interpretation of CSR, domestic companies are able to increase exports, create employment, and ultimately contribute to the growth of the national economy through a national CSR policy. In the case of Canada, the government framed CSR as a competitive advantage of the nation in both the first and enhanced national CSR strategies. The fact that Canada's national CSR strategy has been driven by a business case rationale should not come as a surprise – the strategy was led by the Department of Foreign Affairs and International Trade (DFAIT),[3] hence the prioritization of a market rationale. Similarly, because the department was home to foreign affairs, Canada's national CSR strategy was – and continues to be – framed as an extension of Canadian foreign policy. For example, the strategy explicitly encourages Canadian extractive companies to "embody the Canada brand" and operate in a manner that does not tarnish Canada's reputation abroad (Canada 2014, 3). Indeed, as Gjølberg (2010, 220–1) notes, "the formal ministerial affiliation is decisive for how CSR is interpreted and conceptualized."

The promotion of CSR using economic rationality discourse allows the Canadian government to secure corporate buy-in. Drucker (1984, 59), writing more than three decades ago, asserted that, "in the next decade [the 1990s] it will become increasingly important to stress that business can discharge its 'social responsibilities,' only if it converts them into 'self-interest,' that is, into business opportunities." Consequently, from a government perspective, the business case discourse and the economic policy rationalization of government CSR strategy constitute a creative effort to deliberately rationalize CSR in a particular way; this discourse and rationalization justify and promote a particular economic "truth" that CSR creates win-win outcomes (Vallentin and Murillo 2012). This is despite the fact that numerous empirical studies linking CSR and corporate financial performance have been inconclusive – and some have even suggested a rather negative relationship (Margolis and Walsh, 2003). The broader implication is that the business case approach allows the government to raise awareness of CSR among Canadian extractive companies, consistent with Steurer's (2010) suggestion that raising awareness is a key role of government.

As previously mentioned, Canada's national CSR strategy provides a channel for the government to fulfil its foreign policy objectives, such as delivering development assistance (through, for example, the Canada Investment Fund for Africa). This is in line with Steurer's (2010) explanation that governments may take an interest in CSR when certain business efforts align with their policy objectives. In Canada's case, its first national CSR strategy was phrased within the discourse of capacity building and past financial investments made to host countries. In "Building the Canadian Advantage," the government emphasized the contribution of Canadian extractive companies to development in host countries in the following manner: "Canadian companies have invested over $60 billion in developing countries ... These companies are making a substantial contribution to economic development in their host countries. Indeed, Canadian industry associations and extractive companies have been recognized domestically and internationally for their leadership on these issues." Yet providing foreign aid has several useful benefits; among others, it serves to maintain good relationships with civil society groups and public officials of the host countries where Canadian extractive companies do business. For instance, "Doing Business the Canadian Way" highlights some of the concerns raised by NGOs that heavily criticized the government's approach of linking aid with benefits for Canadian businesses operating in development countries. Similarly, other critics believe that these CSR initiatives amounted to the government's using tax dollars to subsidize the commercial interests of wealthy corporations. As a result, Bodruzic (2015) concluded that the government was allowing Canadian commercial interests to strongly influence and determine international development objectives. Perhaps due to these criticisms, in its enhanced CSR strategy the government noted that "other activities, such as capacity-building, are not undertaken for the benefit of companies, but have an impact on how much host countries can benefit from the activities of responsible extractive sector companies" (Canada 2014, 14).

Furthermore the national CSR strategy is based on an accountability mechanism that allows CSR to be used strategically to avoid the implementation of hard laws in the Canadian extractive industry and possibly to move gradually from public governance to network governance based on self- and co-regulation. This is because, according to Dashwood (2016), the government has a predisposition towards a voluntary, rather than a regulatory, approach to CSR.

A Comparative Analysis of the Canadian Government's CSR Strategies

In its first national CSR strategy, "Building the Canadian Advantage," introduced in 2009, the Canadian government identified four main CSR programs: 1) supporting capacity building in developing countries; 2) promoting "widely-recognized international CSR performance guidelines," such as the Voluntary Principles on Security and Human Rights (VPs) and the Global Reporting Initiative (GRI); 3) setting up the Office of the Extractive Sector CSR Counsellor; and 4) assisting in the development of a CSR Centre of Excellence (Canada 2009). In contrast, the government's 2014 enhanced strategy, "Doing Business the Canadian Way," is based on more comprehensive programs for guiding and promoting CSR, including: 1) promoting and advancing CSR guidance; 2) fostering networks and partnerships; 3) facilitating dialogue towards dispute resolution; and 4) strengthening the environment affecting responsible business practices.

Much like the 2009 strategy, the enhanced 2014 strategy commits to socially responsible investment. Instead of focusing exclusively on maximizing profits, socially responsible investment aims for companies to address the social and environmental issues experienced by host countries due to extractive operations. The main continuity between the two strategies is that both emphasize the promotion of voluntary-based international CSR guidelines for Canadian corporate actors. The key departure is that the 2014 strategy is based on a more comprehensive approach, involving a wider array of relevant actors and targeting a more inclusive goal. While the 2009 strategy focused on the role of companies abroad, the 2014 strategy includes the participation of non-corporate actors such as diplomats and development workers. For example, the 2014 strategy recognizes that Canada's "Trade Commissioner Service ...

officers at Canadian missions around the world promote Canadian industry, and can help Canadian client companies by providing local contacts, helping to solve problems, and assisting with market preparation and assessment" (Canada 2014, 9). This new approach integrates the experiences of expert Canadian state actors with those of Canadian corporate actors to form a hybrid force for promoting and implementing CSR practices abroad, allowing such practices to go beyond financial risk assessments to include social risk analyses or conflict analyses (9).

Although both strategies claim to be proactive, they essentially highlight a reactive framework. First, given that both strategies were attempts to respond to domestic economic and political demands, concerns for the needs of local communities were secondary on the agenda – even though the framing of both documents suggests otherwise. This is because both strategies were the result of the government's accommodation by legitimation approach, evident in the fact that host countries' agency was not initially discussed in the framing of the various government programs mentioned above. For instance, host country capacity building was a privileged program in 2009, meant as a way to address domestic criticisms regarding the lack of institutional capacity in the extractive sectors of developing countries. Similarly, conflict prevention became a privileged program in 2014 to address the reputational crisis of Canadian extractive companies that were facing grievances from local communities. Hence, discussion of local capabilities in host countries occurs in the two documents only when discussing how such local capabilities might serve to advance the objectives of Canada's national CSR strategy abroad, suggesting that the priorities of local communities might be incompatible with the priorities identified in that strategy.

Second, the wider political and socio-economic contexts in Canada have shaped the nature of the programs that the two strategies prioritized. Thus, although an overview of the programs shows that the 2014 strategy includes some accountability mechanisms (which were lacking in the 2009 strategy), this difference reflects the policy environment in which each strategy emerged. For instance, prior to the 2014 revision, the government enacted a new law called the Extractive Sector Transparency Measures Act (ESTMA), which set "to implement Canada's international commitments to participate in the fight against corruption through the imposition of measures applicable to the extractive sector."[4] Given that this regulatory framework was enacted in December 2014, the procedures that led to the enactment must have occurred around the same time as the review process that led to the enhanced 2014 CSR strategy. As such, the enhanced 2014 strategy, with its increased accountability mechanisms, emerged amid a period of increased awareness of the importance of such mechanisms in the extractive sector; this was not the case for the 2009 CSR strategy.

A Comparative Analysis of Government Technologies: Which CSR Policy Instruments Are Used and Why?

As noted, government technologies refer to the instruments through which government programs are realized (Vallentin and Murillo 2012). The emphasis of the 2009 national CSR strategy on capacity building in host countries lacked specific guidelines, however, which explains why many of the criticisms converged around its "lack of concrete action" (Scheinert 2016, para. 1). For instance, although the 2009 strategy promoted *informational* mechanisms through the establishment of the CSR counsellor's office and the CSR Centre of Excellence, it insufficiently elaborated on how government technologies (with a focus on techniques, procedures, vocabularies, and design) would be deployed concretely to oversee the programs. Overall, the procedures promoted in the 2009 strategy revolved around advocating for *legal* reforms in host countries. For instance, the country's former development arm, the Canadian International Development Agency (CIDA), in collaboration with Natural Resources Canada, was to provide technical assistance to host countries so that the latter could reform their extractive sectors. Aside from promoting home state assistance, it was not quite clear how CSR practices were to be fostered in host communities and how that would affect local economies. In that sense, the government technologies in the 2009 strategy remained focused at the macro level (with a focus on home state-company relations), and failed to discuss exactly how potential reforms ultimately would affect the socio-economic welfare of actors at the micro level – namely, local communities.

The 2014 strategy addresses some of the gaps identified in the 2009 strategy by creating a more comprehensive design. The focus of the 2014 strategy is not just on technical procedures, such as legal reforms; instead, it also speaks to social issues in host communities by paying attention to locally identified concerns and seeking to promote a CSR agenda that "take[s] into consideration the project's life cycle from initial exploration to closure and beyond" (Canada 2014, 3). To achieve the goals identified in this comprehensive framework, the 2014 strategy proposes a focus on local capabilities (for example, local procurement) and on joint plans with the host government, which would be taken into account in corporate planning and management structures. In other words, the enhanced strategy emphasizes the importance of partnerships, thus speaking to Steurer's (2010) categorization of *partnering* and *hybrid* mechanisms as instrumental for government implementation of CSR practices. Nonetheless, although these changes appear promising for local communities, the 2014 strategy does not speak to specific local capabilities that can be examined when assessing the long-term potential of these revised government technologies. For instance, the 2014 strategy highlights that Canadian diplomatic missions in host countries have organized over 250 CSR-related initiatives (Canada 2014, 10), but fails to discuss how many of these initiatives were the result of joint action between the home government and the host government. Moreover, because the strategy does not further elucidate the nature of these numerous CSR-related initiatives abroad, it is unclear what the effects of these efforts have been for sustainable development in local communities.

Furthermore, in the 2009 strategy, the role of the CSR counsellor was limited strictly to reviewing CSR practices with the consent of involved parties and then advising the stakeholders. Hence, the counsellor's role lacked any kind of accountability mechanisms to resolve disputes or to secure compliance among Canadian extractive companies. In the 2014 revision, although the powers of the CSR counsellor are still limited, there are now clear accountability mechanisms that both the government and civil society can use to hold Canadian companies accountable:

In line with the Government of Canada's "economic diplomacy" approach, Government of Canada services include the issuance of letters of support, advocacy efforts in foreign markets and participation in Government of Canada trade missions. Canadian companies found not to be embodying CSR best practices and who refuse to participate in dispute resolution processes contained in the CSR Strategy will no longer benefit from economic diplomacy of this nature. Furthermore, such a designation will be taken into account in the CSR-related evaluation and due diligence conducted by the Government of Canada's financing crown corporation, Export Development Canada ..., in its consideration of the availability of financing or other support. (Canada 2014, 12–13)

Indeed, Sagebien et al. (2008) note that, although several members of the corporate accountability movement, such as the Canadian Network on Corporate Accountability, called for such a disciplinary strategy, home states can influence CSR performance abroad significantly by regulating access to finance and insurance. As it stands in practice, however, the accountability mechanisms adopted in the new national strategy can be considered weak because financial disincentives are only efficient when corporations are significantly dependent on government funding. In other words, corporations are faced with "soft rods," rather than "sticks," to use Steurer's (2010) terms. The introduction of an accountability instrument was vital, and signified the government's willingness to resort to soft economic penalties, such as the withdrawal of government diplomatic and financial support, as a way of encouraging Canadian extractive companies to be more socially and environmentally responsible. For example, the government seems to have adopted the strategy of "naming and shaming" as a means of widening the space for civil regulation by NGOs. It was noted that "Canada strongly encourages participation by companies and project-affected stakeholders in the most relevant mechanism as the situation merits. While participation remains voluntary, a decision by either party not to participate in the CSR Counsellor Office's or [National Contact Point's] or review process will be made public" (Canada 2014, 12). This is consistent with Steurer's (2010) claim that government CSR policies tend to push CSR towards a form of mandated self-regulation that is not completely detached from the regulatory state. The Canadian case also supports the assertion by Gond, Kang, and Moon (2011) that the government can use CSR as an indirect market pressure for corporations and civil society.

Conclusions: Implications of Canada's National CSR Strategy for Sustainable Development in Africa

Debates on the CSR-development nexus need to be critically and closely examined, with a particular focus on the extent to which the contemporary CSR agenda affects developing countries (Idemudia 2008). For instance, driven by a business case rationale, Canada's national CSR strategy reinforces the idea that its primary goal is to secure the competitive advantage of Canadian extractive companies, while serving as an extension of Canada's foreign policy goals. Although the CSR strategy seemed to have matured, the extent to which it supports, rather than undermines, sustainable development in Africa remains suspect. This is because of the strategy's minimalist approach to defining CSR and the business case rationale that underpins it. Although the minimalist government definition of CSR sets some minimum standards, it provides no clear guidelines with which poor and marginalized communities can hold Canadian companies accountable for the negative social and environmental externalities they produce. Hence, the definition adds to the opaqueness of CSR by allowing Canadian companies to appropriate the meaning of ethics, redefine the meaning of development, and allow business thinking to dominate a wider sphere of our way of life (Blowfield and Frynas 2005; Frynas 2005; Smith 2003; Utting 2005, 2008). Besides, the business case discourse promotes a particular rationality in which social problems that cannot be translated into business opportunities are likely to be neglected, even if caused by the corporation (Utting 2012; Utting and Clapp 2008). In other words, it allows CSR to become a lever for the creation of opportunities, as opposed to a vehicle for addressing social problems (Vallentin 2015).

As well, both national CSR strategies were driven by significant power dynamics that either ignore or undermine the participation of host communities, thereby negatively affecting their potential to contribute to sustainable development. These power dynamics are rooted in the fact that the strategies, particularly the first, enthusiastically aligned with widely recognized international CSR initiatives, thus leaving host country initiatives behind. For instance, although the 2009 strategy promoted the Canadian government's CSR initiatives, it failed to specify whether CSR initiatives from host countries were equally important. Yet if host governments are to assert ownership over the governance of their natural resources, which is assumed in the capacity-building framework championed by the 2009 strategy, then such capacity building should prioritize host states' initiatives. In fact, both the 2009 and 2014 strategies failed to engage clearly with prominent regional, national, and local knowledge in host countries, in sharp contrast to the numerous international initiatives that both documents promoted. African actors have already enthusiastically embraced important regional and national initiatives designed to help regulate the extractive sectors, yet these were ignored in both strategies. For instance, the Africa Mining Vision (AMV) is an initiative that seeks to use "mineral resources to catalyse broad-based growth and development" on the continent (African Union 2009, 13). Endorsed by the African Union in 2009, the AMV is a regulatory approach to help African countries use their mineral resources to achieve sustainable development by harmonizing the regulatory regimes of their mining sectors. Despite the huge presence of Canadian mining companies in Africa, neither national CSR strategy engaged with the AMV (see also Chapters 7 and 12, in this volume). This shortcoming reflects Canada's treatment of African countries as passive agents of their own development.

Finally, despite some improvements upon the 2009 CSR strategy, a lack of firm guidelines for implementation has meant that the latest version of the strategy does not offer strong prospects for development in host communities. The 2014 strategy recognizes the importance of local capabilities in fostering Canada's CSR strategy abroad as a way to address the limitations of the 2009 strategy on this front. Unfortunately, however, the enhanced strategy continues to be marred by uncertainties of interpretation – for instance, advocating that Canadian companies consider local CSR processes first and foremost, before considering any other process: "If local processes are unavailable or have not succeeded, guidance on Canadian and international mechanisms will be made available to relevant parties" (Canada 2014, 11). It is not clear, however, who, if necessary, will provide guidance for determining the specific guidelines, and one may assume that home governments and extractive companies will make that decision unilaterally in such an instance. Indeed, although the 2014 strategy specifies that international CSR standards may trump those from local countries if the former represent the *most rigorous* standards (Canada 2014, 6), it is not clear *who* will determine the rigour of a given standard and *by what means*. This situation echoes the discussion by Lepoutre, Dentchev, and Heene (2007, 392) of the many uncertainties surrounding the definition and implementation of CSR. In the case of Canada's national CSR strategy, the institutional background of the Canadian government, Canadian mining companies, and host governments can lead to different understandings and framings of the required CSR action. In the same vein, given the lack of specific guidelines even in the revised and enhanced version, the addition of local capabilities on the agenda might fail to yield a significant improvement for local communities if their voices remain unheard. As such, business actors need a clearer and firmer guideline as a basis for action to meet the ultimate goal – making sure that extractive operations yield sustainable benefits for local communities – and that this goal does not get lost in technicalities and power dynamics.

NOTES

1 In addition, he suggested that there are four thematic fields of CSR action by government – namely, raising awareness, improving transparency, fostering socially responsible investment, and leading by example.

2 The chapter adopts a discourse analysis methodology and uses Gill's (2000) notion of "skeptical reading," which means searching for purpose lurking behind the ways something is said or presented. In addition, the chapter is informed by Gill's (2000) suggestion to treat the way something is said as being "a solution to a problem."

3 In March 2013 the Conservatives reorganized the department, by merging the former Canadian International Development Agency with DFAIT, to

54   Corporate Social Responsibility

create the Department of Foreign Affairs, Trade and International Development (DFATD). The 2014 strategy was thus officially led by DFATD.
4 See Extractive Sector Transparency Measures Act, S.C. 2014, c. 39, s. 376,
Available online at http://laws-lois.justice.gc.ca/eng/acts/E-22.7/page-1.
html#h-2, accessed 17 June 2016.

BIBLIOGRAPHY

African Union. 2009. *Africa Mining Vision*. [Addis Ababa], February 2009.
Available online at www.africaminingvision.org/amv_resources/AMV/
Africa_Mining_Vision_English.pdf.
Albareda, Laura, Antonio Tencati, Josep M. Lozano, and Francesco Per-
rini. 2006. "The Government's Role in Promoting Corporate Responsibility:
A Comparative Analysis of Italy and UK from the Relational State Perspec-
tive." *Corporate Governance: The International Journal of Business in Society*
6 (4): 386–400. https://doi.org/10.1108/14720700610689504.
Albareda, Laura, Josep M. Lozano, Antonio Tencati, Atle Midttun, and Francesco
Perrini. 2008. "The Changing Role of Governments in Corporate Social Re-
sponsibility: Drivers and Responses." *Business Ethics: A European Review* 17 (4):
347–63. https://doi.org/10.1111/j.1467-8608.2008.00539.x.
Albareda, Laura, Josep M. Lozano, and Tamyko Ysa. 2007. "Public Policies on
Corporate Social Responsibility: The Role of Governments in Europe."
Journal of Business Ethics 74 (4): 391–407. https://doi.org/10.1007/s10551-007
-9514-1.
Blowfield, Michael, and Jedrzej George Frynas. 2005. "Editorial Setting
New Agendas: Critical Perspectives on Corporate Social Responsibility in
the Developing World." *International Affairs* 81 (3): 499–513. https://doi.
org/10.1111/j.1468-2346.2005.00465.x.
Bodruzic, Dragana. 2015. "Promoting International Development through
Corporate Social Responsibility: The Canadian Government's Partnership
with Canadian Mining Companies." *Canadian Foreign Policy Journal* 21 (2):
129–45. https://doi.org/10.1080/11926422.2014.934862.
Canada. 2005. Parliament. House of Commons. Standing Committee on Foreign
Affairs and International Trade. 38th Parliament, 1st Session. *Fourteenth
Report*. Ottawa.
Canada. 2009. Global Affairs Canada. "Building the Canadian Advantage:
A Corporate Social Responsibility (CSR) Strategy for the Canadian
International Extractive Sector." Ottawa. Available online at https://
www.international.gc.ca/trade-agreements-accords-commerciaux/
topics-domaines/other-autre/csr-strat-rse-2009.aspx?lang=eng,
accessed 22 April 2016.

Canada. 2014. Global Affairs Canada. "Doing Business the Canadian Way: A Strategy to Advance Corporate Social Responsibility in Canada's Extractive Sector Abroad." Available online at https://www.international.gc.ca/trade-agreements-accords-commerciaux/topics-domaines/other-autre/csr-strat-rse.aspx?lang=eng, accessed 8 June 2016.

Canada. 2016. Global Affairs Canada. *Corporate Social Responsibility.* Available online at https://www.international.gc.ca/trade-agreements-accords-commerciaux/topics-domaines/other-autre/csr-rse.aspx?lang=eng, accessed 8 June 2016.

Crane, Andrew. 2010. "From Governance to Governance: On Blurring Boundaries." *Journal of Business Ethics* 94 (1): 17–19. http://dx.doi.org/10.1007/s10551-011-0788-y.

Crouch, Colin 2010. "CSR and Changing Modes of Governance: Towards Corporate Noblesse Oblige?" In *Corporate Social Responsibility and Regulatory Governance: Towards Inclusive Development?* edited by Peter Utting and José Carlos Marques, 26–49. Basingstoke, UK: Palgrave Macmillan.

Dashwood, Hevina. 2016. "Corporate Social Responsibility in Fragile and Stable States: Dilemmas and Opportunities in South Sudan and Ghana." In *From Kinshasa to Kandahar: Canada and Fragile States in Historical Perspective,* edited by Michael K. Carroll and Greg Donaghy, 207–35. Calgary: University of Calgary Press.

Dean, Mitchell. 1999. *Governmentality: Power and Rule in Modern Society.* Thousand Oaks, CA: SAGE.

Dentchev, Nikolay A., Elvira Haezendonck and Mitchell van Balen. 2015. "The Role of Governments in the Business and Society Debate." *Business & Society* 56 (4): 527–44. https://doi.org/10.1177/0007650315586179.

Do, Trinh Theresa 2014. "Canadian Aid for Mining Projects Concerns NGOs." *CBC News,* 26 February. Available online at https://www.cbc.ca/news/politics/canadian-aid-for-mining-projects-concerns-ngos-1.2551201, accessed 26 February 2014.

Drucker, Peter F. 1984. "Converting Social Problems into Business Opportunities: The New Meaning of Corporate Social Responsibility." *California Management Review* 26 (2): 53–63. https://doi.org/10.2307/41165066.

Fox, Tom, Halina Ward, and Bruce Howard. 2002. *Public Sector Roles in Strengthening Corporate Social Responsibility: A Baseline Study.* Washington, DC: World Bank.

Frynas, Jedrzej George. 2005. "The False Development Promise of Corporate Social .Responsibility: Evidence from Multinational Oil Companies." *International Affairs* 81 (3): 581–98. https://doi.org/10.1111/j.1468-2346.2005.00470.x.

Gill, R. 2000. "Discourse Analysis." In *Qualitative Researching with Text, Image and Sound,* edited by M.W. Bauer and G. Gaskell, 172–90. London: Sage.

Gjølberg, Maria. 2010. "Varieties of Corporate Social Responsibility (CSR): CSR Meets the 'Nordic Model.'" *Regulation & Governance* 4 (2): 203–29. https://doi.org/10.1111/j.1748-5991.2010.01080.x.

Gond, Jean-Pascal, Nahee Kang, and Jeremy Moon. 2011. "The Government of Self-Regulation: On the Comparative Dynamics of Corporate Social Responsibility." *Economy and Society* 40 (4): 640–71. https://doi.org/10.1080/03085 147.2011.607364.

Grant, J. Andrew, Dianne Balraj, and Georgia Mavropoulos-Vagelis. 2013. "Reflections on Network Governance in Africa's Forestry Sector." *Natural Resources Forum* 37 (4): 269–79. https://doi.org/10.1111/1477-8947.12028.

Hamann, Ralph. 2006. "Can Business Make Decisive Contributions to Development? Towards a Research Agenda on Corporate Citizenship and Beyond." *Development Southern Africa* 23 (2): 175–95. https://doi.org/10.1080/03768350600707587.

Hamann, Ralph, and Nicola Acutt. 2003. "How Should Civil Society (and the Government) Respond to 'Corporate Social Responsibility'? A Critique of Business Motivations and the Potential for Partnerships." *Development Southern Africa* 20 (2): 255–70. https://doi.org/10.1080/03768350302956.

Idemudia, Uwafiokun. 2008. "Conceptualising the CSR and Development Debate: Bridging Existing Analytical Gaps." *Journal of Corporate Citizenship* 29: 91–110. https://doi.org/10.9774/gleaf.4700.2008.sp.00011.

Lascoumes, Pierre, and Patrick Le Galès. 2007. *Sociologie de l'action publique*. Paris: Armand Colin.

Lepoutre, Jan, Nikolay A. Dentchev, and Aimé Heene. 2007. "Dealing with Uncertainties When Governing CSR Policies." *Journal of Business Ethics* 73 (4): 391–408. https://doi.org/10.1007/s10551-006-9214-2.

Margolis, Joshua D., and James P. Walsh. 2003. "Misery Loves Companies: Rethinking Social Initiatives by Business." *Administrative Science Quarterly* 48 (2): 268–305. https://doi.org/10.2307/3556659.

Moon, Jeremy. 2002. "The Social Responsibility of Business and New Governance." *Government and Opposition* 37 (3): 385–408. https://doi.org/10.1111/1477-7053.00106.

Moon, Jeremy. 2004. "Government as a Driver of Corporate Social Responsibility: The UK in Comparative Perspective." ICCSR Research Paper Series 20. University of Nottingham.

Moore, Jennifer. 2012. "Canada's Subsidies to the Mining Industry Don't Stop at Aid: Political Support Betrays Government Claims of Corporate Social Responsibility." Ottawa: Mining Watch Canada, June. Available online at http://miningwatch.ca/sites/default/files/Canada_and_Honduras_mining_law-June%202012.pdf, accessed 1 June 2012.

Rasche, Andreas, Frank de Bakker, and Jeremy Moon. 2013. "Complete and Partial Organizing for Corporate Social Responsibility." *Journal of Business Ethics* 115 (4): 651–63. https://doi.org/10.1007/s10551-013-1824-x.

Sagebien, Julia, Nicole Lindsay, Peter Campbell, Rob Cameron, and Naomi Smith. 2008. "The Corporate Social Responsibility of Canadian Mining Companies in Latin America: A Systems Perspective." *Canadian Foreign Policy Journal* 14 (3): 103–28. https://doi.org/10.1080/11926422.2008.9673477.

Scheinert, Josh. 2016. "Between Rock and Responsibility: Corporate Responsibility for Canada's Mining Sector." *Open Canada*, 3 June. Available online at https://canada-haiti.ca/content/between-rock-and-responsibility-corporate-responsibility-canadas-mining-sector; accessed 3 June 2016, www.opencanada.org/features/between-rock-and-responsibility/.

Smith, N. Craig. 2003 "Corporate Social Responsibility: Whether or How?" *California Management Review* 45 (4): 52–76. https://doi.org/10.2307/41166188.

Steurer, Reinhard. 2010. "The Role of Governments in Corporate Social Responsibility: Characterising Public Policies on CSR in Europe." *Policy Sciences* 43 (1): 49–72. https://doi.org/10.1007/s11077-009-9084-4.

Utting, Peter. 2005. "Corporate Responsibility and the Movement of Business." *Development in Practice* 15 (3–4): 375–88.

Utting, Peter. 2008. "The Struggle for Corporate Accountability." *Development and Change* 39 (6): 959–75. https://doi.org/10.1111/j.1467-7660.2008.00523.x.

Utting, Peter. 2012. "Activism, Business Regulation, and Development." In *Business Regulation and Non-state Actors: Whose Standards? Whose Development?*, edited by Peter Utting, Darryl Reed, and Ananya Mukherjee Reed, 38–53. New York: Routledge.

Utting, Peter, and Jennifer Clapp, eds. 2008. *Corporate Accountability and Sustainable Development*. Oxford: Oxford University Press.

Vallentin, Steen. 2015. "Governmentalities of CSR: Danish Government Policy as a Reflection of Political Difference." *Journal of Business Ethics* 127 (1): 33–47. https://doi.org/10.1007/s10551-013-1703-5.

Vallentin, Steen, and David Murillo. 2012. "Governmentality and the Politics of CSR." *Organization* 19 (6): 825–43. https://doi.org/10.1177/1350508411426183.

Ward, Halina. 2004. *Public Sector Roles in Strengthening Corporate Social Responsibility: Taking Stock*. Washington, DC: World Bank.

3 Corporate Social Responsibility and Canada's Role in Africa's Extractive Industries: A Critical Analysis

NKETTI JOHNSTON-TAYLOR

Introduction

After the decolonization of African states by Europe, Canada-Africa relations were solidified through Western alliances, and Canada emerged as a "leader" in development and global security, marked by instances of "ethically oriented activism on the global stage" (Black 2015). Canada played a key role in the abolition of South Africa's apartheid in the early 1990s, and in the early 2000s Prime Minister Jean Chrétien helped entrench Africa on the G8 agenda through the facilitation of Africa's Action Plan at the 2002 Kananaskis Summit (Black 2015). Concomitantly, Canada took a greater interest in Africa's extractive sectors, with its assets and investment there increasing from $2.87 billion in 2001 to a staggering $31.6 billion in 2011 (Campbell 2011). These investments were concentrated in South Africa, the Democratic Republic of Congo, Madagascar, Zambia, Tanzania, Ghana, Burkina Faso, and Mauritania (Black and Savage 2015; Campbell 2011). This made Canada the single largest source of foreign investment in Africa's extractive sectors and, with support from the Canadian government, Canadian companies became the dominant face of the country in much of Africa. These investments, however, generated significant controversial ramifications for host communities' development and security prospects that have eroded Canada's reputation as the development and humanitarian champion for Africa (Black and Savage 2015).

Resource extraction historically has been linked to a plethora of social and environmental impacts and development challenges. Too often, the economic benefits of extraction do not stay in the host countries and communities (Bush and Graham 2010; Hilson 2012; Mason 2014). Many observers have argued that the Canadian government has essentially abandoned its "ethical mission" in sub-Saharan Africa to become "an aggressive and unapologetic booster of the extractive sector" (Black and Savage 2015, 153). Canada, as one of the G8 members, adopted a more "liberalized" approach to engagement with Africa beginning in the early 2000s. Critics of this approach argue that these policies have increasingly made African countries susceptible to exploitation by Western extractive companies. Institutions such as the World Bank were pioneers of this liberalized policy environment in Africa's extractive sectors, using their position of lender to reform those sectors and rewrite mining laws and taxation regimes across Africa in the 1980s through structural adjustment programs (SAPs) and other good governance programs in the decades that followed (Bush 2008; Bush and Graham 2010; Campbell 2011; Hilson 2012).

Central to these reforms was the stimulation of greater private sector participation (increased competition) through privatization and the liberalization of trade. These policies were intended to create a more favourable environment for foreign investment, which involved a redefinition of the role of the state in the form of deregulation (Campbell 2011). Upon implementation, the policies increased the flow of foreign private investment into Africa's mines and oil fields. However, they also opened Africa's borders to exploitation by powerful transnational corporations (TNCs) and restricted the ability of local governments to regulate them. Without sufficient complementary strengthening of state institutions and skills, these policies turned bloated weak states into small weak states that were unable to monitor and check malpractice by TNCs and control corruption of its agents (Bush and Graham 2010; Campbell 2011; Hilson 2012; Szeftel 1998). The creation of new market openings in Africa's extractive industry "created opportunities to proliferate monopoly powers with all manner of social, ecological, economic and political consequences" (Harvey 2003, 71).

The disenchantment with this hardline brand of liberalism known as "neoliberalism" gave way to an era of what has been referred to as "compassionate capitalism." Rajak (2011, 2) explains that, under this type of capitalism, corporations act as "midwives offering ... moral ... and spiritual, revitalisation of the 'Market.'" Corporate social responsibility (CSR) claims to provide a happy confluence of economic, legal, ethical, and philanthropic values packed together in the new human (or humane) face of capitalism (Carroll 1999; Rajak 2011). CSR is "a movement promising to harness the global reach and resources of TNCs in the service of local development and social development" (Rajak 2011, 1). As such, central to its mandate is the pursuit of and contribution to sustainable development (Rajak 2011).

CSR has been embedded in a maze of voluntary international codes of conduct, ethical principles and guidelines, management systems, toolkits, and toolboxes that have promised to confront social, security, and environmental challenges. A few of these include the Organisation for Economic Co-operation and Development (OECD) Declaration on International Investment and Multinational Enterprises, which urges companies to adhere to guidelines on business conduct, including disclosure, employment and industrial relations, human rights, the environment, and bribery (OECD 2011). The United Nations Declaration on the Rights of Indigenous Peoples sets "the minimum standards for the survival, dignity and well-being of the Indigenous peoples of the World" (United Nations 2008). The Voluntary Principles on Security and Human Rights also provide guidance on steps that extractive companies can take to minimize the risk of human rights abuses in communities located near extraction sites (Voluntary Principles 2017). According to Rajak (2011), champions of CSR view such guidelines and principles as the long-awaited magic bullet to reduce poverty, which involves companies stepping in where the state has failed to deliver social improvements. The non-binding and voluntary nature of these principles has left observers questioning their effectiveness (Andrews 2016; Butler 2015; Campbell 2011; Mason 2014).

The government of Canada has committed to promoting responsible business practices of Canadian companies abroad. The country's support for CSR dates as far back as 1976, when it signed the aforementioned OECD declaration. Canada has advocated and promoted other CSR guidelines and standard practices for decades. In 2009 Canada developed its official strategy on CSR (Canada 2015). However, the effectiveness of CSR in addressing or improving social and environmental ills around the world has been a source of great debate. According to Campbell (2011), Canadian extractive companies have been the most significant group involved in issues of violence, environmental damage, and human rights abuses in extractive-rich African countries, suggesting that Canada's approach to CSR has been somewhat ineffective.

This chapter explores that conundrum. It critically evaluates Canada's approach to CSR and assesses the role of neoliberalism in constraining and undermining that approach. The chapter draws upon insights I developed from fieldwork and research conducted in Sierra Leone in 2011 and 2015 on that country's mining sector – specifically the relationship among mining companies, local communities, and environmental governance. This fieldwork and research project animates my use of secondary sources in this analysis, as they offer different perspectives on Canada's approach to CSR. It also offers different approaches on the behaviour of Canadian and non-Canadian extractive companies operating in other African countries. These sources are also pivotal in exploring the disparity between CSR rhetoric and reality and in illustrating how neoliberal powers and structures shape Canadian companies' behaviour, as well as their relationship with and treatment of local communities in Africa's extractive sectors. As such, the chapter provides a nuanced critical argument that explores CSR in general, as well as illuminating the role and behaviour of Canadian extractive companies, particularly in Africa. Therefore I was tasked with four objectives. First, I outline Canada's approach to CSR. Second, I explore the disparity between the rhetoric and reality of CSR in Africa. Third, I examine the rationale behind the disparity between rhetoric and reality and, in so doing, look at the role of neoliberal structures, processes, and powers in shaping Canadian and non-Canadian companies' behaviour abroad. As part of the fourth objective, I close with recommendations to bridge the gap between rhetoric and reality.

Canada's Approach to and Support for CSR

Following the results of the World Bank–led Extractive Industries Review in 2003, "the industry worked hard to rebrand itself as a human-rights-respecting engine" (Butler 2015, 12). This led to the emergence of a number of CSR-related initiatives, some of which were noted above. In the Canadian context, Butler (2015, 12) points out that "the Prospectors and Developers Association of Canada (PDAC) developed a voluntary code called Environmental Excellence in Exploration – known as 'E3' – which established best practice guidelines for its member countries." As a result, many companies developed CSR departments and committed to the "triple-E" bottom line – which implies a commitment to profits, people, and the planet. As such, they measured the associated successes in financial, social, and environmental terms (Butler 2015). Other important CSR efforts that aligned with Canada's foreign policy objectives include Natural Resource Canada's "Exploration and Mining Guide for Aboriginal Communities" and the "CSR Implementation Guide for Canadian Business" developed by Industry Canada (Canada 2015).

Canada was one of the original signatories of the OECD declaration in 1976. It has been influential in the development and advancement of other international CSR standards, and has worked to increase the standardization of CSR reporting (Canada 2015). These include the: United Nations Guiding Principles on Business and Human Rights; the Voluntary Principles on Security and Human Rights; the International Finance Corporation's Performance Standards on Social and

Environmental Sustainability; the OECD Due Diligence Guidance for Responsible Supply Chains of Minerals from Conflict-Affected and High-Risk Areas; and the Global Reporting Initiative. The Canadian government's CSR strategy for Canadian extractive companies operating abroad was developed in 2009 and is updated every five years. According to Global Affairs Canada, the government's expectation is that Canadian companies integrate CSR throughout their management structures. As such, companies are expected to understand the impact of their functions on the surrounding economy, community, and environment, and adjust their activities and operations to create value for themselves and other stakeholders. Canada's strategy rests on four pillars: 1) promoting and advancing CSR guidelines; 2) fostering networks and partnerships; 3) facilitating dialogue towards dispute resolution; and 4) strengthening the environment affecting responsible business practices. The fourth pillar incorporates support for host-county resource governance capacity building (Canada 2015; see also Canada 2016).

This strategy was led by the then Department of Foreign Affairs, Trade and Development – now Global Affairs Canada. Global Affairs Canada works closely with other government departments, including Industry Canada, and with the National Contact Point (NCP) for the OECD Guidelines for Multinational Enterprises. The Office of the Extractive Sector CSR Counsellor, the Centre for Excellence in CSR, and Canada's network of missions around the world were central to the implementation of Canada's CSR strategy (Canada 2015, 2016). Central to the role of the CSR counsellor, in turn, was offering advice and guidance for all stakeholders on implementing CSR performance guidelines and reviewing the CSR practices of Canadian extractive companies abroad. The office also had a review process to resolve differences between companies and affected stakeholders (Canada 2015, 2016). Global Affairs Canada further noted:

> With regional offices across Canada and diplomatic missions in more than 100 countries around the world, the Government is well positioned to assist Canadian companies abroad. The Canadian Trade Commissioner Service (TCS) provides on-the-ground intelligence and practical advice on foreign markets to help companies make better, timely, and cost-effective decisions. The TCS can also assist extractive sector companies that are part of the Canadian business community, are actively contributing to Canada's economic growth, have a demonstrated capacity for internationalization, and have strong potential to add value to the Canadian economy ... Canada recognizes that action by industry may not bring about sustainable

positive change in the absence of broader, coordinated efforts at the national and regional levels. The Canadian Government works with interlocutors at international, bilateral, and organizational levels on a range of activities that strengthen the environment affecting business conduct abroad in a way that is conducive to advancing CSR performance and benefits on the ground ... Canada's efforts to promote CSR are also advanced at the bilateral level by the inclusion of voluntary provisions for CSR in all Foreign Investment Promotion and Protection Agreements and Free Trade Agreements signed since 2010 ... The Government of Canada works with host governments to enhance their capacity to manage their own natural resources for economic, social, and environmental sustainability. [Natural Resources Canada's] ability to provide knowledge and expertise in this area is crucial to these efforts, which enhance the capacities of countries to manage both natural resource development and the benefits the sector generates. It includes building and modernizing governance regimes to ensure that natural resources are managed in a technically and environmentally sound manner. Canada recognizes the importance of improving the countries' resource governance as it is pertinent to poverty reduction and creating a business and investment environment that is conducive to responsible corporate conduct in countries where Canadian companies operate ... To get more fulsome [sic] risk assessments for managers and investors, and improve the chances of far-reaching benefits from Canadian investments, the Government of Canada encourages companies to:

• Respectfully engage relevant stakeholders, early on and regularly;
• Understand local customs, culture and expectations, and how they affect, and are affected by the project;
• Work with stakeholders to determine and communicate environmental, social and economic impact solutions;
• Explore opportunities to build local capabilities;
• Work with locals to develop a joint plan to contribute to local development; and
• Strategically incorporate this information throughout their planning and management structures. (Canada 2015, 5, 14–15)

In May 2018 the CSR counsellor's office was replaced by the Canadian Ombudsperson for Responsible Enterprise (CORE). A multistakeholder advisory board was created to provide advice and to support the CORE in fulfilling its mandate. According to Global Affairs Canada, the ombudsperson has a "wider mandate than existing mechanisms, with the ability to: undertake collaborative fact-finding; initiate independent fact-finding, even without the submission of a complaint; and make recommendations to parties involved in the complaint, as well as to the Canadian Government" (Canada 2018b). This position covers the mining and oil and gas sectors and the garment industry. Global Affairs Canada notes that the roles of the Canadian NCP and the new ombudsperson are complementary. The CORE refers cases to the NCP for formal mediation when this is appropriate (Canada 2018a, 2018b; Oved 2018). Since the CORE is a recent creation, determining its effectiveness would be premature. Accordingly I focus on Canada's CSR infrastructure *before* the creation of the CORE in 2018. With that being said, the creation of the CORE does indicate a recommitment by the Canadian government to improving the business practices of Canadian companies operating abroad.

Rhetoric versus Reality

Despite Canada's seemingly robust approach to CSR, Canadian extractive companies have been at the heart of many controversies in Africa. Active in forty-three different African countries, Canadian mining firms have been associated with the dispossession of farmers, the displacement of communities, forced labour, and devastating ecosystem and human rights violations (Engler 2016). The controversy concerning Talisman Energy in Sudan has been a sore point among civil society organizations. Talisman's operations and revenues were seen as aiding the conflict in that country, specifically over oil fields, one result of which was major displacement of civilian populations related to oil extraction from their factors of production (Black 2015). Similarly, in 2002, a UN Security Council Panel of Experts on "the illegal exploitation of natural resources and other forms of wealth in the Democratic Republic of Congo" cited eight Canadian companies for violating leading international CSR standards. After much protesting, all but one of these companies were absolved of any wrongdoing. The swift closing of Bonte Gold Mines in 2004 in Ghana left behind "un-reclaimed degraded land, unpaid compensation, and a debt of about $18 million," with host communities affected by "environmental degradation, uncompensated destruction of farms and land, and the failure to engage in any social responsibility projects in the vicinity of the mine" (Black and Savage 2015, 171). In Mali, investment by the Canada Pension Plan resulted in the displacement of two villages with inadequate replacement land, scarce water resources, and environmental degradation from the mine (Black and Savage 2015, 172). In 2008 Guinea's military killed three people in a bid to drive away small-scale miners from SEMAFO's Kiniero mine in the southeastern region of the country (Engler 2015b). These stories validate claims that Canada has been unwilling to hold Canadian companies accountable in Africa (Black and Savage 2015).

Tanzania sits on $40 billion of gold reserves, and Canada is the largest mining operator in the country – Barrick Gold has operated there since the early 1990s. The then Canadian International Development Agency (CIDA) gave over $1 billion in aid to the country and provided disbursements that increased from $9.8 million in fiscal year 2002/03 to over $119 million in 2011/12 (McMillan 2012). Barrick Gold's involvement in Tanzania, however, has been laced with a number of "corporate irresponsibilities." These include severe job losses as Tanzanians who were once actively employed in the resource sector could not compete with foreign ownership. National policies enable foreign mining companies to hire internationally and, as such, the foreign-dominated mining sector in Tanzania has offered few opportunities for local employment. Articles 8.4 and 8.5 of the Buzwagi mine contract between Barrick and the Tanzanian government provide no restrictions on the number of expatriates Barrick can employ. Consequently, Tanzanians miss out on local job opportunities (McMillan 2012).

Barrick Gold was also cautioned when, in May 2009, toxic sludge from the North Mara mine crept into the Thigithe River. Barrick's chief African spokesperson, Charles Chichester, assured that the toxic waste was quickly cleaned and resulted in no deaths. In contrast, village chairperson Abel Kereman Nyakiha reported that more than forty deaths in three surrounding villages resulted from the contamination. Furthermore a report from the Norwegian University of Life Sciences condemned the life-threatening arsenic levels found near the North Mara mine (Engler 2015a; McMillan 2012).

A Canadian-owned uranium mine in South Africa has also been at the centre of controversy. According to Butler (2015, 92–3), mine workers alleged poor working conditions that included a lack of protective clothing against radiation exposure, inadequate access to health services, lack of compensation for work-related health problems, unfair job dismissals, diagnoses of silicosis, tuberculosis, chronic headaches, and nausea, low wages, and racism in the workplace – with white staff employed in the best-paid, higher-level positions, while the majority Black South African employees and migrant workers from neighbouring African countries carried out the most dangerous and poorly paid jobs. The challenges came to a head when workers went on strike and approximately fourteen hundred workers were dismissed when the company declared the strike illegal (Butler 2015). The remaining workers continued to voice complaints about environmental safety and health matters.

Canadian mining companies have also been accused of bribing officials and tax evasion. According to Engler (2016), in 2015 TSX-listed MagIndustries was accused of paying a bribe of $100,000 to tax officials with the intention of avoiding taxes on its $1.5 billion potash mine and processing facility in Congo-Brazzaville. In April 2016 a Tanzanian tribunal ruled that Barrick Gold had organized a "sophisticated scheme of tax evasion." It was calculated that the Toronto company had failed to pay corporate taxes and cheated the country out of more than $41 million (Engler 2016). Vancouver-based Ivanhoe Mines, operating in South Africa, has also been accused of bribery and corruption of local chiefs to secure land rights over the wishes of residents. According to Scheinert's (2016) account, the company disrespects local grave sites and works to block community members from voicing opposition to their project. There is a belief that the company's desire to stifle opposition led to an attempted assassination of a local protest leader. As a result, South African activists have appealed the environmental approval of the Platreef mine.

These problems are not just prevalent in Africa. Canada has also been at the epicentre of other controversies in Latin America. In the absence of investigations, more extensive research, and analyses of specific case studies, however, it is onerous to assess conclusively the reports of corporate irresponsibility and government complicity in this region. It is also difficult to determine the pervasiveness of these issues.

The Rationale behind the Disparity between Rhetoric and Reality

Insufficient Commitment and Complicity of the Canadian Government

The disparities discussed have led observers to suggest that the Canadian government is insufficiently committed to, and arguably complicit in, the harming of host communities abroad (Bush 2007; Butler 2015; Campbell 2011; Engler 2015a, 2015b; McMillan 2012; Mitchell 2014), evidence that I explore in this section. As highlighted in this volume's introductory chapter, the Harper government opposed legislation modelled on the US Alien Torts Claims Act that would have allowed lawsuits against Canadian companies responsible for major human rights violations or ecological destruction abroad. Similarly the Harper government opposed Liberal MP John McKay's private members bill (C-300), which would have withheld diplomatic and financial support from companies found responsible for significant abuses abroad (Engler 2015a).

Scholars such as Engler (2015a) and McMillan (2012) have argued that, contrary to the rhetoric, Foreign Investment Promotion and

Protection Agreements (FIPPAs) do not provide balanced trade benefits; instead, they have allowed Canadian extractive companies to challenge national and local governments seeking to raise standards in the name of non-discrimination against foreign investors. FIPPAs offer heavy protection of Canadian companies, and give them the right to sue governments internationally for pursuing policies that interfere with profit making (Engler 2015b; McMillan 2012; Newell 2008). Tanzania is a case in point. Following talks to increase royalties and taxes in 2008, the Canadian government pursued a FIPPA with Tanzania to ensure that Canadian investors' capital remained secure. Although both governments agreed upon and finalized a FIPPA, there is an undeniable power imbalance in favour of Canadian companies. Although the Canadian government does not endorse these malpractices, weakened regulations heighten *opportunities* for them to occur (Engler 2015b; McMillan 2012).

As mentioned in the introductory chapter, the development and installation of the CSR counsellor's office was great progress. The inclusion of the withdrawal of economic diplomacy was a promising tool to enhance the human rights and environmental record of Canadian companies operating abroad, and aligned with the original intent of failed Bill C-300 (Blackwood and Stewart 2012). The then CSR counsellor Jeffrey Davidson said, however, that he had not encountered a conflict that warranted withdrawing government support (e.g., from the Trade Commissioner Service) (Mazereeuw 2016), a statement that raised questions about Canada's commitment to ensuring that Canadian companies behave responsibly abroad.

Many observers called for the end of the CSR counsellor and office and advocated for the establishment of an independent ombudsperson with more power, including the ability and mandate to investigate and reprimand malpractice, since Canadian companies' "corporate irresponsibilities" remained pervasive. On 25 April 2016, over 150 Latin American civil society groups sent an open letter to Prime Minister Trudeau asking him to end human rights abuses by Canadian mining companies in Mexico, Guatemala, Honduras, El Salvador, Colombia, Chile, Argentina, and Peru (Coalition of NGOs 2016). Among other requests, these groups asked for the creation of "objective and impartial mechanisms to effectively monitor and investigate complaints of individual and collective human rights violations" (Coalition of NGOs 2016, 3). They also asked the Canadian government to "refrain from promoting international arbitration mechanisms," which they viewed as a powerful tool to "shield foreign investments that profit from the absence of effective accountability measures aimed at preventing human rights violations" (3). These specific recommendations spoke directly to the power and responsibilities of the CSR counsellor.

As mentioned, the UN Guiding Principles on Business and Human Rights are clear that access to judicial and non-judicial grievance mechanisms is a basic human right. However, many victims of human rights abuses by corporations live in jurisdictions where access to effective courts or out-of-court legal remedies is not possible (Coumans 2014; United Nations Human Rights 2011). There were no provisions for this in Canada's CSR strategy, which remains unchanged under the CORE (Canada 2018b). Central to this ombudsperson's role is the investigation of allegations of human rights abuses or violations by Canadian companies operating abroad. Unlike the CSR counsellor, the CORE does not require the permission of a company to investigate. It also has the power to launch its own investigations and publicly report its findings (Canada 2018a, 2018b; Oved 2018). Some observers are optimistic that its creation marks a substantive step towards Canadian companies doing business responsibly abroad, as it moves "the needle" beyond the usual voluntary CSR infrastructure. According to Julia Sanchez, president of the Canadian Council for International Co-operation (as cited in Oved 2018), "[i]t really is momentous ... there's no other such position in the world." Others however question its effectiveness and watch with a, "cautious optimism." It is unclear if the CORE's recommendations will lead to tangible action and if the CORE has the mandate to review old cases. Furthermore, much of the voluntary principles remain.

Insufficient Consideration of Community Needs and Impacts

Often it is not the absence of a CSR strategy that produces the devastating consequences, but rather the approach and strength of the host country to regulate the industry (Andrews 2016; Idemudia 2014; Mason 2014). Although the companies Idemudia (2014) and Johnston-Taylor (2015) explore are not Canadian, they present an important perspective and explanation into the reason for the gap between Canada's pro-CSR rhetoric and the reality in host communities in Africa and Latin American countries.

According to Idemudia (2014) and Johnston-Taylor (2015), infrastructural development is often reserved for the immediate communities, not those nearby, even if the latter experience negative externalities from company operations. Consequently the developmental benefits are not sufficiently distributed among affected communities. This explains why communities often can boast of considerable development while others "have nothing to show for it" (Idemudia 2014, 139). There is also often a wrong targeting of community development needs, which can be attributed partly to the failure of companies to consult sufficiently with a representative sample of community members. According to Idemudia (2014), this is often the case with in-house corporate community investment models that focus on local elites who generally do not reflect the priorities and concerns of ordinary people. Many community members in Kono's mining communities in Sierra Leone lamented that companies often consulted only with local elites (Johnston-Taylor 2015; Mason 2014), and that mining companies have been able to placate local elites, such as local chiefs and local "big men," by offering bribes. In return, traditional leaders have advocated on behalf of companies in a way sometimes at odds with the developmental needs of local communities. Furthermore, companies' failure to deal with the day-to-day consequences of their operations continue to undermine the effectiveness of their CSR strategies. Such failure plants seeds of distrust and engenders conflict. The prohibition of government regulation of corporate behaviour unsurprisingly has facilitated such failure, as I discuss in greater detail in the next section.

Resource Governance Capacity Development with Dire Consequences

As described earlier, structural adjustment programs consisted of multiyear loans and mining sector reforms aimed at creating an attractive investment climate for foreign investors. As part of these reconstruction programs, liberal mining codes were developed at the behest of institutions such as CIDA and the World Bank (Bush 2007; Butler 2015; Campbell 2010, 2011; Hilson 2012). Accompanying these codes were resource governance capacity development programs, which gained momentum after the World Bank commissioned an Extractive Industries Review in 2001 after endless criticism from civil society organizations, activists, and researchers (Extractive Industries Review 2003).

The Extractive Industries Review called for three main enabling conditions: "pro-poor public and corporate governance, including proactive planning and management to maximize poverty alleviation through sustainable development, increased effective social and environmental policies and respect for human rights" (Extractive Industries Review 2003). As a result, environmental governance has taken centre stage in resource governance capacity development, spearheaded by international financial institutions, including the World Bank. Such institutions provided capacity for the development of regulatory and legislative frameworks for the extractive industries, with the aim of promoting socio-economic development, poverty reduction, and environmental protection. The reality, however, has been different (Akabzaa 2009; Bryceson 2002; Bush 2010; Campbell 2010; Hilson 2002; Hilson and Haselip 2004).

The three main components of environmental governance are laws and legislation (e.g., mining, environmental, and land laws), the Environmental Impact Assessment (EIA), and regulatory agencies such as the Environmental Protection Agency (EPA). In line with neoliberal ideology, below-surface lands belong to governments, which can transfer ownership to any third party, including extractive companies. Consequently, anything on the land is disrupted. This is a common provision in the mining laws in Africa – including in Tanzania, South Africa, Nigeria, Ghana, and Sierra Leone (Bryceson 2002; Bush 2010; Butler 2015; Campbell 2011, 2010; Collins, Grant, and Ackah-Baidoo 2019; Grant 2005; Hilson 2002; Johnston-Taylor 2015; Mason 2014). Furthermore the laws often fail to provide explicit, clear, and unambiguous guidelines on issues such as compensation and the resettlement of affected communities. Counterintuitive to the CSR objectives, local laws are undermined, favouring investors and legitimizing the dispossession of host communities.

The implementation of an EIA has been described as the "magic bullet" to address the negative effects of extractive operations. EIAs are often ineffective, however, as they give extractive companies an undue leverage over conducting and reporting impact assessments and proposing strategies to address the declared impacts. Several critical scholars have argued that self-assessment by mining companies as an alternative to state regulation raises problems, particularly because there is no accompanying enforcement mechanism. Many believe that a company that prioritizes profit is unlikely to disclose all the effects of its operations, as this would often translate into greater costs (Akabzaa 2009; Akiwumi and Butler 2008; Belem 2009; Campbell 2010, 2011; Johnston-Taylor 2015). In Mali, for example, Belem (2009) found that there was a failure to declare the long-term effects of mining operations, creating a situation where the state was left to assume responsibility without the means to follow it through. In short, the subjective nature of the EIA process grossly undermines its efficacy, as it allows companies to govern themselves (Jay et al. 2007; Ortolano and Shepherd 1995).

Companies' level of commitment to addressing and managing the impacts of their operations is often vague, ambiguous, and at best difficult to measure, allowing for compliance without necessarily prioritizing the effective management of impacts. Companies do this with little interference from government, which is in line with neoliberal ideology, but counterintuitive to the goals and objectives of environmental governance and CSR (Akabzaa 2009; Andrews 2016; Johnston-Taylor 2015; Mason 2014). This would also support Idemudia's (2014) contention that companies routinely fail to address the direct impact of their operations in the Niger delta, which undermines CSR efforts and is counterintuitive to the goals of responsible corporate behaviour.

Local regulatory institutions such as the EPA are often constrained by inadequate resources and a restricted mandate to regulate the behaviour of mining companies. The role of these agencies is often restricted during the stages where actual environmental and social impact studies are conducted. Without government regulation, involvement, or monitoring during these studies, Canadian companies operating in Africa are essentially free to disclose impacts in the EIA reports as they deem fit (Campbell 2010, 2011; Mason 2014). Africa is also constrained by blurred lines of responsibility and accountability, which make the continent fertile ground for violations and all manner of corruption (Campbell 2011).

Prioritization of Economics

Although the establishment of the CORE indicates progress and a recommitment to Canada's CSR goals, central to the limitations in Canada's approach to CSR and sustainable development has been its prioritization of economics, and thus profits and economic growth and development. Carroll's (1999) CSR triangle outlined that economic development and profits are at the heart of the CSR model, and are therefore at the foundation of any decision making on implementing CSR. This is evident in Canada's current approach. Industry Canada recommends that businesses practise CSR solely on the basis of its benefit to the bottom line (Industry Canada 2011).

Canada's strategy is also revealed in the assistance the Trade Commissioner Service provides Canadian companies operating abroad. In helping to reduce such companies' costs, the TCS enables them to free up funds to increase profits that can be repatriated to Canada to help boost the Canadian economy. As such, critical observers view the TCS as a mechanism strategically intended to increase the profits and further the interests of Canadian extractive companies in Africa (Engler 2015a). Darimani (2005) argues that Canadian government representatives in Africa are, in effect, advocators and facilitators for Canadian extractive companies, with no mandate and little inclination to investigate claims of corporate misconduct in a determined and even-handed way; as he notes, "the foreign missions of the Canadian government are believed to be stop-shops for corporate lobby" (7).

Central to the motivation of CSR is sustainable development. Scholars have argued that the model of sustainability prioritizes economics and therefore economic growth and/or profits. Rajak (2011) compares the idea of sustainable development pursued through initiatives such as CSR to a "Trojan horse" that prioritizes profits, self-regulation, and unfair trade, and African countries inadvertently embrace their own enslavement. According to the "treadmill of production" theory, the challenge is that the pursuit of economic growth and development puts an ever-increasing demand on the environment by extracting natural resources. Advocates of this theory suggest that, to achieve sustainability and poverty reduction, radical restructuring of the political economy and a move away from the economic growth dependence are required. Schnaiberg and Gould (1994), for example, believe that a failure to restructure would result in no real and lasting sustainable social and environmental improvement. Thus, CSR initiatives would become little more than "window dressing" with nothing new to report (Mol 2002), and mechanisms such as the TCS would merely facilitate the "treadmill" of production.

Additionally, the historical composition of international financial institutions is premised on the idea of industrialization and capital accumulation and, as such, these institutions are great advocates of the neoliberal ideology spearheaded by the Bretton Woods institutions, the World Trade Organization, and Global Affairs Canada. Industrial development places the environment and poverty reduction secondary to the pursuit of capital expansion, often at the expense of the Global South (Bush 2007, 2010; Butler 2015; Campbell 2010, 2011; Hilson 2012; Johnston-Taylor 2015; Mason 2014).

Conclusion

Initiatives such as corporate social responsibility, some scholars suggest, are not "compassionate capitalism," but rather "capitalism in new clothes." Therefore the marketization of such initiatives, as Pellizzoni (2011) argues, makes it difficult to be efficient at dealing with social and environmental problems in Africa's extractive sectors. Only recently (in May 2018) did the Canadian government, in line with neoliberal ideology and through the creation of the Canadian Ombudsperson for Responsible Enterprise, take steps to move beyond voluntary codes and standards. Historically the government has refrained from mandating Canadian companies to act responsibly abroad or to institute punitive measures for failing to comply with such as mandate. This rudimentary, laissez-faire approach has undermined socio-economic development in

Africa and allowed dire consequences to proliferate in Africa's mines and oil and gas fields.

The increase in the "globalization of mining" caused by the free market approach characterized by liberalization essentially has left many poor African countries open to exploitation and unable to stand up against big and powerful extractive companies holding on to the purse strings. As such, extractive companies' attempt at CSR is voluntary and involves minimal oversight. It leaves a lot of room for variation of implementation, and creates complexities in measuring and evaluating impact. Weak government and governance issues in many mineral- and energy-rich African countries also compounds the problem. As long as dealings with local communities remain a voluntary act with no real possibility of repercussions (from the Canadian government), problems between host communities and Canadian companies in Africa are likely to persist. The Canadian government has an important role to play in Africa's extractive-rich countries because it engages African governments as development partners and serves as financier for private sector projects. Consequently, the Canadian government is in a great position to regulate Canadian companies' operations abroad and, essentially, to move the needle on voluntary modes of governance. The creation of the CORE represents a substantive development in the country's CSR infrastructure, but it remains to be seen if this newly created institution represents a change in the way Canadian companies conduct business abroad.

In closing, I offer three brief policy-relevant recommendations. First, I suggest a repurposing of Bill C-300 is needed – one that involves a review and rewrite of the bill to ensure greater consultation that would facilitate greater buy-in than before. Second, Canada should legislate access to Canadian courts for civil suits brought by non-Canadian alleged victims of human rights abuses perpetrated by Canadian companies operating abroad. Finally, there needs to be a shift from an infrastructure-based CSR to an approach that engages more directly the communities in which companies are working. According to Idemudia (2014), a CSR strategy based on a community foundation model, where communities are sufficiently represented and participate in the development of CSR projects, can positively affect companies' ability to secure a social licence to operate, improve stakeholder relationships, and reduce distrust. It would also enable them to deliver appropriate development projects that address the needs of the communities in which they operate. These can be embedded in the role of the ombudsperson.

It is states – not private actors – that are signatories to these conventions, so it is imperative that Canada do more to ensure that businesses operating through agreements such as FIPPAs meet international standards of practice. In this way, Canada can ensure that its FIPPAs are truly bilateral agreements, rather than unilateral ones. Even amid the need for companies to maximize profits and for the economy to grow, what is required is a fundamental ontological shift characterized by "an ethic of mutuality and of respect for Others as Self" (Butler 2015, 293). As such, Canada needs to "move the needle" on its approach to CSR and on regulating Canadian companies' behaviour abroad.

BIBLIOGRAPHY

Akabzaa, Thomas. 2009. "Mining in Ghana: Implications for National Economic Development and Poverty Reduction." In *Mining in Africa: Regulation
and Development*, edited by Bonnie Campbell, 25–65. London; New York:
Pluto Press.
Akiwumi, Fenda, and David Butler. 2008. "Mining and Environmental
Change in Sierra Leone, West Africa: A Remote Sensing and Hydrogeo-
morphological Study." *Environmental Monitoring and Assessment* 142 (1–3):
309–18. https://doi.org/10.1007/s10661-007-9930-9.
Andrews, Nathan. 2016. "Challenges of Corporate Social Responsibility (CSR)
in Domestic Settings: An Exploration of Mining Regulation vis-à-vis CSR in
Ghana." *Resources Policy* 47 (March): 9–17. https://doi.org/10.1016/
j.resourpol.2015.11.001.
Belem, Gisèle. 2009. "Mining, Poverty Reduction, the Protection of the Envi-
ronment and the Role of the World Bank Group in Mali." In *Mining in
Africa: Regulation and Development*, edited by Bonnie Campbell, 119–49.
London; New York: Pluto Press.
Black, David, ed. 2015. *Canada and Africa in the New Millennium: The Politics of
Consistent Inconsistency*. Waterloo, ON: Wilfrid Laurier University Press.
Black, David, and Malcom Savage. 2015. "Canadian Extractive Companies
in Africa: Exposing the Hegemonic Imperative." In *Canada and Africa in the
New Millennium*, edited by David Black, 151–82. Waterloo, ON: Wilfrid
Laurier University Press.
Blackwood, Elizabeth, and Veronika Stewart. 2012. "CIDA and the Mining
Sector: Extractive Industries as an Overseas Development Strategy." In
Struggling for Effectiveness: CIDA and Canadian Foreign Aid, edited by Stephen
Brown, 217–45. Montreal; Kingston, ON: McGill-Queen's University Press.
Bryceson, Deborah. 2002. "The Scramble in Africa: Reorienting Rural
Livelihoods." *World Development* 30 (5): 725–39. https://doi.org/10.1016/
s0305-750x(02)00006-2.

Bush, Ray. 2007. *Poverty and Neoliberalism: Persistence and Reproduction in the Global South*. London: Pluto Press.

Bush, Ray. 2008. "Scrambling to the Bottom? Mining, Resources and Underdevelopment." *Review of African Political Economy* 35 (117): 361–6. https://doi.org/10.1080/03056240802410968.

Bush, Ray. 2010. "Conclusion: Mining, Dispossession, and Transformation in Africa." In *Zambia, Mining and Neoliberalism: Boom and Bust on the Globalized Copperbelt*, edited by Alastair Fraser and Miles Larmer, 237–68. New York: Palgrave Macmillan.

Bush, Ray, and Yao Graham. 2010. "Mining Companies Are Not Interested in Africa's Development." *Guardian*, 2 December.

Butler, Paula. 2015. *Colonial Extractions, Race, and Canadian Mining in Contemporary Africa*. Toronto: University of Toronto Press.

Campbell, Bonnie. 2010. "Revisiting the Reform Process of African Mining Regimes." *Canadian Journal of Development Studies* 30 (1–2): 197–217. https://doi.org/10.1080/02255189.2010.9669288.

Campbell, Bonnie. 2011. "Canadian Mining in Africa: 'Do As You Please' Approach Comes at High Cost." *Canadian Dimension* 45 (1): 28–32.

Canada. 2015. "Canada's Enhanced Corporate Social Responsibility Strategy to Strengthen Canada's Extractive Sector Abroad." Ottawa: Global Affairs Canada. Available online at https://www.international.gc.ca/trade-agreements-accords-commerciaux/topics-domaines/other-autre/csr-strat-rse.aspx?lang=eng, accessed 30 May 2016.

Canada. 2016. "Corporate Social Responsibility." Ottawa: Global Affairs Canada. Available online at https://www.international.gc.ca/trade-agreements-accords-commerciaux/topics-domaines/other-autre/csr-17-rse.aspx?lang=eng, accessed 1 May 2016.

Canada. 2018a. "Responsible Business Conduct Abroad.: Ottawa: Global Affairs Canada. Available online at https://www.international.gc.ca/trade-agreements-accords-commerciaux/topics-domaines/other-autre/csr-rse.aspx?lang=eng, accessed 2 November 2018.

Canada. 2018b. "Responsible Business Conduct Abroad – Questions and Answers." Ottawa: Global Affairs Canada. Available online at https://www.international.gc.ca/trade-agreements-accords-commerciaux/topics-domaines/other-autre/faq.aspx?lang=eng, accessed 2 November 2018.

Carroll, Archie. 1999. "Corporate Social Responsibility Evolution of a Definitional Construct." *Business & Society* 38: 269–95. https://doi.org/10.1177%2F000765039903800303.

Coalition of NGOs. 2016. "Open Letter on Mining to Canadian Prime Minister Trudeau." Available online at https://aida-americas.org/sites/default/files/publication/letter_to_trudeaueng.pdf, accessed 6 February 2017.

Collins, Andrea M., J. Andrew Grant, and Patricia Ackah-Baidoo. 2019. "The Glocal Dynamics of Land Reform in Natural Resource Sectors: Insights from Tanzania." *Land Use Policy* 81 (February): 889–96. https://doi.org/10.1016/j.landusepol.2017.05.027.

Coumans, Catherine. 2014. "Submission to the Government of Canada's Review of Corporate Social Responsibility Strategy for the Canadian Extractive Sector." Available online at http://miningwatch.ca/sites/default/files/submission_to_the_government_of_canada_on_csr_jan-2014.pdf, accessed 30 May 2016.

Darimani, Abdulai. 2005. *Impacts of Activities of Canadian Mining Companies in Africa*. Accra, Ghana: Third World Network – Africa.

Engler, Yves. 2015a. Canada *in Africa: 300 Years of Aid and Exploitation*. Black Point, NS: Fernwood Publishing.

Engler, Yves. 2015b. "Canadian Mining Abuses in Africa." *Canadian Dimension*, 30 November. Available online at https://canadiandimension.com/articles/view/canadian-mining-abuses-in-africa, accessed 30 May 2016.

Engler, Yves. 2016. "The Hypocrisy of Canadian Ownership in Africa." *Huffington Post*, 14 June.

Extractive Industries Review. 2003. "Striking a Better Balance: The Extractive Industries Review, Executive Summary." Available online at http://wman-info.org/wp-content/uploads/2012/08/World-Bank-EIR-Exec-Summary.pdf, accessed 1 August 2013.

Grant, J. Andrew. 2005. "Diamonds, Foreign Aid, and the Uncertain Prospects for Post-Conflict Reconstruction in Sierra Leone." *Round Table: The Commonwealth Journal of International Affairs* 94 (381): 443–57. https://doi.org/10.1080/00358530500243690.

Harvey, David. 2003. *The New Imperialism*. Oxford: Oxford University Press.

Hilson, Gavin. 2002. "An Overview of Land Use Conflicts in Mining Communities." *Land Use Policy* 19 (1): 65–73. https://doi.org/10.1016/s0264-8377(01)00043-6.

Hilson, Gavin. 2012. "Corporate Social Responsibility in the Extractive Industries: Experiences from Developing Countries." *Resources Policy* 37 (2): 131–7. https://doi.org/10.1016/j.resourpol.2012.01.002.

Hilson, Gavin, and James Haselip. 2004. "The Environmental and Socioeconomic Performance of Multinational Mining Companies in the Developing World Economy." *Minerals and Energy - Raw Materials Report* 19 (3): 25–47. https://doi.org/10.1080/14041040410027318.

Idemudia, Uwafiokun. 2014. "Corporate-Community Engagement Strategies in the Niger Delta: Some Critical Reflections." *Extractive Industries and Society* 1 (2): 154–62. https://doi.org/10.1016/j.exis.2014.07.005.

Jay, Stephen, Carys Jones, Paul Slinn, and Christopher Wood. 2007. "Environmental Impact Assessment: Retrospect and Prospect." *Environmental*

Impact Assessment Review 27 (4): 287–300. https://doi.org/10.1016/j.eiar.2006.12.001.

Johnston-Taylor, Nketti. 2015. "The Resource Curse and Natural Resource Environmental Governance in Sierra Leone, Case Study Kono District." PhD diss., University of Leeds.

Mason, Nketti. 2014. "Environmental Governance in Sierra Leone's Mining Sector: A Critical Analysis." *Resources Policy* 41 (September): 152–9. https://doi.org/10.1016/j.resourpol.2014.05.005.

Mazereeuw, Peter. 2016. "Liberals 'Seriously' Considering Mining Ombudsperson, Says Federal Corporate Social Responsibility Adviser." *Hill Times*, 9 November. Available online at https://www.hilltimes.com/2016/11/09/feds-seriously-considering-mining-ombudsman-says-canadas-corporate-social-responsibility-envoy/86691.

McMillan, Leah. 2012. "The Canada-Tanzania FIPA: Bilateral Relationship or Unilateral Advantage?" Available online at https://www.cardus.ca/article/the-canada-tanzania-fipa-bilateral-relationship-or-unilateral-advantage/, accessed 7 May 2016.

Mitchell, Terry. 2014. "Introduction." In *The Internalization of Indigenous People, UNDRIP in the Canadian Context Special Report*. Waterloo, ON: Centre for International Governance Innovation.

Mol, Arthur. 2002. "Ecological Modernization and the Global Economy." *Global Environmental Politics* 2 (2): 92–115. https://doi.org/10.1162/15263800260047844.

Newell, Peter. 2008. "The Marketization of Global Environmental Governance. Manifestations and Implications." In *The Crisis of Global Environmental Governance. Towards a New Political Economy of Sustainability*, edited by Jacob Park, Ken Conca, and Matthias Finger, 77–95. London; New York: Routledge.

OECD (Organisation for Economic Co-operation and Development). 2011. *OECD Guidelines for Multinational Enterprises*. Paris: OECD. Available online at http://www.oecd.org/corporate/mne/48004323.pdf, accessed 4 March 2016.

Ortolano, Leonard, and Anne Shepherd. 1995. "Environmental Impact Assessment: Challenges and Opportunities." *Impact Assessment* 13 (1): 3–30. https://doi.org/10.1080/07349165.1995.9726076.

Oved, Marco. 2018. "Ottawa Creates Office to Investigate Human Rights Abuses Linked to Canadian Companies Abroad." *Toronto Star*, 17 January. Available online at https://www.thestar.com/news/canada/2018/01/17/ottawa-creates-office-to-investigate-human-rights-abuses-linked-to-canadian-companies-abroad.html.

Pellizzoni, Luigi. 2011. "Governing through Disorder: Neoliberal Environmental Governance and Social Theory." *Global Environmental Change* 21 (3): 795–803. https://doi.org/10.1016/j.gloenvcha.2011.03.014.

Rajak, Dinah. 2011. *In Good Company: An Anatomy of Corporate Social Responsibility*. Stanford, CA: Stanford University Press.

Scheinert, Josh. 2016. "Between Rock and Responsibility: Corporate Responsibility for Canada's Mining Sector." Canada Haiti Action Network. Available online at https://canada-haiti.ca/content/between-rock-and-responsibility -corporate-responsibility-canadas-mining-sector.

Schnaiberg, Allen, and Kenneth Gould. 1994. *Environment and Society: The Enduring Conflict*. New York: St Martin's Press.

Szeftel, Morris. 1998. "Misunderstanding African Politics: Corruption and the Governance Agenda." *Review of African Political Economy* 25 (76): 221–40. https://doi.org/10.1080/03056249808704311.

United Nations. 2008. *United Nations Declaration on the Rights of Indigenous Peoples*. New York: United Nations.

United Nations Human Rights. 2011. "Guiding Principles on Business and Human Rights." In *Implementing the United Nations 'Protect, Respect and Remedy' Framework*. New York; Geneva: United Nations.

Voluntary Principles. 2017. *Voluntary Principles on Security and Human Rights*. Available online at https://www.voluntaryprinciples.org/, accessed 4 March 2017.

4 Canadian Perspectives on the Voluntary Principles on Security and Human Rights in Africa: Assessing the Legitimacy of Multistakeholder Initiatives in the Extractive Sectors

CHARIS ENNS

Introduction

In April 2016 the government of Canada assumed the chair of the Voluntary Principles on Security and Human Rights Initiative (VPI), a multistakeholder initiative that provides standards for the provision of security in the extractive sectors. As chair the Canadian government promoted the Voluntary Principles on Security and Human Rights (VPs) and advanced discussions on their implementation, and was also involved in growing the initiative's membership and developing its next strategic plan. Indeed, the Canadian government has become an increasingly strong proponent of the VPs in recent years, introducing new measures domestically to encourage industry actors to comply with this set of standards and undertaking bilateral and multilateral efforts to advance the implementation of the VPs globally.

Canadian extractive companies have also demonstrated a new degree of commitment to the VPs, and have become more engaged in the VPI as of late. In fact, Canadian-headquartered companies currently account for nearly 15 per cent of the VPI's corporate membership.[1] Numerous Canadian companies have developed security management systems that integrate the VPs into their practices on the ground. For example, Barrick Gold has implemented a Security Management System that involves risk assessments, data analysis, and incident management and investigations, while Kinross Mining has developed a Human Rights Adherence and Verification Program that includes risks assessments and stakeholder engagement strategies – consistent with the human rights and security approach promoted by the VPs. Moreover, most major publicly listed Canadian extractive companies endorse the VPs to some extent, even if they are not officially members of the initiative.

Yet during the same period in which many Canadian actors have be-come stronger proponents of the VPs, some Canadian non-governmental organizations (NGOs) have raised concerns about the initiative. In this chapter, I examine conflicting perspectives about the VPI among differ-ent Canadian stakeholder groups, including the federal government, extractive companies, and NGOs. Drawing primarily on examples from the extractive sectors in sub-Saharan Africa, I demonstrate that, although Canadian extractive companies are engaging with the VPs "on the ground" and the Canadian government is actively promoting them both domestically and globally, Canadian civil society has raised important concerns about the transparency, efficacy, and enforcement of this initiative. Employing a conceptual framework developed by Mena and Palazzo (2012), I argue that the critiques levied by NGOs against the VPI ultimately challenge its legitimacy. As the success of any multistakeholder initiative depends on its legitimacy (Bernstein and Cashore 2007; Grant, Balraj, and Mavropoulos-Vagelis 2013; Mena and Palazzo 2012), addressing these critiques is essential if the VPI is to be a successful venue for addressing human rights and security con-cerns in the extractive sectors.

Theoretically, my analysis contributes to scholarly work that exam-ines the legitimacy of multistakeholder initiatives by applying Mena and Palazzo's (2012) conceptual framework to a new case study. How-ever, my analysis is also relevant to ongoing policy-practitioner dis-cussions in Canada about how best to regulate the Canadian extractive sectors, pinpointing possible areas where the VPI could be reformed to enhance its perceived legitimacy. In terms of the geographic focus of the chapter, examining how Canadian stakeholders use and engage with the VPs around extractive sites in sub-Saharan Africa is of inter-est for two additional reasons. First, the VPs have great significance in sub-Saharan Africa, as conflicts between extractive companies, security providers, and communities are particularly prevalent in this region. Moreover, given that Canadian companies have a large presence in sub-Saharan Africa, it is important to understand how the VPs are used, advanced, and critiqued by Canadian actors. Second, as the Canadian government recently served as chair of the VPI, it is timely to discuss Canadian perspectives of the VPI, as well as steps that could be taken to address critiques against the initiative moving forwards.

The following analysis is based on close examination of relevant doc-uments produced by the Canadian government, Canadian extractive companies, Canadian NGOs, and the VPI itself. These documents in-clude reports, policies, strategies, press releases, meeting minutes, and website materials. Further insights have been garnered through fifteen interviews with representatives from Canadian extractive companies, Canadian NGOs, a Canadian industry association, and the Canadian government. My analysis is also informed by discussions with academic, legal, and policy experts with knowledge of the VPs, as well as by auditing a professional development course on the VPs offered by Edumine – the world's leading provider of training and education to the mining industry. Once collected, data were analysed by coding key themes and ideas that emerged during a close reading of the texts and interview transcripts.

To begin the chapter, I briefly review scholarly debates about the legitimacy of multistakeholder initiatives, and introduce the conceptual framework I use to frame my analysis. Next, I provide a brief overview of the VPI. I then present a case study of the VPs in the Canadian context, and describe Canadian involvement in the VPI to date. Finally, I use Mena and Palazzo's (2012) conceptual framework to evaluate the legitimacy of the VPI, supporting my analysis with examples from Canadian extractive operations in sub-Saharan Africa. Using this framework, it is possible to show specific areas where the VPI appears to lack legitimacy, thereby revealing why some Canadian NGOs remain sceptical about the potential of this governance initiative. I conclude the chapter by considering the practical implications of this analysis.

The Legitimacy of Multistakeholder Initiatives

In areas where "national and international regulation of significant global social and environmental problems has been absent or weak, an array of voluntary, self-regulatory, shared governance, and private arrangements are beginning to fill the policy void" (Bernstein and Cashore 2007, 347). These governance arrangements fit under the umbrella term of multistakeholder initiatives. Well-known examples of such initiatives in the extractive sectors include: the Voluntary Principles on Security and Human Rights; the Extractive Industries Transparency Initiative; the Publish What You Pay campaign; the Kimberley Process Certification Scheme (KPCS) to prevent the trade of conflict diamonds; and the Sustainable Development Framework of the International Council on Mining and Metals (ICMM). Each of these initiatives differs in its purpose, reach, and scope. Some provide learning platforms where organizations can exchange experiences and ideas; others set rules and develop mechanisms for monitoring compliance. Despite their differences, multistakeholder initiatives share certain common characteristics: they are the result of cooperation between stakeholders (e.g., governments, corporations, and civil society), and they aim to influence the governance and regulation of transnational business (Bernstein and Cashore 2007; Grant 2013).

When multistakeholder initiatives become involved in rules setting and monitoring compliance, they take on a state-like function (Mena and Palazzo 2012). Some scholars have acclaimed these initiatives as an ideal approach to governing and regulating in an increasingly globalized world, arguing that they have the potential to fill governance gaps in areas where states are weak or absent (Bäckstrand 2006; Ruggie 2014). However, the role of multistakeholder initiatives in global governance has also been subject to criticism. In particular, some scholars have shared a concern that such initiatives escape traditional conceptions of legitimacy and accountability (Hahn and Weidtmann 2016; Klijn and Skelcher 2007; Sørensen and Torfing 2005, 2007). This concern relates to the fact that stakeholders who participate in multistakeholder initiatives are not elected through democratic processes, and cannot always be held accountable by those they govern (Klijn and Skelcher 2007; Sundström, Furusten, and Soneryd 2010).

However, the fact that the legitimacy and accountability of multistakeholder initiatives cannot be measured using conventional approaches does not necessarily mean that those stakeholders lack the authority to govern. Instead it can be argued simply that new ways of defining and understanding legitimacy are needed in a globalizing world. As Hahn and Weidtmann (2016, 92) suggest, "[s]ince traditional elements conveying legitimacy (such as elections, democratic representations, and public control) do not apply to the novel elements of governance in question," new ways of establishing legitimacy must be discussed and better understood. Mena and Palazzo (2012) have proposed a conceptual framework for measuring and testing the legitimacy of multistakeholder initiatives that is inspired by the Habermasian idea of deliberative democracy. This framework makes criteria used to evaluate the legitimacy of governments relevant to debates on the legitimacy of multistakeholder initiatives.

Mena and Palazzo's (2012) framework suggests that a multistakeholder initiative is legitimate if: 1) it is shaped by processes and structures that are justified, transparent, fair, and credible; and 2) it effectively solves the issues that it targets without creating negative externalities. These two dimensions of legitimacy are referred to respectively as input legitimacy and output legitimacy. Breaking down these dimensions further, Mena and Palazzo outline four criteria to measure input legitimacy: a) stakeholder inclusion; b) procedural fairness of deliberations; c) consensual decision making; and d) transparency of structures and processes. They propose an additional three criteria to measure output legitimacy: (e) coverage of membership; (f) efficacy; and (g) enforcement and monitoring of rules. In the later sections of this chapter, I use Mena and Palazzo's (2012) conceptual framework to evaluate the legitimacy of the VPI. I suggest that the VPI is a particularly useful case study for advancing discussions on multistakeholder initiative legitimacy as so many of the critiques facing this particular governance initiative in the Canadian context relate directly to the issue of (il)legitimacy. Before evaluating the legitimacy of the VPI, I provide important background information about the VPI, and outline how the VPs have been used, advanced, and critiqued by various Canadian stakeholders.

The Voluntary Principles on Security and Human Rights

The Voluntary Principles on Security and Human Rights emerged in 2000, when the UK Foreign Office and the US State Department invited a number of large transnational extractive companies and NGOs to "initiate a 'continuing dialogue among diverse stakeholders' on the pressing issue of corporate security and human rights" (Hofferberth 2010, 11). Out of this dialogue, a set of principles was created to serve as a standard for maintaining the security of extractive operations within a framework that ensures respect for human rights. According to Pitts (2011, 357), the VPs were created to address "one of the most persistent patterns of human rights abuse and violations of corporate social responsibility standards: the deaths, kidnappings, torture and physical harm historically caused by oil, gas, mining and extractive companies attempting to protect their assets in host countries." They act as a mode of soft-regulation to address human rights abuses at extractive sites – an issue area where national and international regulation historically has been lacking.

The VPs are overseen by a multistakeholder initiative called the Voluntary Principles on Security and Human Rights Initiative, which is comprised of three "pillars," or types of members: extractive companies, governments, and NGOs. Although the United States and the United Kingdom were important actors in establishing the VPI, other early members included companies – notably Chevron, Texaco, and Shell – and NGOs such as Amnesty International, Human Rights Watch, and International Alert. In March 2017, VPI membership consisted of twenty-nine companies, ten governments, and ten NGOs. In recent years, corporate and government participation in the initiative has gown slowly, while NGO membership has waxed and waned. The VPs set standards in relation to three primary areas:

- *Risk assessment*: The VPs guide extractive companies in identifying and analysing risks and developing mitigation strategies. Company members of the VP must complete risk assessments, focusing particularly on assessing risks with human rights–related effects.
- *Relations with public security forces*: The VPs outline how police or public forces and extractive companies should interact. They encourage companies to work with public security forces to help them act in accordance with international norms.
- *Interactions with private security providers*: The VPs also outline standards for private security providers, and offer guidance on how they and extractive companies should interact.

When the initiative launched in 2001, it was strictly a set of principles, with no corresponding guidance on implementation. It was not until the annual Plenary Meeting in 2010 that a commitment was made to grow the influence of the initiative by increasing its participant base and developing better implementation processes. This was the same year that Foley Hoag's CSR Practice was elected to take over as secretariat for the VPI – in place of the Business for Social Responsibility and the International Business Leaders Forum, which had jointly served as secretariat since 2004 – and that Canada assumed the chair of the VPI for the first time.

Under Canada's term as chair, a joint project was initiated by the International Finance Corporation, the International Council on Mining and Metals, IPIECA, and the International Committee of the Red Cross and to develop implementation guidelines to accompany the VPs (Baumann-Pauly and Nolan 2016). Key Performance Indicators (KPI) to help companies monitor progress on implementation were developed the following year. In 2015 a reporting and auditing framework for member companies was released that elaborates on the KPI and provides guidance materials to help companies measure or audit their security performance in relation to the VPs. In short, the activities of the VPI have evolved and expanded over the past several years, after a relatively slow first decade of existence.

The VPs in the Canadian Context

The Canadian Government and the VPs

The Canadian government was not an early member of the VPI; in fact Canada did not formally sign on as a member of the initiative until 2010. Over the past several years, however, the Canadian government has become an important and influential member of the VPI. As noted, between 2011 and 2012 the Canadian government assumed the role of chair of the VPI. In this role, it was responsible for advancing discussions on the implementation of the VPs and seeking out new members. It also worked to expand the scope and effectiveness of the initiative. Under Canada's leadership the first implementation guide for the VPs, entitled "Voluntary Principles on Security and Human Rights: Implementation Guidance Tools," was also developed.

In April 2016 the Canadian government assumed the role of chair once again, as a way to demonstrate "Canadian leadership on sustainable natural resource management and respect for human rights" (Canada 2016a, 7). Priorities for its tenure as chair included streamlining the work of the VPI, seeking out new members, and facilitating discussions about implementation and verification of the VPs (interview with government representative, 4 May 2016). In 2015 and 2016, the Canadian government also supported a Canadian working group to develop a reporting and auditing framework for the VPs, entitled "Auditing Implementation of Voluntary Principles on Security and Human Rights." These activities reflect the clear leadership role the government has played in the VPI in recent years, influencing the direction and priorities of the initiative.

In addition to participating in the VPI, the Canadian government has made noteworthy efforts to promote and advance the implementation of the VPs both at home and abroad. Domestically, the government promotes the VPs through Canada's Corporate Social Responsibility (CSR) strategy, which encourages Canadian companies to align their policies and practices with six international CSR guidelines, including the VPs (Canada 2015). The government has also introduced complementary measures to support the uptake of this CSR strategy. For example, Canadian extractive companies are now required to demonstrate their adherence with international CSR guidelines, including the VPs, when requesting loans from Export Development Canada. Global Affairs Canada also positioned the implementation of the VPs and the Extractive Industries Transparency Initiative as a priority in its *Report on Plans and Priorities 2016–17* (Canada 2016b), reflecting the government's commitment to implementing the VPs across Canada's extractive sectors.

Internationally, the Canadian government has promoted the VPs through various multilateral forums, such as the Organisation for Economic Co-operation and Development, the G7, and the G20. It systematically supports the implementation of the VPs through its nine-hundred-plus trade commissioners in diplomatic missions abroad (Canada 2016a). Trade commissioners are given training on the six international CSR standards, including the VPs, which the government endorses before the commissioners are posted. Moreover, diplomatic support from trade commissioners for Canadian extractive companies operating abroad is reported to be contingent on adherence to the federal CSR strategy, including the implementation of the VPs (Canada 2015).

Canadian diplomatic missions are also active in establishing working groups and networks to support the implementation of the VPs in host countries. For example, the High Commission of Canada in Kenya has provided support for the Nairobi Process, a multistakeholder working group that provides guidance to extractive companies with operations in East Africa, on how to deploy public and private security in ways consistent with the VPs. As was explained during an interview, "the Canadian government is friends of the Nairobi Process. They have provided support to the initiative and assisted us with hosting meetings by helping to convene Canadian companies. They help get Canadian companies to these meetings" (interview with Kenyan NGO, 3 March 2015). Canadian diplomatic missions have also supported similar types of activities in other countries, including Tanzania and the Democratic Republic of Congo (DRC).

The Canadian government sees the VPs as an "extremely useful tool" for promoting corporate social responsibility, explaining that, "from the corporate side, the VPs are well thought-out" (interview with government representative, 4 May 2016). This positive assessment regarding the potential of the VP to yield constructive results for both companies and communities is reiterated in the government's 2016 *Annual Report to the Voluntary Principles on Security and Human Rights Initiative*, which states: "Our active engagement in the Voluntary Principles is part of Canada's continued engagement in a range of multi-stakeholder initiatives to actively promote international standards, guidelines, and responsible business practices with the objective of increasing effective governance in resource-rich developing countries and enabling communities to maximize benefits from natural resources development, while respecting human rights and the environment" (Canada 2016a, 6).

Ultimately, the Canadian government's commitment to the VPs is demonstrated in its public discourse and its active role in the VPI, particularly in the steps it has taken to implement the VPs both domestically and internationally. Importantly, this commitment to the VPs can be understood, at least in part, as a way of protecting and securing Canadian interests and investments in natural resources. The government has described the VPs as a "risk mitigation" strategy for Canadian investors and a means of managing the social and environmental risks of extractive operations abroad (Canada 2009, 2015). Interestingly, the active involvement of the Canadian government in promoting the VPs supports the argument made by Idemudia and colleagues (Chapter 2, in this volume), who suggest that the shift towards governing the extractive sectors through global governance initiatives does not necessarily imply the reduction of state power and influence.

Canadian Extractive Companies and the VPs

As stated previously, Canadian-headquartered companies now account for nearly 15 per cent of the VPI's corporate membership. Barrick Gold was the first Canadian mining company to become a member of the VPI, in 2010. The following year Barrick Gold faced a number of serious allegations related to security and human rights, including "highly disturbing allegations of sexual assaults by the police and [African Barrick Gold] security against local women" at its North Mara mine in Tanzania, which was operated by a subsidiary (Barrick Gold 2011). In response to these events, Barrick Gold employed the VPs to revise its security policies, standards, and procedures. The company also began to promote the VPs in communities around its operating sites and in its host countries more broadly. At its North Mara mine, for example, the company engaged "with senior Tanzanian government officials and local law enforcement agencies to encourage and support the provision of Voluntary Principles training to these agencies" (Acacia Mining Plc 2016.). Barrick Gold also implemented a comprehensive Security Management System across all of its operations to manage and respond to security challenges in accordance with the VPs.

Since 2010 other Canadian-headquartered companies have followed Barrick Gold's lead and joined the VPI, including Goldcorp, Pacific Exploration & Production Corporation, and Sherritt International. These companies have taken similar steps to align their policies with the VPs and to demonstrate publicly their commitment to upholding this set of principles. For example, Sherritt International has aligned its security practices with the VPs, and conducts third-party security and human rights risk assessments on an annual basis. In the case of its operating site in Madagascar, the company has embedded the VPs into Memorandums of Understanding with both private security contractors and public security forces. It also delivers security and human rights awareness training based on the VPs for Madagascar's armed forces and defence authorities, in partnership with the United Nations, the International Committee of the Red Cross (ICRC), and Madagascar's Ministry of Justice. These types of activities illustrate the degree of commitment and the amount of resources that some VPI member companies dedicate towards implementing the VPs at their operating sites.

Beyond implementing the VPs in and around their sites of operation, Canadian extractive companies have participated in advancing them domestically. Sherritt International, Goldcorp, and Barrick Gold were all involved in the working group that developed the reporting and auditing framework for the VPs, entitled "Auditing Implementation of Voluntary Principles on Security and Human Rights." Barrick Gold also assisted the Mining Association of Canada in developing requirements related to VPs for its members (Barrick Gold 2016). Notably, Barrick Gold also has played a key leadership role in the VPI itself, having served as a board member of the VPI for several years and, in 2016, reassuming its position as one of the four companies on the VPI's Steering Committee.

A particularly interesting trend in relation to the VPs in the Canadian context is that many Canadian extractive companies refer to them in their public discourse and policies even if they are not officially members of the initiative. For example, although not formally a member of the corporate pillar, Kinross has implemented a comprehensive Human Rights Adherence and Verification Program based on the VPs. This program "helps ensure that all security personnel, as well as key site management, understand and are consistently compliant with the Voluntary Principles on Security and Human Rights" (Kinross 2016). Similarly, the Lundin Mining Corporation works with an NGO, Search for Common Ground, around its operating site in the DRC to align its security practices with the VPs (Search for Common Ground 2016). As well, all members of the Mining Association of Canada, whether or not they are official members of the VPI, now report on their implementation of the VPs annually in the association's *TSM Progress Report*.

For extractive companies operating in complex environments, managing security in a way that ensures respect for human rights is often a significant challenge. Moreover, failing to overcome this challenge presents substantial personal and financial risks to all stakeholders involved, including the company, its shareholders, its security contractors, the host government, and community members in the vicinity of extractive operations. For this reason, the VPs were often highly praised during my interviews with Canadian extractive companies. While other CSR instruments were described as "simply nice to have," the VPs were described as "easy to implement ... a tangible link to human rights that the oil and gas industry could really get behind," and a "useful risk mitigation instrument" (interviews with Canadian extractive companies, 4 September 2014; 22 September 2014; 18 September 2014).

Another representative from a Canadian extractive company explained that, although the company aimed to uphold all relevant international guidelines and standards, the VPs provided "the most effective means of dealing with risk" (interview with Canadian extractive company, 6 January 2015). Arguably, much like the Canadian government, Canadian extractive companies are making public commitments to adhere to the standards set by the VPs because these principles can serve as a sound risk-management strategy if well implemented.

Canadian NGOs and the VPs

When it comes to governance initiatives like the VPI, "the multi-stakeholder nature of these initiatives is what gives them their strength and credibility, and ongoing NGO participation is an essential element of their success" (Baumann-Pauly and Nolan 2016, 118). From the outset, however, the VPI has struggled to maintain sufficient and representative NGO membership. There are currently ten NGO participants in the VPI, compared with twenty-nine extractive companies. Moreover, only one NGO participant, Partnership Africa Canada, is based in Canada.

NGOs involved in the VPI have different opinions about the effectiveness of the initiative. Some NGOs, such as Search for Common Ground, International Alert, and Partnership Africa Canada, demonstrate a strong level of support for the VPs and serve as active participants within the VPI. They promote the VPs as a good model for addressing security and human rights issues, and they have been involved in creating guidance and tools to assist companies in implementing the VPs. Other NGOs, however, are more cautious about their participation. For example, the ICRC has elected to participate in the VPI as an "observer," rather than as an official member (Voillat 2012). The ICRC argues that the VPI has "so far delivered rather poorly in terms of having its members work together to tackle Voluntary Principles-related challenges at the level of the various countries where extractive operations are taking place" (Voillat 2012, 1099). Other research reiterates these findings. For example, Pitts (2011, 360) found that NGO members of the VPI were critical of the VPs, deeming them "'worthless' in their current incarnation."

The fact that some NGOs have withdrawn their support from the VPI altogether also suggests there are internal rifts within the initiative. As Pitts (2011) writes, even strong friends of the VPI have been compelled to withdraw their support in recent years. In May 2013 Amnesty International notified the secretariat of the VPI of its decision to terminate its membership, stating that the decision was a result of concerns about the credibility and effectiveness of the initiative. During the same year, Oxfam issued a similar statement explaining its resignation from the VPI, stating: "Our decision stems in large part from our frustration at the lack of meaningful progress in independent assurance, despite more than ten years of deliberation and discussion" (Oxfam 2013).

Canadian NGOs not officially involved in the VPI have also expressed concerns, questioning whether the initiative is proving an effective governance tool. For example, a MiningWatch Canada report on the use of the VPs in Tanzania and the DRC, entitled "Principles Without Justice: The Corporate Takeover of Human Rights," argues that the VPs have been "misused to encourage companies to enter into, or continue to operate in, unstable situations where their security is dependent on public law enforcement bodies which routinely perpetrate human rights violations and where the rule of law is weak" (RAID 2016, 75), and calls on the Canadian government to use its position as chair of the VPI to correct this misuse of the VPs. The concerns emanating from Canadian civil society about the VPI and the standards it promotes raise important questions about the legitimacy of the initiative.

Assessing the Legitimacy of the VPs

In the final section of this chapter, I use the idea of legitimacy to explain the conflicting perspectives about the VPI among different stakeholder groups, and argue that these different perspectives exist because the VPI – in its current formation – lacks legitimacy in some areas. I frame my discussion using a conceptual framework developed by Mena and Palazzo (2012), which allows for the evaluation of multistakeholder initiative legitimacy using seven criteria. Table 4.1 summarizes the discussion that follows.

Input Legitimacy

A multistakeholder initiative with input legitimacy must include all stakeholders that are affected by the issue. Importantly, an inclusive initiative is not simply a large one, as "even if [a multistakeholder initiative] includes a large number of stakeholders, its legitimacy might be low, because it does not involve the relevant ones" (Mena and Palazzo 2012, 539). In the case of the VPI, all members are included in the decision-making processes, and the highest decision-making body – the Steering Committee – is comprised of companies, governments, and NGOs. At the surface, this might suggest that the VPI is *inclusive*, but some NGOs remain concerned about the degree of its inclusivity. For example, the ICRC chose not to become an official member because of what it perceived as the initiative's lack of inclusivity, arguing that "formal membership in an initiative that was constituted exclusively of Western governments, companies, and organisations was not suitable with regard to the institution's principle of neutrality" (Voillat 2012, 1099). Although more members from the Global South have since joined the VPI, many NGOs argue that this is not enough. As one interviewee explained, although the VPI might be recruiting governments from the Global South to participate, there is still little space for community-level NGOs or affected communities to influence the initiative (interview with Canadian NGO, 30 October 2014). Moreover, even if such groups were openly welcomed into the initiative, many community-level NGOs lack the resources (such as funds to travel) and organizational capacity needed to participate.

A second criterion when assessing the input legitimacy of a multistakeholder initiative is *procedural fairness*: whether included stakeholders are able to influence the decision-making processes. Within the VPI all members are able to vote and, therefore, influence decisions in the Plenary; in the Steering Committee at least two members from each pillar must vote affirmatively for a vote to pass. With this in mind, the VPI demonstrates procedural fairness, as deliberations are structured in a way that aims to "neutralize" power imbalances between different stakeholders (Mena and Palazzo 2012). Of course, as Dingwerth (2008) argues, even when the procedures in place are fair, decision-making processes do not always unfold fairly. For example, one interviewee argued that stakeholders with more resources have a greater ability to influence the direction and priorities of the VPI as they can attend every meeting, whereas stakeholders with fewer resources are often not able to do so (interview with government representative, 15 June 2016; see also Baumann-Pauly and Nolan 2016).

A multistakeholder initiative with input legitimacy also aspires for *consensual orientation* and *transparency*, whereby consensual decisions are arrived at through open and inclusive deliberation. Upon arriving at an agreement, an initiative is transparent if external stakeholders are provided information that allows them to evaluate "how a rule was decided upon and judge its appropriateness" (Mena and Palazzo 2012, 541). It seems the VPI, however, has been relatively ineffective at achieving consensual orientation among its stakeholders. As a result of dissenting positions, NGO members have defected from the initiative. The initiative has also been accused of lacking transparency when it comes to decision-making processes, including around the admission

Table 4.1. Assessment of the Democratic Legitimacy of the VPI, 2017

Dimension	Criterion	Definition	Assessment of Criterion in VPI
Input legitimacy	Inclusion	Involvement of all stakeholders affected by the issue in decision-making structures and processes	• The Plenary involved in decision making includes members from each pillar: government, corporate, and NGO • The Steering Committee includes members from each pillar • Lack of representation from the Global South and community-level stakeholders
	Procedural fairness	Neutralization of power differences so all stakeholders can influence decisions and priorities of initiative	• All members of the Plenary have an equal vote • All members of the Steering Committee have an equal vote • Participation in initiative requires access to sufficient resources to attend meetings
	Consensual orientation	Decisions are arrived at through cooperation and compromise	• Members have left based on disagreements
	Transparency	Structures, processes, and decisions are open and transparent	• Members submit annual reports • Annual reports often lack detail and, more important, disclosure remains optional • Recap from annual conference is made public • Certain decision-making processes are not disclosed (e.g., admissions process)
Output legitimacy	Coverage	Number of rule targets; following the rules	• Percentage of firms and governments covered by rules is low • Growing number of firms voluntarily adhere to principles without becoming an official member
	Efficacy	Fit of the rules to the issue and ability of the rules to induce change	• Standard has the potential to induce social and political change if properly implemented • Disagreement about whether rules fit problem, and concerns about potential negative externalities

(Continued)

Table 4.1. (Continued)

Dimension	Criterion	Definition	Assessment of Criterion in VPI
	Enforcement	Measures in place to ensure rules are followed	• Self-monitoring permitted; third-party monitoring optional • Few enforcement mechanisms in place, though members can be expelled for failing to submit annual report

Source: Dimension, criteria, and definitions by Mena and Palazzo (2012).

and refusal of members to the VPI, as these decisions are not made public. NGOs have also questioned why participants have the option of keeping their annual reports for the VPI confidential, suggesting that this "lends credence to the argument that these reports are compiled as a compliance exercise," rather than to encourage "genuine dialogue with those impacted by operations or demonstrate a commitment to public accountability" (RAID 2016, 16).

Output Legitimacy

A multistakeholder initiative with output legitimacy binds as many firms as possible to the same rules. Mena and Palazzo (2012) refer to this as *coverage*. The coverage of the VPI remains low, but is slowly growing. Interviews with Canadian extractive companies revealed one important reason for low coverage: membership is costly, which creates an entry barrier for smaller companies. As Bernstein and Cashore (2007) suggest, companies must perceive the costs of participating in a multistakeholder initiative as less than the economic benefits if the initiative's membership is to grow. This also partly explains why some companies agree in principle to comply with the VPs but never seek formal membership in the initiative – however, this cannot be included in an assessment of the coverage of the initiative, as these companies are not bound by its rules.

In terms of *efficacy*, legitimate multistakeholder initiatives create rules that fit the problem at hand. These rules are meant to induce change, and must avoid creating negative externalities (Mena and Palazzo 2012). During interviews, Canadian extractive companies often described the VPs as inducing political and social change in relation to the provision of security. For example, one company reported on how its approach to working with public law enforcement around its extractive sites in East Africa has changed for the better since implementing the VPs – particularly in relation to avoiding conflicts with artisanal miners (interview with Canadian extractive company, 14 October 2014). Another company explained how it was using the VPs to shape its security policies in order to "avoid the problems that the oil and gas sector has dealt with in Nigeria" (interview with Canadian extractive company, 5 January 2015).

Yet some NGOs question the efficacy of the VPs. They argue that Canadian extractive companies use the VPs to address the symptom of the problem, rather than to address the problem itself. As one interviewee explained: "Companies identify security as a major issue and see the VPs as the clear fix. We keep saying though, 'You cannot address security unless you first address underlying issues.' Most of the security issues are not even security issues. They are engagement issues" (interview with Kenyan NGO, 3 March 2015). Similarly, other NGOs report that implementing the VPs rarely results in tangible changes to security practices at extractive sites. A Canadian legal expert on the VPs agreed, stating: "When the VPs appear to be working for companies and delivering good results, the company was probably already doing really well with security to begin with" (interview with government representative, 15 June 2016). Ultimately, NGOs that are sceptical about the efficacy of the VPs argue that, although the VPs have been designed to serve as a pragmatic, ready-made solution for companies dealing with security and human rights challenges, in many cases they fail to make a difference on the ground (RAID 2016). The Geneva Centre for the Democratic Control of Armed Forces has argued that this might be because existing guidance and tools on implementing the VPs are often "under-developed" or "ignore" "user-needs and field realities," along with the most "challenging aspects of engagement with host governments or with public and private security" (DCAF 2016, 2). This claim is further supported by McSparren (Chapter 5, in this volume), who suggests that extractive companies' security policies are more likely to adhere to certain aspects of the VPs than others.

Finally, a legitimate multistakeholder initiative has measures in place to ensure that members follow the rules. Much of the criticism directed at the VPs relates to poor *enforcement*. All members of the VPI are required to report on their implementation of the VPs on an annual basis, and members can be expelled for failing to submit their annual report. As RAID (2016, 26) notes, however, "[a]fter allowing an applicant to join, the VPs effectively rely upon a company reporting its own performance and there is no external monitoring or verification of whether it is complying with the VPs." Moreover, companies write their own reports, and have control over much of the content. The fact that annual reports are not required to be independently verified and third-party monitoring remains optional has been a major source of contention. For example, RAID, MiningWatch Canada, and Human Rights Watch have all critiqued the VPI for its lack of enforceable rules, pointing to specific examples of Canadian extractive companies, such as Barrick Gold and Nevsun, that have failed to uphold aspects of the VPs at their operating sites, yet in their corporate policies and annual reports still claim to have implemented the VPs. These examples have been used to raise questions around whether the initiative can contribute to solving the complex security and human rights issues facing the extractive sectors without adequate enforcement measures.

Conclusion

Over the past fifteen years, the reach and scope of the Voluntary Principles on Security and Human Rights has expanded globally. Today there is all but an expectation in the Canadian context that Canadian extractive companies will use the VPs to shape their approach to security in and around their operating sites. The Canadian government has embedded the VPs into its corporate social responsibility strategy, and has linked compliance with the VPs to commercial diplomacy. The government is also working with other countries to promote and advance the implementation of the VPs. At the same time, many Canadian extractive companies have taken noteworthy steps to align their security policies and procedures with the VPs, and some are also playing a leadership role in the Voluntary Principles on Security and Human Rights Initiative.

Yet, as the Canadian government and Canadian extractive companies have become stronger proponents of these principles, some segments of Canadian civil society have become more vocal about their concerns with this governance initiative, particularly in relation to Canadian extractive sites in sub-Saharan Africa – a region that faces complex security and human rights challenges. Although industry actors are embracing the VPs as a pragmatic solution to the security challenges they face in this region, many NGOs remain sceptical about whether these principles will solve long-standing conflicts among extractive companies, security providers, and communities. In fact some NGOs have so little faith in the potential of the VPI that they have withdrawn from participating in the initiative altogether.

The analysis in this chapter, using the conceptual framework developed by Mena and Palazzo (2012), reveals that, although the VPs are generally accepted as legitimate in some areas, such as procedural fairness, they lack legitimacy in others, particularly in relation to transparency, efficacy, and enforcement. Pinpointing these specific areas helps to show why some people remain sceptical about the initiative's potential to address complex security and human rights issues. At the same time, it also serves to direct attention towards areas of the VPI that sit at the centre of critiques and that could benefit from reforms.

Addressing critiques and implementing reforms, however, is easier said than done. This is particularly true when it comes to improving the legitimacy of a multistakeholder initiative, since improving one aspect of legitimacy could negatively affect another (Mena and Palazzo 2012). For example, critics of the VPs often argue that standards should be better enforced. This is, in fact, one of the most persuasive critiques of the VPs – it is widely agreed that, without strong compliance mechanisms and sanctions in cases of non-compliance, "the probability of compliance by companies and their business partners decreases, thus also lowering codes' credibility" (van Tulder and Kolk 2001, 276). Companies might resist efforts to improve enforcement, however, as this would make them more susceptible to public scrutiny and raise the cost of non-compliance; thus, improving enforcement could lower coverage if companies decided to defect from the initiative as a result. This example illustrates the complex interplay between different aspects of legitimacy, and demonstrates why improving the legitimacy of a multistakeholder initiative can be difficult. Perhaps for this very reason, the VPI has been slow in responding to many of its critics, and only minor reforms of the initiative have been made over the past fifteen years.

This being said, individual stakeholders have sought ways to address criticisms levied against the VPs. Important work is taking place – often outside the VPI – that uses the VPs to improve the provision of security at extractive sites in a way that ensures respect for human rights. For example, a multistakeholder working group has been formed by the Global Compact Canada Network to provide guidance and help companies measure and improve their implementation of the VPs. This group functions outside the purview of the VPI. Similarly the Nairobi Process is working to implement the VPs in East Africa's growing extractive sectors by providing guidance to governments and companies on implementing and "localizing" the VPs (interview with Kenyan NGO, 3 March 2015). As one interviewee confirmed, "sometimes the most important work is happening outside of the dysfunctional [multistakeholder initiative]" (interview with government representative, 15 June 2016). This ultimately raises important questions about the future of the VPI and where resources should be directed. Is it time to reform how the VPI functions to improve the transparency, efficacy, and enforcement of the initiative? Or, if the most important work towards implementing the VPs is happening outside the VPI, would it be useful to direct fewer resources towards the VPI and more towards supporting localizing the VPs in various national contexts? Are efforts to localize the VPs "on the ground" proving more effective? These are questions that the next chair of the initiative must take seriously if the VPI is to be a successful venue for addressing human rights and security concerns in the extractive sectors, and might be useful avenues for future research on the VPI as well.

NOTE

1 Canadian-headquartered companies that are members of the VPI include Barrick Gold, Goldcorp, Pacific Exploration & Production Corporation, and Sherritt International.

BIBLIOGRAPHY

Acacia Mining plc. 2016. *Security and Human Rights – Human Rights.*
Bäckstrand, Karin. 2006. "Multi-stakeholder Partnerships for Sustainable Development: Rethinking Legitimacy, Accountability and Effectiveness." *European Environment* 16 (5): 290–306. https://doi.org/10.1002/eet.425.
Barrick Gold. 2011. "Statement from Barrick Gold Corporation Concerning the North Mara Mine, Tanzania." 30 May.
Barrick Gold. 2016. *2015 Annual Report to the Voluntary Principles on Security and Human Rights.* Toronto.
Baumann-Pauly, Dorothée, and Justine Nolan. 2016. *Business and Human Rights: From Principles to Practice.* New York: Routledge.
Bernstein, Steven, and Benjamin Cashore. 2007. "Can Non-State Global Governance Be Legitimate? An Analytical Framework." *Regulation & Governance* 1 (4): 347–71. https://doi.org/10.1111/j.1748-5991.2007.00021.x.
Canada. 2009. *Export Development Canada (EDC) Financial Services – Corporate Social Responsibility Requirements.* Presented to Canada-South Africa Chamber of Business and MineAfrica Seminar, Toronto, 22 October.
Canada. 2015. *Canada's Enhanced Corporate Social Responsibility Strategy to Strengthen Canada's Extractive Sector Abroad.* Ottawa.
Canada. 2016a. *Government of Canada Annual Report to the Voluntary Principles on Security and Human Rights Initiative.* Ottawa.
Canada. 2016b. Global Affairs Canada. *Report on Plans and Priorities 2016–17.* Ottawa.

DCAF (Geneva Centre for the Democratic Control of Armed Forces). 2016. *Addressing Security and Human Rights Challenges in Complex Environments Toolkit.* 3rd ed. Geneva: DCAF.

Dingwerth, Klaus. 2008. "North-South Parity in Global Governance: The Affirmative Procedures of the Forest Stewardship Council." *Global Governance* 14 (1): 53–71. https://doi.org/10.1163/19426720-01401005.

Grant, J. Andrew. 2013. "Consensus Dynamics and Global Governance Frameworks: Insights from the Kimberley Process on Conflict Diamonds." *Canadian Foreign Policy Journal* 19 (3): 323–39. https://doi.org/10.1080/1192 6422.2013.844909.

Grant, J. Andrew, Dianne Balraj, and Georgia Mavropoulos-Vagelis. 2013. "Reflections on Network Governance in Africa's Forestry Sector." *Natural Resources Forum* 37 (4): 269–79. https://doi.org/10.1111/1477-8947.12028.

Hahn, Rüdiger, and Christian Weidtmann. 2016. "Transnational Governance, Deliberative Democracy, and the Legitimacy of ISO 26000 Analyzing the Case of a Global Multistakeholder Process." *Business & Society* 55 (1): 90–129. https://doi.org/10.1177%2F0007650312462666.

Hofferberth, Mattias. 2010. "The Binding Dynamics of Non-binding Governance Arrangements: The Emergence and Development of the Voluntary Principles on Security and Human Rights." Conference paper presented at the American Political Science Association, Washington, DC, 2–5 September.

Kinross. 2016. *Corporate Responsibility – Commitments and Recognition.*

Klijn, Erik-Hans, and Chris Skelcher. 2007. "Democracy and Governance Networks: Compatible or Not?" *Public Administration* 85 (3): 587–608. https://doi.org/10.1111/j.1467-9299.2007.00662.x.

Mena, Sébastien, and Guido Palazzo. 2012. "Input and Output Legitimacy of Multi-Stakeholder Initiatives." *Business Ethics Quarterly* 22 (3): 527–56. https://doi.org/10.5840/beq201222333.

Oxfam. 2013. "Oxfam Leaves Voluntary Principles for Security and Human Rights Multi-Stakeholder Initiative." Press release, 17 April.

Pitts, Chip. 2011. "Voluntary Principles on Security and Human Rights." In *Handbook of Transnational Governance*, edited by Thomas Hale and David Held, 357–63. Cambridge, UK: Polity.

RAID. 2016. *Principles without Justice: The Corporate Takeover of Human Rights.* Oxford, UK: Rights and Accountability in Development.

Ruggie, John Gerard. 2014. "Global Governance and 'New Governance Theory': Lessons from Business and Human Rights." *Global Governance* 20 (1): 5–17. https://doi.org/10.1163/19426720-02001002.

Search for Common Ground. 2016. "Search for Common Ground's 2015 Sustainable Business Practice & the Voluntary Principles on Security and Human Rights." 18 March.

Sørensen, Eva, and Jacob Torfing. 2005. "The Democratic Anchorage and Governance Networks." *Scandinavian Political Studies* 28: 195–218.

Sørensen, Eva, and Jacob Torfing. 2007. "Introduction: Governance Network Research: Towards a Second Generation." In *Theories of Democratic Network Governance*, edited by Eva Sørensen and Jacob Torfing, 1–21. Basingstoke, UK: Palgrave Macmillan.

Van Tulder, Rob, and Ans Kolk. 2001. "Multinationality and Corporate Ethics: Codes of Conduct in the Sporting Goods Industry." *Journal of International Business Studies* 32 (2): 267–83. https://doi.org/10.1057/palgrave.jibs.8490952.

Voillat, Claude. 2012. "Pushing the Humanitarian Agenda through Engagement with Business Actors: The ICRC's Experience." *International Review of the Red Cross* 94 (887): 1089–114. https://doi.org/10.1017/s1816383113000507.

5 The Impact of the Voluntary Principles on Security and Human Rights on Corporate Social Responsibility Policies: An Assessment of Canadian Mining Firms

JASON J. MCSPARREN

Introduction

Canada is a global leader in the mining sector. As of 2013, 57 per cent of the world's publicly listed exploration and mining companies were headquartered in Canada (Canada 2015a), and Canada was the source of 62 per cent of the global mining equity raised in 2014 (Mining Association of Canada 2016). The Canadian mining "footprint" globally is estimated to be upwards of 1,500 enterprises that own interest in some 8,000 properties across 107 countries (Canada 2015a). The global proliferation of Canadian mining enterprises ramped up in the mid-1990s. This coincided with the 1992 publication of the World Bank's *Strategy for African Mining*, which is characterized as an export-led development plan that encouraged African governments to overhaul national mining legislation in line with liberal economic theory by providing generous incentives for prospective mining and mineral exploration companies, privatizing mine parastatals, and reducing government intervention in the sector (African Union 2009, 12; Ayee 2014; Campbell 2013; Hilson 2011; Jacobs 2013). Canadian firms are among the top-five producers globally of key minerals such as uranium, cobalt, aluminum, titanium, platinum, tungsten, sulphur, diamonds, nickel, and potash (Bhushan and Heidrich 2013). The scale of Canadian firms' proliferation globally has a significant impact on development trends in host-countries and also on the normalization of industry values, strategies, and practices.

Developing states benefit from the revenues, taxes, and other fees generated by foreign direct investment (FDI) from extractive firms. The mining sector, however, is fraught with negative externalities, and many transnational corporations (TNCs) have been complicit in human rights abuses and environmental degradation in communities adjacent to mining sites; moreover, mining companies, including those from Canada, have contributed to the propagation of corruption at the national and municipal levels of government.

The abusive behaviour of Canadian mining companies overseas was documented in a 2010 report by the Canadian Centre for the Study of Resource Conflict.[1] The report was critical of the operational practice and attitudes of Canadian extractive corporations towards local communities, stating, as quoted in the *Toronto Star*, that, "of the 171 companies identified in incidents involving mining and exploration companies over the past ten years, 34 per cent are Canadian" (Whittington 2010; see also MiningWatch Canada 2010). Furthermore, the study compared Canadian firms to those from the United Kingdom, the United States, and Australia, and determined that Canadian firms were more likely to be engaged in community conflict, environmental destruction, and unethical behaviour, but less likely to be involved in incidents related to occupational issues. These findings support Oshionebo's (2009, 25) that some TNCs based in countries that are members of the Organisation for Economic Co-operation and Development "adhere to lower business, human rights, and environmental standards in Africa than they do in their own home countries." Beginning in the late 1990s, the natural resource extractive sectors – oil and gas drilling and mining for metals and minerals – garnered international attention for their negative effects on sustainable development by contributing to official corruption, localized conflict, human rights abuses, and environmental degradation in host communities.[2] The approach taken by the international community to address these problems since the early 2000s has been to create and implement initiatives based on transparency and multistakeholder governance.

This chapter examines the influence of one such global governance initiative, the Voluntary Principles on Security and Human Rights (VPs), on the development of corporate social responsibility (CSR) policies. Across the sample, CSR policies reference the VPs along with other relevant global governance initiatives such as the Extractive Industries Transparency Initiative (EITI), the United Nations Global Compact, and ISO 26000. This suggests that the movement is influencing a shift in corporate outlook. Moreover, it is important to qualify this shift as "measured" and "protracted." The shift is measured in that the governance initiatives are influencing the design of CSR policies, and corporations are now acknowledging the demand for change in corporate norms of stakeholder interactions. Corporate practice, however, has yet to embrace the paradigm shift, as evident in the enduring legacy of industrial production ahead of community protection in multiple cases.

I begin by explaining the purpose of the VPs and their characterization as a global governance framework. I then present the methodology, including the selection criteria and the discourse analysis framework. Following the methodology, I present the findings and, in the final section, I discuss the implications of shifting norms in the mining sector.

The Voluntary Principles on Security and Human Rights

The Canadian government is cognisant that perceptions of Canadian TNCs reflect upon the country's international image. Both domestic and international pressure has spurred the government to enhance its support for corporate responsibility abroad. In 2009 Canada's first national CSR policy, "Building the Canadian Advantage: A Corporate Social Responsibility Strategy for the Canadian Extractive Sector Abroad," was introduced. This policy was updated in 2014 as "Doing Business the Canadian Way: A Strategy to Advance Corporate Responsibility in Canada's Extractive Sector Abroad" (Canada 2015a). Canada has also supported the VPs from the onset, and took a second turn as chair in 2016–17. As a means of assisting corporations abroad, and also cajoling them to act as better corporate citizens, the government has put political and diplomatic resources to work promoting both Canadian business and CSR expansion globally (Canada 2015b).

The VPs are designed specifically to guide extractive corporations as they negotiate stakeholder interactions abroad. A multitude of states, corporations, and non-governmental organizations (NGOs) officially support the program even as the VPs accommodate the neoliberal preferences of TNCs. The VPs are a voluntary initiative. This allows corporations to self-regulate in a private governance arrangement; however, the VPs strongly encourage consultation with local stakeholders. As the liberalization of mining codes in Africa has severely curtailed state regulation (see, for example, Campbell 2004), Bernstein and Cashore (2007, 347) contend that global/private governance "offers the strongest regulation and potential to socially embedded global markets" and "encourages compliance by recognizing and tracking, along the market's supply chain." As private companies pursue "political legitimacy," firms, social actors, and stakeholders may unite into a community that accepts "shared rule as appropriate and justified" (347). The VPs encourage corporations to advance a multistakeholder approach that includes local communities, government, and both public and private security forces. The multistakeholder arrangement is intended to create a cooperative security situation by providing a forum where discourse may alleviate tensions, avoid misunderstandings and overreach, and enhance accountability among the interest groups. Moreover, Carbonnier, Brugger, and Krause (2011, 260) applaud multistakeholder governance for its potential as a vehicle that "facilitates collective learning and raises awareness" among members.

The VPs are part of a broad international effort within the extractive sectors to instil new norms that advance sustainable development through cooperative stakeholder relations and away from what is characterized as "strictly business" and "practical partnership" approaches. More specifically, the VPs aim to "address the critical nexus between the legitimate security needs of companies in the extractive sector and the human rights of people in the surrounding communities, which can be and often have been abused by security forces" (Business & Human Rights Resource Centre 2006, 48). They promulgate the right of a corporation to protect its investments in equipment, personnel, and territory on the one side, and the protection of human rights and the environment on the other.

The VPs promote security by encouraging a corporation to conduct due diligence prior to initiating an exploration or exploitation project. This entails a risk assessment study of the socio-political context to prevent the corporation from unwittingly inserting itself into localized conflict or instigating existing or latent conflicts in the area. Additionally the VPs recommend that the information from the risk assessment be used for three other related purposes: corporations should implement procedures to minimize the incidence of perceived abuses of power; security personnel should be trained in ways to mitigate human rights infractions; and the project design should minimize environmental degradation.

Methodology

This qualitative study relies on discourse analysis techniques, and is divided into two stages of analysis, a methodology that facilitates the study of the corporate side of the bargain between the firm and the local community regarding the discourse around mining companies' role in sustainable development. Dashwood (2012, loc. 349) informs us that the majority of major mining companies frame their CSR policies and practices in relation to the global norm of sustainable development, a concept that "implies that profit maximization must be squared with measures that promote ecological and human well-being." The CSR policies and reports constitute a form of discourse – the use of language through speech and writing as a "social practice." Wodak and Meyer (2009, 5) advance that "[d]escribing discourse as a social practice implies a dialectical relationship between a particular discursive event and the situation(s), institution(s) and social structure(s), which frame it." To that end, the research sample includes five Canadian mining corporations operating eleven gold mines in seven West African countries. The structure and content of their CSR policies replicate industry trends. Additionally, the stakeholder disputes presented are indicative of clashes that may occur in any country when corporations disrupt local societies. Lastly, the power dynamics and strategies employed in the disputes reflect the realities of the extractive industry at large. Generally speaking, the data presented here reflect the state of the global industry, making this study a baseline for further empirical investigation.

The sample selection is primarily concerned with controlling for the mining company's country of origin (Canada), the region of operation (West Africa), and sector (gold mining). The logic is that a sector and regional focus allows for similar, although not exact, comparisons of factors across national contexts. The five Canadian-based mining companies and their mines featured in this study are: First Quantum Minerals (one mine – Guelb Moghrein in Mauritania); SEMAFO (three mines – Kiniero in Guinea, Mana in Burkina Faso, and Samira Hill in Niger); IAMGOLD (three mines – Essakane in Burkina Faso, and Sadiola and Yatela in Mali); B2Gold (two mines – Fekola in Mali and Kiaka in Burkina Faso); and Kinross Gold (two mines – Tasiast in Mauritania and Chirano in Ghana).

In the first stage, I apply discourse analysis to the CSR policies and reports published by these companies on their websites in 2015 and 2016, with the addition of supplementary documents from earlier years in some cases.[3] The CSR policies and reports are not uniformly designed; therefore, it is necessary to identify specific language targets and concepts as markers for the discourse analysis. The analytical framework incorporates elements of the VPs that inform corporations how to avoid infringing on human rights while also maintaining a sufficient level of security. The review of these policies seeks to identify language related to the concepts presented in the three overarching categories of the VPs: *conduct risk assessments, interact with public and private security providers, and engage with stakeholders from the host communities* (ICMM et al. 2012, 8, emphasis added).

The analytical framework encapsulates these constituent elements of the VPs, and is used to identify references to: 1) risk assessments that recognize security risks, potential for violence, human rights records of state and local law enforcement, the rule of law, conflict analysis, and equipment transfers; 2) evidence of corporate interaction with both public security and private security forces employed to secure company assets, including security arrangements, deployment and conduct, consultation and advice, and responses to human rights abuses; and 3) stakeholder engagement in the form of opportunities for local input, consultation, and mechanisms for the settlement of grievances.

Additionally the analytical framework includes the "Protect, Respect, and Remedy" framework adopted by the VPs. The analysis looks for examples of policies that demonstrate how corporations extend protection and respect to the community as well as ways that corporations may remedy community grievances. Although the protection of human rights is the duty of the government, businesses operating in a host country should act as a partner in providing a reasonable level of protection in the localities where they operate. For instance, corporations may *protect* local communities by employing due diligence, such as conducting a risk analysis to gain contextual information that can be used to avoid infringing on the rights of those directly affected by the mining operations in the first place. They can express a sense of *respect* by inviting civil society consultation during the pre-planning stages of the project and by adhering to policies that promote ethical decision making and take into consideration the potential impact of their operations on communities. Since the nature of the mining industry is disruptive, along with efforts to avoid confrontation, TNCs should also create a system to *remedy* infractions. This system should respond to local grievances in a timely manner, and remediation should be directed at the ground level as a community outreach mechanism. The second stage of analysis examines published accounts of conflicts between corporations and communities. The objective is to evaluate the extent to which corporations voluntarily adhere to their own responsibility policies in situations of conflict with local stakeholders. The first part of the analysis reveals which elements of the VPs influence mining corporations' policies, while the second evaluates the level of accountability corporations hold themselves to in a self-regulated, private governance system.

Findings

Many African states court FDI and seek to divert such investment towards their extractive industries. Revenues derived from the sectors fund the state system, and reinvestment is a prevailing strategy for socio-economic development (African Union 2009; Lin 2012). The scope of global investment in the extractive industries is estimated to surpass US$2 trillion by 2030 in "resource-rich, lower-income countries" (Dobbs et al. 2013). These societies could end the cycle of *sustainable poverty*, potentially moving 540 million people out of a prolonged period of economic marginalization. Canadian mining assets in Africa alone totalled C$27 billion in 2014 and C$31.3 billion in 2015, an increase of 15.9 per cent (Canada 2014).

Researchers have identified a range of attitudes and approaches on the part of corporations with respect to their CSR policies. Evidence of a gap between corporations' public acknowledgement of the VPs and their actual implementation is a common example, perhaps because the level of accountability is not always adequate in the absence of "hard" sanctions for non-compliance. Tangentially, some corporations are using emerging norms of CSR policy because, in their view, positive outreach makes good business sense. Quijada (2014) identifies two situations where corporations are implementing the VPs yet their operationalization fails to include community outreach. This baseline study, conducted in one village in Nigeria and another in Ghana, questioned 109 villagers about local knowledge of human rights, the VPs, and related corporate programs. A majority of the respondents' claimed that rights in extractive host communities have either "not been adhered to" or "only partially so" by corporations. Additionally, the study found no attempts at corporate outreach: local populations were not aware of any attempts by the companies to engage the community about human rights effects, nor did the respondents notice any indication that a risk assessment had been conducted. Lastly, respondents were unaware of the existence of an official grievance mechanism, notwithstanding that these communities had confronted government and corporations about rights abuses. These findings suggest that there is a continued privileging of corporate interests over those of affected communities, a lack of corporations' commitment to the VPs and their own CSR policies, and an unwillingness to be held accountable for the negative effects of their operations.

Quijada (2014) suggests a lack of corporate due diligence; Kirschke (2016) sees it differently, claiming CSR is emerging as a "core nontechnical function" of mineral extraction companies. This might indicate a degree of evolution, since Kirschke's assertion stands in stark contrast to the conclusion of Frynas (2005, 597) a decade earlier that "there are fundamental problems about the capacity of private firms to deliver development, and the aspiration of achieving broader development goals through CSR may be flawed." Additional support comes from the International Finance Corporation (IFC), which finds evidence of a "new communications landscape" where the dynamics of business are affected by the function of information sharing. "Strategic communication" methods are being used in the context of managing risk and adding value for all stakeholders. The IFC claims companies have realized that expanding their communications with local stakeholders presents returns framed as a "social licence" to operate that extends from improved company reputation (IFC, ICMM, and Brunswick Group n.d.).

These four studies represent varying degrees of corporate commitment to CSR and its strategic use. CSR policy can be a means for corporations to outline the parameters of their accountability. The "good corporate citizen" utilizes CSR policy to guide decision making. Many corporations, however, continue to pursue profitability above stakeholder relations. Notably, a distinction has been made "as to whether companies adhere to a voluntary standard strictly because they believe doing so will produce reputational benefits, [or] do so because their managers recognize an obligation to internalize negative social and environmental externalities" (King and Lennox 2000, cited in Dashwood 2014, 575–6). To improve our understanding of the approaches to CSR by mining companies operating in developing states, it is necessary to analyse their actual CSR policies.

CSR Analysis

Analysis of the corporate responsibility webpages of Canadian mining companies B2Gold, Kinross, First Quantum, IAMGOLD, and SEMAFO reveals that the policies dictating corporate interactions with outside stakeholders are grounded in multiple internationally recognized global governance frameworks. The influence of the VPs and other governance frameworks reveals two things; first, it was necessary for the international community – NGOs, industry groups, and state-sponsored development agencies – to influence and (re)shape corporate practices; second, it is possible that corporations are accepting this guidance and incorporating it into their self-regulating structures.

Each mining corporation in this dataset publishes numerous policies that cover multiple aspects of concern, for instance: Code of Business Ethics, Anti-Corruption, Labour Policy, Human Rights Policy, and Environmental Policy, among others. Additionally, all companies publish annual CSR reports that tend to highlight corporate-funded projects that contribute to improving the well-being of workers and local communities. As mentioned in the IFC study above, these reports are a means for "strategic communication," by which the companies project a positive image as "good corporate citizen" and "environmental steward." For instance, they highlight macro-economic benefits and corporate-sponsored charitable projects, investments that often concentrate on disease prevention, education programs, and infrastructure development such as water delivery systems, road construction, and agricultural projects. A notable absence from these CSR reports is any reference to a problem solved or avoided through a risk assessment or local stakeholder consultation.

Regarding the premise of the "Respect, Protect, and Remedy" framework, corporations use the term "respect" much more prominently than the other two concepts in their publications. The companies' approach is often characterized as an "attitude of respect" for local domestic laws, communities and cultures, other stakeholders, and the environment. For example, respect is featured prominently at the top of Kinross Gold's Corporate Responsibility webpage: "Respect: ... For Kinross this means responsibly managing our impacts while leveraging economic opportunity to generate sustainable long-term benefits for host communities ... it means approaching everything we do with an attitude of respect for the people, laws and cultures where we do business" (Kinross 2016). In a more succinct manner, SEMAFO's corporate values statement lists respect among the following group of terms: "Respect and integrity; Excellence; Know-how; Teamwork" (SEMAFO n.d.). In fact, every corporation in this sample attaches its brand to the concept of respect, which, by definition, indicates esteem and the attribution of value and excellence to a person, quality, or ability.

The corporate focus on respect and the lack of it on protection and remediation invoke a sense of distance, rather than collaboration. In corporate-community relations, the corporation has substantially more power to promote its interests than does the host community. Furthermore it does not necessarily take collaboration or consensus for one to respect another; respect can be offered from a distance. Protection and remediation, on the other hand, require a relationship and engagement by both parties. This engagement with the local community is not natural to corporations that are ontologically rooted in the concept that "the business of business is business"; this engagement identifies the shareholders, not local stakeholders, as the object of corporate responsibility (Friedman 1970) and, thus, negative externalities such as human rights and environmental abuses may be treated as part of the cost of conducting business.

Another example of the corporation's power over the relationship with stakeholders is exemplified by SEMAFO's public statement of accountability found in a report titled *Honouring Our Commitments* (SEMAFO 2015): "this report serves as the principle means of communicating SEMAFO's accountability with respect to sustainable development." Accepting responsibility is the epitome of what the international community is requesting through global governance initiatives such as the VPs; however, this statement is also the actualization of self-regulation in that the company is assuring its own unchecked accountability. Whether the company's practices hold up to outside scrutiny is irrelevant in relation to this report because it is the company that is framing how accountability is to be perceived. Rhetorically the report adheres to tenets of the VPs; it offers details of three analytical stages of due diligence: the materiality of social, environmental, and economic issues. It further includes the analytical process: a) identification; b) prioritizing the issues; and c) analysis and reporting concerning its business practice, which includes environmental stewardship, stakeholder relations (employees and community), economic contributions to the communities, and other issues focused on maintaining "social licence to operate."

In a section of SEMAFO's report titled "Respect for Human Rights," many of the precepts of the VPs are mentioned. The company prefers "clear communication," and implements a "measured approach to mitigate negative social and economic impacts"; additionally, "SEMAFO compensates villagers from neighbouring communities for loss of agricultural land or if they need to be displaced due to the expansion of the corporation's projects" (SEMAFO 2015, 18–19). However, the process to quantify the monetary value of these tangible and intangible losses is not detailed. Moreover, details concerning remediation are absent, although there is mention of a liaison, who "listens, communicates, collects complaints and resolves disputes on a daily basis" (SEMAFO 2015, 19). This vague description is the most detailed account of a remediation process of the five sample corporations.

IAMGOLD's report, titled *Human Rights Indicators*, concedes there was only a single incident of discrimination with actions taken in 2014. It gives no further details other than stating: "[The] Remediation plan has been implemented and results reviewed through routine internal management review process" (IAMGOLD 2015, sec. HR4). The report also claims that "during 2014 there were no incidents of violations involving the rights of indigenous peoples" (IAMGOLD 2015, n.p.). The report does not mention IAMGOLD's West African mining sites, but does include its Rosebel mine in Suriname and the Côté gold project in Canada, where working agreements are in place and accepted by the indigenous population. No explanation is given for the exclusion of such agreements at IAMGOLD's West African mines.

The corporate responsibility websites of the five companies mention risk assessment and risk management, but exclude details regarding the process, findings, and strategies implemented, with one exception: B2Gold's Feasibility Report for the Fekola mine in Mali (B2Gold 2015a). The report publicizes information related to ownership and mineral tenure, tailings disposal, surface water management, river flood assessment and water supply, sewage, and solid waste management. B2Gold is exemplary in this respect because no other company of the sample released a report of this nature, yet there is a discernible silence in the report concerning the potential for conflict or any other socio-political issue.

The VPs might be influencing companies to conduct risk assessments, but the results generally are not available for public scrutiny. For instance, IAMGOLD claims that "100% of investments and potential investments in properties undergo a thorough due diligence process, which includes a community relations and human rights screening" (IAMGOLD 2015, sec. HR1). In 2014, according to the company, this due diligence for the Essakane mine in Burkina Faso determined that "0% of contracts with significant suppliers, contractors, and other business partners were either declined or imposed performance conditions, or were subject to other actions as a result of human rights screenings" (sec. HR2). The limited nature of this public information is insufficient, however, to determine whether local stakeholders were involved and whether the VPs are being adhered to in a meaningful and transformative way. Furthermore, the apparent absence of local input underscores the power differentials that further undermine the preservation of local interests.

First Quantum Minerals is the only company reviewed that names the VPs explicitly. Its "Human Rights Policy" is "guided by the principles of internationally recognized human rights norms," and lists four frameworks, including the VPs (First Quantum Minerals 2013). The policy mentions the VPs by name, but there is no mention of risk assessment or security and human rights approaches. The company's stated policies reflect the high standards expected by the international community – for example, the environmental policy declares that, "[i]n countries where legislation does not meet our standards ... the company will apply management practices under the Equator Principles and IFC Standards with the objective of advancing environmental protection and managing risks and impacts" (First Quantum Minerals 2013a). Such a statement bodes well for corporate self-regulation as long as it is consistently put into practice.

Mining projects can instigate violent conflict to arise, re-emerge, or intensify. This reality should elevate the VPs as a priority, yet none of the publications reviewed contains any evidence of concern about conflict or violence – past, current, or potential – even though the companies report (though scantily) on the training of their security forces.

Interactions between company and public and private security forces were mentioned by two companies. Kinross Gold has implemented a Human Rights Adherence and Verification Program to train security personnel and site managers to understand and act in compliance with the VPs. The company also has a program that focuses on developing constructive community-security relationships by training employees and public security personnel regarding matters of allegation reporting and verification, investigation and resolution, and monitoring of investigations conducted by public officials. In 2014 Kinross reported that it put 100 per cent of its security employees through this program; in 2011 only 60 per cent, and in 2013 81 per cent, of these personnel had been so trained (Global Compact n.d.a).

IAMGOLD similarly offers brief details regarding its approach to security, but still makes no reference to conflict. The company mentions two operations where a significant security presence is maintained: Essakane in Burkina Faso and Rosebel in Suriname. Security personnel there do interact with external stakeholders (community, artisanal miners, etc.), and have been trained on various components of "appropriate engagement," which includes a human rights component (IAMGOLD 2015). The company explains that, in 2014, as part of the new employees' orientation, 124 security agents at the Essakane mine (6 per cent of the workforce) had 186 total hours of human rights training that acknowledged the VPs. Additional data indicate that security personnel training at Essakane has included human rights policies since at least 2011 and that each year more security personnel were hired: in 2011, 35 out of 70 of company security personnel and 189 third-party security personnel received training; in 2012, all 119 company security personnel and all the third-party security personnel were trained; and in 2013, all 181 company security personnel and all third-party security personnel were trained (IAMGOLD 2015). It appears that security is a priority for the company, yet the nature of the threat is not stated.

This analysis of CSR policies and related documents reveals two things. First, the VPs and other governance initiatives are influencing the design of corporate policies. Corporations are conducting some sort of risk assessment in some cases, but the results are not transparent. This leads to gaps in public knowledge regarding the extent to which corporations are consulting with local communities and considering local interests when planning a project. Second, a few corporations have published information regarding the substance of training for security personnel, yet they failed to include any details pertaining to the threat and level of insecurity they face. The ensuing analysis of disputes between corporations and local communities presents additional insight into corporate fidelity towards the VPs.

Human Rights Issues in the Mining Sector

Multiple Canadian mining corporations, including all of those in the sample, have been implicated in human and environmental rights abuses in West Africa or elsewhere (Mining-Technology.Com 2017; MiningWatch Canada 2016). Accordingly, it is worth comparing the discourse presented in their CSR policies and the actualization of corporate strategy when mired in dispute.

To begin, NGOs have identified three types of corporate complicity in human rights abuses. *Silent complicity* exists when companies fail to speak out against clear patterns of human rights violations perpetrated by the state, public or private security, or a militia. *Beneficial complicity* pertains to situations where companies are the beneficiaries of human rights abuses committed by state security forces. *Direct complicity* occurs when a company violates the rights of communities by failing to comply with regulations meant to protect them (Tamufor n.d.). Other researchers have gone beyond the identification of "types" of complicity to identifying actual actions, practices, and decisions that either "directly" or "indirectly" contribute to human rights offences (Belem 2009, 122; Boocock 2002; Pegg 2003; Reed 2002; Snell 2007, 196–8).

A report published by the Center for World Indigenous Studies documenting human rights abuses involving Canada's mining corporations (Schertow 2009) cites corporate complicity in the eviction of indigenous peoples from their homelands and their displacement without compensation. The report documents cases where people were held at gunpoint while villages and property – including graveyards, sacred sites, farmland, and other areas connected to cultural and physical survival – were destroyed. Instances of environmental degradation include water and food source contamination from hazardous chemicals such as arsenic, cyanide, mercury, and uranium, among others used in mining operations. In some cases, communities attempted to confront mining corporations through protests and court challenges, or simply tried to engage the company in discourse. In many cases, these civil actions turned individuals into targets for abuse, including kidnapping, rape, torture, and execution. In still other cases, companies have used bribery, coercion, and extortion to gain concessions to operate on land inhabited by indigenous groups.

Some mining companies, however, are working to improve their relations with local communities. For example, SEMAFO has had both positive and negative experiences with community relations in Burkina Faso. On a positive note, in 2015 the company was granted the grand prize for CSR of Mining Companies in that country by Groupe Redevabilité (Accountability Group), a consortium of civil society organizations in Burkina Faso (SEMAFO n.d.). The award recognized the company's commitment to human rights, the environment, communities, and local development. This laudable corporate reputation is much improved from a decade earlier.

At SEMAFO's Mana mine site in Burkina Faso in July 2006, three young shepherds drowned in an open pit dug by the company just a hundred metres outside the village. People close to this case allude to the company's having political protection against reprisal. Community members claim that the mayor refused to criticize the company for negligence. The administrative head (*préfet*), on the other hand, attempted to take action by presenting the company with a formal grievance. Shortly after contacting the company, however, the *préfet* was transferred out of the municipality in retaliation, the community believes, for confronting the company. In this case, SEMAFO began operations without relocating or compensating the community despite a government-generated public enquiry report stating that SEMAFO was obligated to do so before destroying the village. The company showed little regard for the welfare of villagers, however, forcing them to quit their settlements before completing the construction of a new village and leaving them in limbo while mining operations continued unabated (Tamufor n.d.).

These details of the incident from 2006 indicate SEMAFO did not meet the expectations embedded in the VPs. There is no indication that the company conducted a risk assessment or consulted with the community, which could have prevented the loss of life. More significantly, the company showed that expanding the project was more important to it than relocating the village and its people. The case illustrates the level of insecurity that mining activity can produce, in addition to the inequity of power between corporations and communities. By 2015, however, SEMAFO had achieved a much-improved level of corporate accountability than the one on display in 2006. Perhaps the company learned from its mistakes and shifted its policies accordingly.

For its part, IAMGOLD has implemented an extensive corporate responsibility program titled "Zero Harm Vision" across its global operations, and the company's CSR program in Burkina Faso has been recognized for its best practices (IAMGOLD n.d.c). Despite the company's efforts, however, it still manages to inflict harm on people and the environment. A 2016 report by Action de Carême (Swiss Catholic Lenten Fund) and the Swiss NGO Pain pour le prochain (Bread for All) states that villages relocated by IAMGOLD in Burkina Faso have less agricultural land and less access to clean water, and have been separated from their cultural and social foundations. Additionally, the remote location of the company-provided settlement makes it more difficult for villagers, particularly women, to make a living. NGOs are calling on Switzerland to act in defence of the displaced people because 90 per cent of Burkina Faso's gold is refined there (Business & Human Rights Resource Centre 2016). These allegations have arisen even though IAMGOLD received an award for CSR and despite the company's claims that "100% of investments and potential investments in properties undergo a thorough due diligence process, which includes a community relations and human rights screening" (IAMGOLD 2015, sec. HR1), and that as recently as 2014 (the latest publicly available data), no incidents at the Essakane mine involved human rights infringements. This example depicts the complexity of analysing relations between corporations and communities; evidence suggests that, in IAMGOLD's case, the company sometimes acts as a good corporate citizen and sometimes not.

Of the companies in the sample, the one accused of the largest degree of malfeasance in West Africa is Kinross Gold Corporation, which was charged with withholding compensation to Ghanaian farmers displaced by the Chirano gold mines in 2004. In 2006 the local farmers took the company to court for not paying a government-negotiated compensation rate for the cocoa trees lost to the mining operation. The farmers settled out of court, but sued again because Kinross's subsidiary, Chirano Gold Mines Ltd., still remained non-compliant with the agreed-upon compensation package for the displaced farmers, despite producing 261,846 ounces of gold in 2011 from Chirano worth $200 million (MiningWatch Canada 2012). The case was still in the court system in 2014 when a fourteen-member executive board was created in an Accra Fast Track High Court (GhanaWeb 2014). In mid-2015 Chirano Gold Mines Ltd. paid restitution in the sum of GH₵3,400,000 as compensation to 1,124 farmers in the region (GhanaWeb 2015).

In 2015 Kinross Gold's operations in West Africa became the focus of an investigation by the US Securities and Exchange Commission (SEC) for corruption. Internal Kinross documents and letters from a whistleblower detail allegations of bribery, corruption, and other financial crimes associated with the Tasiast (Mauritania) and Chirano (Ghana) gold mines. Allegations first arose in 2013 of improper payments made to government officials and certain internal control deficiencies (Faucon 2015; MiningWatch Canada 2015). In 2018 the SEC found Kinross in violation of the internal accounting controls provisions of the Foreign Corrupt Practices Act of 1977. The company was sanctioned with civil penalty of $950,000 and the company's African operations were subjected to a requisite one-year term for oversight in which training and testing of relevant controls relating to collection and analysis of compliance data are to be monitored by the Commission (SEC 2018).

Based on these two issues, the "Respect, Protect, and Remedy" framework appears to be outside Kinross Gold's corporate strategy. In the first case, the discrepancy between the large amount of money generated for the company and the miniscule amount slated to compensate farmers is an illustration of the inequity between corporate and community interests that permeates the industry. The compensation rate the government agreed upon with Chirano Gold was less than US$2 per tree – a very low value for an agricultural commodity that takes five years from seed to maturity to produce a crop. The mining company directly and completely disrupted the livelihoods of this community, yet refused to provide state-ordered restitution. Moreover, stakeholder engagement was neglected, as the company conducted negotiations with the government, not with community representatives. Perhaps the community did not want to participate as a form of protest or perhaps they were not given the opportunity and the government filled the role from the onset. Either way, the power differential clearly favoured the mining company over the indigenous population both in the process and the outcome. In the second case, corporate interests took precedence to the point of engaging in what the SEC deemed illegal activity. Corruption of the sort alleged here corrodes the entire system, and chokes off any possibility for sustainable development because the ill-gained money is concealed from the public and, therefore, cannot be reinvested in the community.

Conclusion

An analysis of CSR policies and reports shows that global governance initiatives, such as the Voluntary Principles on Security and Human Rights, have influenced the rhetoric and discourse of Canadian mining corporations operating overseas, particularly in Africa. In some respects, their modes of operations have improved, but improvements have not been institutionalized consistently across contexts even within a single corporation. We have encountered two examples where companies seem to have improved their relations with local communities, perhaps exemplifying a shift towards a commitment to sustainable development from that of a "business as usual" logic. Yet both companies have also had recent experiences of allegations of rights abuses within their scope of influence.

It has also been impossible to evaluate fully the policies and actions related to security forces and their interactions with local people. This is because of a lack of corporate transparency in regard to the findings of risk analyses – specifically, in terms of how they avoid inciting conflict and what contingency plans exist in the event conflict arises. A media search conducted for this study failed to identify any high-profile cases in the past few years of abuse in West Africa by security forces protecting mining sites. This could be due to improvements in relations, but it could also be due to a lack of media resources to cover rural mining areas or to other, overshadowing security issues in the region – such as hostile militia groups, which are of more interest to the public. Assuredly it is not because of a monumental shift in corporate approach. Abuses continue to occur, just elsewhere. In South Africa, for instance, the 2012 "Marikana massacre" is a major point of discussion in mine security circles. A report by the Toronto-based Justice and Corporate Accountability Project at York University documents accusations of human rights abuses in over a dozen Latin American countries by twenty-eight Canadian mining corporations, some of which allege complicity in the murder of indigenous activists (Imai, Gardner, and Weinberger 2016).

In sum, it is notable that global governance initiatives are having some influence on the production of corporate responsibility policies, and corporations are implementing the VPs to some extent. They are conducting risk analyses, but not releasing the data; they are training their security personnel, but not publicizing the security threats that make them necessary. There is little evidence that stakeholder engagement is being institutionalized or that norm-shifts towards respect, protection, and remediation are well recognized in corporate public documents. It is not that corporations lack the know-how or guidelines to enhance the security of local people; rather, in a self-regulating system, corporations expectedly choose production over stakeholder rights. Although efforts are being made to promote the business case for sustainable development, progress is uneven across contexts, and local communities continue to bear the brunt of the shortcomings.

NOTES

1 According to MiningWatch Canada, the report was not made public.
2 See for example Human Rights Watch (1999) and Global Witness (1999).

3 Companies	Data Sources
First Quantum Minerals	First Quantum Minerals 2013a, 2013b, 2014, 2016a, 2016b, 2016c, 2016d; First Quantum Minerals and IAMGOLD 2013
SEMAFO	SEMAFO n.d.
IAMGOLD	IAMGOLD 2012a, 2012b, 2013, 2015, n.d.a, n.d.b, n.d.c
B2Gold	B2Gold 2013, 2015a, 2015b, 2015c
Kinross Gold	Global Compact n.d.b; Kinross 2016, n.d.; Kinross Gold Corporation 2013

BIBLIOGRAPHY

African Union. 2009. *Africa Mining Vision*. February. Available online at http://www.africaminingvision.org/amv_resources/AMV/Africa_Mining_Vision_English.pdf.

Ayee, Joseph. 2014. "The Status of Natural Resource Management in Africa: Capacity Development Challenges and Opportunities." In *Managing Africa's Natural Resources: Capacities for Development*, edited by Kobena T. Hanson, Cristina D. D'Alessandro, and Francis Owusu, 15–38. New York: Palgrave Macmillan.

B2Gold. 2013. "Code of Business Conduct and Ethics, Effective May 13, 2013." Available online at https://www.b2gold.com/_resources/corporate_governance/B2Gold-Code-of-Business-Conduct-and-Ethics-May-13-2013.pdf.

B2Gold. 2015a. "NI 43-101 Technical Report Feasibility Study on the Fekola Gold Project in Mali." 30 June. Available online at https://www.b2gold.com/_resources/Fekola_Technical_Report_2015.pdf.

B2Gold. 2015b. "Corporate Responsibility: Responsible Mining." Available online at https://www.b2gold.com/corporate-responsibility/index.php#responsible.

B2Gold. 2015c. "Corporate: Vision and Values." Available online at https://www.b2gold.com/corporate/vision_values/.

Belem, Gisele. 2009. "Mining, Poverty Reduction, the Protection of the Environment and the Role of the World Bank Group in Mali." In *Mining in Africa: Regulation and Management*, edited by Bonnie Campbell, 119–49. Ottawa; London: International Development Research Centre and Pluto Press.

Bernstein, Steven, and Benjamin Cashore. 2007. "Can Non-State Global Governance Be Legitimate? An Analytical Framework." *Regulation and Governance* 1 (4): 347–71. https://doi.org/10.1111/j.1748-5991.2007.00021.x.

Bhushan, Aniket, and Pablo Heidrich. 2013. "Canadian Mining in Africa and Latin America: A Comparison Based on Mine Output and Asset Valuation." Ottawa: North-South Institute.

Boocock, Colin Noy. 2002. "Environmental Impact of Foreign Direct Investment in the Mining Sector in Sub-Saharan Africa." In *Foreign Direct Investment and the Environment: Lessons from the Mining Sector*, 19–49. Paris: Organisation for Economic Co-operation and Development.

Business & Human Rights Resource Centre. 2006. "John Ruggie Interim Report to Human Rights Council, Feb 2006." Available online at http://business-humanrights.org/en/john-ruggie-interim-report-to-human-rights-council-feb-2006.

Business & Human Rights Resource Centre. 2016. "Profit over Human Rights? Gold Mining in Burkina Faso and Switzerland's Responsibility." Available online at https://www.business-humanrights.org/en/%E2%80%9Cprofit-over-human-rights-gold-mining-in-burkina-faso-and-switzerland%E2%80%99s-responsibility%E2%80%9D.

Campbell, Bonnie, ed. 2004. *Regulating Mining in Africa: For Whose Benefit?* Uppsala, Sweden: Nordiska Afrikainstitutet.

Campbell, Bonnie, ed. 2013. *Modes of Governance and Revenue Flows in African Mining*. Basingstoke, UK: Palgrave Macmillan.

Canada. 2014. Natural Resources Canada. "Canadian Mining Assets: The Global Presence of Canadian Mining Companies." Ottawa, December. Available online at https://www.nrcan.gc.ca/mining-materials/publications/17072.

Canada. 2015a. Global Affairs Canada. "Canada's Enhanced Corporate Social Responsibility Strategy to Strengthen Canada's Extractive Sector Abroad." Ottawa. Available online at www.international.gc.ca/trade-agreements-accords-commerciaux/topics-domaines/other-autre/csr-strat-rse.aspx?lang=eng.

Canada. 2015b. Global Affairs Canada. "Responsible Business Conduct Abroad." Ottawa. Available online at https://www.international.gc.ca/trade-agreements-accords-commerciaux/topics-domaines/other-autre/csr-rse.aspx?lang=eng#CSRSupport.

Carbonnier, Gilles, Fritz Brugger, and Jana Krause. 2011. "Global and Local Policy Responses to the Resource Trap." *Global Governance* 17 (2): 247–64. https://doi.org/10.1163/19426720-01702010.

Dashwood, Hevina S. 2012. *The Rise of Global Corporate Social Responsibility: Mining and the Spread of Global Norms*. Cambridge: Cambridge University Press.

Dashwood, Hevina S. 2014. "Sustainable Development in Industry Self-Regulation: Developments in the Global Mining Sector." *Business & Society* 53 (4): 551–82. https://doi.org/10.1177/0007650313475997.

Dobbs, Richard, Jeremy Oppenheim, Adam Kendall, Fraser Thompson, Martin Bratt, and Fransje van der Marel. 2013. "Reverse the Curse: Maximizing the Potential of Resource-Driven Economies." McKinsey & Company, December. Available online at https://www.mckinsey.com/industries/metals-and-mining/our-insights/reverse-the-curse-maximizing-the-potential-of-resource-driven-economies.

Faucon, Benoît. 2015. "SEC, Justic Department Investigate Corruption Allegations at Kinross Gold." *Wall Street Journal*, 2 October. Available online at https://www.wsj.com/articles/sec-justice-department-investigate-corruption-allegations-at-kinross-gold-1443830877.

First Quantum Minerals. 2013a. "Environmental Policy." Available online at http://s1.q4cdn.com/857957299/files/policies/Environmental%20Policy%20Revised%20December%209%202013%20(Final).pdf.

First Quantum Minerals. 2013b. "Social Policy." Available online at http://s1.q4cdn.com/857957299/files/policies/FQM Social Policy December 9 2013.pdf.

First Quantum Minerals. 2014. *Respect: The Common Thread Uniting Social, Economic and Environmental Sustainability*. Available online at http://s1.q4cdn.com/857957299/files/doc_presentations/2014/2014_FQM-Sustainability-Report_English-Online.pdf.

First Quantum Minerals. 2016a. "Corporate Responsibility." Available online at https://www.first-quantum.com/Corporate-Responsibility/default.aspx.

First Quantum Minerals. 2016b. "Economics." Available online at www.first-quantum.com/Corporate-Responsibility/Economics/default.aspx.

First Quantum Minerals. 2016c. "Environment." Available online at www.first-quantum.com/Corporate-Responsibility/Environment/default.aspx.

First Quantum Minerals. 2016d. "Labour." Available online at www.first-quantum.com/Corporate-Responsibility/Labour/default.aspx.

First Quantum Minerals. 2013. "Human Rights Policy." Available online at https://s1.q4cdn.com/857957299/files/doc_downloads/FQM%20Human%20Rights%20Policy%20-%20December%209%202013.pdf.

Friedman, Milton. 1970. "The Social Responsibility of Business Is to Increase Its Profits." *New York Times Magazine*, 13 September. Available online at www.umich.edu/~thecore/doc/Friedman.pdf.

Frynas, Jedrzej G. 2005. "The False Developmental Promise of Corporate Social Responsibility: Evidence from Multinational Oil Companies." *International Affairs* 81 (3): 581–98. https://doi.org/10.1111/j.1468-2346.2005.00470.x.

GhanaWeb. 2014. "Chirano Gold Mines Compensation Saga." 20 July. Available online at https://www.ghanaweb.com/GhanaHomePage/business/Chirano-Gold-Mines-compensation-saga-317710#.

GhanaWeb. 2015. "1,000 Farmers Receive Compensation." 18 May. Available online at https://www.ghanaweb.com/GhanaHomePage/ NewsArchive/1-000-farmers-receive-compensation-358608.

Global Compact. n.d.a. "Human Rights and Business Dilemmas Forum: Security Forces and Human Rights." Available online at http://hrbdf.org/case_studies/ security-forces-and-human-rights/#.VxpwPDArKaF, accessed 4 February 2016.

Global Compact. n.d.b. "Kinross Gold." Available online at https://www.un-globalcompact.org/what-is-gc/participants/11171, accessed 1 January 2016.

Global Witness. 1999. *A Crude Awakening: The Role of Oil and Banking Industries in Angola's Conflict*. London: Global Witness.

Hilson, Gavin. 2011. "'Inherited Commitments: Do Changes in Ownership Affect Corporate Social Responsibility (CSR) at African Gold Mines?" *African Journal of Business Management* 5 (9): 10921–39. https://doi.org/ 10.5897/AJBM10.1608.

Human Rights Watch. 1999. *The Price of Oil: Corporate Responsibility and Human Rights Violations in Nigeria's Oil Producing Communities*. New York: Human Rights Watch.

IAMGOLD. 2012a. "Anti-Bribery and Anti-Corruption Policy." Available online at http://s1.q4cdn.com/060001837/files/doc_downloads/ policies/2014/2 Anti-Bribery and Anti-Corruption Policy.pdf.

IAMGOLD. 2012b. "Code of Business Conduct and Ethics." Available online at http://s1.q4cdn.com/060001837/files/doc_downloads/policies/2014/1 Code of Business Conduct and Ethics.pdf.

IAMGOLD. 2013. "Human Rights Policy." Available online at http://s1.q4cdn. com/060001837/files/doc_downloads/hhs/Human Rights Policy.pdf.

IAMGOLD. 2015. "Human Rights Indicators: 2014 Health, Safety and Sustainability Report." Available online at http://www.iamgold-hssreport. com/2014/human.php.

IAMGOLD. n.d.a. "Evolution of HSS: About HSS." Available online at http:// hss.iamgold.com/English/about-hss/evolution-of-hss/default.aspx, accessed 1 January 2016.

IAMGOLD. n.d.b. "Voluntary Initiatives." Available online at http://hss.iam-gold.com/English/industry-participation/voluntary-initiatives/official-participation/default.aspx, accessed 1 January 2016.

IAMGOLD. n.d.c. "Zero Harm Vision: What Drives Us." Available online at http://hss.iamgold.com/English/about-hss/zero-harm-vision/what-drives-us/default.aspx., accessed 1 January 2016.

ICMM, ICRC, IFC, and IPIECA. 2012. *Voluntary Principles on Security and Human Rights: Implementation Guidance Tools*. Available online at https:// www.icmm.com/en-gb/publications/mining-and-communities/voluntary-principles-on-security-and-human-rights-implementation-guidance-tools.

Imai, Shin, Leah Gardner, and Sarah Weinberger. 2016. "The 'Canada Brand': Violence and Canadian Mining Companies in Latin America." Osgoode

Legal Studies Research Paper 17/2017. Available online at https://papers. ssrn.com/sol3/papers.cfm?abstract_id=2886584.

IIFC (International Finance Corporation), ICMM (International Council on Mining and Metals), and Brunswick Group. n.d. *Changing the Game: Communications & Sustainability in the Mining Industry.*

Jacobs, John. 2013. "An Overview of Revenue Flows from the Mining Sector: Impacts, Debates and Policy Recommendations." In *Modes of Governance and Revenue Flows in African Mining*, edited by Bonnie Campbell, 16–46. London: Palgrave Macmillan.

King, Andrew, and Michael Lennox. 2000. "Industry Self-Regulation without Sanction: The Chemical Industry's Responsible Care Program." *Academy of Management Journal* 43: 698–716. https://doi.org/10.5465/1556362.

Kinross. 2016. "Corporate Responsibility." Available online at https://www. kinross.com/corporate-responsibility/default.aspx.

Kinross. n.d. "Ten Guiding Principles for Corporate Responsibility." Available online at http://s2.q4cdn.com/496390694/files/doc_downloads/our_ approach/k-4-4-cr-brochure_english.pdf, accessed 1 January 2016.

Kinross Gold Corporation. 2013. "Code of Business Conduct and Ethics." Available online at http://s2.q4cdn.com/496390694/files/doc_downloads/reports_ and_downloads/kgc-codeofbusinessconductandethics-13feb2013.pdf.

Kirschke, Joseph. 2016. "Mining Companies Bring Sustainability to the Surface." *Barron's*, 12 March. Available online at https://www.barrons.com/ articles/mining-companies-bring-sustainability-to-the-surface-1457759958? shareToken=st08fa3b4b453943a0b1d619f06fb69c31.

Lin, Justin Yifu. 2012. *New Structural Economics: A Framework for Rethinking Development and Policy.* Washington, DC: World Bank.

Mining Association of Canada. 2016. *Facts and Figures of the Canadian Mining Industry.* Available online at http://mining.ca/sites/default/files/ documents/Facts-and-Figures-2016.pdf.

Mining-Technology.com. 2017. "Canada's Mining Ombudsman: Oversight at Last But Is It Too Little Too Late?" 23 January. Available online at https://www.mining-technology.com/features/ featurecanadas-mining-ombudsman-has-it-come-too-late-5715514/.

MiningWatch Canada. 2010. "Suppressed Report Confirms International Violations by Canadian Mining Companies." News release. Available online at http://miningwatch.ca/news/2010/10/18/suppressed-report-confirms- international-violations-canadian-mining-companies.

MiningWatch Canada. 2012. "Ghanaian Farmers Run Out of Patience with Kinross/ Chirano Gold Mines." Blog, 26 November. Available online at http:// miningwatch.ca/blog/2012/11/26/ghanaian-farmers-run-out-patience- kinrosschirano-gold-mines.

MiningWatch Canada. 2015. "NGOs Urge RCMP to Investigate Kinross over Reports of Corruption in Africa." Blog, 10 December. Available online at http://miningwatch.ca/news/2015/12/10/ngos-urge-rcmp-investigate-kinross-over-reports-corruption-africa.

MiningWatch Canada. 2016. "New Law Would Create Human Rights Ombudsperson to Investigate Violations Associated with Canadian Mining, Oil and Gas Operations Overseas." Blog, 2 November. Available online at http://miningwatch.ca/news/2016/11/2/new-law-would-create-human-rights-ombudsperson-investigate-violations-associated.

Oshionebo, Evaristus. 2009. *Regulating Transnational Corporations in Domestic and International Regimes*. Toronto: University of Toronto Press.

Pegg, Scott. 2003. "Poverty Reduction or Poverty Exacerbation? World Bank Group Support for Extractive Industries in Africa." Indianapolis: Indiana University. Available online at https://www.laohamutuk.org/OilWeb/Bground/Africa/PRPE_eng.pdf.

Quijada, Jessica Jester. 2014. *Improving Extractive Industry Governance: Implementing the Voluntary Principles to Human Rights in Nigeria and Ghana: Baseline Study*.

Reed, Darryl. 2002. "Resource Extraction Industries in Developing Countries." *Journal of Business Ethics* 39 (3): 199–226. Available online at https://www.jstor.org/stable/25074839.

Schertow, John Ahni. 2009. "Briefing on the Human Rights and Environmental Abuses of Canadian Corporations." *IC Magazine*. Available online at https://intercontinentalcry.org/briefing-on-the-human-rights-and-environmental-abuses-of-canadian-corporations/.

SEC (Securities and Exchange Commission). 2018. "United States of America before the Securities and Exchange Commission: Order Instituting Cease-and-Desist Proceedings, Pursuant to Section 21C of the SEC Act of 1934, Making Findings, and Imposing a Cease-and-Desist Order." Release No. 82946. Washington, DC, 26 March.

SEMAFO. 2015. "Sustainable Development Report: Honouring Our Commitments." Available online at http://s2.q4cdn.com/795832262/files/reports_CSR_EN/RDD-2014-FINAL-EN-low-res.pdf.

SEMAFO. n.d. "Honouring Our Commitments." Available online at www.semafo.com/English/corporate-responsibility/default.aspx, accessed 1 January 2016.

Snell, Darryn. 2007. "Beyond Workers' Rights: Transnational Corporations, Human Rights Abuse, and Violent Conflict in the Global South." In *Global Unions*, edited by Kate Bronfenbrenner. Ithaca, NY: Cornell University Press.

Tamufor, Lindlyn. n.d. "Human Rights Violations in Africa's Mining Sector." Accra, Ghana: Third World Network Africa. Available online at http://twnafrica.org/twnaf_humanrights-compilation.pdf.

Whittington, Les. 2010. "Canadian Mining Firms Worst for Environment Rights: Report." *Toronto Star*, 19 October. Available online at https://www.thestar.com/news/canada/2010/10/19/canadian_mining_firms_worst_for_environment_rights_report.html.

Wodak, Ruth, and Michael Meyer. 2009. "Critical Discourse Analysis: History, Agenda, Theory and Methodology." In *Methods for Critical Discourse Analysis*, 2nd ed., edited by Ruth Modak and Michael Meyer, 1–33. London: Sage.

6 Canada, Human Security, and Artisanal and Small-Scale Mining in Africa

TIMOTHY ADIVILAH BALAG'KUTU

Introduction

Efficient natural resource governance is key for development. Many states with abundant resources are among the least developed in the world due fundamentally to poor resource management. This trend has led to the phenomenon scholars have described as the "resource curse" (Auty 2002) or "paradox of plenty" (Karl 1997). Although minerals, oil, gas, timber, and many other essential natural resources from Africa have contributed to the development of many parts of the world, the continent remains one of the least developed world regions. This is because many states have failed consistently to manage their natural resources efficiently.

Concerned about the resource curse and growing impoverishment in resource-rich parts of the world, global development actors have sought to help states improve governance of their natural resources. Before the emergence of the notion of resource curse in mainstream development scholarship in the 1990s, stakeholders had started to contemplate measures to curtail observed characteristics of the phenomenon. The 1972 United Nations Conference on Human Environment (UNCHE) in Stockholm is one landmark event that drew global attention to the implications of unsustainable development practices (Smith 1984). The conference emphasized the need for sustainable development, which the Brundtland report re-echoed a decade later in *Our Common Future* (World Commission on Environment and Development 1987). Consequently, sustainability became a central theme in global development discussions. Inspired by this idea and the imperative to reverse the resource curse, governments and other stakeholders in the extractive sector began to address socio-environmental externalities of resource extraction (Campbell 2012; Hilson 2012). However, while these efforts mainly target large-scale operations, the use of artisanal methods for resource extraction has become popular and widespread globally (Armah et al. 2016; Hilson 2016; Van Bockstael 2014).

Today, artisanal and small-scale mining (ASM) is a vibrant and expanding economic activity in many rural communities of the developing world (Hilson 2016; Seccatore et al. 2014; Van Bockstael 2014). Although operations vary in size, level of technology, and across locations, ASM is mostly labour-intensive (Ferring, Hausermann, and Effah 2016; Hilson 2016; Seccatore et al. 2014). ASM is still largely informal, but it contributes considerably to communities, states, and the global economy: about a third of total gold production in Ghana comes from ASM (Ghana 2015; Wilson et al. 2015); over 100 million people depend directly on the sector worldwide (Intergovernmental Forum on Mining, Minerals, Metals and Sustainable Development 2017); and it generates other forms of economic activity that supplement household incomes (Hinton, Veiga, and Beinhoff 2006; Nyame and Grant 2014).

At the same time, however, ASM causes social and environmental problems for local communities, states, and the global community. Common in the ASM sector are deforestation, pollution, mercury contamination and related health issues; increased proneness of individuals to physical harm and death; child labour exploitation; violent conflicts; and sexual offences (Hilson 2010; Hilson and Yakovleva 2007; Rustad, Østby, and Nordås 2016). Overall, the sector's activities undermine the seven categories of human security outlined in the 1994 United Nations Development Programme (UNDP) report: environmental, economic, personal, community, health, political, and food security (UNDP 1994; see also Owen 2004). Therefore, although ASM is a source of livelihood for many individuals and communities around the world, it is also a site of grave global human insecurity, requiring concerted governance.

The social and environmental problems of ASM elude existing resource governance processes (Ferring, Hausermann, and Effah 2016). The capacity, design, and scope of mainstream resource governance mechanisms are unsuited for the informal extractive sector. Various scholars have drawn attention to the challenge and need to adopt appropriate and methodical approaches to governing ASM (Hilson 2016; Jønsson, Appel, and Chibunda 2009; Spiegel et al. 2015; Spiegel and Veiga 2009). This chapter extends this observation from the point of view of critical security theory (Booth 1997). I argue for the use of the human security paradigm (UNDP 1994) to address insecurity in the ASM sector. Although some analysts discuss critical security and human security as different concepts (Newman 2010), I use human security in the context of Booth's (1997) depiction of an idea that is critical of the mainstream statist security thought. This critical stance and the changing global reality have influenced post–Cold War theorizing on security to extend beyond state-centrism (Booth 1997). Departing from statist security thinking, the 1994 UNDP framework emphasized the centrality of individual security and well-being in development thinking, policy, and practice (UNDP 1994). The emphasis on the individual is the basis for the chapter's discussion on governance of ASM in Africa and Canada's role in it.

The chapter examines the importance of Canada in advancing a human-centred approach to governing ASM in Africa. Canada is a global champion of human security (Axworthy 1997, 2000) and a major actor in Africa's extractive industry (Black 2016; Campbell 2012; Kinsman 2015). In the context of traditional security, specialized state agencies are responsible for crafting and executing security policy (Buzan, Wæver, and de Wilde 1998). With respect to human security, however, a set of criteria might help determine the actors, processes, and mechanisms that matter for effective governance: 1) the specific development sector in which the security threat exists; 2) the expertise and influence of actors involved in the sector; 3) the availability of resources (human and material) for appropriate policy and governance instruments to address the situation; and 4) the will to act. The chapter builds on these criteria to explain the significance of Canada's role in adopting and applying the human security paradigm to governing ASM in Africa.

The rest of the chapter consists of four sections. The first discusses the rise and governance of modern ASM in Africa. The second section, which builds on critical security theory, examines the imperative for the human security paradigm in resource governance broadly and, focusing on the insecurity in ASM operations, re-emphasizes the recommendation to rethink resource governance (Hilson 2016). The third looks at how, through various state and non-state efforts, Canada's experience and expertise could facilitate human-centred resource governance in Africa. This section also discusses the response of key African actors to human-centred ASM governance initiatives across the continent. In the concluding section, I re-emphasize the link between ASM and human security and the rationale for Canada's role in promoting human-centred governance of ASM in Africa.

The Rise and Governance of ASM in Africa

The rise of modern ASM can be described as dramatic. Although it is an old practice in some African communities (Hilson 2002; Wilson et al. 2015), the rate and nature of the activity in its modern form has evolved considerably. Global development policy, the rise in the world price of gold and other minerals, and various natural factors have contributed to the drastic growth of modern ASM. For instance, the structural adjustment programs of the World Bank and International Monetary Fund in the 1970s and 1980s that targeted extractive industries in the developing world led to massive retrenchments, which in turn drove many individuals into artisanal mining (Banchirigah 2006, 2008; Hilson 2016; Hilson and Potter 2005). Poor agricultural yields and the rise in world gold prices further motivated many individuals to venture into ASM as a new source of livelihood (*Economist* 2016; Nyame and Grant 2012, 2014). Across Africa, Asia, and Latin America, ASM takes place in hundreds of communities in more than eighty countries (Intergovernmental Forum on Mining, Minerals, Metals and Sustainable Development 2017). In Africa, ASM now complements, competes with, and even threatens to replace agriculture as the mainstay in many rural communities (*Economist* 2016; Hilson 2016).

ASM continues to expand globally and the scope and nature of operations constantly evolve. As a result, various scholars have described it differently (Ferring, Hausermann, and Effah 2016), and ascribe various reasons for its attractiveness and growth. While some relate its emergence to poverty and the quest for survival (Aryee, Ntibery, and Atorkui 2003; Barry 1996; Hilson and Pardie 2006), others contend that the practice is, in some cases, a manifestation of entrepreneurial spirit (Banchirigah and Hilson 2010). In its modern form, ASM might have affected agricultural activity, but it also complements and connects effectively to farming (Hilson 2016). However, irrespective of the difference in scope, motivation for entry into the trade, and levels of economic contribution across states and regions, a common feature of modern ASM is the sector's inherent and pervading threat to human security.

Owing to its crude nature and the absence of prior expert study to determine site suitability before most ASM operations, several kinds of fatal accidents occur in the sector. In Ghana's ASM sector, researchers report the cause of death between 2007 and 2012 as 4 per cent from suffocation, 4 per cent from clashes, 9 per cent from burning, 9 per cent from shooting, 13 per cent from crushing, 13 per cent from falling, 17 per cent from drowning, and 31 per cent from entrapment (Kyremateng-Amoah and Clarke 2015). In addition, the "slow violence" (Nixon 2011) of mercury contamination from ASM constitutes a major human security threat to many communities. Mercury releases and emissions into the environment from ASM spread far beyond the locations of mining activity (Cordy et al. 2011; Kirby et al. 2013). This is particularly worrying because ASM is currently the largest source of anthropogenic mercury release into the environment, at 37 per cent, with fossil fuel combustion coming second at 24 per cent (UNEP 2013).

The myriad security issues and generally complex nature of ASM make mainstream resource governance mechanisms inefficient for the sector. Across Africa, various governments have adopted several measures to address the challenges in ASM, but without any significant impact. Alternative livelihood projects in agriculture have been mostly unattractive to miners because, compared to mining, agriculture is unreliable and crops take longer to provide a net income that is often smaller (Banchirigah and Hilson 2010). Although governments and other development actors have tried to introduce environmentally friendlier and less harmful methods of mining, they have failed to reduce mercury use in the sector because miners mostly prefer mercury amalgamation in the extractive process (Davies 2014). Crime and illegality have also become rampant in the sector because miners flout laws and evade licensing in most cases (Banchirigah 2008).

Scholars and policy makers continue to explore better governance mechanisms for ASM. Some have argued for the incorporation of indigenous knowledge systems into the crafting of ASM policy and governance instruments (Spiegel et al. 2015; Spiegel and Veiga 2009). Drawing from De Soto's (2006) concept of "extralegality," which argues for the absorption of indigenous informal practices into mainstream legal and economic processes, Spiegel and Veiga (2009) reaffirm that community engagement offers an opportunity for policy makers to better understand the issues pertaining to ASM. The complexity of the sector and lack of political will to address its governance challenges in many communities have undermined the effect of various policies and programs (Banchirigah 2008; Hilson 2016). The desire for financial gain that drives individuals along the ASM value chain also contributes to further weaken already-deficient ASM governance efforts. Hilson (2016) has observed that negative official perceptions of and attitudes towards artisanal mining and the individuals in the trade have also impeded governance efforts. The insecurity resulting from ASM operations necessitates innovative governance ideas for the sector.

Governing ASM, however, requires methodical policy considerations. As Hilson (2016) has suggested, a "rethink" of attitude and approach to governing ASM is a necessary first step. It is undeniable that ASM is entrenched, extensive, and expanding – in Africa and other parts of the world. The artisanal mining sector has become a key part of the modern extractive industries. Being both a source of livelihood and a threat to human survival, its significance and viability are connected to the global sustainability imperative. In this regard, formal resource governance processes need to cover issues in ASM as well. Indeed, some have argued for the formalization of ASM and its inclusion in mainstream governance mechanisms such as the Extractive Industries Transparency Initiative (EITI) (Garrett 2007; Geenen 2012; Hilson 2016). In line with this, I argue that it is important to adopt approaches that address the sector's threat to human security. Thus, although mainstream resource governance mechanisms mostly target fiscal propriety, ASM governance should focus considerable attention on individual well-being and security.

The human security paradigm, which emphasizes individual well-being, would suitably inform policy and the crafting of appropriate governance mechanisms for ASM. The next section expands on the imperative for human-centred ASM governance, showing the link between the two, in the broad context of natural resource governance.

Rethinking Resource Governance: ASM and Human Security

Issues of insecurity in the extractive industries have attracted various scholarly discussions (Andrews 2015; Balag'kutu, McSparren, and VanDeveer 2018; Hilson 2010; Rustad, Østby, and Nordås 2016). In his exploration of the human security imperative in ASM, Andrews (2015) underscores the link between ASM and human survival, land deprivation, and the pursuit of justice. This chapter extends this link and, from a critical security viewpoint, discusses the relationship between ASM and human security and outlines Canada's (potential) contribution to human-centred governance of Africa's informal extractive sector.

Critical security draws attention to direct human suffering. Scholars of this orientation contend that traditional security theories are insufficient for explaining new (post–Cold War) security challenges (Booth 1997; Buzan, Wæver, and de Wilde 1998; Newman 2010). The relevance of this argument is manifest in the extractive industries, where some have long observed that human suffering is rife (Axworthy 2001). The use of a critical security viewpoint in the extractive sector is especially significant to ASM because of the extent of its embedded human insecurity (Balag'kutu, McSparren, and VanDeveer 2018).

The literature on ASM governance examines several important ideas: attitudinal change, the use of alternative environmentally friendly methods, the incorporation of indigenous knowledge systems, and the engagement of miners, among others. In line with mainstream resource governance approaches, attention to the fiscal component of ASM is often predominant in discussions, and constitutes the main objective of policy instruments and governance mechanisms (Hilson 2016). This exclusive focus on the fiscal component of resource governance has contributed to a governance deficit, especially regarding issues of human security in the larger extractive industry (Balag'kutu 2017). Insufficient attention to human security in resource governance also affects the attitudes of various actors in the extractive industries, including government officials, towards ASM.

Yet currently, ASM is arguably more dangerous than it is profitable. Exposure to human insecurity in the sector is particularly high in Africa, where millions engage in it (Hilson 2016) and, hence, endanger their lives in the process. Scholars have documented various threats to human security in ASM operations around Africa. In Ghana various kinds of fatal accidents occur in the sector (Kyremateng-Amoah and Clarke 2015). In the Democratic Republic of Congo, militia groups terrorize and extort artisanal miners to support their activities (*Economist* 2016). All over the continent, miners' preference for the use of mercury over environmentally-friendlier methods of extraction puts individuals and communities at risk of contamination (Davies 2014).

Although some policy and governance mechanisms might have targeted insecurity in ASM, a deliberate effort to use a human-centred approach could highlight the extent of the problem better and help to craft more appropriate policy instruments and governance mechanisms. As I have argued elsewhere, widening the scope of mechanisms such as the EITI to include social and environmental externalities of resource extraction not only would highlight the insecurity, but also galvanize citizen engagement to improve resource governance generally (Balag'kutu 2017). Thus, in the "rethink" of resource governance in general (Hilson 2016), policy makers need not only to pay attention to ASM, but also to consider seriously the human security question in the sector's operations.

The 1994 UNDP report, which formalized the concept of human security in mainstream development discourse, underscored the importance of dignified human existence devoid of "fear" and "want" (UNDP 1994; see also Alkire 2003). The centrality of the individual in development thinking and practice is the main feature of this new development paradigm (Axworthy 2001; Newman 2010). The idea has attracted different reactions from scholars and policy makers. Some have questioned the concept's theoretical and policy utility (Christie 2010; Thomas and Tow 2002). Also, various expressions of doubt over the notion of a worldwide acceptance of human security result from suspicions of biopolitics, the concept's vagueness and ambiguity, as well as its practical incoherence in terms of implementation, among other reasons (Acharya 2001; Chandler 2012; Delvoie 2001; Grayson 2008; Owen 2004; Paris 2001). For others however, human security is revolutionary and a significant addition to global development (Gasper 2005).

Unlike mainstream security thought, which is concerned primarily with state safety from external aggression (Booth 1997), human security privileges the survival of individuals (UNDP 1994). A human security lens is more holistic than the exclusive fiscal focus of existing resource governance mechanisms. ASM governance that is informed by the human security paradigm would highlight aspects of the sector that affect the survival of individuals and communities and enable policy makers to craft suitable instruments.

To better appreciate the pervading (human) insecurity situation in ASM and to adopt effective mechanisms to address it, input from actors with the necessary expertise, as well as the capacity and willingness to support the approach, is fundamental. The next section examines how one such actor, Canada, could help advance a human-centred ASM governance in Africa and why that would be important both for resource governance broadly and for development relations between Canada and Africa.

Canada, Human Security, and Governance of ASM in Africa

The new development paradigm based on the privileging of human survival (UNDP 1994) has gained support from various influential global actors, including Canada. The people and government of Canada have pioneered the global advocacy for human security since the emergence of the concept in global development discourse (Axworthy 1997; Paris 2001). Lloyd Axworthy is a notable voice on various platforms in Canada's campaign to spread the values of this new development paradigm (Axworthy 2000; see also Black 2016; Donaghy 2003).

It is important to note, however, that despite Canada's endorsement of human security in its foreign policy and development outlook (Axworthy 1997; Paris 2001; Small 2001), the concept has not always enjoyed the same favourable attention from different Canadian governments (Delvoie 2001). The kind of government, liberal or conservative, has been a major determiner of Canada's adherence to the centrality of humans in development policy and practice. The tenure of a more traditionalist (realist) security-minded government under Prime Minister Stephen Harper ignited debates on, doubts over, and criticisms of human security (Chapnick and Kukucha 2016; Kinsman 2015; see also Chapter 1, in this volume).

The return to power of the Liberals under Prime Minister Justin Trudeau reinvented Canada's resolve and commitment to human-centred development. Canada has portrayed this position in various ways, including a demonstration of support for the empowerment of vulnerable populations in the world (Black 2016; Canada 2016; Smith 2016). This renewed commitment also extends to the extractive sector. As Black (2016, 7) explains, Canada's engagement in Africa's extractive industries is an expression of its interest and obligation "to maximize the social benefits from their extractive sectors, and minimize the harms associated with extractive sector developments." Although the main reference here is large-scale resource extraction, a commitment to the minimization of harm is an important gesture to Canadian organizations working in the sector and to Canada's development partners in Africa. It shows a willingness to adhere to the notion of human security in engagements within the extractive industries; it also inspires Canadian organizations engaged in efforts that enhance human security in ASM.

Through several global initiatives, Canada has already demonstrated the capacity to promote a human-centred approach to governance in many development areas, including the resource sector. The Human Security Network (HSN), which has become an important vehicle for global development, is a major example of Canada's leading role in the promotion of human security. In collaboration with Norway and other actors, Canada created the HSN to galvanize a global coalition for the promotion of human survival and well-being (Paris 2001; Small 2001). Inspired by discussions on the Ottawa Treaty on Landmines, Lloyd Axworthy and Knut Vollebaek, the past foreign ministers of Canada and Norway, respectively, initiated discussions that led to the establishment of this network. Since its launch in 1998 through the Lysøen Declaration, the HSN has grown steadily and affected the development agendas of several states and global institutions (Krause 2008). The values of the HSN, as a collective group and through the efforts of individual member states, have also contributed to the advancement of human well-being globally (Krause 2008). For example, the network's advocacy of the "responsibility to protect" has engendered efforts towards safeguarding the rights and dignities of vulnerable individuals and groups in crisis situations (Krause 2008). In the extractive industries, the initiative has contributed to the creation of the Kimberley Process Certification Scheme for diamonds (Grant 2013a).

Canada's contribution to global development has also led to the development of initiatives that specifically target insecurity in the extractive sector. The Voluntary Principles on Security and Human Rights Initiative (VPs) is an international effort to promote adherence to human-centred values as a guide to resource extraction (Börzel and Hönke 2010; Freeman, Pica, and Camponovo 2000; Voluntary Principles 2017). Canada is a major partner and leader in the development and implementation of the VPs, serving twice as chair (see Chapters 1, 4, and 5, in this volume). Moreover Canada has further demonstrated the commitment to human well-being in the extractive sector by incorporating the VPs into its corporate social responsibility (CSR) programs (Campbell 2008). Although the lack of independent studies on corporate compliance with the VPs that examine issues beyond company policies leaves the application and effect of the initiative still in doubt (Börzel and Hönke 2010; Global Compact Network Canada n.d.), its existence is an important testament to Canada's contribution to the promotion of human-centred resource governance globally. Although CSR targets large-scale mechanized extractive processes (Dashwood 2012; Jenkins 2006) and its implementation is still a challenge (Butler 2015), it has become a major component of resource governance in many African countries (Campbell 2008, 2012).

Non-state Canadian development actors are also making noteworthy contributions to the promotion of human security in Africa's extractive sector. IMPACT (formerly Partnership Africa Canada) is a Canadian non-state organization that has designed measures to address insecurity in Africa's mineral sector (IMPACT 2019). IMPACT's "Just Gold" program, which focuses specifically on ASM operations, provides technical assistance to artisanal miners to help reduce their reliance on mercury and proneness to conflict, as well as enable them to gain access to markets. It currently serves ASM operators in Africa's Great Lakes region, where many communities have experienced extensive resource-related insecurity.

The Diamond Development Initiative International (DDII)[1] also aims to enhance human security in the extractive industries. Based in Ottawa, DDII emerged out of a 2005 meeting of representatives of the United Nations, governments, non-governmental organizations (NGOs), aid agencies from the United States and the United Kingdom, and the global diamond industry. It aims to ensure an enabling, safe, and dignified environment for artisanal miners around the world to enhance their contribution to the global economy. In this effort, DDII works to improve the "sub-standard" working conditions of artisanal miners by developing and implementing various projects (DDII n.d.; Grant 2009, 12–13; 2013b, 328). DDII's initiatives entail: 1) working within the Kimberley Process Certification Scheme to address issues of conflict diamonds; 2) assisting local governments to register artisanal miners in order to accord them legal recognition and participation in the formal economy; 3) organizing miners into cooperatives for bargaining and providing necessary skills training and education on several aspects of the sector; 4) certifying diamonds by artisanal miners to meet its Maendeleo Diamond Standards certification criteria; and 5) providing support in various forms, including social amenities to improve the living and working conditions of miners. Through the Maendeleo Diamond Standards program, DDII has empowered artisanal miners in Sierra Leone and continues to reach other mining communities in Africa (DDII 2016).

MiningWatch Canada is another important actor whose work has had direct effects on Africa's extractive industries. A Pan-Canadian non-governmental initiative concerned with the adverse human and environmental implications of irresponsible mining, MiningWatch Canada focuses on four key issues in resource governance: 1) compliance with the goals of "sustainable communities and ecological health" in mineral development; 2) improvement of technical and strategic skills among communities and groups dealing with the effects of mineral development; 3) protection of areas of ecological, economic, and cultural significance; and 4) risk minimization and efficiency enhancement in mineral development (MiningWatch Canada n.d.). Its activities guide Canadian mining companies operating in Africa and elsewhere, and can also influence and complement Canada's foreign development interests and activities, especially in the extractive industries.

The willingness among members of the Canadian mining communities to adopt humane methods of resource extraction is probably the most significant signal yet. Although some members of the Mining Association of Canada already participate in the VPs, the association formally announced its collective commitment to the initiative, which is the first by a national mining association (Mining Association of Canada 2017). The commitment enjoins members to submit regular reports on the implementation of the VPs. Although some have observed that Canada's mining companies relegate the artisanal process to the margins (Butler 2015), a commitment to the VPs is in line with Canada's broad development outlook and strategy in the extractive industries (Black 2016). It is an important gesture and a major boost to the advancement of human-centred governance in the extractive industry, which eventually could affect attitudes towards and governance of ASM positively.

Axworthy (2001) made a key observation on the rising trend of insecurity in the resource sector over a decade and a half ago. He noted emphatically that extractive industries, whose activities are geared towards enhancing human welfare, sometimes tend to expose individuals to extensive suffering. This observation is most vivid in ASM today. As stated earlier, while serving as an important source of liveli-hood for millions in Africa (Hilson 2016), ASM also causes extensive harm and death (Rustad, Østby, and Nordås 2016; Wilson et al. 2015). The social and environmental consequences in Africa's ASM would con-tinue to exacerbate the insecurity in the larger extractive sector unless relevant stakeholders adopt a concerted effort to address them.

It is important also that some key global and especially African actors have shown interest in improving governance of ASM. The Africa Mining Vision (AMV), which Shaw (2013, 4) has described as "a new form of African agency," underscores the need for efficient govern-ance mechanisms to enhance the contribution of ASM to continental development (African Union 2009). The AMV recognizes that, although ASM is a potential poverty-alleviating activity, its unsustainable nature undermines its economic value (African Union 2009, 27). ASM was also highlighted during a 2002 joint seminar by the United Nations Economic Commission of Africa and the United Nations Department of Economic and Social Affairs held in Yaoundé, Cameroon. The sem-inar, titled "Artisanal and Small-Scale Mining in Africa: Identifying Best Practices and Building Sustainable Livelihoods of Communities," concluded with the adoption of the Yaoundé Vision on ASM: it is this vision that inspired the inclusion of ASM in the AMV (African Union 2009). As well, a coalition of members of the Africa-Canada Forum and the Canadian Network on Corporate Accountability has acknowledged the centrality of ASM in development relations between the two regions (Africa-Canada Forum n.d.).

Moreover, and perhaps more important, the artisanal mining com-munity in Africa is beginning to acknowledge openly the human security threat of ASM and to welcome new and sustainable methods of operation. For instance, the Ghana National Association of Small-Scale Miners (GNASSM) has joined a national call for environmentally friendly mining (News Ghana 2017). With GNASSM's affiliation to the budding Association of Small Scale Miners Africa-Network, the gesture has the potential to affect ASM operations around Africa.

These are important developments that could benefit from the influence and expertise of a global leader in human-centred develop-ment. Canada has just such expertise. As an influential global leader in human security and a major actor in Africa's extractive industries, Canada could play a central role in the promotion of human-centred ASM governance on the continent. As discussed earlier, non-state Canadian organizations have adopted governance mechanisms that target human insecurity in Africa's ASM sector. The response to and overall effect of these initiatives is encouraging. A further deliberate human-centred national policy effort targeting ASM governance in Africa would be a major boost to the combined efforts of these Canadian organizations and the efforts of individual African states. With the huge and active presence of Canadian interests in Africa's extractive industries (Black 2016; Campbell 2012; Kinsman 2015), an efficiently governed ASM sector and the extractive industries more broadly in Africa would benefit both Canada and Africa (Africa-Canada Forum n.d.; Black 2016).

Conclusion

Artisanal and small-scale mining is a major subject in contemporary global development discussions. Scholars have described ASM in Africa as "an indispensable – and potentially, *the* most important – economic activity" (Hilson and McQuilken 2014, 117). Canadian policy experts have observed that ASM is central to development engagements between Africa and Canada (Africa-Canada Forum n.d.; Black 2016; Campbell 2008). In Africa, however, ASM governance is generally poor. Efficient and appropriate ASM governance mechanisms are necessary and urgent. Some analysts have asserted that governing ASM is a "matter of approach" (Jønsson, Appel, and Chibunda 2009). The question is: what approach would best address the varied socio-environmental problems and general human insecurity in the sector?

I have sought to demonstrate that an approach founded on and motivated by the human security paradigm would be most ideal. A human-centred approach to governing ASM could help address key aspects of the resource curse phenomenon. Addressing this trend requires expertise in and commitment to human-centred resource governance and development. Canada has played an influential leadership role in developing and promoting the human security paradigm in global development. The current Trudeau Liberal government's global outlook suggests a strong commitment to the promotion of human security (Black 2016; Canada 2016; Smith 2016). More important, Canada has the needed expertise to facilitate human-centred resource governance in Africa. Canadian civil society initiatives in Africa's ASM sector would be an important additional resource. IMPACT's "Just Gold" program, DDII's Maendeleo Diamond Standards, and other ASM governance mechanisms are making important contributions to the enhancement of the well-being of individuals and communities in parts of Africa. MiningWatch Canada's monitoring of resource extraction is another boost to Canadian leadership on a human security approach to resource governance. African response to the human-centred ASM governance initiatives by Canadian organizations is positive. The Africa Mining Vision's focus on ASM has awakened state-level interests among actors across the continent.

Canada's involvement in Africa's extractive sector, the country's global development outlook, and its role in promoting human security worldwide are key reasons to anticipate its involvement in and potential impact on the promotion of human-centred ASM governance in Africa. The Africa-Canada Forum recommends that Canada focuses on ASM in its resource development engagement with Africa (Africa-Canada Forum n.d., 11). Although a conservative reversal to *realpolitik* security policy in Canada remains a possibility (Delvoie 2001), and I acknowledge that one or more of my projections might not come to pass, Canadians' preference for human-centred development (Kinsman 2015) is an important indication that the paradigm can endure in Canada's development interactions with Africa. Moreover the Canadian civil society and business communities have shown significant interest in development engagements that prioritize human well-being (Black 2016; Grant 2014). More important, Canada has shown the capacity and willingness to provide the necessary leadership in the global promotion of human security (Axworthy 1997). As Black (2016) convincingly argues, a human-centred approach to governing resource extraction, especially ASM, ultimately would benefit both Canada and African states. Pursuing this interest is a matter of choice: Canada *can* encourage its mining firms to move Africa's ASM sector from the margins to the core of the governance equation. These progressive actions are something that Canadian NGOs and forums such as the DDII and members of the Devonshire Initiative,[2] respectively, could support. Whichever direction the decision goes, ASM is sure to remain a part of development relations between Canada and Africa, at least with respect to the extractive industries.

NOTES

1 See the website of the Diamond Development Initiative International, at http://www.ddiglobal.org/. For a scholarly analysis of DDII's contribution to diamond sector governance, see, for example Grant (2009, 2012, 2018).
2 For the latest list of Devonshire Initiative members, see the website at https://www.devonshireinitiative.org/members.

BIBLIOGRAPHY

Acharya, Amitav. 2001. "Human Security: East versus West." *International Journal* 56 (3): 442–60. https://doi.org/10.2307/40203577.
Africa-Canada Forum. n.d. "The African Mining Vision: Transformative Agenda for Development – Backgrounder." Available online at https://www.ccic.ca/_files/en/working_groups/2013-04-02-AMV_backgrounder_EN.pdf, accessed 10 April 2017.
African Union. 2009. *Africa Mining Vision*. Addis Ababa: African Union.
Alkire, Sabina. 2003. "A Conceptual Framework for Human Security." Centre for Research on Inequality, Human Security and Ethnicity Working Paper 2. Oxford: University of Oxford, Queen Elizabeth House.
Andrews, Nathan. 2015. "Digging for Survival and/or Justice? The Drivers of Illegal Mining Activities in Western Ghana." *Africa Today* 62 (2): 3–24. https://doi.org/10.2979/africatoday.62.2.3.
Armah, Frederick Ato, Sheila A. Boamah, Reginald Quansah, Samuel Obiri, and Isaac Luginaah. 2016. "Working Conditions of Male and Female Artisanal and Small-Scale Goldminers in Ghana: Examining Existing Disparities." *Extractive Industries and Society* 3 (2): 464–74. https://doi.org/10.1016/j.exis.2015.12.010.
Aryee, Benjamin N.A., Bernard K. Ntibery, and Evans Atorkui. 2003. "Trends in the Small-Scale Mining of Precious Minerals in Ghana: A Perspective on Its Environmental Impact." *Journal of Cleaner Production* 11 (2): 131–40. https://doi.org/10.1016/S0959-6526(02)00043-4.
Auty, Richard. 2002. *Sustaining Development in Mineral Economies: The Resource Curse Thesis*. London: Routledge.
Axworthy, Lloyd. 1997. "Canada and Human Security: The Need for Leadership." *International Journal: Canada's Journal of Global Policy Analysis* 52 (2): 183–96. https://doi.org/10.1177/002070209705200201.
Axworthy, Lloyd. 2000. Notes for an Address to the Woodrow Wilson International Center for Scholars, Washington, DC. 16 June. Available online at http://www.peace.ca/axworthyaddresstwoodrow.htm, accessed 16 April 2017.
Axworthy, Lloyd. 2001. "Human Security and Global Governance: Putting People First." *Global Governance* 7 (1): 19–23. https://doi.org/10.1163/19426720-00701004.
Balag'kutu, Timothy Adivilah. 2017. "Enhancing Citizen Engagement in Natural Resource Governance: Scope, Content and Input in the Operation of the Extractive Industries Transparency Initiative." *Extractive Industries and Society* 4 (4): 775–8. https://doi.org/10.1016/j.exis.2017.10.003.
Balag'kutu, Timothy Adivilah, Jason J. McSparren, and Stacy D. VanDeveer. 2018. "Extractives and Environmental Governance Research." In *A Research

Agenda for Global Environmental Politics, edited by Peter Dauvergne and
Justin Alger, 65–83. Cheltenham, UK: Edward Elgar. https://doi.org/10.433
7/9781788110952.00011.
Banchirigah, Sadia Mohammed. 2006. "How Have Reforms Fuelled the
Expansion of Artisanal Mining? Evidence from Sub-Saharan Africa."
Resources Policy 31 (3): 165–71. https://doi.org/10.1016/j.resourpol.2006.
12.001.
Banchirigah, Sadia Mohammed. 2008. "Challenges with Eradicating Illegal
Mining in Ghana: A Perspective from the Grassroots." *Resources Policy*
33 (1): 29–38. https://doi.org/10.1016/j.resourpol.2007.11.001.
Banchirigah, Sadia Mohammed, and Gavin Hilson. 2010. "De-agrarianization,
Re-agrarianization and Local Economic Development: Re-orienting
Livelihoods in African Artisanal Mining Communities." *Policy Sciences*
43 (2): 157–80. https://doi.org/10.1007/s11077-009-9091-5.
Barry, Mamadou. 1996. "Regularizing Informal Mining – A Summary of
the Proceedings of the International Roundtable on Artisanal Mining."
Washington, DC: World Bank.
Black, David. 2016. "Canada in Africa: Finding Our Footing?" Policy Paper.
Calgary: Canadian Global Affairs Institute. Available online at https://
www.cgai.ca/canada_in_africa_finding_our_footing, accessed 6 April 2017.
Booth, Ken. 1997. "Security and Self: Reflections of a Fallen Realist." In *Critical
Security Studies: Concepts and Cases*, edited by Krause Keith and Michael C.
Williams, 83–120. Minneapolis: University of Minnesota Press.
Börzel, Tanja, and Jana Hönke. 2010. "From Compliance to Practice: Mining
Companies and the Voluntary Principles on Security and Human Rights
in the Democratic Republic of Congo." SSRN Scholarly Paper ID 1642073.
Rochester, NY: Social Science Research Network. https://papers.ssrn.com/
abstract=1642073.
Butler, Paula. 2015. *Colonial Extractions: Race and Canadian Mining in
Contemporary Africa*. Toronto: University of Toronto Press.
Buzan, Barry, Ole Wæver, and Jaap de Wilde. 1998. *Security: A New Framework
for Analysis*. Boulder: Lynne Rienner.
Campbell, Bonnie. 2008. "Regulation & Legitimacy in the Mining Industry
in Africa: Where Does Canada Stand?" *Review of African Political Economy*
35 (117): 367–85. https://doi.org/10.1080/03056240802410984.
Campbell, Bonnie. 2012. "Corporate Social Responsibility and Development
in Africa: Redefining the Roles and Responsibilities of Public and Private
Actors in the Mining Sector." *Resources Policy, Corporate Social Responsibility
in the Extractive Industries: Experiences from Developing Countries*, 37 (2):
138–43. https://doi.org/10.1016/j.resourpol.2011.05.002.
Canada. 2016. "Canada Renews Its Security Support and Development
Assistance to Afghanistan." Press release, 11 July. Available online at

http://pm.gc.ca/eng/news/2016/07/09/canada-renews-its-security-support-and-development-assistance-afghanistan, accessed 30 March 2017.

Chandler, David. 2012. "Resilience and Human Security: The Post-Interventionist Paradigm." *Security Dialogue* 43 (3): 213–29. https://doi.org/10.1177/0967010612444151.

Chapnick, Adam, and Christopher J. Kukucha. 2016. *The Harper Era in Canadian Foreign Policy: Parliament, Politics, and Canada's Global Posture.* Vancouver: UBC Press.

Christie, Ryerson. 2010. "Critical Voices and Human Security: To Endure, to Engage or to Critique?" *Security Dialogue* 41 (2): 169–90. https://doi.org/10.1177/0967010610361891.

Cordy, Paul, Marcello M. Veiga, Ibrahim Salih, Sari Al-Saadi, Stephanie Console, Oseas Garcia, Luis Alberto Mesa, et al. 2011. "Mercury Contamination from Artisanal Gold Mining in Antioquia, Colombia: The World's Highest per Capita Mercury Pollution." *Science of the Total Environment* 410–11 (December): 154–60. https://doi.org/10.1016/j.scitotenv.2011.09.006.

Dashwood, Hevina S. 2012. *The Rise of Global Corporate Social Responsibility: Mining and the Spread of Global Norms.* Cambridge: Cambridge University Press.

Davies, George R. 2014. "A Toxic Free Future: Is There a Role for Alternatives to Mercury in Small-Scale Gold Mining?" *Futures* 62 (Part A): 113–19. https://doi.org/10.1016/j.futures.2013.11.004.

De Soto, Hernando. 2006. "The Challenge of Connecting Informal and Formal Property Systems: Some Reflections Based on the Case of Tanzania." In *Realizing Property Rights,* edited by Hernando de Soto and Francis Cheneval, 18–67. Zurich: Rüffer & Rug.

Delvoie, Louis. 2001. "Curious Ambiguities: Canada's International Security Policy." *Policy Options* 22 (1): 36–42.

DDII (Diamond Development Initiative International). 2016. "Maendeleo Diamond Standards (MDS): Frequently Asked Questions." Available online at http://www.ddiglobal.org/login/resources/mds-maendeleo-diamond-standards-faqs.pdf.

DDII (Diamond Development Initiative International). n.d. "About DDI." Available online at http://www.ddiglobal.org/who-we-are/about, accessed 29 March 2017.

Donaghy, Greg. 2003. "All God's Children: Lloyd Axworthy, Human Security and Canadian Foreign Policy, 1996–2000." *Canadian Foreign Policy Journal* 10 (2): 39–58. https://doi.org/10.1080/11926422.2003.9673326.

Economist. 2016. "Jobs in Africa: In Praise of Small Miners." 7 May. Available online at https://www.economist.com/middle-east-and-africa/2016/05/07/in-praise-of-small-miners.

Ferring, David, Heidi Hausermann, and Emmanuel Effah. 2016. "Site Specific: Heterogeneity of Small-Scale Gold Mining in Ghana." *Extractive Industries and Society* 3 (1): 171–84. https://doi.org/10.1016/j.exis.2015.11.014.

Freeman, Bennett, Maria B. Pica, and Christopher N. Camponovo. 2000. "A New Approach to Corporate Responsibility: The Voluntary Principles on Security and Human Rights." *Hastings International and Comparative Law Review* 24: 423–50.

Garrett, Nicholas. 2007. "The Extractive Industries Transparency Initiative (EITI) and Artisanal and Small-Scale Mining (ASM): Preliminary Observations from the Democratic Republic of the Congo (DRC)." Extractive Industries Transparency Initiative. October. Available online at https://eiti.org/sites/default/files/documents/Garrett_EITI_10_2007.pdf.

Gasper, Des. 2005. "Securing Humanity: Situating 'Human Security' as Concept and Discourse." *Journal of Human Development* 6 (2): 221–45. https://doi.org/10.1080/14649880500120558.

Geenen, Sara. 2012. "A Dangerous Bet: The Challenges of Formalizing Artisanal Mining in the Democratic Republic of Congo." *Resources Policy* 37 (3): 322–30. https://doi.org/10.1016/j.resourpol.2012.02.004.

Ghana. 2015. Minerals Commission. *Artisanal and Small Scale Mining (ASM) Framework.* Accra: Ministry of Finance. Available online at https://www.mofep.gov.gh/sites/default/files/reports/economic/ASM%20FRAMEWORK.pdf.

Global Compact Network Canada. n.d. *Auditing Implementations of VPs on Security and Human Rights: A Guidance Document to Assist Companies and Their Auditors Assess Implementation of the Voluntary Principles on Security and Human Rights.* Available online at https://globalcompact.ca/wp-content/uploads/2016/08/Auditing-Implementations-of-VPs-on-Security-and-Human-Rights.pdf, accessed 29 March 2017.

Grant, J. Andrew. 2009. *Digging Deep for Profits and Development? Reflections on Enhancing the Governance of Africa's Mining Sector.* Johannesburg: South African Institute of International Affairs.

Grant, J. Andrew. 2012. "The Kimberley Process at Ten: Reflections on a Decade of Efforts to End the Trade in Conflict Diamonds." In *High-Value Natural Resources and Post-Conflict Peacebuilding,* edited by Päivi Lujala and Siri Aas Rustad, 159–79. New York: Earthscan/Taylor & Francis.

Grant, J. Andrew. 2013a. "Commonwealth Cousins Combating Conflict Diamonds: An Examination of South African and Canadian Contributions to the Kimberley Process." *Commonwealth & Comparative Politics* 51 (2): 210–33. https://doi.org/10.1080/14662043.2013.774197.

Grant, J. Andrew. 2013b. "Consensus Dynamics and Global Governance Frameworks: Insights from the Kimberley Process on Conflict Diamonds." *Canadian Foreign Policy Journal* 19 (3): 323–39. https://doi.org/10.1080/11926422.2013.844909.

Grant, J. Andrew. 2014. *How Can Canada's Natural Resource Sector Remain Globally Competitive?* Toronto: Canadian International Council.

Grant, J. Andrew. 2018. "Eliminating Conflict Diamonds and Other Conflict-Prone Minerals." In *African Actors in International Security: Shaping Contemporary Norms,* edited by Katharina P. Coleman and Thomas K. Tieku, 51–71. Boulder, CO: Lynne Rienner.

Grayson, Kyle. 2008. "Human Security as Power/Knowledge: The Biopolitics of a Definitional Debate." *Cambridge Review of International Affairs* 21 (3): 383–401. https://doi.org/10.1080/09557570802253625.

Hilson, Gavin. 2002. "Harvesting Mineral Riches: 1000 Years of Gold Mining in Ghana." *Resources Policy* 28 (1–2): 13–26. https://doi.org/10.1016/S0301-4207(03)00002-3

Hilson, Gavin. 2010. "Child Labour in African Artisanal Mining Communities: Experiences from Northern Ghana." *Development and Change* 41 (3): 445–73. https://doi.org/10.1111/j.1467-7660.2010.01646.x.

Hilson, Gavin. 2012. "Corporate Social Responsibility in the Extractive Industries: Experiences from Developing Countries." *Resources Policy* 37 (2): 131–7. https://doi.org/10.1016/j.resourpol.2012.01.002.

Hilson, Gavin. 2016. "Farming, Small-Scale Mining and Rural Livelihoods in Sub-Saharan Africa: A Critical Overview." *Extractive Industries and Society* 3 (2): 547–63. https://doi.org/10.1016/j.exis.2016.02.003.

Hilson, Gavin, and James McQuilken. 2014. "Four Decades of Support for Artisanal and Small-Scale Mining in Sub-Saharan Africa: A Critical Review." *Extractive Industries and Society* 1 (1): 104–18. https://doi.org/10.1016/j.exis.2014.01.002.

Hilson, Gavin, and Sandra Pardie. 2006. "Mercury: An Agent of Poverty in Ghana's Small-Scale Gold-Mining Sector?" *Resources Policy* 31 (2): 106–16. https://doi.org/10.1016/j.resourpol.2006.09.001.

Hilson, Gavin, and Clive Potter. 2005. "Structural Adjustment and Subsistence Industry: Artisanal Gold Mining in Ghana." *Development and Change* 36 (1): 103–31. https://doi.org/10.1111/j.0012-155X.2005.00404.x.

Hilson, Gavin, and Natalia Yakovleva. 2007. "Strained Relations: A Critical Analysis of the Mining Conflict in Prestea, Ghana." *Political Geography* 26 (1): 98–119. https://doi.org/10.1016/j.polgeo.2006.09.001.

Hinton, Jennifer, Marcello M. Veiga, and Christian Beinhoff. 2006. "Women and Artisanal Mining: Gender Roles and the Road Ahead." In *The Socio-economic Impacts of Artisanal and Small-Scale Mining in Developing Countries,* edited by Gavin M. Hilson, 149–88. Lisse, Netherlands: A.A. Balkema.

IMPACT. 2019. "Transforming National Resource Management; Empowering Communities." Available online at https://impacttransform.org/en/, accessed 14 May 2019.

Intergovernmental Forum on Mining, Minerals, Metals and Sustainable Development. 2017. *Global Trends in Artisanal and Small-Scale Mining: A Review of Key Numbers and Issues*. Winnipeg: International Institute for Sustainable Development. Available online at www.iisd.org/sites/default/files/publications/igf-asm-global-trends.pdf.

Jenkins, Heledd. 2006. "Small Business Champions for Corporate Social Responsibility." *Journal of Business Ethics* 67 (3): 241–56. https://doi.org/10.1007/s10551-006-9182-6.

Jønsson, Jesper Bosse, Peter W.U. Appel, and Raphael Tihelwa Chibunda. 2009. "A Matter of Approach: The Retort's Potential to Reduce Mercury Consumption within Small-Scale Gold Mining Settlements in Tanzania." *Journal of Cleaner Production* 17 (1): 77–86. https://doi.org/10.1016/j.jclepro.2008.04.002.

Karl, Terry Lynn. 1997. *The Paradox of Plenty: Oil Booms and Petro-States*. Berkeley: University of California Press.

Kinsman, Jeremy. 2015. "Harper's Foreign Policy: Hard Realism or Empty Posturing?" *OpenCanada*. 5 January. Available online at https://www.opencanada.org/features/harpers-foreign-policy-hard-nosed-realism-or-empty-posturing/, accessed 18 March 2017.

Kirby, Alex, Ieva Rucevska, Valentin Yemelin, Christy Cooke, Otto Simonett, Viktor Novikov, and Geoff Hughes. 2013. *Mercury: Time to Act*. New York: United Nations Development Programme. Available online at http://cwm.unitar.org/cwmplatformscms/site/assets/files/1254/mercury_timetoact.pdf.

Krause, Keith. 2008. "Building the Agenda of Human Security: Policy and Practice within the Human Security Network." *International Social Science Journal* 59 (September): 65–79. https://doi.org/10.1111/j.1468-2451.2008.00635.x.

Kyeremateng-Amoah, Emmanuel, and Edith E. Clarke. 2015. "Injuries among Artisanal and Small-Scale Gold Miners in Ghana." *International Journal of Environmental Research and Public Health* 12 (9): 10886–96. https://doi.org/10.3390/ijerph120910886.

Mining Association of Canada. 2017. "Canadian Miners to Implement Voluntary Principles on Security and Human Rights." 2 March. Available online at www.mining.com/web/canadian-miners-to-implement-voluntary-principles-on-security-and-human-rights/, accessed 2 March 2017.

MiningWatch Canada. n.d. "MiningWatch Canada – Changing Public Policy and Mining Practices to Ensure the Health of Individuals, Communities and Ecosystems." Available online at http://miningwatch.ca/, accessed 29 March 2017.

Newman, Edward. 2010. "Critical Human Security Studies." *Review of International Studies* 36 (1): 77–94. https://doi.org/10.1017/S0260210509990519.

News Ghana. 2017. "GNASSM to Support Government to Flush Out Illegal Miners." 11 April. Available online at https://www.newsghana.com.gh/gnassm-to-support-government-to-flush-out-illegal-miners/, accessed 15 April 2017.

Nixon, Rob. 2011. *Slow Violence and the Environmentalism of the Poor.* Cambridge, MA: Harvard University Press.

Nyame, Frank K. and J. Andrew Grant. 2012. "From Carats to Karats: Explaining the Shift from Diamond to Gold Mining by Artisanal Miners in Ghana." *Journal of Cleaner Production* 29 (1): 163–72. https://doi. org/10.1016/j.jclepro.2012.02.002.

Nyame, Frank K. and J. Andrew Grant. 2014. "The Political Economy of Transitory Mining in Ghana: Understanding the Trajectories, Triumphs, and Tribulations of Artisanal and Small-Scale Operators." *Extractive Industries and Society* 1(1): 75–85. https://doi.org/10.1016/j.exis.2014.01.006.

Owen, Taylor. 2004. "Human Security – Conflict, Critique and Consensus: Colloquium Remarks and a Proposal for a Threshold-Based Definition." *Security Dialogue* 35 (3): 373–87. https://doi.org/10.1177/0967010604047555.

Paris, Roland. 2001. "Human Security: Paradigm Shift or Hot Air?" *International Security* 26 (2): 87–102. https://doi.org/10.1162/016228801753191141.

Rustad, Siri Aas, Gudrun Østby, and Ragnhild Nordås. 2016. "Artisanal Mining, Conflict, and Sexual Violence in Eastern DRC." *Extractive Industries and Society* 3 (2): 475–84. https://doi.org/10.1016/j.exis.2016.01.010.

Seccatore, Jacopo, Marcello Veiga, Chiara Origliasso, Tatiane Marin, and Giorgio De Tomi. 2014. "An Estimation of the Artisanal Small-Scale Production of Gold in the World." *Science of the Total Environment* 496 (October): 662–7. https://doi.org/10.1016/j.scitotenv.2014.05.003.

Shaw, Timothy. 2013. *Post-2015 Natural Resource Governance in Africa: African Agency and Transnational Initiatives to Advance Developmental States.* Ottawa: North-South Institute.

Small, Michael. 2001. "The Human Security Network." In *Human Security and the New Diplomacy: Protecting People, Promoting Peace,* edited by Robert G. MacRae and Don Hubert, 231–5. Montreal; Kingston, ON: McGill-Queen's University Press.

Smith, George P., II. 1984. "The United Nations and the Environment: Sometimes a Great Notion?" *Texas International Law Journal* 19: 335–65. https://ssrn.com/abstract=2265463.

Smith, Joanna. 2016. "PM Trudeau in Africa Recognizes Different Pace in Respecting Human Rights." *CTV News,* 24 November. Available online at https://www.ctvnews.ca/politics/pm-trudeau-in-africa-recognizes-different-pace-in-respecting-human-rights-1.3174529, accessed 30 March 2017.

Spiegel, Samuel, and Marcello M. Veiga. 2009. "Artisanal and Small-Scale Mining as an Extralegal Economy: De Soto and the Redefinition of 'Formalization.'" *Resources Policy* 34 (1): 51–6. https://doi.org/10.1016/j.resourpol.2008.02.001.

Spiegel, Samuel, Susan Keane, Steve Metcalf, and Marcello Veiga. 2015. "Implications of the Minamata Convention on Mercury for Informal Gold Mining in Sub-Saharan Africa: From Global Policy Debates to Grassroots Implementation?" *Environment, Development and Sustainability* 17 (4): 765–85. https://doi.org/10.1007/s10668-014-9574-1.

Thomas, Nicholas, and William T. Tow. 2002. "The Utility of Human Security: Sovereignty and Humanitarian Intervention." *Security Dialogue* 33 (2): 177–92. https://doi.org/10.1177/0967010602033002006.

UNDP (United Nations Development Programme). 1994. *New Dimensions of Human Security*. New York: Oxford University Press.

UNEP (United Nations Environment Programme). 2013. *Global Mercury Assessment: Sources, Emissions, Releases and Environmental Transport*. Number 42. Geneva: UNEP Chemicals Branch.

Van Bockstael, Steven. 2014. "The Persistence of Informality: Perspectives on the Future of Artisanal Mining in Liberia." *Futures* 62 (October): 10–20. https://doi.org/10.1016/j.futures.2014.02.004.

Voluntary Principles on Security and Human Rights. 2017. *What Are the Voluntary Principles?* Available online at https://www.voluntaryprinciples. org/what-are-the-voluntary-principles, accessed 30 March 2017.

Wilson, Mark L., Elisha Renne, Carla Roncoli, Peter Agyei-Baffour, and Emmanuel Yamoah Tenkorang. 2015. "Integrated Assessment of Artisanal and Small-Scale Gold Mining in Ghana – Part 3: Social Sciences and Economics." *International Journal of Environmental Research and Public Health* 12 (7): 8133–56. https://doi.org/10.3390/ijerph120708133.

World Commission on Environment and Development. 1987. *Our Common Future*. New York: Oxford University Press.

SECTION III

Corporate Social Responsibility, Norms, and Development

7 Global Governance via Local Procurement? Interrogating the Promotion of Local Procurement as a Corporate Social Responsibility Strategy

PAULA BUTLER

Introduction

In March 2017 Tanzania's Ministry of Energy and Minerals announced a ban on exports of unprocessed gold, silver, nickel, and copper. The government's stated objective was "to make sure that mineral value addition activities are carried out within Tanzania as emphasized in the Mineral Policy of 2009 and Mining Act of 2010. Mineral value addition activities will provide employment opportunities, revenues and technology transfer, hence more benefits to the nation" (Tanzania 2017). In subsequent months, following explosive allegations by government investigators of underreported volumes and values of mineral exports from two majority Canadian-owned gold mines (Bulyanhulu and Buzwagi, both owned by UK-listed Acacia), the government introduced major amendments to the legislative framework for the mining sector with a view to dramatically increasing political control over, and economic benefit from, the country's substantial mineral wealth. In addition to increased royalties and a 16 per cent minimum state equity provision, "Mining Development Agreements," which had long provided a legislative loophole for companies to broker special arrangements and guarantees, were discontinued. The 2017 legal changes also introduced local content and local sourcing requirements. Barrick Gold, with its 64 per cent ownership stake in Acacia Mining, entered into negotiation with the Tanzanian government. Acacia, however, filed notice with the International Court of Arbitration in London, challenging Tanzania's right to pass legislation that voided aspects of existing mining licences and changed the rules mid-contract. This case, which remains unresolved, appears to pit a low-income African government aggressively pursuing "resource nationalism" against foreign-owned (Canadian and British) mining companies attempting to protect shareholders' interests.[1] It thus provides a compelling snapshot of the frequently conflicted terrain of foreign private resource extraction in African countries, and sets a political context for this chapter's focus on local procurement as part of the global mining industry's corporate social responsibility (CSR) paradigms.

The Tanzanian government's actions can be seen as a response to the discontent of African citizens who have not enjoyed developmental benefits from resource wealth. The paucity of backward and forward economic linkages associated with foreign-owned mines operating in African countries has long been cited as a major barrier to realizing greater socio-economic benefits from mineral resource extraction (African Union 2009; Lanning 1979; Mkandawire and Soludo 1999; Yachir 1988). Thus, from a development or poverty-reduction perspective, any steps towards improving linkages could be regarded in a positive light. What I argue in this chapter, however, is that local procurement has been taken up by the industry as one way to head off the kind of widespread local and elite discontent that could lead to more substantive forms of resource nationalism.

My initial interest in local procurement was catalyzed by a talk entitled "Procurement as a Means for Mining Firms to Secure Their Social License to Operate" (Geipel and D'Souza 2014), which took place in October 2014 at Ryerson University's Institute for the Study of Corporate Social Responsibility (located in the Ted Rogers School of Management). In this case, the CSR program was located in a business studies department, rather than in international development studies. Moreover, the emphasis in the presentation was not primarily on local procurement as a benefit for Global South communities, but as a strategically smart choice for mining firms. The speakers represented a non-governmental organization (NGO), Engineers Without Borders Canada, and a Canadian mining company, Centerra Gold. At the time, the fact that one aspect of backward linkages – local procurement – appeared to be gaining visibility within the field of CSR piqued both my curiosity and my scepticism. Further investigation revealed that local procurement in African mining had been the subject of a new series of World Bank and International Finance Corporation studies from 2011 to 2014. Moreover, from 2014 to 2017, local procurement continued to be featured at major mining events such as the Prospectors & Developers Association of Canada (PDAC) annual convention in Toronto and the Mining Indaba in Cape Town, South Africa. Local procurement was one of the first themes addressed by the CSR Forum set up in Burkina Faso by the Canadian government–funded Plan Canada-IAMGOLD pilot project.[2] Clearly, a new theme had entered the CSR field of discourse.

This chapter presents a structured enquiry into the meaning of these developments. As a scholar who draws on critical political economy, post-colonial studies, and critical race theory, I am interested in how a new field of ideas emerges, gains traction in the public domain, and engenders new institutional practices and policies. I am equally interested in discerning whether these emergent discourses and practices have a transformative or domesticating effect in resource-rich African communities and countries. The emergence of local procurement as a discursive field and as a practical field of policy intervention – especially one that purports to be highly beneficial for African communities – presents an important opening for examining continuing and new modalities of neoliberal governance of mining in African countries. This chapter thus explores the following questions: What institutional strategies and interests have fostered the emergence of local procurement as a new dimension of CSR? What institutions are involved and why? What are the salient characteristics of the institutional discourses pertaining to local procurement as they have emerged since 2011? Finally, in order to stimulate future research on the topic, I reflect on what alternate strategies and perspectives might be suppressed or rendered less tenable as local procurement gains prominence.

Before proceeding, it is important to state clearly that the purpose of this chapter is *not* to evaluate the economic potential of local procurement in African countries and communities. Rather, I analyse *why* and *how* local procurement has emerged in recent years as a locus of international policy attention and, more specifically, as part of the discourse of CSR. Data for this analysis draw on one key informant interview and three institutional framings of local procurement: 1) the African Union and United Nations Economic Commission on Africa's "Africa Mining Vision"; 2) Engineers Without Borders Canada's "Mining Shared Value" project; and 3) Foundation Strategy Group's "Shared Value Initiative" on local procurement. First, however, I locate my analysis with reference to critical literatures on CSR and global governance and review recent political economy literature on local procurement and backward linkages. In the final section, I suggest that the manner in which local procurement engages the legitimacy challenges facing the extractive sector reveals a characteristic tendency of neoliberal power: to colonize agency and foreclose alterity.

Manifestations of Power: Neoliberalism, Global Governance, and CSR

For Michel Foucault, "governmentality is not about the institutional power of states; rather it is a relational and discursive power that permeates society.... Governmentality is a process of defining what practices, mechanisms and institutions are needed for ... societies to be governed or made governable" (quoted in Banerjee 2008, 68). The concept of governmentality aids in assessing the nature of power that operates in the contemporary global governance of "developing nations." Operating to advance both market capitalism and liberal rights, global governance is diffuse, disaggregated, thick, and horizontal rather than hierarchical; it operates discursively; and consists of multilateral, quasi-state, corporate, financial, NGO, and civil society actors (Finkelstein 1995; Rosenau 1995; Strange 1996). Despite the horizontality among global governance institutions, as a system of rule it is non-democratic. It variously counters, supersedes, influences, and dominates state authority, and installs "commonsense" neoliberal practices at the micro- and meso-levels. Citizens of Global South nations have no constitutionally guaranteed access to or voice in these supra- and extra-national governance institutions.

In the African extractive sector, a multitude of actors have jockeyed to fill the governance vacuum created by the structural adjustment program-induced shackling of the post-colonial African state (Campbell 2004, 2013; Ferguson 2006). Global governance of African resources is thus dominated by a range of for-profit and not-for-profit, public sector, and private sector entities, including: the World Bank, the UN Economic Commission on Africa, the International Finance Corporation, the African Development Bank, the Organisation for Economic Co-operation and Development (OECD), the African Minerals Development Centre, Natural Resources Canada, the Extractive Industries Transparency Initiative, the International Council on Mining and Metals, the International Institute for Sustainable Development, the PDAC, chambers of commerce, chambers of mines, and schools of business and mining engineering; academic research centres such as the Canadian International Resources and Development Institute; CSR consulting firms such as rePlan; and a host of private consultants. Such organizations govern through policy influence, networking, research, technologies, and access to human and financial resources – even while having no formal accountability to African publics. They present as sources of sociological and scientific expertise, and thus occupy political space as legitimate authorities.

In this context of private, transnational governance of Africa's extractive sector, CSR has emerged as a key discourse and set of social technologies. Critical literatures on CSR identify it as a new form of the colonial "civilizing mission" whereby enlightened and compassionate Westerners purport to bring development and a "fair deal" to mining-affected communities (Adanhounme 2011; Banerjee 2008; Munshi and Kourian 2007). But relations of power within CSR programming are typically asymmetrical. Adanhounme (2011) notes that when structural adjustment programs enabled foreign extractive firms to return to post-colonial African countries on terms that were highly beneficial, CSR programs were offered "in return." These programs were developed, however, by extractive sector corporations in alignment with the institutional culture of their home states. Banerjee (2008, 52) presents a scathing assessment of CSR as "an ideological movement intended to legitimize the power of large corporations" and "to maintain entrepreneurial freedom through voluntary initiative rather than regulatory coercion" (66). He further notes that the purported participatory design of CSR initiatives involving community and corporate stakeholders often does not give community members genuine power or choice. Referring to interviews conducted in an Australian CSR mining forum with indigenous participants who stated that their wish was for the multinational mining company to pack up, leave, and never return, Banerjee (2008, 64) notes that this option is never really on the table in CSR community consultations. If local procurement has emerged as a new focus of CSR, it will be subject to similarly rigorous scrutiny.

The question of agency exercised by globally governed African peoples is addressed by Kamola (2015). He argues that analyses of agentive resistance to, and engagement with, neoliberal governance rarely draw on the work of Black African anti-colonial scholars such as South African freedom fighter Steve Biko. Although Biko's analysis was grounded in the experience of apartheid, Kamola asserts that his insights are relevant to contemporary contexts. Biko asserted that, when "white liberals" took anti-apartheid leadership roles, they detracted from an African politics of self-determination by enacting "governance on behalf of others." Despite their identity as colour-blind "do-gooders," they "retained a political vision originating in the social order under which they benefitted" (Kamola 2015, 64). Limits to their political thinking became visible when they exhibited dismay with forms of autonomous Black resistance they deemed too "militant" – as, more recently, South Africa's Mining Charter or Tanzania's ban on exports of unprocessed ores have been decried by the mining industry as extreme or provocative. Applying Biko's critiques to the contemporary context, Kamola (2015, 63) advises that "contemporary white liberals should instead work to identify their own complicity with the existing 'global' order and seek to make imaginable a world governed by the world's majority – namely, those currently marginalized under the existing 'global' order." He concludes that "radical and transformative projects cannot originate from those concerned with the governance of others" (73). This view presents an important challenge to the contemporary institutionalization of CSR as a form of "white liberal" activity.[3]

Assessing the Impact of Local Procurement

Attention to mining industry linkages has been a focus of economists for decades, and it plays an important role in some of the recent literature on local procurement to which I now turn. Forward linkages refers to the manufacturing and other value-added procedures ("beneficiation") that occur to the resource once it is extracted. Processed minerals and metals are considerably more valuable than raw minerals and metals; countries that have mineral/metals processing or manufacturing sectors garner greater economic value from their resource endowments than those that do not. When diamonds were discovered in Canada's north, in order to capture economic benefit for citizens in their respective jurisdictions, the governments of the Northwest Territories and Ontario required diamond producers to allocate a portion of their raw gemstones to locally owned diamond-cutting and -polishing firms. Such industries, along with diamond jewellery making, were thus established in Yellowknife and Sudbury, even though Canada had no prior industrial knowledge of or experience in diamond cutting or polishing.[4] Presumably, this is the same motivation that inspired Tanzania's recent ban on unprocessed mineral exports.[5]

Backward linkages refers to all the supply-side goods and services required to enable the resource extraction to occur through exploration, mine construction, operations, and reclamation. Local procurement refers to the purchase of goods and services from local and/or national businesses, while local content encompasses local procurement, the employment of local and national people, and goods and services (value addition) from local or national firms. As Morris, Kaplinsky, and Kaplan (2012, 413) note, "It is important to recognize that linkage development is both a matter of the breadth of linkages (the proportion of inputs sourced locally or outputs processed locally) and the depth of linkages (how 'thick' the linkages are, that is, their domestic value-added)."

In African contexts the mining industry has been labelled an enclave industry because of the weak backward and forward linkages into local, national, and continental economies. With only a few exceptions, such as South Africa and Botswana, African countries export most of their minerals and metals in unprocessed form. Drawing on United Nations data, Bocoum-Kaberuka (1999, 238–41) reported that, while sub-Saharan Africa (excluding South Africa) exported 41.9 per cent of the world's bauxite, it exported only 0.2 per cent of the world's aluminum alloys; while it exported 39.4 per cent of the world's copper matte, it exported only 0.5 per cent of copper semi-manufactures; and while it exported 80.8 per cent of the world's cobalt, it exported only 7.2 per cent of processed cobalt. More recent research shows no significant change in these trends (Hansen 2014; OECD 2016; Otchia 2015; Ramdoo and Bilal 2014). It also remains the case that, with the exception of low-value-added products such as food or cleaning services, most equipment, vehicles, technologies, and services required for large-scale mining in Africa are sourced and imported from non-African firms (e.g., those domiciled in the United States, United Kingdom, Germany, Japan, France, China, and Canada). In 2010, US and Chinese firms were the leading sources of mining equipment imports by sub-Saharan countries, supplying 19.1 per cent and 15 per cent, respectively (Farooki 2012, 422). In that year, South African firms supplied 8 per cent of sub-Saharan countries' mining equipment needs, but other countries of the region had not established any significant presence in the capital- and technology-intensive mining equipment manufacturing sector (Farooki 2012; Kaplan 2012).

Despite this evidence of the enclave nature of industrial mining on the African continent, Morris, Kaplinsy, and Kaplan (2012) argue that there is much to be hopeful about concerning the scope and potential of industrial mining-related linkages in sub-Saharan Africa. They point to evidence of three main elements in enhancing linkages: select policy interventions and leadership from government; market forces (which, for instance, they suggest eventually will make competitively priced local products and services more cost effective for mining companies); and time (e.g., the number of years of established mining). This third element, time, leads Morris and colleagues (2012) to contend that countries with long-established mining sectors (e.g. South Africa, Zambia, and Ghana) tend to have greater backward linkages. They do note, however, that linkage development is static in countries such as Tanzania and Gabon, and that there is evidence of "a shallowing of linkages" in South Africa and Zambia. Lydall (2009) analyses the state of backward linkages in the platinum mining industry of South Africa, and reaches a similar conclusion: while South Africa historically has had a vibrant and well-developed mining supply-side industry (largely owned by white South African firms), Lydall (2009) and Kaplan (2012) find that this vibrancy is being eroded. Fessehaie's (2012) study of backward linkages in the Zambian mining sector also supports Morris and colleagues' identification of a "shallowing" of linkages in some historic mining countries. She notes that Zambia had a good record of building the mining industry supply-side sector during the early post-colonial era of nationalization, when the government actively invested in research and development (R&D) for mining-related technologies. With the advent of the structural adjustment era and its wave of privatizations, many local suppliers lost access to R&D and skills development as new foreign mining companies (re-)entered the country and contracted goods and services from known and trusted international suppliers. In this context, the supply-side industry that remained in Zambia was reduced to the provision of services with low-value-added content and a general decline in manufacturing. Taken together, one conclusion that could be drawn from these studies is an association between the advent of neoliberal policies and the erosion of domestic linkages in the mining sector.

Bloch and Owusu's (2012) discussion of backward linkages in the Ghanaian mining economy presents a slightly different picture from the discussions of Zambia and South Africa. Bloch and Owusu document a fairly extensive supply-side industry in Ghana involving a large number of local firms, which they attribute not only to the lengthy history of mining in Ghana, but also to private sector (versus state) initiatives. They highlight the efforts of multinational mining companies, such as Newmont and Golden Star, to source goods and services locally and the role of the Ghanaian Chamber of Mines in promoting a vibrant supply-side industry. They also acknowledge that backward linkages are concentrated in low-skill, low-value-added areas (such as catering and cleaning) and note that, despite the length of time mining has been established in Ghana, relatively little by way of forward linkages, such as in-country mineral processing, has developed. Nigeria is identified as one African country that has successfully used legislation to compel local content in the extractive sector (Ramdoo 2016, 5).

A common theme of these studies concerns the appropriate roles of African states in creating policy frameworks to promote backward and forward linkages. Jacobs (2013) cites examples of countries such as Chile that have not only operated state-owned mines, but also used policy and legislative mechanisms (such as required minimum local content) to foster the development of the domestic mining supply sector. Jacobs highlights the importance of strong state administrative and legislative capacity in order to ensure national benefit from the resource industry. Ado (2013) and Nwapi (2016) concur in observing that, although all industrialized mining nations were able, in the past, to use policy measures such as import restrictions, export taxes, technology-transfer stipulations, and performance requirements to protect and grow national industries, these measures today are largely prohibited for African countries by the World Trade Organization's (WTO's) Trade-Related Investment Measures and Articles III and XI of the General Agreement on Tariffs and Trade. Moreover, bilateral investment treaties, such as Canada's foreign investment promotion and protection agreements (FIPAs), prohibit performance requirements such as local content and technology transfer. The 2015 Canada-Burkina Faso FIPA presents a clear example of these prohibitions, stating under "Performance Requirements" (Article 9: 2–3) that: "A Party may not impose the requirement ... to achieve a given level or percentage, in terms of volume or value, of domestic content; to purchase, use or accord a preference to a good produced or service provided in its territory, or to purchase a good or service from a person in its territory." Although export taxes – which African states may use to encourage in-country beneficiation of minerals and metals – are allowed under WTO rules, they are increasingly prohibited in bilateral and multilateral trade agreements such as the European Union's Economic Partnership Agreements with various African countries (OECD 2016; Ramdoo and Bilal 2014). Grynberg (2013) notes that recent World Bank and World Bank–funded research studies actively discourage African countries from using export taxes and export bans on minerals and metals as a way to increase in-country value-added opportunities. The same can be said of various OECD studies.[6]

A nationalist or developmentalist African state will experience constrained policy space as a result of these pressures and influences within the overall framework of foreign aid, international trade, and investment law. If stronger states are associated with the development of a full range of linkages for maximum national benefit from industrial sectors such as mining, then the weakening of African states, and the limitations placed on policy measures available to them, might partially explain the paucity of intra- and inter-African linkages in the current era. This is the source of the scepticism I expressed at the outset with reference to the new interest in local procurement options: procurement is conducted by those who are positioned within the same system of global governance and whose actors oppose legislated and contractual performance requirements and lobby against export taxes. It is against this backdrop that I examine three textual framings of local procurement in the next section of the chapter.

The African Union and UNECA: Local Procurement in the "Africa Mining Vision"

The 2009 Africa Mining Vision (AMV) and 2014 Africa Mining Vision Strategy were developed by the United Nations Economic Commission on Africa (UNECA) with a number of academic and civil society experts, input from the African Development Bank, and endorsement and adoption by the African Union Heads of State. I contend that the AMV represents the most politically feasible compromise between those who wanted to keep the governance of African mining clearly within the parameters of a private investor–led, neoliberal paradigm (following the trajectory of the World Bank's 1992 *Strategy for African Mining*) and those who aspired to a more self-determined, African-led and Africa-prioritized approach to the use of lands and resources. Strategically the AMV is couched as principally a technical, rather than an ideological or political, approach. Although the AMV is rhetorically framed as designed to harness resource wealth for the benefit of African peoples and nations, it does not fundamentally disrupt the free market or neoliberal foreign-investor-led model. With enormous resource values at stake, the document is inevitably of intense political importance. As it was being developed, the AMV had minimal grassroots or nationally organized input; only now, through UNECA's promotion of "country mining visions" (Pedro 2016), are efforts being made to popularize (or, as Pedro calls it, "domesticate") the AMV among citizens and parliamentarians at the national level. The process and the set of documents and institutions that emerged from this initiative – the AMV itself, the AMV Strategy, the International Study Group Report of 2011, and the creation of the African Minerals Development Centre – exemplify the top-down nature of African resource governance.

Despite these caveats and the political complexity of its production, the AMV merits serious consideration, and is often referenced by the CSR community, albeit selectively. One of the AMV's nine areas of strategic focus is the development of backwards, forwards, and "sideways" economic linkages. Although local procurement is mentioned, other means of enhancing linkages are given much more space and attention in this section of the AMV. The bulk of recommendations aimed at national, subregional, and regional levels concern enhanced beneficiation and value addition – that is, downstream linkages that are known to add the greatest economic value to the resource. Furthermore, many recommendations have to do with tax measures and legal changes that imply a more interventionist state than is typically appreciated by international mining capital. Some of the specific policy changes recommended, such as greater state equity in mining ventures as well as taxes on the export of raw materials, are policies that would affect Western mining companies negatively and that they would actively resist. To be specific, the AMV advises the "judicious use of export taxes to encourage beneficiation"; assurance that "WTO [environmental protection agreements, free trade agreements, bilateral investment treaties] and other bilateral, regional or international agreements *do not constrain policy space for mineral resource based industrialization and value addition*" (emphasis added); the alignment of "international agreements to create space for mineral resource-based industrialization"; and a review of "best practice in state equity participation" (African Union 2009, 35–6). In fact, none of the action items in the linkages section of the AMV specifically mentions the promotion of supply-side local procurement. Rather, the emphasis is on obtaining political space for African state governance of the sector using many of the same policy tools available in the past to industrialized nations. This raises important political questions about the attention that local procurement has garnered from the World Bank, the International Finance Corporation, Engineers Without Borders, and the Shared Value Initiative since the release of the AMV. Why has local procurement emerged as a vigorous field of discourse and policy action among the latter, while resource-based beneficiation and industrialization, support for African state equity in mining, and reform of international trade and investment laws have garnered minimal interest or advocacy from the industry-linked CSR community? One can reasonably conclude that, when faced with a conflict of interest between African nations' development priorities and Western companies' business priorities, Western CSR for-profit and not-for-profit firms will side with the latter.

Engineers Without Borders Canada: "Mining Shared Value"

Engineers Without Borders Canada (EWBC) is a registered charity founded in 2000 by two energetic, young, white, male engineers who wanted to "mobilize" engineers "to address the root causes of poverty in rural Africa."[7] Based mainly on university campuses across Canada, it grew rapidly and now has forty-four chapters.[8] EWBC can be dubbed a "corporate NGO" to differentiate it from an earlier generation of Canadian NGOs that were informed, at least in their early decades (1960s to 1980s) by structural analyses of global poverty and inequality, according to which the transnational corporate sector was seen as central to a colonial and neocolonial pattern of Northern exploitation of Southern resources, lands, and labour.[9] Since the turn of the twenty-first century there has been a notable increase in NGOs in Canada that identify entrepreneurship as a means of addressing poverty, which, in their view, can be eliminated through private sector technological innovation, rather than via structural changes in the transnational political economy. "Corporate NGOs"[10] typically receive significant funding from large corporations, have business, law and finance sector representatives on their board of directors, espouse social change theories compatible with ideologies of big business, and partner with them. In a related critique of philanthropic organizations that use "ethical shopping," celebrities, and billionaires to promote social change, Ilan Kapoor suggests that such approaches depoliticize and dehistoricize global inequality, mask corporate harm, and thus "decaffeinate capitalism" (Kapoor 2013, 63).

In Canada, EWBC was a pioneer among NGOs experimenting with social entrepreneurship – a concept and approach that uses techniques from the field of business and management to address social problems. EWBC adapted the model of the business endeavour to launch and institutionalize creative action on a range of social issues. Its webpage asserts that these ventures "challenge the status quo and provide radical alternatives to unjust systems."[11] One of its early ventures was "Mining Shared Value" (MSV), with a focus on promoting local procurement within the Canadian global mining sector. The project was to be self-financing and profitable, generating income through the provision of research and expertise on local procurement while also building a knowledge-based brand and producing "measurable results" in the form of increased action on, and recognition of, local procurement as a CSR issue by industry and other key stakeholders. MSV's clients and collaborators consist mainly of Western governments, universities, professional engineering associations, mining associations, and multilateral institutions.

EWBC's launch of its work on local procurement arose in the context of a strong Canadian government push, under the Harper Conservatives, for the Canadian mining industry to rebrand itself as a responsible and ethical industry through CSR programming. In 2009 the government released its CSR policy, "Building the Canadian Advantage," and soon after initiated a set of controversial CSR pilot projects featuring collaborations between mining companies and NGOs. In this political climate, some of EWBC's industry partners, including SNC-Lavalin, suggested the promotion of increased local procurement by Western mining firms in African countries (and elsewhere) as an area where EWBC could "add value" by developing expertise in this emerging aspect of CSR. Although some student members of EWBC chapters expressed uneasiness about working on issues that might appear to support the mining industry,[12] EWBC proceeded to create Mining Shared Value "to increase local procurement by the global mining industry so that host countries gain more economic and social benefits from mining activity."[13]

From 2014, MSV began actively promoting local procurement, making presentations at key mining conferences, and producing research on the reporting of local procurement by Canadian mining firms. One of its first strategies was to document and publish a baseline study (in 2014) on the extent of reporting on local procurement by Canadian companies operating in the Global South. This was followed by a larger study in the subsequent year of public reporting trends across the global mining industry, with a supplementary study on the Canadian industry's practices. The supplementary study showed a 50 per cent increase between 2012 and 2013 in the number of Canadian companies publicly reporting on local procurement programming (from 10 to 15 companies); while these numbers were still low, they appeared to indicate some success on the part of MSV in bringing this issue to the attention of the Canadian mining industry (MSV 2015, 14). It was noted that mid-size companies in particular were receptive to guidance on better institutionalizing their CSR commitments.

In 2015, MSV became a founding member of the World Bank's "Extractives for Local Content Development – Community of Practice" (CoP) – a by-invitation-only forum for exchange of information among researchers, development institutions, and industry on local content. MSV also initiated collaborative work to develop a global standardized reporting framework for industry on local procurement, and began testing the framework with key stakeholders. This framework would introduce common ways of defining and quantifying local content so that reliable and comparative data could be collected. The development of this kind of standardized template can be identified as a classic device of global neoliberal governance.

MSV also conducted a study on the effectiveness of state-legislated regulatory frameworks for local content – a major concern of the industry – using South Africa and Namibia as contrasting case studies. The study revealed that rates of reporting of local procurement were higher in South Africa, where the government had instituted targets for procurement from South African businesses with prescribed levels of non-white South African ownership. Namibia, by contrast, had no state-regulated local-content requirements, and the mining industry there showed lower levels of reporting on local procurement. Significantly, Namibia's international investment attractiveness ranking was much higher than South Africa's (MSV and CIRDI 2017, 23). The report highlighted non-regulatory measures and "informal tools" that, according to industry informants, offer better incentives to companies to increase local procurement than do "imposed rules." Through this type of research, MSV positioned itself as able to offer expert advice to mining companies facing an environment of increasing state interest in local-content legislation. MSV's panel at the 2017 PDAC conference on local-content regulations promised that "participants will develop a better understanding of what pitfalls can occur with problematic regulations, and how to engage with government to steer laws in the right direction."[14]

Although MSV's mission statement states that the venture aims to secure benefits from mining for (African) "host states," its public presentations and reports are mainly pitched to, and facilitate conversations with, Canadian and other Western mining firms. Three main arguments in favour of local procurement are typically presented: 1) it will benefit the company's bottom line; 2) it will bring employment, income, and economic dynamism to local communities; and 3) it will enhance the company's "social licence" to be present in the area. Considerable attention is often given to corporate financial benefit: companies are encouraged to plan for, and invest in, local procurement on the grounds that local services and supplies will be more cost effective (cheaper labour; the reduction or elimination of import and transportation costs) and more efficient (the time saved if sources are local). The value of an improved "social licence" is also emphasized on the grounds that a happier local populace means less conflict, fewer work stoppages, and smoother operation. Indeed the MSV presentation, "Local Procurement: Benefits for Development and Mining Companies," at the 2014 PDAC convention concludes with the statement that "local procurement ... offers mining companies an effective way to respond to rising expectations of what mining activity should contribute to economic and social development."[15]

Foundation Strategy Group: The "Shared Value Initiative"

Although there is no formal institutional relationship between "Mining Shared Value" and "Shared Value Initiative," the overlap in language is not purely coincidental, but indicates a shared field of discourse and ideology. The Shared Value Initiative (SVI) is a project of the US-based Foundation Strategy Group, a non-profit consulting firm launched by two business studies academics, Michael Porter and Mark Kramer, authors of an influential article, "Creating Shared Value," published in *Harvard Business Review* (Porter and Kramer 2011). Foundation Strategy Group, now a massive hub for foundations and wealth managers, developed the SVI as a platform to promote the concept across sectors. Shared value is defined as "policies and activities that measurably improve socio-economic outcomes and improve related core business performance" (SVI and FSG 2014, 3). The basic tenet is that desirable social and business outcomes could be pursued in harmony, not conflict. Importantly, expertise in conceptualizing and implementing a shared value paradigm is asserted to be "the next competitive advantage." *Extracting with Purpose: Creating Shared Value in the Oil and Gas and Mining Sectors Companies and Communities* (October 2014) is one of a series of studies that envision and detail shared value opportunities, and was financed by major mining, oil, and gas companies (Chevron, Gold Fields, Hess, Newmont, Pacific Rubiales, Rio Tinto, Shell, and Suncor), with support from Mercy Corps and the International Finance Corporation. Research for the study involved travel to Canada and ten countries in Asia, Africa, South America, and the Middle East.

Extracting with Purpose stands out from other governance documents on backward linkages in that it presents a dense, complex, and carefully crafted narrative that moves resource governance discourse onto new terrain. The authors begin by noting that most greenfield resource extraction occurs in "remote, impoverished and underdeveloped" regions of the world where there is "limited economic activity" (SVI and FSG 2014, 2) and "per capita income levels [are] below the global average" (5). Moreover, high levels of conflict "with local communities that see no benefits from resource extraction" (6) are occurring in these areas at significant cost to extractive sector industries in terms of project delays, operational disruptions, and negative publicity from protests and violence. After creating this caricature of Global South communities, the authors depict extractive companies as rashly pouring funds into CSR-identified community projects to mitigate opposition and gain a minimal social licence to operate. This is described as a "transactional, if not adversarial" relationship that fails to address the root causes of conflict and opposition, identified as "lack of economic opportunity, health problems, environmental degradation and ineffective government" (2). Indeed the authors refer to this situation, in which angry communities purportedly gain the upper hand over an ostensibly beleaguered industry, as a "status quo" that has to change. They then propose the development of a shared value approach as a fundamentally different response to this impasse.

As *Extracting with Purpose* explains, shared value differs from obtaining a social licence to operate because it takes a longer-term view, integrates social goals into the company's business model, positions the company as a "development partner," and seeks relationships of trust with communities. As the authors note, "the importance of establishing and sustaining trust is difficult to overstate" (SVI and FSG 2014, 34). There is an implicit acknowledgement of the degree of cynicism felt by local communities. The shared value approach purports to treat the local community's well-being as seriously as the company's profitability. Companies are encouraged to devote time and resources to investing in skills training of local people and capacity building of local suppliers. Shared value is depicted as "win-win": local people will experience greater benefit from private foreign investment, and the company will secure a more stable work environment, along with cost savings in the form of qualified, inexpensive local labour and cheaper goods and services from local suppliers. Such measures sound very appealing. In the shared value paradigm, there is a productive alignment of interests between social and business goals, and between local people and foreign companies. The enclave nature of foreign extractive industries gives way to an integrated, development-oriented presence. It is assumed that most sources of conflict, dissent, and opposition to the foreign company can be overcome through the use of appropriate interventions.

Two strategies proposed to implement shared value are of particular significance. One has to do with the development of metrics of quantification pertaining to the social costs and benefits of the extractive operation. It is asserted that extractive companies do not account adequately for the costs of not building relationships of trust with local communities or for the longer-term financial benefits of investing in backward linkage development. To make business sense, these costs and benefits must be measurable, quantifiable, and reportable. The document draws attention to the Sustainability Accounting Standards Board, which developed an industry-specific set of accounting standards to measure the state of community relations, security, human rights, issues pertaining to indigenous peoples, and so on. Once such societal concerns and issues are translated into measurable financial terms, they are more likely to be seen as relevant factors in relation to the corporate "bottom line." A similar project, "Beyond Zero Harm Framework," was initiated in Canada by IAMGOLD, developed with NGOs and industry personnel, and hosted by the Devonshire Initiative.[16] Within the scope of CSR programming, these constitute some of the latest social neoliberal governance strategies regarding Global South resources.

The second significant strategy proposed in *Extracting with Purpose* relates to the problem of allegedly weak or ineffective host-country governments. The authors assert that "[m]any of these countries lack strong governments at the national, regional and local levels" (SVI and FSG 2014, 13), but offer no context to explain the nature or causes of this lack. According to the SVI, companies desire governments to establish effective regulatory frameworks, conduct research, identify best practices in CSR, and create forums to bring together disparate stakeholders to address social impacts. They want governments to establish national development visions with clear priorities, including shared value requirements in mining contracts. In short, they desire governments that espouse neoliberal market-led growth and that will facilitate the productive operation of foreign-investment-led mining, channelling enough of its profits into sustainable development to legitimize the system. In the alleged absence of such capacity, companies are advised to move into these gaps and use shared value technologies to build the requisite state governance capacity. On the other hand, some governments are seen as leading the nation astray, introducing problematic policy and regulatory frameworks such as ill-conceived local-content requirements – an example is Tanzania, which introduced such requirements as part of the wider package of reforms described at the outset of this chapter. Companies are advised to head off legislated requirements for local content within the dreaded paradigm of "resource nationalism" by voluntarily initiating backward linkages, and to engage with nationalist-leaning governments to co-develop reasonable and effective local-content regulations. Although *Extracting with Purpose* insists that companies do not wish to replace host-country governments, the document envisions extractive companies playing comprehensive roles in governance at international, national, and local levels.

Conclusions: Global Governance via Local Procurement

At the outset of this chapter I raised the general question as to whether the new interest by industry and CSR actors in local procurement is potentially transformative or domesticating. The data and analysis I have presented here suggest the latter – that is, that the promotion of local procurement is being used to maintain and legitimize a leading role for private foreign investors in the African mining sector and to actively discourage mandatory local-content (and other) regulations by African states. However, the fact that local procurement has emerged as a field of discourse and practice reflects some movement in the power relations between foreign mining firms and African states and communities. It also reflects financial realities, such as low global commodity prices that push firms to identify cost savings that can be achieved via increased local procurement. This is what Morris, Kaplinsky, and Kaplan (2012) identified as the role of market forces in fostering greater linkages.

This chapter also provided a glimpse into how the global neoliberal governance of African resources occurs. Specifically, the chapter showed the scale of human and financial resources – the plethora of research studies, reports, documents, networking, and conference presentations – that go into fashioning and disseminating a new field of thought and practice: in this case, the promotion of local procurement by foreign mining firms. The question as to what alternative strategies and perspectives might be consequently suppressed or rendered less tenable was also raised. Review of the content on linkages in even a moderate policy approach such as the Africa Mining Vision identified numerous policies that have not been taken up by the international mining industry or by Western development agencies. Indeed, there is active opposition on the part of non-African mining interests to many AMV strategies to enhance linkages in a manner that would strengthen the continent's political control of, and economic benefit from, its mineral resource wealth.

One is led to conclude that the focus on voluntary backward linkages by industry is at least partially designed to further entrench, normalize, and legitimize the private, foreign investment-led extractives model as the only viable model for Africa's extractive sector and to dissuade African states from the aggressive pursuit of resource nationalism on the grounds that the foreign-led extractives model is already serving national ("host-country") interests. Suppressed or marginalized are any number of alternatives: development visions that do not prioritize the extractive sector at all; mining sector management that features strategic nationalized ownership or state-run beneficiation industries; or models that prioritize the artisanal mining sector and invest in its capacity building. There is much evidence to demonstrate that many communities do not wish foreign-owned industrial mines, preferring rather to protect their lands from industrial pollution and to maintain access to lands for food production, livestock grazing, or artisanal mining operations.[17] Indeed, given that the artisanal sector is much more integrated ("linked") into local communities and generates greater local social and economic benefits than does large-scale industrial mining, it is quite striking that none of the global governance documents or presentations on local procurement mentions the artisanal and small-scale mining sector. In short, the deployment of significant financial resources for research, travel, workshops, production of documents, and policy recommendations by major and minor global governance institutions on the issue of local procurement might flood out or circumscribe opportunities for more substantively democratic, bottom-up, contextually shaped African determination of land and resource use. A cynical reader might conclude that this is precisely the goal.

Earlier I highlighted Kamola's (2015) use of Steve Biko's theories of African self-determination, with particular reference to Biko's assessment of the roles of "white liberals." These actors could, in his view, play a useful role, but not by taking leadership in the struggle for liberation or in the post-colonial/post-apartheid society. Rather, they should prepare ("lubricate") their own oppressor society to relinquish power and to sit with the "Other" on the Other's terms. Although Engineers

Without Borders Canada does not employ the discourse of North-South power relations in its documents and presentations, one could ask whether they play such a lubricating role. Through its Mining Shared Value, EWBC could be seen as a broker between the interests and needs of Global South communities and the interests of the Canadian mining industry. In fact, however, Mining Shared Value has invested in establishing cordial and productive relationships with the mining industry, receives financing from mining companies, and shares with them a common worldview. At the time the research was conducted, it had established no comparable relations with mining-affected African communities nor had it been commissioned by any African governments to produce research on local procurement.[18] Moreover the industry itself, as evidenced in the input MSV collected from it, maintains both a sense of entitlement to pursue profitable extractive opportunities throughout the African continent[19] and to be as unencumbered as possible by African state authorities and regulations. In a basic manner, foreign firms continue to bristle at manifestations of genuinely democratic African sovereignty.[20] There is little sign here of the kind of transformed mentality that Biko observed as necessary. In this sense, neither the Canadian mining industry nor its CSR affiliates can yet be seen as genuine allies of African self-determination.

Finally, I have theorized the global governance of African resource extraction as effectively non-democratic in nature – as a webbed system of governance that bypasses African citizens and hollows out the substance of citizenship. At the same time, I also noted that the very fact that local procurement has emerged as a field of discourse and practice reflects some shift in the power relations between foreign mining firms and African states and communities. That is, demands that the mining of African resources benefit Africans have required some kind of response from the industry. Agentive actions of members of affected communities in African countries and elsewhere have compelled reforms in the global mining industry. Neither dominated populations nor dominated states are powerless – especially when their nations host highly sought-after minerals and metals.

It is in relation to this fact that the Shared Value Initiative requires some additional concluding reflections. In my assessment, the SVI is most acutely aware of the depth of the differences in interests among local communities, mine employees, citizens, and even some parliamentarians of "host states" on the one hand, and foreign mines and their shareholders and investors on the other. Harassed by the spectre of resource nationalism and disturbed by the documentation of continuing and growing anti-mining resistance throughout the Global South, the SVI senses the depth of what is at stake and counters this threat with a carefully crafted response: a strong "charm offensive." If unrealized desires for sovereignty, substantive citizenship, and justice are the real root causes of mine-site conflict, these demands cannot be met. But they must *appear* to be met. They must therefore be refashioned and reconstructed. There is a difference between developing local suppliers – and legislatively requiring such development – for an African-owned and -controlled mining sector and doing so merely to generate cost efficiencies and obtain a greater degree of local acceptance (acquiring the social licence) for foreign-owned mines whose profits largely return to their home states. But through a discursive and ontological sleight-of-hand, the SVI recasts this difference as a commonality. The most significant aspect of the discourse of the SVI is that it fashions a mythology of a deep alignment of interests between communities/ citizens and foreign capital, as well as between social goals and business profits. This is achieved by appearing to welcome and invite agentive self-determination of the Other through joint problem solving and building relationships of trust. It is striking that relationships of trust emerge as central in the discursive repertoire of CSR, both in *Extracting with Purpose* and in the PDAC's 2017 CSR workshops.[21] Trust dissolves distrust, turning an enemy into an ally. Fashioning a discursive terrain of trust, common values, and "win-win" pursuits has the effect of absorbing and thus neutering difference and opposition. In this appealing narrative, everyone is on the same page.

Sustaining this conceptual sleight-of-hand requires a disavowal of the historical and continuing power and resource disparities between Western mining companies and African states and communities, and of the vigorous political and legal efforts to implement mining laws and international investment laws that benefit Western companies and make possible their presence in African countries. It requires not asking why linkages were not supported or promoted by Western global governance institutions when, following decolonization, African countries nationalized their mining sectors or had nationalistic or Pan-Africanist visions of development – but only when Western companies had resumed a dominating presence in the sector. Because the greatest risk to Western miners is the threat of losing access to African resources – of being forced out – the SVI's worldview is aimed at ensuring that no one can be positioned as "enemy" or "Other." Radical alterity – actual differences of cultural or spiritual values, visions, and ways of being; the rejection of free market neoliberalism; pan-Africanist continentalism; outrage at exploitation – these must be gently but firmly eliminated or neutralized. This signals a new modality of neoliberal violence: the death not of the Other, but of Otherness. The notion of shared value requires and produces sameness, friendliness, and relationships of trust – while operating insidiously to domesticate the politics of out-rage at exploitation, plunder, inequitable access to resources, and so on. Moreover, if everyone is on the same page and there are no mean-ingful asymmetries of power, governance itself becomes a legitimately technocratic, apolitical process in which industry accountability, rights of African states, and democratic control by African citizens are moot. Moreover, nothing material need be relinquished. There is no operative notion of privilege or dispossession – just of business rationales and "financials." Social benefits and risks can be quantified, expressed and dealt with via reporting rubrics and financial metrics.

With this collapsing of difference, conflict, and alterity into commonality – into an "alignment of values" through which the African continent now finally will benefit from its remarkable mineral wealth – the private foreign-investor-led industrial mining model is collectively reaffirmed as what is best for Africa. If EWBC can describe its ventures as "providing radical alternatives to unjust systems," this study of local procurement shows that neoliberal power responds to threat – that is, to expressions of self-determination – by embracing and recasting threat. It absorbs and retrofits transformative and oppositional ideas, harnessing them to capitalist advance and stability; it flows into the most radical and progressive spaces and discourses and occupies them; chameleonic, it changes its colours (but not its intentions) to adapt to its environment, even, and most especially, environments of perceived threat. It thus looks and sounds at times highly progressive – as does much of the current discourse on local procurement. Thus a central effect of neoliberal power as it operates in African resource governance is the productive manner in which the simulacrum of self-determina-tion and economic justice is differentiated, only with the most intense scrutiny and scepticism, from the actual thing.

NOTES

1 Indeed the value of Acacia shares was reported in June 2018 to have dropped by 80 per cent since March 2017; see "Barrick Won't Set Deadline for End of Acacia Tax Dispute with Tanzania," *Globe and Mail*, 25 June 2018, available online at https://www.theglobeandmail.com/business/industry-news/energy-and-resources/article-barrick-wont-set-deadline-for-end-of-acacia-tax-dispute-with-tanzania/, accessed 27 October 2018.

2 This two-day workshop was held in June 2013 in Ouagadougou. This information was obtained from Access to Information and Privacy (ATIP) Request A2401401809_2015_03_31_08-38-09, p. 319.

3 Under apartheid, white identity was a legal category tied to phenotype and ancestry. For critical race scholars today, whiteness signifies a social position of racial, political, and economic dominance linked to a history of colonial and capitalist exploitation. See also the work of Melissa Steyn.

4 Both Ontario and the Northwest Territories acted quickly to harness diamond discoveries to provincial and territorial value-added beneficiation and job creation. According to Ontario's Ministry of Energy, Northern Development and Mines, "Under an agreement with the Ontario government, De Beers Canada ... is making 10 per cent of its annual rough diamond production from the Victor mine, by value, available for cutting and polishing activities in Ontario"; see Ontario, "Sudbury gives shine to Ontario diamonds," News release, Toronto, 6 April 2009, available online at https://news.ontario.ca/mndmf/en/2009/04/sudbury-gives-shine-to-ontario-diamonds-1.html, accessed 25 April 2017. The Northwest Territories does not specify a percentage, but does require all diamond producers to allocate "a portion of rough diamonds ... for manufacturing by Approved NWT Diamond Manufacturers"; see Northwest Territories, "Diamond Policy Framework," available online at https://www.iti.gov.nt.ca/sites/iti/files/2018_-_diamond_policy_framework_0.pdf, accessed 25 April 2017. In recent years, Botswana has also struck deals with De Beers to have diamonds cut and polished in-country; this has created 3,200 jobs for Botswana's citizens (Grynberg 2013).

5 On 12 January 2014, Indonesia's president ordered a ban on all exports of unprocessed minerals such as bauxite, nickel, tin, chromium, gold, and silver. These ores were to be processed in Indonesia. In January 2017 this ban was revised to allow limited exports of bauxite and nickel ores.

6 See, for example, Korinek (2015); OECD (2010).

7 See Engineers Without Borders Canada, "About Us," http://legacy.ewb.ca/en/whoweare/accountable/introduction.html

8 See Engineers Without Borders Canada, "Chapters," https://www.ewb.ca/en/chapters/, accessed 26 October 2018.

9 In making these observations, I draw on personal work experience with CUSO and the faith-based international development sector from 1982 to 2000. See also Barry-Shaw and Jay (2012); Ismail and Kamat (2018).

10 Shared Value Initiative (SVI and FSG 2014, 16) differentiates "activist NGOs" from "implementing NGOs," the latter being those that are "increasingly willing to engage with the extractive sector to promote economic development."

11 See Engineers Without Borders Canada, "Investing in Ventures," https://www.ewb.ca/ventures

12 Author's interview with key informant, 16 May 2016.

13 See the website at http://miningsharedvalue.org

14 Prospectors & Developers Association of Canada, "Integrating Local Content Regulations: A Win-Win for Communities and Companies?" Toronto, 2017.

15 Jeff Geipel, "Local Procurement: Benefits for Development and Mining Companies," PowerPoint presentation at PDAC, Toronto, March 2014, slide 14, available online at https://static1.squarespace.com/static/54d667e5e4b05b179814c788/t/55a55e3ce4b09a8bb04bab9c/1436900924331/EWB-PDAC+Convention+LP+Panel+Presentation+-+2014-03-02.pdf, accessed 21 March 2017.

16 See Devonshire Initiative, "Beyond Zero Harm Framework," available online at http://devonshireinitiative.org/beyond-zero-harm/, accessed 21 March 2017.

17 A graphic example of recent grassroots community resistance to a proposed mine is described by Pearce (2017).

18 Author's interview with key informant, 16 May 2016.

19 As an example of this sense of entitlement, see the comments of Robert Friedland, CEO of Ivanhoe Mines, concerning new opportunities in the Democratic Republic of Congo, in York (2017, B1–B2).

20 Burr (2014) notes that foreign mining firms in Mozambique tacitly supported more authoritarian parties because they were better able to work attractive deals with them.

21 A workshop hosted by the International Council on Mining and Metals at the PDAC conference in Toronto, 6 March 2017, was entitled "Where Is the Trust? Redefining Mining's Social Contract," available online at www.pdac.ca/convention/programming/csr-event-series/sessions/csr-event-series/where-is-the-trust-redefining-mining-s-social-contract, accessed 21 March 2017.

BIBLIOGRAPHY

Adanhounme, Armel Brice. 2011. "Corporate Social Responsibility in Postcolonial Africa: Another Civilizing Mission?" *Journal of Change Management* 11 (1): 91–110. https://doi.org/10.1080/14697017.2011.548945.

Ado, Rabiu. 2013. "Local Content Policy and the WTO Rules of Trade-Related Investment Measures (TRIMS): The Pros and Cons." *International Journal of Business and Management Studies* 2 (1): 137–46.

African Union. 2009. *Africa Mining Vision*. Addis Ababa: AU.

Banerjee, Subhabrata Bobby. 2008. "Corporate Social Responsibility: The Good, the Bad and the Ugly." *Critical Sociology* 34 (1): 51–79. https://doi.org/10.1177/0896920507084623.

Barry-Shaw, Nikolas, and Dru Oja Jay. 2012. *Paved with Good Intentions: Canada's Development NGOs from Idealism to Imperialism*. Halifax: Fernwood Press.

Bloch, Robin, and George Owusu. 2012. "Linkages in Ghana's Gold Mining Industry: Challenging the Enclave Thesis." *Resources Policy* 37 (4): 434–42. https://doi.org/10.1016/j.resourpol.2012.06.004.

Bocoum-Kaberuka, Brigitte. 1999. "The Significance of Mineral Processing Activities and Their Potential Impact on African Economic Development." *African Development Review* 11 (2): 233–64. https://doi.org/10.1111/1467-8268.00010.

Burr, Lars. 2014. *The Development of Natural Resource Linkages in Mozambique: The Ruling Elite Capture of New Economic Opportunities.* Copenhagen: Danish Institute for International Studies.

Campbell, Bonnie, ed. 2004. *Regulating Mining in Africa: For Whose Benefit?* Uppsala, Sweden: Nordiska Afrikainstitutet.

Campbell, Bonnie, ed. 2013. *Modes of Governance and Revenue Flows in African Mining.* New York: Palgrave Macmillan.

Farooki, Masuma. 2012. "The Diversification of the Global Mining Equipment Industry – Going New Places?" *Resources Policy* 37 (4): 417–24. https://doi.org/10.1016/j.resourpol.2012.06.006.

Ferguson, James. 2006. *Global Shadows: African in the Neoliberal World Order.* Durham, NC: Duke University Press.

Fessehaie, Judith. 2012. "What Determines the Breadth and Depth of Zambia's Backward Linkages to Copper Mining? The Role of Public Policy and Value Chain Dynamics." *Resources Policy* 37 (4): 443–51. https://doi.org/10.1016/j.resourpol.2012.06.003.

Finkelstein, Lawrence. 1995. "What Is Global Governance?" *Global Governance* 1 (3): 367–72. https://doi.org/10.1163/19426720-001-03-90000007.

Geipel, Jeff, and Kevin D'Souza. 2014. "Procurement as a Means for Mining Firms to Secure Their Social License to Operate." PowerPoint presentation, Toronto, 9 October. Available online at at http://www.ryerson.ca/content/dam/csrinstitute/key_dates/Procurement-Oct9-2014.pdf, accessed 10 April 2017.

Grynberg, Roman. 2013. "Some Like Them Rough: The Future of Diamond Beneficiation in Botswana." Discussion Paper 142. Maastricht, Netherlands: European Centre for Development Policy Management. Available online at http://ecdpm.org/wp-content/uploads/2013/11/DP-142-Future-of-Diamond-Beneficiation-Botswana-2013.pdf, accessed 26 April 2017.

Hansen, Michael W. 2014. "From Enclave to Linkage Economies? A Review of the Literature on Linkages Between Extractive Multinational Corporations and Local Industry in Africa." DIIS Working Paper 2. Copenhagen: Dansk Center for Internationale Studier og Menneskerettigheder.

Ismail, Feyzi, and Sangeeta Kamat. 2018. "NGOs, Social Movements and the Neoliberal State: Incorporation, Reinvention, Critique." *Critical Sociology* 44 (4–5): 569–77. https://doi.org/10.1177/0896920517749804.

Jacobs, John. 2013. "An Overview of Revenue Flows from the Mining Sector: Impacts, Debates and Policy Recommendations." In *Modes of Governance and Revenue Flows in African Mining*, edited by Bonnie Campbell, 16–46. New York: Palgrave Macmillan.

Kamola, Isaac. 2015. "Steve Biko and a Critique of Global Governance as White Liberalism." *African Identities* 13 (1): 62–76. https://doi.org/10.1080/14725843.2014.961281.

Kaplan, David. 2012. "South African Mining Equipment and Specialized Services: Technological Capacity, Export Performance and Policy." *Resources Policy* 37(4): 425–33. https://doi.org/10.1016/j.resourpol.2012.06.001.

Kapoor, Ilan. 2013. *Celebrity Humanitarianism: The Ideology of Global Charity.* New York: Routledge.

Korinek, Jane. 2015. "Export Restrictions in Raw Materials Trade: Facts, Fallacies and Better Practices." Prepared for UNCTAD Global Commodities Forum, 13–14 April. Available online at https://unctad.org/meetings/en/Presentation/SUC%20GCF2015%20Jane%20Korinek.pdf.

Lanning, Greg. 1979. *Africa Undermined: A History of the Mining Companies and the Underdevelopment of Africa.* With Marti Mueller. Harmondsworth, UK: Penguin.

Lydall, Marian. 2009. "Backward Linkage Development in the South African PGM Industry: A Case Study." *Resources Policy* 34 (3): 112–20. https://doi.org/10.1016/j.resourpol.2009.01.001.

MSV (Mining Shared Value). 2015. *Local Procurement and Public Reporting Trends across the Global Mining Industry: An Analysis of Company Reporting 2012–2013.* Toronto: Engineers Without Borders Canada.

MMSV and CIRDI (Mining Shared Value and Canadian International Resources and Development Institute). 2017. *The Relationship between Local Procurement Strategies of Mining Companies and Their Regulatory Environments: A Comparison of South Africa and Namibia.* Toronto: Engineers Without Borders Canada.

Mkandawire, Thandika, and Charles C. Soludo. 1999. *Our Continent, Our Future: African Perspectives on Structural Adjustment.* Dakar, Senegal: CODESRIA.

Morris, Mike, Raphael Kaplinsky, and David Kaplan. 2012. "'One Thing Leads to Another' – Commodities, Linkages and Industrial Development." *Resources Policy* 37 (4): 408–16. https://doi.org/10.1016/j.resourpol.2012.06.008.

Munshi, Debashish, and Priya Kurian. 2007. "The Case of the Subaltern Public: A Postcolonial Investigation of the Corporate Social Responsibility's (O)missions." In *The Debate over Corporate Social Responsibility*, edited by Steven May, George Cheney, and Juliet Roper, 438–47. Oxford: Oxford University Press.

Nwapi, Chilenye. 2016. "A Survey of the Literature on Local Content Policies in the Oil and Gas Industry in East Africa." SPP Technical Paper 9 (16). Calgary: University of Calgary, School of Public Policy.

OECD (Organisation for Economic Co-operation and Development). 2010. *The Economic Impact of Export Restrictions on Raw Materials.* Paris: OECD Publishing. http://dx.doi.org/10.1787/9789264096448-en.

OECD (Organisation for Economic Co-operation and Development). 2016. "Exports of Mineral Commodities: Contributing to Economy-Wide Growth?" Paris: OECD Trade Policy Note. Available online at http://www. oecd.org/tad/policynotes/exports-mineral-commodities-english.pdf, accessed 26 April 2017.

Otchia, Christian S. 2015. "Mining-Based Growth and Productive Transformation in the Democratic Republic of Congo: What Can an African Lion Learn from an Asian Tiger?" *Resources Policy* 45: 227–38. https://doi. org/10.1016/j.resourpol.2015.06.003.

Pearce, Fred. 2017. "Murder in Pondoland: How a Proposed Mine Brought Conflict to South Africa." *Guardian,* 28 March. Available online at https:// www.theguardian.com/environment/2017/mar/27/murder-pondoland-how-proposed-mine-brought-conflict-south-africa-activist-sikhosiphi-rhadebe?utm_source=esp&utm_medium=Email&utm_campaign=%20 Green+Light+2016&utm_term=219836&subid=12871078&CMP=EMCENVEML1631, accessed 26 April 2017.

Pedro, Antonio. 2016. "The Country Mining Vision: Towards a New Deal." *Mineral Economics* 29 (1): 15–22. https://doi.org/10.1007/s13563-015-0075-y.

Porter, Michael E., and Mark R. Kramer. 2011. "Creating Shared Value." *Harvard Business Review* (January–February). Available online at https://philoma.org/wp-content/uploads/docs/2013_2014_Valeur_actionnariale_a_partagee/Porter__Kramer_-_The_Big_Idea_Creating_Shared_Value_HBR.pdf.

Ramdoo, Isabelle. 2016. "Local Content Policies in Mineral-Rich Countries: An Overview." Discussion Paper 193. Maastricht, Netherlands: European Centre for Development Policy Management. Available online at https:// ecdpm.org/wp-content/uploads/ECDPM-Discussion-Paper-193-Local-Content-Policies-Mineral-Rich-Countries-2016.pdf.

Ramdoo, Isabelle, and San Bilal. 2014. "Extractive Resources for Development: Trade, Fiscal and Industrial Considerations." Discussion Paper 156. Maastricht, Netherlands: European Centre for Development Policy Management. Available online at http://ecdpm.org/wp-content/uploads/DP-156-Extractive-Resources-for-Development-2014.pdf.

Rosenau, James. 1995. "Governance in the Twenty-First Century." *Global Governance* 1 (1): 13–43. https://doi.org/10.1057/9780230245310_2.

SVI and FSG (Shared Value Initiative and Foundation Strategy Group). 2014. *Extracting with Purpose: Creating Shared Value in the Oil and Gas and Mining Sectors Companies and Communities*. New York: Foundation Strategy Group.

Strange, Susan. 1996. *The Retreat of the State: The Diffusion of Power in the World Economy*. Cambridge: Cambridge University Press.

Tanzania. 2017. Ministry of Energy and Minerals. "Export Ban of Metallic Mineral Concentrates and Ore." Press release, 3 March. Available online at http://extractives-baraza.com/media-center/news/2017/03/07/press-release-export-ban-of-metallic-mineral-concentrates-and-ore/, accessed 15 March 2017.

World Bank. 1992. *Strategy for African Mining*. Technical Paper 181. Washington, DC: World Bank Group.

Yachir, Faysal. 1988. *Mining in Africa Today: Strategies and Prospects*. New York: Zed Books.

York, Geoffrey. 2017. "Canadian Mining Companies Turn Bullish on Congo, Despite Its Violence." *Globe and Mail*, 20 March. Available online at https://www.theglobeandmail.com/report-on-business/international-business/canadian-mining-companies-lured-by-congos-mineral-wealth/article34344168/, accessed 26 April 2017.

8 Examining the Dynamics of Global Corporate Social Responsibility Frameworks and Canadian Mining Firms: Insights from Ghana and South Africa

Introduction

Over the past two decades, we have witnessed the proliferation of powerful non-state actors such as transnational corporations (TNCs) on the global stage (Coolidge, Seyle, and Weiss 2013; Jenkins 2013). Despite evidence pointing to the socio-economic contributions of TNCs, there have also been numerous reports of business complicity in human rights abuses in the context of globalization (Kobrin 2009; Orellana 2012; Payne and Pereira 2016; Wettstein 2009, 2012). As a result, global governance initiatives such as the Extractive Industries Transparency Initiative (EITI) and the Voluntary Principles on Security and Human Rights (VPs) have emerged to promote corporate social responsibility (CSR). The most recent and most authoritative global governance initiative that focuses on CSR and human rights is the United Nations Guiding Principles on Business and Human Rights (UNGPs), which rests on three principles: the state's duty to protect against human rights abuses by third parties such as firms; the responsibility of business to respect human rights; and greater access by victims to effective remedies (Ruggie 2011). The existence of inalienable human rights has been accepted by the 193-member countries of the United Nations in the 1948 Universal Declaration on Human Rights, but cases of human rights abuses still occur in the mining sectors of the Global South. Within the business literature, relatively modest attention has been paid to the role of global governance norms – and very little study of how such norms are diffused. While international relations (IR) scholarship tends to offer empirical analyses of the extent to which civil society organizations affect *large* firms in the national context, little attention has been given to their effect on *small* and *mid-sized* companies (Del Baldo 2012; Johnson 2015); Lyons, Bartlett, and McDonald 2016).

The above gap generates two main questions that guide this chapter: First, how do institutional dynamics in Ghana and South Africa facilitate (or hinder) the on-the-ground CSR performance of large, mid-tier, and junior Canadian firms in the mining sector? Second, what are the drivers of CSR commitments and/or reporting among these TNCs? This analysis is more important than ever, as research indicates that the extent to which firms *differ* in their organizational cultures and business ethics, and the extent to which they advance CSR (Matten and Crane 2005), matter for global governance discourse. In other words, examining variation in commitments to CSR based on firm *size* is vital given the emerging consensus in the IR literature on private actors as "global governors" (Avant, Finnemore, and Sell 2010; Büthe 2010). Overall, although there has been emphasis on the economic power of *large* transnational firms in the Global South, there is a dearth of research on the extent to which variation in the *size* of firms could affect security and human rights norms at the domestic level. It is therefore important to reflect on the mechanisms of norm operationalization at the domestic level vis-à-vis corporate actors.

When it comes to the domestic adoption of international norms, O'Faircheallaigh (2014) asserts that a key issue in the literature involves the question of how norms come to operate and influence domestic political systems through policies, legislation, and decisions. This is in line with Gurowitz's (1999, 416) assertion that "international norms can matter only when they are used domestically and they work their way into the political process." O'Faircheallaigh (2014) further contends that "corporate actors are *almost entirely absent* from the literature on domestic norm adoption" (158, emphasis added); however, firms are often featured as targets by social movement groups in the international norms literature (see also Haufler 2010; Keck and Sikkink 1998). It is also important to note the tendency to assume only global-to-local connections when examining norms (e.g., firms as norm takers). In practice, however, the activities of actors (such as firms) in a domestic context could also influence the policy attitudes of states in the international system through what is described as a "feedback loop" (O'Faircheallaigh 2014, 158).

In an article focusing on the Global South, Lyons, Bartlett, and McDonald (2016, 204) note that CSR discourse has focused primarily on the world's largest transnational firms, while "little is known about the meaning and practice of CSR in junior and mid-tier companies, and how this translates into a social licence to operate." Nevertheless, small and medium-sized firms form 90 per cent of the worldwide population of firms and employ more than 50 per cent of all labour in the private sector (United Nations 2002). Campbell (2006) also contends that it is unclear whether differences in CSR adoption are due to specific national institutions. It is therefore vital to examine the CSR practices of TNCs by considering institutional factors that hinder or enable CSR adoption across countries.

This chapter aims to contribute to the existing scholarly IR literature on global governance regimes in the mining sector and their influence on the CSR of Canadian TNCs operating in sub-Saharan Africa. I argue that, in order to understand how firms differ in their adoption of voluntary governance norms (specifically, the VPs and UNGPs), it is imperative *first* to examine the domestic *institutional* dynamics of where these firms operate. In other words, firms do not operate in a vacuum. As such, a study focusing on their CSR commitments and practices requires an understanding of institutional factors that could enable or constrain these firms as actors. I also argue that commitments to security and human rights norms and stakeholder approaches by large, mid-tier, and junior TNCs are influenced by visibility and legitimacy.

Multistakeholder Governance, Institutional Theory, and the VPs and UNGPs as Multistakeholder Governance Initiatives

Multistakeholder Governance Theory and Institutional Theory

Hemmati (2002, 2) defines "stakeholders as those who have an interest in a particular decision, either as individuals or representatives of a group. This includes people who influence a decision, or can influence it, as well as those affected by it." Furthermore, he asserts that "the term multi-stakeholder processes describe processes which aim to bring together all major stakeholders in a new form of communication, decision-finding (and possibly decision-making) on a particular issue" (2). These multistakeholder processes or initiatives are generally based on principles of accountability, transparency, and participation to ensure that diverse views are represented in decision-making processes, and are fertile grounds for multistakeholder governance – also known as "collaborative governance" (Huxham et al. 2000), "hybrid governance" (Risse 2004), or "polycentric governance" (Ruggie 2014). This form of governance promises to address more complex social problems than the traditional forms of governance through creative, innovative, and inclusive means. Dashwood and Puplampu (2015) describe multistakeholder partnership as a "round table" or "symposium" of interest groups and stakeholders. The aim of these partnerships is to take all the issues around a particular issue into discussion and to develop appropriate strategies that are inclusive. To be sure, these discussions give actors the opportunity to engage in constructive dialogue and decision making. They also help to break down barriers and tackle conflicting interests at the discussion table. For example, Pero and Smith (2014), examining the functioning of multisector dialogue in two rural regional natural resource management bodies in Queensland, Australia, conclude that such dialogue was instrumental in promoting greater acceptance of community-based natural resource governance by local people and by governments. In these cases, multistakeholder governance broke down traditional intra-commodity silos of dialogue, promoting not only a greater interdependency between rural sectors, but also common community values and norms.

Although the term *governance* remains contested, the Commission on Global Governance (1995, 5) defines it as: "the sum of the many ways individuals and institutions, public and private, manage their common affairs. It is a continuing process through which conflicting or diverse interests may be accommodated and cooperative action may be taken. It includes formal institutions and regimes empowered to enforce compliance, as well as informal arrangements that people and institutions either have agreed to or perceive to be in their interest." Similarly, Rosenau (1995, 14) argues that governance "encompasses the activities of governments, but it also includes the many other channels through which 'commands' flow in the form of goals framed, directives issued, and policies pursued." A common thread linking these definitions is a focus on collaboration among diverse actors to find solutions to problems. Central to this common thread is the vital role that international regimes or institutions – the collection of "principles, norms, rules and decision making procedures around which the expectations of authors converge in a particular issue area" Krasner (2012, 93) – play in enabling or constraining actors as they strive to address problems (North 1990).

This chapter also draws insights from institutional theory, which is particularly useful for understanding differences in corporate governance (Aguilera and Jackson 2003). Institutional perspectives examine the dynamics of stakeholder demands and legitimacy (Hooghiemestra 2000). To be more specific, companies want to be seen as legitimate actors among various stakeholders as a result of institutional pressures. Considering that social expectations to behave in a responsible fashion are driven by "soft" law mechanisms (Adeyeye 2011) such as the UNGPs and the VPs, institutional theory helps to highlight the conditions under which firms are able to "walk" their CSR "talk" in a particular context. Brammer, Jackson, and Matten (2012, 12) note that "in some instances, institutions may support a 'business case' for activities through which business lives up to these expectations – resulting in what (certainly in the management literature) is commonly referred to as CSR. But more often than not, business responds to these expectations by reflecting and shaping those wider institutions which govern the broader economic, social and political systems." Overall, institutional theory complements multistakeholder governance as it brings a robust understanding of context, rules, and norms that shape behaviour through strategic interactions and the inclusive participation of various actors.

The VPs and UNGPs as Multistakeholder Governance Initiatives

The Voluntary Principles on Security and Human Rights and UN Guiding Principles on Business and Human Rights are clearly multistakeholder governance initiatives. The VPs,[1] launched in 2000 with strong support from the US State Department and the UK Foreign Office, bring together extractive sector (mining and oil and gas) firms, governments, and NGOs to promote and maintain the safety and security of operations that are consistent with human rights. The key components of this voluntary initiative include comprehensive risk assessment with regard to security and human rights issues and engagement with private and public security forces. Today the VPs are widely supported by public, private, and civil sector members, demonstrating its multistakeholder nature. For instance, as of 1 May 2017, the membership of the initiative consisted of ten governments, twenty-nine companies, and eleven NGOs. Overall, the VPs offer a solid foundation for dialogue and creative partnerships among industry, government, and civil society.

Similar to the VPs, the foundation of the UNGPs was based on extensive pilot projects, research on legal issues, and broad consultations with diverse stakeholders. In a resolution endorsing the UNGPs, the Human Rights Council highlighted "the importance of multi-stakeholder dialogue and analysis to maintain and build on the results achieved to date and to inform further deliberations of the Human Rights Council on business and human rights" (United Nations General Assembly 2011, para. 5). The Council also established a multistakeholder Forum on Business and Human Rights, with the objective of promoting dialogue and cooperation on issues relating to business and human rights. As the most authoritative multistakeholder global governance framework, the UNGPs have influenced many stakeholders, including firms, investors, civil society organizations, governments, industry and professional associations, and international organizations (see Figure 8.1). For instance, some governments, especially in Europe, are in the process of creating National Action Plans to implement the UNGPs; others are pushing for legally binding mechanisms. For example, on 22 February 2017, France adopted a corporate duty of care law for parent and subcontracting companies.[2] This law was viewed as a historic step by French civil society groups. In March 2017 the African Union (AU), supported by the European Union, held a two-day validation workshop on the Draft AU Policy Framework on Human Rights and Business in Addis Ababa, Ethiopia, in order to influence businesses to become more responsive to business and human rights issues. The UNGPs have also influenced international organizations to align their business and

Figure 8.1. The UN Guiding Principles on Business and Human Rights as a Global Influencer

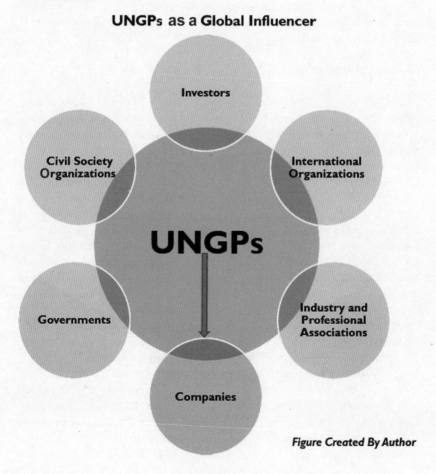

UNGPs as a Global Influencer

Investors

Civil Society Organizations

International Organizations

UNGPs

Governments

Industry and Professional Associations

Companies

Figure Created By Author

human rights policies. Professional associations such as the International Bar Association and Chartered Global Management Accountant have published guidance materials on the UNGPs to help their members incorporate them into their business practices. In Figure 8.1, the arrow is a depiction of the UNGPs and their influence on several stakeholders, with a particular focus on how the UNGPs (and VPs) influence companies.

Given the existence of these kinds of multistakeholder initiatives and principles, how are Canadian TNCs putting them into practice in their activities in the African mining sector? The next section looks specifically at Ghana and South Africa, two countries where Canadian gold-mining companies have a sizable presence. These two countries are also excellent candidates for comparative analysis as both are considered stable, resource-rich democracies with a long history of gold mining, and both have witnessed increased foreign investment in their extractive resource sector.

Ghana: Voluntary Initiatives in the Domestic Context

On 26–27 March 2014 the Swiss government hosted the Voluntary Principles on Security and Human Rights Initiative Annual Plenary Meeting in Montreux. It was during this meeting that Ghana announced its intention to join the VPs initiative pending parliamentary approval. Ghana joined the initiative in April 2014, the first (and *only*) African country to do so,[3] and a workshop was held to draw up an action plan for implementation.[4] The Ghanaian government, supported by the Commission on Human Rights and Administrative Justice, also held three workshops on the UNGPs.[5] Although no National Action Plan has actually yet been created, Ghana's efforts are commendable, its membership in the VPs and UNGPs workshops signalling a commitment to security and human rights norms. Even so, challenges continue to hinder the institutionalization of these voluntary CSR initiatives.

In November 2014 Global Rights Partners for Justice conducted a baseline study to determine the level of knowledge and degree of implementation of the VPs in Nigeria and Ghana (Global Rights Partners for Justice 2014). Survey data were requested from three key stakeholder groups – communities and civil society organizations, companies, and government bodies. Information from communities and civil society organizations was based on their perceptions of the penetration of the VPs. The study revealed that there was little awareness of the VPs due to limited engagement with them among stakeholders. Obviously, the lack of meaningful engagement has implications for the general level of awareness and productive debates regarding security, safety, risk assessments, and human rights violations.

Why there should be such limited engagement with the VPs among stakeholders in Ghana requires reflection on the historical context of mining in that country. More specifically, a focus on the regulatory context, neoliberal economic policies, and government-company-community relations can provide insight into a relationship characterized by a top-down approach of centralization and mistrust. Garvin et al. (2009) provide a good historical overview of the post-independence mining industry. To summarize, following independence in 1957, Ghana underwent a nationalization exercise, and mines primarily became state owned. Between 1960 and 1985, however, there was a decline in output in the mineral sector due to production, technical, and financial constraints, and state-owned companies could not compete globally with their counterparts. As a result, Ghana sought relief from the World Bank and the International Monetary Fund through structural adjustment policies (SAPs), leading to a set of economic and social policies that had positive and negative outcomes. During the SAPs period, the mining sector received considerable attention due to its importance to the national economy. In order to bolster investment and development, "a set of regulatory institutions and a new legal framework was initiated in 1986 which streamlined the mineral rights licencing procedures and gave mining companies, among other things, general tax allowances, exemption from customs duties, a rebate on royalties, and fewer foreign ownership restrictions" (Garvin et al. 2009, 572). The establishment of these regulatory institutions was partly responsible for the country's rapid and significant economic growth between 1983 and 1998, resulting in the substantial growth in export earnings for the national government, particularly from gold and diamonds. Overall, despite trade liberalization and economic growth, control over mineral resource development and the distribution of revenues from mines in Ghana remains *highly centralized*, favouring the national government. For instance, Akabzaa and Darimani (2001) assert that applications for an exploration or mining licence go through a series of centralized committees and government agencies relating to mining. Moreover, discussions relating to the mineral sector generally take place among national agencies that engage only minimally with local communities and their leaders (Garvin et al. 2009). When communities are informed of a potential development, it is usually by the mining companies themselves, rather than by national agencies or actors. Considering that there are generally pre-existing tensions between transnational mining companies and local community members who mostly focus on small-scale mining, these dynamics exacerbate the potential for conflict in local communities when it comes to the state-led implementation of global governance frameworks such as the VPs and UNGPs. For example, there are ongoing debates about the impact of illegal small-scale mining (referred to as *galamsey*); see, for example, Grant et al. (2013); Grant, Mitchell, and Nyame (2011); Nyame et al. (2009); Nyame and Grant (2012, 2014). Recently, concerns have been raised about the influx of illegal Chinese gold miners (see Aidoo 2016; Hilson, Hilson, and Adu-Darko 2014), resulting in the mechanization of the small-scale mining sector and violent clashes with community members. In addition, wider public exposure to the devastating environmental and socio-economic effects of illegal small-scale mining has resulted in media coalitions and campaigns (e.g., #StopGalamsey-Now) to curb the issue.[6] These efforts have led to support from diverse stakeholders, including government officials, chiefs, religious leaders, and teachers. In the context of transnational mining firms, *galamsey* operations continue to pose significant threats to assets, security, and human rights. However, the drive to engage with key actors through multistakeholder dialogue is promising.

In terms of the dynamics of *state-business relations* and implications for policy making, Handley (2008) examines the mineral resources sectors in four African countries, including Ghana and South Africa, emphasizing the importance of "political and economic capacity to constructively engage the state in economic policy issues" (259). She notes that state-business relations in Ghana depict the characteristics of a neo-patrimonial state, in which a weak business community's economic growth is dependent on personal ties to the political leadership, and, further, that Ghana inherited a weak, virtually non-existent business community post-independence. From an analytical standpoint, this is arguably a key reason the national government is able to make autonomous decisions regarding participation in global CSR initiatives without the consent of regional or local actors. In other words, in Ghana, constructive contestation is weak when it comes to the implications of voluntary global CSR initiatives, since business elites depend on the patronage of the state to the extent that they have little influence in decision making. Furthermore, attracting foreign direct investment in the mining sector is a major motivator for the government to adopt these initiatives. International investors are likely to see the country in a favourable light, and the state is most likely to avoid international or domestic pressure from civil society organizations. In short, the adoption or institutionalization of global CSR initiatives at the domestic level helps to attract foreign direct investment and secure social legitimacy among stakeholders.

To address these challenges and to ensure adequate and trustworthy engagement with diverse stakeholders, the Ghanaian government needs to reconsider current institutional arrangements regarding security and human rights and the effects of mining on local communities. Ideally, a robust degree of state-community-company engagement prior to making decisions about these global initiatives would help understand local issues of private and public security and risk management for companies. Overall, multistakeholder governance, an approach that promises collaboration and inclusion, is essential for generating trust among actors and for creating space for meaningful public debates and conflict resolution.

South Africa: Voluntary Initiatives in the Domestic Context

A 2016 report by the Centre for Human Rights at the University of Pretoria highlights that "South Africa has been quiet on matters involving soft law, especially in the context of business and human rights ... While many States have openly expressed support for the ... UNGPs, the South African government is currently prioritizing the process around a treaty on business and human rights at the UN level" (Loots 2016, 2). As a 2014 report by the Dutch government notes, South Africa has been a priority country since the 2012 March Annual Plenary Meeting of the VPs, but there has been limited outreach to the South African government (Netherlands 2015). Overall, the South African government has been reluctant to discuss the VPs with all VP members, even though the UK government, which chaired the VPs in 2014, conducted outreach efforts.

Having experienced devastating conflicts in the mining sector (e.g., the Marikana tragedy in 2012) and having assumed a role as the "proxy voice" for Africa on international matters, South Africa might be assumed to be a signatory to the VPs, but this is not in fact the case, at least from a national-level perspective. From an institutional perspective, the short answer to this puzzle is that regulations are already stringent (most of them are legally binding) for corporate social investments in the mining sector. As such, there is no appetite for voluntary CSR initiatives focusing on security and human rights.

To elaborate on why the South African government is hesitant about voluntary ("soft law") mechanisms but pushing for a treaty ("hard law") on business and human rights, one needs to reflect on the institutional context and take historical influences into account. When it comes to the institutional context, it is important to note that, even though the preamble of the Mineral and Petroleum Resources Development Act (2002) acknowledges that mineral and petroleum resources belong to the whole nation, the state serves as the sole custodian of these resources. As regulator, the state has the power to award mining rights to companies, and the promotion of mineral rights occurs through the "use it or lose it" principle (Cawood 2004, 55). The idea behind this principle is to encourage the exploitation of mineral resources for the benefit of all members of society, especially historically disadvantaged South Africans. Furthermore, to address the long history of inequality in the mineral sector and to ensure that mine workers and mining communities benefit from resources, mining companies are required to submit legally binding social and labour plans as part of their application for mining rights. Other regulatory mechanisms in place to promote good corporate governance include the Socially Responsible Investment Index for all companies listed on the Johannesburg Stock Exchange, and voluntary rules known as the King Code "Report on Corporate Governance" (see also Chapter 9, in this volume). For instance, a key emphasis of King Code IV, released in 2016, is a stakeholder approach that is inclusive in nature. It is fair to state that regulatory mechanisms that require social investments in the mineral sector complement the broad human rights approach of the bill of rights in the South African constitution.

As for the relationship among stakeholders in the mineral sector, a deep sense of mistrust exists, especially between state and business actors. This can be attributed to South Africa's historical context, in which corporations, including mining firms, violated human rights during the apartheid era. Hönke and colleagues (2008) provide a compelling historical account of South Africa's corporate social responsibility strategies. Like other accounts of South Africa's socio-economic history, they posit that the current discourse on corporate responsibility and the interaction of various actors in the South African context is closely related to the role of business during the apartheid era: "Dominated by white Afrikaner business, the South African corporate sector during apartheid was based on an exploitative as well as a *highly segregated system of forced labour*, which initially was supported by foreign investment and later subject to trade sanctions in the wake of South African isolationism" (Hönke et al. 2008, 10, emphasis added). To be clear, mining simply trumped surface land rights. This context gave mining companies tremendous legal power to acquire mineral rights over agricultural lands and environmentally sensitive communal and tribal areas. Natural resources were simply exploited without paying attention to social and environmental effects or sustainable practices.

Hönke et al. (2008) also note that, during South Africa's period of transition to democracy, businesses were "extremely apprehensive" about large-scale national redistribution measures that might bring radical economic change. As such, they adopted effective monitoring and lobbying practices to influence the government. Even though businesses, especially mining companies, have been influential in many ways, they have never truly been held responsible for complicity in human rights abuses or any other malpractice under the official reconciliation process. This has created an atmosphere of mistrust among various stakeholders in the mining industry, resulting in several regulatory frameworks to hold companies accountable for their operations. This sense of mistrust has also contributed to the reason the state is hesitant to promote or adopt *voluntary* ("soft law") mechanisms.

Handley (2008, 243) notes that South Africa exhibits the characteristics of "constructive contestation," arguing that economic success in South Africa is based on the way ethnicity "historically separated out" the political and economic elites. Unlike in Ghana, this separation allowed for "contestation" between the business class and the state, leading to efficient and effective economic decision making. Similar to the views of Hönke et al. (2008), Handley also notes that "there is little doubt that the business community in South Africa was powerful, diversified, well institutionalized, and willing to engage with government" (Handley 2008, 173), and points out that, despite the structural strength of business, it was *constrained* by its "ethnic profile and political past" – specifically, its association with apartheid. This connection has affected the broader political legitimacy of the business community.

Today's South Africa faces the challenge of redressing years of institutionalized inequality. Redistributive policies, such as Black economic empowerment, have been established to address the historical legacy of apartheid. Even so, South Africa continues to be under pressure to attract foreign direct investment to the mining industry and to be competitive as a global player. One key challenge to attracting foreign direct investment remains mining-related violence.[7] Labour leaders are frequently accused of being authoritarian, rather than fully engaging all members in decision-making processes. Intense competitions between rival unions also make bargaining processes more challenging and lead to issues of violence in the mining sector. The government has intervened in mining strikes and protests by using the military and the police, and has often blamed the mining companies for these issues. As Hönke et al. (2008) show, at first glance South Africa has surprisingly far-reaching and well-developed environmental legislation, but it has limited capacity in terms of implementation and enforcement. For instance, crime and illegal mining – "*zama zama*" (see Mills 2016) – have led to the growth of the private security industry, and some of these security companies have become key suppliers of services to the mining industry. Despite these challenges, the South African Human Rights Commission has used multistakeholder dialogues to promote collaboration among government, civil society, and mining companies. In one example, an investigative hearing sought the perspectives of all actors to address challenges facing unregulated artisanal mining. The commission has also been a strong advocate of security and human rights initiatives in the South African context (South African Human Rights Commission n.d.). Although it is generally difficult to reach a consensus when bringing diverse stakeholders together, it is important for initiating critical debates, including marginalized voices in discussions, building trust among actors, and securing social legitimacy.

The above sections on Ghana and South Africa focused on the level of commitment to the VPs and UNGPs, and institutional and multi-stakeholder governance dynamics. The subsequent section delves into the level of commitment to security and human rights policies and multi-stakeholder approaches by Canadian firms. More specifically, the section examines.

Canadian Mining Firms in Ghana and South Africa: Commitment to Security and Human Rights Policies and Multistakeholder Approaches

To what extent are large, mid-tier, and junior Canadian mining firms in Ghana and South Africa committed to security and human rights norms? In this section, I focus on six Canadian gold-mining firms: one large, two mid-tier, and three junior (Table 8.1).

Table 8.1. Overview of Selected Canadian Gold-Mining Firms in Ghana and South Africa

Host State	Firm	Size	Assets
Ghana	Kinross Gold	large (among "Big Ten" in world)	over $1 billion
	Golden Star Resources	mid-tier	$100 million–$500 million
	Castle Peak Mining Ltd.	junior	$5 million–$25 million
South Africa	Superior Mining International	junior	under $5 million
	Caledonia Mining Corporation Plc	mid-tier	$25 million–$100 million
	Giyani Gold	junior	under $5 million

Source: Author's compilation based on data from the System for Electronic Document Analysis and Retrieval (SEDAR), the electronic filing system for the disclosure of . documents of public companies and mutual funds across Canada.

Large Firms

As indicated in Table 8.1, Kinross (with its Chirano mine in Ghana) is one of the largest mining companies in the world. It has made commitments to security and human rights policies in its reports; for instance, the company supports both the VPs and the UNGPs. When it comes to the VPs, the company has also implemented a Human Rights Adherence and Verification Program. This is to ensure that security personnel and site management personnel are consistently compliant with the VPs. Turning to the UNGPs, the company's website states that: "Kinross uses the United Nations Guiding Principles for Business and Human Rights to help identify priorities based upon the nature of our operations, the context of the host countries where we operate, and the list of human rights as defined by the Universal Declaration of Human Rights, International Labour Organization Core Conventions, Convention on Economic Social and Cultural Rights, and Convention on Civil and Political Rights" (Kinross n.d). A key observation from a multistakeholder perspective is that the company also has a long list of stakeholders with which it interacts in the countries where it operates (Kinross 2013). A 2013 company report makes it quite clear that the company is multistakeholder driven, noting, for example, that, "across all Kinross sites, we engaged with over 84,000 stakeholders in 2013 and reviewed a total of 27 community grievances" (Kinross 2013, 12). In that report, the company also raised specific stakeholder concerns and how it responded to them.

Apart from Ivanhoe Mines Ltd.'s platreef project – a tier one palladium-platinum-nickel-copper-gold-rhodium mine development project – no large Canadian gold-mining firm operates in South Africa, but insights in that context can be drawn from a major non-Canadian firm, Anglogold Ashanti, which has operations in both Ghana and South Africa. Interviews with Anglogold Ashanti's senior executives focusing on security and sustainability confirmed that the company is driven by its value-based systems and built-in multistakeholder mechanisms to implement security and human rights initiatives. For example, Anglogold Ashanti is a signatory to the VPs, and it supports the UNGPs. Similar to Kinross, Anglogold Ashanti's stakeholder approach is extensive. For instance, the company's 2015–16 community report reveals a broad level of consultation with diverse internal and external stakeholders.

The reality is that mining is a controversial business. As such, the operations of mining firms are generally under scrutiny. The implications of this is that mining firms must gain legitimacy in the contexts in which they operate. Deegan, Rankin, and Tobin (2002) and Slack (2012) note that the bigger an industry's effect in a particular or global context and the more vulnerable it is to criticism, the more likely that it will use CSR as a means to demonstrate *legitimacy*. This assertion confirms the detail-oriented nature of the reports released by Kinross, including emphasis on Ghana and specific stakeholders. Furthermore, large firms with a high public profile are *visible* to powerful external stakeholders (Crane et al. 2008) – visibility that serves as an incentive to report on global CSR initiatives. Moreover, large firms have the personnel to deliver on CSR reporting and signal legitimacy to their stakeholders, although further research might reveal that the bureaucratic nature of large firms tends to delay the training of employees on these policies and procedures.

Mid-Tier Firms

As Table 8.1 shows, Golden Star Resources (Ghana) and Caledonia Mining Corporation (South Africa) are mid-tier Canadian firms. Golden Star Resources outlines on its website that it supports the VPs and UNGPs, stating that "the Guiding Principles and the Voluntary Principles both help ensure that we do not negatively impact the human rights of our stakeholders. At the same time, our operations and corporate responsibility initiatives can also have a positive impact on human rights" (Golden Star Resources 2015, 18). Although the company engages in some other forms of CSR initiatives that can be seen as philanthropy, there seems to be a clear commitment to security and human rights norms. Reports of Caledonia Mining Corporation, in contrast, largely target investors. They simply highlight relevant trends and the company's position, and there is less or no emphasis on security and human rights issues. In the South African context, this implies that mid-tier companies find it difficult to keep up with the stringent regulatory environment and key challenges outlined in the minerals sector.

Although large firms have greater visibility, mid-tier firms clearly are also driven to gain legitimacy where they operate, as evident in their support of global CSR initiatives. Their CSR reporting, however, seems to aim at reassuring specific external stakeholders, including investors and the media. This demonstrates that visibility serves as a driver in reporting on global CSR norms. Moreover, mid-tier firms give less attention to the multiplicity of stakeholders in the mining industry – although this is not surprising, as mid-tier firms are generally at the production stage and are driven to meet certain stakeholder needs that are quite different from those of large firms that might be operating for several years.

Junior Firms

As Table 8.1 shows, three junior Canadian mining firms operating in Africa are Castle Peak Mining (Ghana), Superior Mining International (South Africa), and Giyani Gold (South Africa). Unlike a large or mid-tier mining company that typically would have a mining operation in place (mineral production), a junior mining company does not own an operation. Instead a junior mining company is generally an exploration company searching for new mineral deposits; it is neither a producing company nor the recipient of significant income from production. Due to the scarcity of public capital for exploration companies and the high risk of failure, the websites of these companies focus heavily on investor-related information, with little or no reference to issues such as security and human rights. Both Giyani Gold and Superior Mining International have a lot of information targeting investors, while Castle Peak's website notes that the company is "a proud supporter" of World Malaria Day and the Foundation for African Children's Education.[8]

One could argue that it is reasonable for junior mining firms not to have committed to the VPs and UNGPs, particularly firms that have not yet started production. It is possible that they have internal documents demonstrating these norms, but are not willing to make them public until they reach a point of production. Meyer and Rowan (1977) proposed that, although organizations are compelled to adopt particular practices in order to demonstrate legitimacy, it can be expensive or inefficient for organizations to make major changes to their underlying business operations to improve their social or environmental performance. This is applicable to junior mining firms, as they consider public reporting quite costly. In an interview, however, a senior executive in the South African gold-mining industry argued that "security and human rights initiatives can be done at a *minimum* cost ... Not everything costs money, so if you are a junior player, begin the conversation at the top and make a commitment to these initiatives based on your value system."[9]

Junior mining firms are more likely to take opportunistic approaches (e.g., short-term initiatives) to enhance their legitimacy in the communities in which they conduct their exploration activities. Moreover, given that junior firms are not as visible as the large and mid-tier firms, they are subject to less criticism. Hence, there is less motivation to declare publicly their commitments to security and human rights norms. Table 8.2 summarizes the discussion on the commitment to security and human rights policies and the stakeholder approaches of firms of different sizes.

Table 8.2. Summary of Firms' Commitment to Security and Human Rights Policies and Stakeholder Approaches

Company	UNGPs Support?	VPs Support?	Public Human Rights and Security Policy?	Stakeholder Approach	Size, Visibility, Legitimacy
Kinross Gold (large)	yes	yes	yes	very broad + holistic	visibility + vulnerability = high
Golden Star Resources (mid-tier)	yes	yes	yes	limited stakeholders + reassurance	visibility + vulnerability = medium
Caledonia Mining Corp. (mid-tier)	N/A	N/A	unavailable	limited stakeholders + reassurance	
Castle Peak (junior)	N/A	N/A	N/A	very limited – investor driven	visibility + vulnerability = low
Superior Mining International (junior)	N/A	N/A	N/A	very limited – investor driven	
Giyani Gold (junior)	N/A	N/A	N/A	very limited – investor driven	

Source: Author's compilation from publicly available reports and SEDAR.

Concluding Remarks

Using multistakeholder governance and institutional theories, this chapter has examined the institutional dynamics in Ghana and South Africa that facilitate (or hinder) *voluntary* security and human rights initiatives (VPs) and the drivers of CSR commitments and/or stakeholder reporting approaches of large, mid-tier, and junior Canadian TNCs. I argued that, in order to understand how firms differ in their commitment to voluntary governance norms, it is imperative first to examine the domestic *institutional* dynamics of the countries in which these firms operate. In both Ghana and South Africa, mineral rights are vested in the state and the degree of centralization is quite high, but they differ in the national level of commitment to voluntary security and human rights norms in the mineral sector. Ghana, depicting the characteristics of the neo-patrimonial state and demonstrating a high level of centralization, has made efforts to embrace voluntary initiatives – indeed, it is the only African government participant of the VPs. South Africa, characterized by constructive contestation, has been hesitant about voluntary ("soft law") mechanisms, but has made efforts at the international level towards a treaty ("hard law") on business and human rights. A key reason for South Africa's reluctance to engage with voluntary initiatives is that its regulations are already stringent based on historical experiences in the mineral sector – a legacy of apartheid. In general, these institutional contexts shed some light on why Canadian TNCs in the Ghanaian gold-mining sector are in a better position to demonstrate commitment to voluntary initiatives on security and human rights than those operating in South Africa. Unlike in Ghana, the complex regulatory landscape in South Africa poses several challenges, so firms must strive to keep their mining rights and adhere to corporate governance initiatives through both binding and non-binding mechanisms.

I further argued that commitment to security and human rights norms (the VPs and UNGPs) and stakeholder approaches by large, mid-tier, and junior TNCs is influenced by visibility and legitimacy. As evident in the analyses presented in Table 8.2, domestic context and firm size influence the dynamics of legitimacy, stakeholder approaches, and public commitment to voluntary security and human rights norms. Large and mid-tier firms are more visible and subject to more intense scrutiny than are junior mining firms. As a result, large firms tend to take broad, holistic approaches to their stakeholder engagements and interactions, while mid-tier firms focus mostly on their investors and the media as stakeholders in committing to security and human rights norms – a finding consistent with the view that the greater the scrutiny of a company's activities, the more likely it is to conform with industry norms in order to appear legitimate (Campbell 2006; DiMaggio and Powell 1983). Junior mining companies, in contrast, are less visible and focus solely on their investors during their exploration stage. As such, they have little public commitment to security and human rights norms, and are likely to see less value in reporting on these norms as the cost of doing so would take away from their exploration budgets. Spence (2004) notes, however, that small and mid-sized firms might have informal reporting mechanisms that focus on face-to-face interactions, rather than formal written documents that are made public, an observation that suggests that the drivers of commitment to global CSR initiatives are more nuanced and more complex than is generally thought (Lyons, Bartlett, and McDonald 2016).

NOTES

1 See the website at https://www.voluntaryprinciples.org/
2 "France Adopts Corporate Duty of Care Law," Friends of the Earth International, 22 February 2017, available online at https://www.foei.org/press/france-adopts-corporate-duty-care-law, accessed 27 February 2017.
3 "The Voluntary Principles on Security and Human Rights Initiative Welcomes Ghana," Business and Human Rights Resource Centre, 3 April 2014, available online at https://business-humanrights.org/en/the-voluntary-principles-on-security-and-human-rights-initiative-welcomes-ghana, accessed 10 January 2017.
4 "Ghana to Implement Voluntary Principles," *Ghana Business News*, 24 July 2015, available online at https://www.ghanabusinessnews.com/2015/07/24/ghana-to-implement-voluntary-principles/, accessed 10 January 2017.
5 "Workshop on the United Nations Guiding Principles ends," *Modern Ghana*, 14 July 2014, available online at https://www.modernghana.com/news/556108/workshop-on-the-united-nations-guiding-principles-ends.html, accessed 10 January 2017.
6 "Ghana at War with Chinese 'Economic Guerrillas' – Prof Martey." *New Statesman*, 10 April 2017. Available online at http://www.thestatesmanonline.com/index.php/news/3360-ghana-at-war-with-chinese-economic-guerrillas-prof-martey, accessed 12 April 2017.
7 "South Africa Rape: 'Shocking' Levels of Violence in Mining Area." *BBC News*, 16 August 2016, available online at https://www.bbc.com/news/world-africa-37097941, accessed 16 March 2017.
8 Castle Peak Mining. "Social Responsibility," available online at https://castlepeakmining.com/corporate/social-responsibility, accessed 10 January 2017.
9 Author's interview with senior corporate executive (global security), Johannesburg, South Africa, 27 March 2017.

BIBLIOGRAPHY

Adeyeye. Adefolake. 2011. "The Role of Global Governance in CSR." *Santa Clara Journal of International Law* 9 (1): 147–68. https://digitalcommons.law.scu.edu/scujil/vol9/iss1/5
Aguilera, Ruth V., and Gregory Jackson. 2003. "The Cross-National Diversity of Corporate Governance: Dimensions and Determinants." *Academy of Management Review* 28 (3): 447–65. https://doi.org/10.2307/30040732
Aidoo, Richard. 2016. "The Political Economy of Galamsey and Anti-Chinese Sentiment in Ghana." *African Studies Quarterly* 16 (3/4): 55–72. https://doi.org/10.2307/30040732

Akabzaa, Thomas, and Abdulai Darimani. 2001. *The Impact of Mining Sector Investment: A Study of the Tarkwa Mining Region*. Draft Report. Accra, Ghana: Structural Adjustment Participatory Review International Network.

Avant, Deborah, Martha Finnemore, and Susan K. Sell. 2010. "Who Governs the Globe?" In *Who Governs the Globe?* edited by Deborah Avant, Martha Finnemore, and Susan K. Sell, 1–31. Cambridge: Cambridge University Press.

Brammer, Stephen, Gregory Jackson, and Dirk Matten. 2012. "Corporate Social Responsibility and Institutional Theory: New Perspectives on Private Governance." *Socio-Economic Review* 10 (1): 3–28. https://doi.org/10.1093/ser/mwr030

Büthe, Tim. 2010. "Global Private Politics: A Research Agenda." *Business and Politics* 12 (3): 1–24. https://doi.org/10.2202/1469-3569.1345

Campbell, John L. 2006. "Institutional Analysis and the Paradox of Corporate Social Responsibility." *American Behavioural Scientist* 49 (7): 925–38. https://doi.org/10.1177/0002764205285172

Cawood, Frederick T. 2004. "The Mineral and Petroleum Resources Development Act of 2002: A Paradigm Shift in Mineral Policy in South Africa." *Journal of the South African Institute of Mining and Metallurgy* 104 (1): 53–64. https://www.saimm.co.za/Journal/v104n01p053.pdf

Commission on Global Governance. 1995. *Our Global Neighbourhood*. Oxford: Oxford University Press.

Coolidge, Kelsey, Conor Seyle, and Thomas G. Weiss. 2013. *The Rise of Non-State Actors in Global Governance: Opportunities and Limitations*. One Earth Future Foundation. https://doi.org/10.18289/OEF.2013.003

Crane, Andrew, Dirk Matten, Abigail McWilliams, Jeremy Moon, and Donald S. Siegel. 2008. "The Corporate Social Responsibility Agenda." In *The Oxford Handbook of Corporate Social Responsibility*, edited by Andrew Crane, Dirk Matten, Abigail McWilliams, Jeremy Moon, and Donald S. Siegel, 3–15. New York: Oxford University Press.

Dashwood, Hevina S., and Bill Buenar Puplampu. 2015. "Multi-Stakeholder Partnerships in Mining: From Engagement to Development in Ghana." In *New Approaches to the Governance of Natural Resources: Insights from Africa*, edited by J. Andrew Grant, W.R. Nadège Compaoré, and Matthew I. Mitchell, 131–51. London: Palgrave Macmillan.

Del Baldo, Mara. 2012. "Corporate Social Responsibility and Corporate Governance in Italian SMEs: The Experience of Some 'Spirited Businesses'." *Journal of Management and Governance* 16 (1): 1–36. https://doi.org/10.1007/s10997-009-9127-4

Deegan, Craig, Michaela Rankin, and John Tobin. 2002. "An Examination of the Corporate Social and Environmental Disclosures of BHP from 1983–1997: A Test of Legitimacy Theory." *Accounting Auditing and Accountability Journal* 15 (3): 312–43. http://dx.doi.org/10.1108/09513570210435861

DiMaggio, Paul J., and Walter W. Powell. 1983. "The Iron Cage Revisited: Institutional Isomorphism and Collective Rationality in Organizational Fields." *American Sociological Review* 48 (2): 147–60. http://dx.doi.org/10.2307/2095101.

Garvin, Theresa, Tara K. McGee, Karen E. Smoyer-Tomic, and Emmanuel Ato Aubynn. 2009. "Community-Company Relations in Gold Mining in Ghana." *Journal of Environmental Management* 90 (1): 571–86. https://doi.org/10.1016/j.jenvman.2007.12.014

Global Rights Partners for Justice. 2014. "Improving Extractive Industry Governance: Implementing the Voluntary Principles to Promote Human Rights in Nigeria and Ghana." Available online at www.voluntaryprinciples.org/wp-content/uploads/2015/01/Global-Rights-VPs-Baseline-Study-Nigeria-Ghana-Final-2014.pdf, accessed 10 December 2016.

Golden Star Resources. 2015. "2015 Corporate Responsibility Report." Available online at https://s1.q4cdn.com/789791377/files/doc_downloads/CSR/Final-Golden-Star-CR-Report-2015__Web-Spreads.pdf, accessed 16 December 2016.

Grant, J. Andrew, Matthew I. Mitchell, and Frank K. Nyame. 2011. "New Regionalisms, Micro-Regionalisms, and the Migration-Conflict Nexus: Evidence from Natural Resource Sectors in West Africa." In *The Ashgate Research Companion to Regionalisms*, edited by Timothy M. Shaw, J. Andrew Grant, and Scarlett Cornelissen, 375–96. Aldershot, UK: Ashgate.

Grant, J. Andrew, Matthew I. Mitchell, Frank K. Nyame, and Natalia Yakovleva. 2013. "Micro-Regionalisms, Information and Communication Technologies, and Migration in West Africa: A Comparative Analysis of Ghana's Diamond, Cocoa, and Gold Sectors." In *Mapping Agency: Comparing Regionalisms in Africa*, edited by Ulrike Lorenz-Carl and Martin Rempe, 149–74. Aldershot, UK: Ashgate.

Gurowitz, Amy. 1999. "Mobilizing International Norms: Domestic Actors, Immigrants and the Japanese State." *World Politics* 51 (3): 413–45. https://doi.org/10.1017/s0043887100009138

Handley, Antionette. 2008. *Business and the State in Africa: Economic Policy-Making in the Neo-Liberal Era*. Cambridge: Cambridge University Press.

Haufler, Virginia. 2010. "Corporations in Zones of Conflict: Issues, Actors, and Institutions." In *Who Governs the Globe?* edited by Deborah D. Avant, Martha Finnemore, and Susan K. Sell, 102–31. Cambridge: Cambridge University Press.

Hemmati, Minu. 2002. *Multi-stakeholder Processes for Governance and Sustainability: Beyond Deadlock and Conflict*. Hoboken, NJ: Taylor and Francis.

Hilson, Gavin, Abigail Hilson, and Eunice Adu-Darko. 2014. "Chinese Participation in Ghana's Informal Gold Mining Economy: Drivers,

Implications and Clarifications." *Journal of Rural Studies* 34: 292–303. https://doi.org/10.1016/j.jrurstud.2014.03.001

Hönke, Jana, Nicole Kranz, Tanja A. Börzel, and Adrienne Héritier. 2008. "Fostering Environmental Regulation? Corporate Social Responsibility in Countries with Weak Regulatory Capacities – The Case of South Africa." SFB-Governance Working Chapter Series 9. Berlin: DFG Research Center.

Hooghiemstra, Reggy. 2000. "Corporate Communication and Impression Management: New Perspectives Why Companies Engage in Corporate Social Reporting." *Journal of Business Ethics* 27(1–2): 55–68. https://doi.org/10.1023/a:1006400707757

Huxham, Chris, Siv Vangen, Christine Huxham, and Colin Eden. 2000. "The Challenge of Collaborative Governance." *Public Management Review* 2 (3): 337–58. https://doi.org/10.1080/14719030000000021

Jenkins, Rhys. 2013. *Transnational Corporations and Uneven Development: The Internationalization of Capital and the Third World*. New York: Routledge.

Johnson, Matthew P. 2015. "Sustainability Management and Small and Medium-Sized Enterprises: Managers' Awareness and Implementation of Innovative Tools." *Corporate Social Responsibility and Environmental Management* 22: 271–85. https://doi.org/10.1002/csr.1343

Keck, Margaret E., and Kathryn Sikkink. 1998. *Activists beyond Borders: Advocacy Networks in International Politics*. Ithaca, NY: Cornell University Press.

Kinross. 2013. "Corporate Responsibility Summary Report." Available online at http://2013corporateresponsibilityreport.kinross.com/files/8914/0587/8867/Kinross_2013_CR_Summary_Report.pdf, accessed 12 December 2016.

Kinross. n.d. "Assessing Our Policy Framework." Available online at http://2013corporateresponsibilityreport.kinross.com/our-approach-responsible-mining/human-rights/assessing-our-policy-framework/, accessed 10 January 2017.

Kobrin, Stephen J. 2009. "Private Political Authority and Public Responsibility: Transnational Politics, Transnational Firms and Human Rights." *Business Ethics Quarterly* 19 (3): 349–74. https://doi.org/10.5840/beq200919321

Krasner, Stephen D. 2012. "Structural Causes and Consequences of International Regimes: Regimes as Intervening Variables." *Revista de sociologia e política* 20 (42): 93–110. https://doi.org/10.1590/s0104-44782012000200008

Loots, Joshua. 2016. "Shadow" National Baseline Assessment of Current Implementation of Business and Human Rights Frameworks: South Africa. Pretoria: University of Pretoria, Centre for Human Rights and International Corporate Accountability Roundtable. Available online at https://mk0globalnapshvllfq4.kinstacdn.com/wp-content/uploads/2018/08/south-africa-shadow-sa-nba-final.pdf, accessed 1 January 2017.

Lyons, Margaret, Jennifer Bartlett, and Paula McDonald. 2016. "Corporate Social Responsibility in Junior and Mid-Tier Resources Companies Operating in Developing Nations – Beyond the Public Relations Offensive." *Resources Policy* 50: 204–13. https://doi.org/10.1016/j.resourpol.2016.10.005

Matten, Dirk, and Andrew Crane. 2005. "Corporate Citizenship: Toward an Extended Theoretical Conceptualization." *Academy of Management Review* 30 (1): 166–80. https://doi.org/10.5465/amr.2005.15281448

Meyer, John W., and Brian Rowan. 1977. "Institutionalized Organizations: Formal Structure as Myth and Ceremony." *American Journal of Sociology* 83 (2): 340–63. https://doi.org/10.1086/226550

Mills, Greg. 2016. "Take a Chance: Welcome to the Golden Underground World of Zama-Zamas." *Business Maverick*, 5 July 2016. Available online at https://www.dailymaverick.co.za/article/2016-07-05-take-a-chance-welcome-to-the-golden-underground-world-of-zama-zamas/#.WPjRL865qSo, accessed 15 March 2017.

Netherlands. 2015. *Annual Report of the Government of the Netherlands: The Initiative on the Voluntary Principles on Security and Human Rights*. Available online at www.voluntaryprinciples.org/wp-content/uploads/2015/04/Government-of-the-Netherlands-Annual-Report-2014.pdf, accessed 10 January 2017.

North, Douglass C. 1990. *Institutions, Institutional Change and Economic Performance*. Cambridge: Cambridge University Press.

Nyame, Frank K., and J. Andrew Grant. 2012. "From Carats to Karats: Explaining the Shift from Diamond to Gold Mining by Artisanal Miners in Ghana." *Journal of Cleaner Production* 29–30: 163–72. https://doi.org/10.1016/j.jclepro.2012.02.002

Nyame, Frank K., and J. Andrew Grant. 2014. "The Political Economy of Transitory Mining in Ghana: Understanding the Trajectories, Triumphs, and Tribulations of Artisanal and Small-Scale Operators." *Extractive Industries and Society* 1 (1): 75–85. https://doi.org/10.1016/j.exis.2014.01.006

O'Faircheallaigh, Ciaran. 2014. "IR Theory and Domestic Adoption of International Norms." *International Politics* 51 (2): 155–76. https://doi.org/10.1057/ip.2013.23.

Orellana, Adriana. 2012. "Conceptualizing the Notion of Corporate Complicity with Human Rights Abuses." International Conference on Business Strategy and Organizational Behaviour (Bizstrategy) Proceedings.

Payne, Leigh A., and Gabriel Pereira. 2016. "Corporate Complicity in International Human Rights Violations." *Annual Review of Law and Social Science* 12 (1): 63–84. https://doi.org/10.1146/annurev-lawsocsci-110615-085100

Pero, Lionel V., and Timothy F. Smith. 2014. "Facilitating Multi-Sector Dialogue for Natural Resource Management: Examples of Rural Governance in Two Queensland Regions." *Rural Society* 16 (3): 236–53. https://doi.org/10.5172/rsj.351.16.3.236

Risse, Thomas. 2004. "Global Governance and Communicative Action." *Government and Opposition* 39 (2): 288–313. https://doi.org/10.1111/j.1477-7053.2004.00124.x

Rosenau, James N. 1995. "Governance in the Twenty-First Century." *Global Governance* 1 (1): 13–43. https://doi.org/10.1057/9780230245310_2

Ruggie, John. 2011. *Human Rights Council Seventeenth: Session Agenda Item 3 – Promotion and Protection of All Human Rights, Civil, Political, Economic, Social and Cultural Rights, Including the Right to Development.* New York: United Nations General Assembly. 21 March. Available online at https://www.ohchr.org/Documents/Issues/Business/A.HRC.17.31.pdf, accessed 1 October 2016.

Ruggie, John. 2014. "Global Governance and 'New Governance Theory': Lessons from Business and Human Rights." *Global Governance* 20 (1): 5–17. https://doi.org/10.1163/19426720-02001002

Slack, Keith. 2012. "Mission Impossible? Adopting a CSR-Based Business Model for Extractive Industries in Developing Countries." *Resources Policy* 37 (2): 179–84. https://doi.org/10.1016/j.resourpol.2011.02.003

South African Human Rights Commission. n.d. *Report of the SAHRC Investigative Hearing: Issues and Challenges in Relation to Unregulated Artisanal Underground and Surface Mining Activities in South Africa.* Braamfontein, SA: SAHRC. Available online at http://www.sahrc.org.za/home/21/files/Unregulated%20Artisanal%20Underground%20and%20Surface%20Mining%20Activities%20electronic%20version.pdf, accessed 10 March 2017.

Spence, Laura J. 2004. "Small Firm Accountability and Integrity." In *Corporate Integrity and Accountability*, edited by George Brenkert, 115–28. London: Sage.

United Nations. 2002. "Corporate Social Responsibility: Implications for Small and Medium Enterprises in Developing Countries." New York. Available online at http://195.130.87.21:8080/dspace/bitstream/123456789/1169/1/Corporate%20social%20responsibility%20%20implications%20for%20small%20and%20medium%20enterprises%20in%20developing%20countries.pdf., Accessed 26 November 2018.

United Nations General Assembly. 2011. Seventeenth Human Rights Council Session: Promotion and Protection of All Human Rights, Civil, Political, Economic, Social and Cultural Rights, including the Right to Development. A/HRC/RES/17/4. New York. Available online at https://www.business-humanrights.org/sites/default/files/media/documents/un-human-rights-council-resolution-re-human-rights-transnational-corps-eng-6-jul-2011.pdf, accessed 15 December 2016.

Wettstein, Florian. 2009. *Multinational Corporations and Global Justice: Human Rights Obligations of a Quasi-Governmental Institution*. Stanford, CA: Stanford University Press.

Wettstein, Florian. 2012. "Silence as Complicity: Elements of a Corporate Duty to Speak Out against the Violation of Human Rights." *Business Ethics Quarterly* 22 (1): 37–61. https://doi.org/10.5840/beq20122214

9 Golden Expectations: Corporate Social Responsibility and Governance in South Africa's Mining Sector

DAVID W. ORR

Introduction

Mining is deeply intertwined with the South African national psyche. Employing more South Africans than any other industry save agriculture, mining has played an integral role in the country's economic development (Rogerson 2011). Mining also holds historical importance; South Africa's Truth and Reconciliation Commission, set up to address the transgressions of the apartheid regime,[1] concluded that "the blueprint for *grand apartheid* was provided by [mining companies]" (Hamann 2004, 279). Indeed South African mining giant Anglo American became one of the world's largest companies during apartheid, "expanding into every facet of the South African industrial economy" (Freund 1998, 228). However, scant corporate social responsibility[2] (CSR) expenditures and a reliance on low-cost Black African labour during the apartheid era fostered popular resentment towards the mining industry. Following the country's transition to democracy in 1994, racially discriminate policies became intolerable, and new legislative, voluntary, and corporate governance frameworks for the mining sector were established to redress such inequalities.

Fuelled by the belief that responsibility rests with the mining industry to remedy the oppression of the apartheid era, mining firms operating in South Africa must comply with a wealth of domestic and international legislation to aid communities affected by mining operations. Yet mining firms in South Africa have often engaged in voluntary social and environmental development initiatives via CSR that surpass their compliance requirements. It is this phenomenon that forms the basis of this chapter: the rationales and implications of why and how mining firms operating in South Africa have voluntarily developed CSR norms and initiatives.

This points to the notion of private authority, which expands upon the neo-institutionalist obligations that firms have as integrated members of an interdependent and socialized world. As a relatively new framework of analysis within international relations, private authority explicitly rejects the state-centred traditional focus of the discipline and instead explores "the degree to which the institutions created by the private sector [operate] autonomously or in coordination with governments and intergovernmental organisations" (Cutler, Haufler, and Porter 1999, xi). In essence, private authority analyses the manifestations and implications of non-sovereign actors in the regulatory sphere. This does not necessarily diminish the importance of the state; instead, it examines how the state coalesces alongside private actors in the creation and cascading of norms and regulation.

CSR norms among mining firms emerged in the early 2000s. Dashwood (2012) argues that criticism by non-governmental organizations (NGOs), greater societal awareness of the environmental degradation caused by mining, and financial institutions' refusal to provide capital to mining firms that exhibited only cursory community and environmental concerns effectively compelled mining companies to engage in more sincere CSR provisions. Elbra (2014) notes that extractive firms might pursue private governance for other reasons, such as to minimize corporate risk and to improve their reputation. Moreover, firms might embrace private authority to enhance their profitability, to maintain a social licence to operate, or as a response to more stringent regulatory regimes. Mining firms also might choose to self-regulate for normative reasons. The inherent nature of the mining industry sees firms exploit the environments of the communities where they operate, leading many firms to have both a normative obligation to the local community and "a moral imperative and commitment to best practice" (Elbra 2014, 217).

It should be noted that this chapter's focus on the corporate actor precludes a deeper analysis of how communities, civil society groups, and other non-state actors experience corporate-led CSR policies. The experiences of local beneficiaries of CSR are frequently at odds with the rosy development-grounded CSR logics extolled by extractive firms, and considerable ink has been spilled to examine CSR's limited effect for local communities (see Idemudia 2010; Ololade and Annegarn 2013; and Chapters 2 and 3, in this volume, for incisive critiques of CSR). Although these critical contributions to the literature are highly valuable for exposing CSR's inadequacies, they focus more on the implications of CSR provision, rather than affording a deeper understanding of mining firms' rationales for engaging in CSR. This chapter opts instead for an amended approach, treating mining firms operating in South Africa as the key variable of analysis to examine how apartheid's legacy has informed their CSR strategies in the post-1994 era.

Additionally, although the scope of this chapter is restricted to examining how apartheid's legacy affected the evolution of CSR in South Africa's mining sector, this focus should not insinuate that apartheid is the sole driver for mining companies' adoption of CSR policies. The literature and my interviews with corporate stakeholders suggest that the evolution of CSR in South Africa has numerous causes, involving financial, moral, and compliance rationales. For example, financial institutions' introduction of more socially conscious conditionalities coupled with the public relations fallout of the 2012 Marikana incident[3] and the need to redress the inequalities of apartheid have spurred enhanced CSR provision. Space constraints, however, unfortunately prevent an in-depth analysis of these other significant explanatory factors.

South Africa presents a fascinating case to explore how a change in political circumstance can usher in dramatic changes for both the expectations and manifestations of CSR. Moreover, as sub-Saharan Africa's commercial and diplomatic hub, South Africa serves as a bellwether to predict the successful implementation of CSR policies in other African states (Grant and Hamilton 2016). Drawing on in-person interviews and the existing resource governance literature, this chapter traces CSR's evolution in the South African context, commencing with an overview of mining in the country prior to Nelson Mandela's victory in 1994. I then turn towards the country's unique post-apartheid conception of CSR before exploring domestic legislation and mechanisms pertaining to CSR. In the final section I examine how transnational natural resource regimes have affected this phenomenon, before offering a conclusion about what lessons can be learned from the South African mining industry's relationship with CSR.

Mining in Pre-1994 South Africa

The mining industry catalysed the industrialization of modern South Africa, both before and after the country's transition to a racially inclusive democracy in 1994. The discovery of diamonds in the Northern Cape in the late 1860s, glamorized by the discovery of the 48-carat Star of South Africa in 1869, stimulated the country's mineral revolution. "[B]y February 1871 two thousand whites and two thousand Blacks were panning the [Vaal River], while an estimated thirteen thousand whites and fifteen thousand Blacks worked the dry diggings" (Smalberger 1976, 420). The largest discovery came in 1886, when gold was discovered in the Witwatersrand region of northeast South Africa near modern-day Johannesburg, triggering what became known as the Witwatersrand "Gold Rush." Much like the Kimberley "Diamond Rush" two decades prior, the Witwatersrand Gold Rush saw tens of thousands of Boers and European expatriates flock to the region with hopes of profiting from these precious minerals.

South Africa enjoys the richest mineral trove ever to be discovered in a confined region, with nearly every known mineral and precious stone found in various quantities – the Witwatersrand gold fields are the richest in the world (Beck 2013). The country is also unique in the depths of its deposits: gold veins run deeper in South Africa than in any other country – to a depth of four thousand metres – leading late nineteenth-century mining companies to seek capital to develop deep and expensive underground mines to further exploit these minerals. Despite these geological challenges, what made South African gold mining commercially viable was the "immense, unequalled quantity of gold ore" (Beck 2013, 78).

The original gold prospectors could readily access capital to develop these expensive gold mines. A dynamic mining finance structure already existed, generated by capital from European and British banks during the earlier Kimberley diamond rush. Powerful entrepreneurs, including the "Randlords" Cecil Rhodes and Barney Barnato, had the expertise and financial means to exploit the gold (Wheatcroft 1985). Mining companies' constant thirst for capital also ushered in mining finance houses that blended financial services and extraction expertise. By 1917 major mining houses were well established, including Anglo American, Randgold, and Gold Fields of South Africa. These houses provided the foundations for the gold industry that hastened the country's economic development.

The discovery of minerals represented a turning point for South Africa. Before 1886, the Transvaal was a poor Boer republic. Following the gold rush, it swiftly became the richest gold-mining area in the world (Beck 2013). Mining camps blossomed into cities; the mining camp of Johannesburg became the country's economic powerhouse and the country's largest city. New gold reefs were discovered every few decades: Gold Fields located the West Wits Line near Johannesburg in the 1930s, and Anglo American exploited the Orange Free State Field beginning in 1946 (Mining Artifacts 2017). The consolidation of mining firms in the latter half of the nineteenth century led to the evolution of supermines, which benefited from economies of scale and allowed for the folding of a new mine into an existing one. Most notably, Rhodes acquired Barnato's mining companies in 1888 and merged them with his own holdings, creating De Beers Consolidated Mines and offering Rhodes a near-monopoly on the international diamond trade (Beck 2013).

Prior to US President Richard Nixon's abandoning the gold standard in 1971, the price of gold was internationally controlled and remained fixed. Despite increases in the cost of gold production, these costs could not be transferred to the customer. To ensure their continued profitability, mining companies looked to reduce the cost of production by securing cheap, unskilled labour. For South African mining companies, poor, Black Africans matched this profile. Working together, the Boer and British governments imposed "hut taxes" on Africans that were the equivalent of three months of work, effectively forcing Africans to work in mines (Shillington 2005). Between 1890 and 1899, the number of African mineworkers rose from fourteen thousand to one hundred thousand (First 1982). Migrant labour came from across southern colonial Africa, including from the British colonies of Bechuanaland (Botswana), Basutoland (Lesotho), Swaziland (eSwatini), Southern Rhodesia (Zimbabwe), and lusophone Mozambique. To keep costs low, the richer mining companies flooded the market with recruited workers, keeping labour supply high while decreasing labour costs (Shillington 2005). Whites took the skilled, supervisory, and well-paid positions while Black Africans performed unskilled, low-wage tasks, fostering a racially divided labour force that would persist until the formal abolition of apartheid in 1994. Thus, from the 1880s through 1990, poor labour conditions, low pay, and negligible CSR expenditures maintained firms' profitability and hindered the economic development of the country's African majority. Moreover, to ensure that the supply of labour was regulated and to prevent Africans immigrating *en masse* to urban areas, the Boer-dominated government implemented a pass system for Africans, effectively confining them to regions where they had government or employer approval to work (Beck 2013). Variants of the pass system remained in place for nearly a century until 1986.

The South African economy benefited massively from these resources. Coupled with the country's enjoying the world's highest diamond and gold ore grades, gold mining became the largest and most important contributor to the economy, with 61.9 per cent of the world's gold produced in the Transvaal in 1982 (First 1982, 8). Until the 1990s South Africa also enjoyed the world's largest mining industry. Naturally this meant significant profits for the South African government, which earned royalties from the mining houses. Following the official introduction of apartheid by the Afrikaner Nationalists in 1948, which called for the segregation of South Africans of white and non-white descent, the wealth generated from mining ensured that South Africa could remain largely solvent until the 1980s, despite boycotts by member states of the Organization of African Unity (OAU) that bordered

South Africa. Indeed, although South Africa's political regime was predicated on racial segregation, the world continued to trade with apartheid South Africa, "for the country's mineral wealth could not be ignored" (Beck 2013, 156). By the 1960s, Johannesburg-based Anglo American was an international mining giant (Freund 1998). Beck (2013) argues that, despite worldwide condemnation of the apartheid regime by civil rights groups, international commerce with South Africa increased during the 1970s, when the country produced 60 per cent of the world's gold and 80 per cent of its diamonds.

In 2019 mining remains vital to the South African economy, but the importance attached to certain minerals has changed. Gold and diamond yields are in decline, having been overtaken by the growth of coal and iron production.[4] Yet mining has not wavered in economic importance. *Business Monitor International*'s 2015 report of the South African mining industry finds that the country possesses "significant untapped mineral reserves, which supports the domestic mining sector's long-term growth outlook" (*Business Monitor International* 2015, 9).

Corporate Social Responsibility in the South African Context

South Africa was selected as the case study for this chapter because of its highly diversified economy and the importance of the mining sector to its historical and contemporary development. Its position as Africa's largest economy and its breadth of expertise in mining, financial services, tourism, and logistics further renders South Africa worthy of investigation. The country also has a "preoccupation with its standing within and outside the African continent," and can be viewed as Africa's norm leader in diplomatic and commercial matters (Grant and Hamilton 2016, 176). Such international investment and scrutiny has also encouraged South Africa to develop strict CSR provisions.

This high expectation for CSR was compounded by the historical circumstances in which the country found itself in 1994. Bereft of a government that was generating racially divisive legislation, mining firms were encouraged to adopt CSR to redress the inequalities of apartheid. The negative connotations associated with the mining industry during the apartheid era led firms to balk at the idea of being associated with such oppression, as a mining firm's reputation follows it across international borders – Dashwood (2012) finds that engaging in CSR can mitigate assaults on a firms' reputation and, by extension, its business success. Consequently mining firms in South Africa have tailored CSR towards a distinctly South African flavour. Known as "corporate social investment" (CSI), the *responsibility* aspect of CSR is removed and is replaced by a novel way to address the relationship between corporate and state actors. CSI is also more focused than CSR, "encompassing factors such as business ethics and good governance, health and safety issues at work, labour relations, and environmental standards" (Hinson and Ndhlovu 2011, 340). CSI's targeted approach illustrates the more pragmatic understanding of CSR in the South African context, relative to other sources of mining investment on the continent. For example, mining firms operating in other states in sub-Saharan Africa with a "governance deficit" frequently flout domestic labour and environmental regulations with paltry recourse from the government (Elbra 2014). By contrast, interviews with select corporate actors in the South African mining industry establish their belief that mining firms' exposure to so much change in a short time forced them to engage with communities in a more sincere and sustainable manner than firms operating in other emerging market mining jurisdictions.

The introduction of CSI in South Africa also illustrates the power of private authority to alter public perceptions of the industry. In this instance, the negative connotations of apartheid responsibility were replaced by more inclusive norms and values in order to demonstrate the industry's more sustainable engagement with communities near mining operations. By divorcing themselves of responsibility for apartheid-era violations, mining firms have begun to develop a novel identity of corporate citizenship that enhances the social contract with government (Hinson and Ndhlovu 2011). However, whereas Dashwood (2012) believes that pressure from NGOs and widespread media coverage of mining environmental disasters fuelled demands for CSR provision by mining firms in the 1990s, these factors were not as prevalent in South Africa. Instead the domestic institutional legacy of apartheid helped to foment the creation of CSR – more specifically, CSI.

South African Mining Legislation and Voluntary Initiatives

State legislation, industry charters, and voluntary initiatives have further compelled firms to adopt CSR activities to redress the inequalities of apartheid. Since 1994 the government has championed provisions that require firms to engage in social and environmental activities to justify their social licence to operate. These mechanisms are, at least in theory, some of the most stringent in the world for protecting affected communities, a sentiment echoed by private sector actors.[5] Moreover, they are often voluntary. However, as I explore in the Broad-Based Black Economic Empowerment (BBBEE) and King III Codes below, firms typically match and exceed these ostensibly voluntary initiatives;

in practice, they have become de facto binding compliance legislation (Dashwood 2012).

Historical impetus first arose in South Africa's 1996 racially indiscriminate constitution, which guaranteed social services to all citizens. This clause was a significant departure from the apartheid era. Prior to 1994, the public and private spheres functioned separately, with limited government intervention in company affairs, particularly with regard to a firms' social obligations, as evidenced by the oppressive pass system then in place (see Ramlall 2012). Indeed, although common law fiduciary duties applied to firms in pre-1994 South Africa, the Companies Act of 1973 held no specific CSR provisions (Ramlall 2012). Where CSR did exist, it was largely limited to ad hoc philanthropic contributions.

The introduction of a racially inclusive democracy in South Africa in 1994 was a fortuitous time for the development of CSR in the country. Dashwood (2012, 79) argues that the mid-1990s represented a "critical juncture" for the global dissemination of CSR norms because mining firms' operations became truly global in the 1990s. The decade saw the advent of "green," environmentally considerate conditionalities attached to mining financing, a source of funding vital for mining firms to secure because of their low day-to-day cash flows. By the early 2000s, most major mining firms had converged around the norm of sustainable development in their operations. Dashwood (2012) also contends that some mining companies have adopted leadership roles in the global dissemination of CSR norms, illustrating the power of norm cascades among competitors and supporting the conviction that companies are governance actors in their own right (i.e., private authority). However, unlike the modern-day conception of CSR that integrates both social and environmental considerations, the global CSR narrative of the 1990s was largely predicated on environmental concerns, leaving out social stakeholder groups.

The Mineral and Petroleum Resources Development Act and Mining Charter

The pre-eminent legislation that guides the South African mining industry is the Mineral and Petroleum Resources Development Act of 2002 (MPRDA), whose purpose is "to make provision for equitable access to and sustainable development of the nation's mineral and petroleum resources; and to provide for matters connected therewith." The MPRDA is important for the social emancipation of previously disadvantaged groups, and thus illustrates the South African government's commitment to redressing the inequalities of apartheid by encouraging mining firms to increase their engagement with affected communities. Under section 10 of the act, mining firms must consult with interested and affected parties within fourteen days of receiving a licence to operate. The need to redress apartheid's inequalities is paramount in the MPRDA. As the legislation states: "To ensure the attainment of Government's objectives of redressing historical, social and economic inequalities as stated in the Constitution, the Minister must within six months from the date on which this Act takes effect develop a broad-based socio-economic empowerment Charter that will set the framework for targets and time table for effecting the entry into and active participation of historically disadvantaged South Africans into the mining industry, and allow such South Africans to benefit from the exploitation of mining and mineral resources and the beneficiation of such mineral resources" (MPRDA, s.100.2.a).

The charter mentioned in the MPRDA was launched in 2004 as the "Mining Charter," and was amended in 2010. A new version was approved in December 2018. The Mining Charter affects section 100.2.a of the MPRDA and section 9 of the South African constitution, which guarantees the equality of all South Africans. With the objective of "[promoting] sustainable growth and meaningful transformation of the industry," the Mining Charter requires at least 26 per cent ownership (increased to 30 per cent in the 2018 version) by historically disadvantaged South Africans, local procurement guarantees, resource beneficiation concerns, and community development initiatives (South Africa 2010, 4). I discuss these requirements and their effect in more detail below.

Although the MPRDA contains no direct definition of what specific services mining companies are required to provide, it is clear that its "prescribed social and labour plan," in line with requirements under the government's Broad-Based Black Economic Empowerment initiative, is vital to securing production licences (s. 84.1.i). Moreover a consistent theme in the MPRDA is the amelioration of historical inequalities, which the mining industry – by virtue of continuing operations and paying royalties to the apartheid regime – helped to support. As part of the process to secure a mining licence, a mining firm is required to submit a Social and Labour Plan (SLP) that stipulates the firm's commitment to engage with workers and communities in a sustainable manner (Rogerson 2011). The SLP must also include a plan for the mine's closure and human resource development. The draft SLP is then submitted to the Department of Mineral Resources for approval, and remains confidential. If targets need to be revised, it is the responsibility of the mining firm to approach the department with justification for the revision. These plans are a confidential agreement between the mining firm and the government, making it challenging for communities to access a company's commitments and to hold it accountable. It should be noted, however, that SLPs are sometimes disclosed in firms' sustainability reports, which are publicly available online.

A major aspect of an SLP consists of an Integrated Development Plan (IDP), which is effectively a cooperative agreement between the social service provision ambitions of the municipality where the firm operates and the planned CSR provision of the mining firm (Rogerson 2011). If the municipality is satisfied with the firm's intended CSR activities, it will issue a letter to the Department of Mineral Resources stating that the firm's draft SLP is compliant with the IDP. The IDP thus, at least in theory, forces mining firms to consult with municipalities and to align their CSR activities with the goals of the municipality. Once this consultative process to engage stakeholders concludes and the IDP is issued, third-party consultants may be hired to verify the feasibility and transparency of the SLP. An executive at a South African–owned mining firm recounted in an interview that the IDP process provides opportunities for partnerships between local community organizations and mining firms, allowing companies to provide more targeted CSR initiatives.[6]

Broad-Based Black Economic Empowerment and CSR

Since the 1990s, South African CSR generally has focused more on social empowerment than on environmental concerns. Rather than creating legislation that directly forces companies to be socially responsible, the government instead has opted to develop mechanisms that encourage businesses, including mining firms, to engage "voluntarily" in CSR (Ramlall 2012). The government's flagship policy is the Broad-Based Black Economic Empowerment (BBBEE) Act, which seeks to redistribute wealth and create job opportunities for those groups (primarily Black and coloured[7] South Africans) that previously had been disadvantaged by the apartheid regime. Ramlall (2012) argues that Black Economic Empowerment (BEE) initially was introduced to encourage Black ownership and management of companies. This narrow definition, however, prevented the realization of widespread income gains for Black South Africans, and instead wealth became centralized among the connected political and business elite. For example, 60 per cent of BEE deals in 2003 went to three individuals: Cyril Ramaphosa (now president of South Africa), Tokyo Sexwale, and Patrice Motsepe (Ramlall 2012, 278). Recognizing the failure of BEE to promote widespread wealth redistribution, the government ushered in

BBBEE. Unlike the narrow definition of BEE, BBBEE includes human aspects of economic development. Binding both the public and private sectors, BBBEE attempts "to empower not only Black shareholders, but also Black employees, Black-owned entities within a supply chain or industry, and communities at large through, *inter alia*, human resource development, employment equity, enterprise development and preferential procurement" (Milanovic 2010).

Unfortunately, some mining firms view BBBEE as "merely another cost of doing business in South Africa," failing to grasp its emancipatory potential (Milanovic 2010). When a draft BEE document was leaked in 2002 that envisaged 51 per cent Black ownership of mining firms, severe discontent within the industry emerged. Within the day, the Johannesburg Stock Exchange fell to its lowest level in eight months (Ramlall 2012). A new target for Black ownership of mining firms was then announced, halved to 26 per cent by 2014 (Ramlall 2012). The new 2018 Mining Charter now requires an increase from 26 to 30 per cent within five years. Thus, although BBBEE introduced emancipatory measures for previously disadvantaged populations, several industries – including mining – initially met it with an embrace that can be described as lukewarm at best. Moreover, although the global mining industry has participated in the development of voluntary initiatives to spur sustainable development, including the Voluntary Principles on Security and Human Rights (VPs) and the UN Global Compact, South African mining firms' poor response to the 51 per cent Black ownership requirement in 2002 illustrates the importance of the state, at least in the short term, in stimulating business practices in the direction of social transformation.

Frustration has also emerged in the mining industry regarding BBBEE compliance. Although an executive at a large international financial institution noted that mining and finance houses are comfortable with the initiative, they are less comfortable with BBBEE partners.[8] The representative stated that, although sustainability, including BBBEE initiatives, has become important to firms' operations in South Africa, implementation is difficult because it can be challenging to finance BBBEE partners. This arises because, in line with BBBEE requirements, firms operating in South Africa must ensure that at least 26 per cent of their shares are Black owned, with up to 11 per cent offset for local beneficiation. However, BBBEE partners – particularly if they are community-based trusts in rural areas with low financial literacy – frequently sell their shares in a mining project without informing the issuing company. For example, when it was incorporated in 2003, 33 per cent of a South African–owned mining firm was held by the host community,[9] but the community then sold off the majority of these shares for liquid funds. As of February 2016, the host community owned just 4.5 per cent of the company, with other BBBEE partners owning the remainder.[10] Thus, mining firms must seek new partners to ensure compliance with the 26 per cent (and now 30 per cent) threshold, rendering BBBEE compliance a major challenge for multinationals in South Africa.

The King Code of Governance Principles of 2009 (King III)

More explicitly tied to CSR than the BBBEE initiatives, the 2009 King Code of Governance Principles for South Africa (King III) is a voluntary attempt by South African firms to ensure strengthened and broader stakeholder accountability. It has been a significant driver of CSR practice since its introduction in 2009. King III developed from the original and "ground-breaking" King Code of Governance Principles for South Africa of 1994 (King I), which sought to provide a framework for firms to comply with best practices for social, ethical, environmental, and inclusive corporate governance. King III extended these principles by expanding stakeholder accountability to integrate "CSR risks and opportunities into their core business strategies" (Ackers and Eccles 2015, 517). The key principles of King III maintain that "good governance is essentially about effective leadership; sustainability is a primary moral and economic imperative and is one of the most important sources of opportunities and risks for business; and the concept of corporate citizenship is a consequence of a company being a legal person who should operate in a sustainable manner" (Institute for Directors in Southern Africa 2009, 9–10).

Even though King III is a voluntary code and thereby legally unenforceable by the South African state, regulation 8.63(a) of the Johannesburg Stock Exchange requires all listed companies to abide by its principles (Ackers and Eccles 2015, 517). Indeed, King III compliance forms the preliminary threshold to adjudicate a company's inclusion on the stock exchange's Social Responsibility Index.[11] Ackers and Eccles (2015) argue that King III has become the de facto mandatory requirement for all companies listed on the exchange. Moreover, firms must ensure that their CSR compliance reports are independently audited, leading Ackers and Eccles to contend that the King III principles have made South Africa one of the first countries "to not only disclose their CSR-related performance, but also to provide independent assurance thereon" (Ackers and Eccles 2015, 516). Due to this requirement, firms' CSR contributions can be scrutinized to a higher degree than in other jurisdictions, providing an incentive for greater compliance. The third-party verification prerequisite also compels firms to "match" each other's contributions, thereby reducing a firm's reputational risk of being branded a pariah for poor social services provision (Ackers and Eccles 2015). This illustrates the norm cascade of private authority within the South African mining sphere. However, even though most firms comply with the King III, Ackers and Eccles (2015) argue that the independent CSR assurance rate remains low.

Yet there is hope for strengthened compliance; with the Johannesburg Stock Exchange leading the adoption of independently assured CSR reports, it is predicted that more and more South African firms will independently assure their CSR commitments to mitigate their reputational risk. The largely positive voluntary response by firms to the King III principles and the Johannesburg Stock Exchange's Social Responsibility Index suggest that it can remain a voluntary initiative, reducing the need for government resources to develop and monitor formal legislation for CSR initiatives beyond what is stipulated in the MPRDA and the South African constitution. Ackers and Eccles (2015, 542) disagree, however, arguing that the standardized codification and framework of King III is required to "improve the quality of assurance engagements, facilitate the comparability of CSR reports and enhance the confidence of users about the veracity of the underlying CSR disclosures." Nevertheless the King Codes look to be further entrenched. In April 2017 an updated version of King III, termed King IV, came into effect with the aim of further improving the governance outcomes and practices outlined in King III. This manifestation should serve to spur further study of the implications of King IV for CSR compliance in South Africa's mining sector.

Thus it appears that voluntary compliance and general enthusiasm of firms for the principles espoused in BBBEE and King III encompass several tenets associated with private authority. First, they align with Dashwood's (2012) argument that CSR promotion was a primarily voluntary initiative in the mining industry, prompted by the aforementioned "critical juncture" of the mid-1990s. Second, compliance with the King III principles and the Johannesburg Stock Exchange's Social Responsibility Index attest to the role of firms as norm entrepreneurs that use multilateral forums to disseminate norms on an industry-wide scale (Cutler, Haufler, and Porter 1999).

Transnational Natural Resource Governance Regimes

Although South Africa's mining legislation and voluntary initiatives are strong in comparison to those of its regional neighbours, the late twentieth century witnessed growing concern about the inability of sovereign governments in developing states to craft and implement emancipatory and transparent mining codes. Consequently, since the late 1990s, there has been "a new wave of international natural resource governance initiatives" developed to mitigate the perceived shortcomings of previous mining codes (Besada and Martin 2015, 269). In line with broader pan-industry acceptance of the neo-institutional conception of CSR and the obligations that firms have to the communities in which they operate, new private and transnational authority has emerged to promote greater accountability in the extractive sphere. Besada and Martin (2015) term this development the "fourth generation" of African mining codes because the emergence of international governance regimes transports mineral codes from the domestic to the international realm.

This "fourth generation" has moved beyond host governments towards multistakeholder dialogue among mining firms, investment partners, and civil society groups. Further illustrating the power of private authority in the mining sector, many of these initiatives are voluntary and are grounded in the popularization of CSR that swept the industry after the mid-1990s. Indeed the inauguration in 1998 of the Global Mining Initiative to enhance industry-wide CSR alignment was spearheaded by mining firms and absent government involvement (Besada and Martin 2015). Additionally the 2002 World Summit on Development in Johannesburg reaffirmed sustainable development as central to the international extractive industry's agenda. Dashwood (2012) notes that the success of the Global Mining Initiative and the World Summit on Development meetings saw "best practices" in environmental management systems and community engagement protocols become a marked feature of the mining industry in the early 2000s.

Beyond advocating for strengthened CSR performance among competitors, a key component of international resource governance initiatives has been engaging in multistakeholder dialogue under transparent and equal terms. This involvement is "essential to coping with the challenges of translating natural resource endowments into wealth, economic development and social empowerment" (Besada and Martin 2015, 270). A key global governance initiative to enhance accountability is the Extractive Industries Transparency Initiative (EITI), which was initiated in 2002 and launched in 2003 to enhance domestic governance in resource-rich countries through strengthening revenue stream accountability (Sovacool et al. 2016). Characteristic of the "fourth generation" of mineral codes, the EITI is structured as a transnational tripartite partnership involving stakeholders from the sovereign, corporate, and civil society spheres. Aimed at the extractive spheres of oil and mining, the EITI relies on unencumbered access to reports and dialogue to determine the extent of stakeholders' accountability. By February 2017, fifty-one countries were implementing the EITI, with over ninety companies committed to EITI norms (EITI 2017). Illustrating its broad-based and international appeal as a transnational governance regime, Sovacool et al. (2016, 179) note that "the European Union, African Union, G-8 and G-20, and the United Nations have all endorsed the EITI."

However, although the EITI provides a useful benchmark to assess countries' and companies' accountability and transparency mechanisms, the extent of its success has been hotly debated. Despite their significant and well-developed mineral sectors, several countries, notably Canada and South Africa, are neither "EITI Compliant" nor "EITI Candidates." This is particularly ironic for South Africa because the EITI was launched by former UK prime minister Tony Blair at the 2002 World Summit on Development in Johannesburg (Compaoré 2013, 2015). The relative reluctance by developed countries to embrace the EITI is a key reason South Africa has failed to become a signatory. Nevertheless, as Compaoré (2013) notes, countries of the Global North have encouraged the South African government to sign on to the EITI in order to enhance South Africa's transparency initiatives and cement its legitimacy as a member of the so-called BRICS – the group of emerging economies comprising Brazil, Russia, India, China, and South Africa. It is also worth noting that Compaoré's (2013, 8) interview with a South African Department of Mineral Resources representative illustrates that the EITI is not a policy priority for the South African government, as the official believed that "[South Africa is] transparent enough in terms of how we account for the mineral resources revenues that come to us."

The EITI's perceived inapplicability to South Africa also appears to permeate the country's private sector. This sentiment was captured in an interview undertaken with an executive at a large international financial institution with exposure to South African mining projects, who argued that the country's resource codes are strong enough that they do not need to comply with transnational regulatory regimes like the EITI.[12] There might be some merit to this argument. A statistical analysis by Sovacool et al. (2016, 180) finds that, "in most metrics EITI countries do not perform better during EITI compliance than before EITI compliance, and that in most metrics they do not outperform other countries" because of its voluntary nature, stakeholder resistance, absence of strong civil society actors, and limited mandate.

Other transnational natural resource governance initiatives have emerged to enhance accountability and CSR provision in the African mining sphere. Some are spearheaded by multilateral forums such as the Kimberley Process, the VPs, and the African Union's Africa Mining Vision (AMV) – see also Chapters 2, 6, 7, and 12, in this volume. The AMV is particularly notable because it provides a holistic framework for African governments to integrate mining into the continent's long-term development at all government levels – from municipal to national – through capacity building (Besada and Martin 2015). It is also worth noting the irony that, although South Africa has not officially endorsed the VPs, many South African corporations are proponents. Indeed, demonstrating the pervasive power of private authority in the mining sector, other initiatives are industry led, including the Equator Principles and the International Finance Corporation's Performance Standards, which both provide frameworks for financial institutions to manage environmental and social issues surrounding project financing. Others are inspired by civil society, including Publish What You Pay and the Revenue Watch Institute, which Besada and Martin (2015) argue inspired the EITI.

Despite the wide-ranging origins and mandates of these transnational governance initiatives, they share the fundamental characteristic that they are all ostensibly voluntary. However, most of these CSR and accountability initiatives effectively compel particular behaviours by corporations, and illustrate the power of private authority for disseminating norms on an industry-wide scale. Indeed these frameworks not only can guide mining firms, but also reward them by providing them with more favourable access to capital, enhanced investor and public goodwill, and a more positive image in the eyes of the host government where they operate.

Conclusion

South Africa has experienced an intimate and challenging relationship with mining and CSR. Although the advent of financial institutions' "green conditionalities" in the 1990s transported CSR to the forefront of global mining operations, calls for enhanced CSR in South Africa were further strengthened by the need to redress the inequalities exacerbated by the apartheid era and that mining companies implicitly had helped to sustain. CSR accordingly has become one of the country's leading vehicles to realize social development. Indeed the South African case illustrates that a historical imperative can stimulate a dramatic paradigm shift in expectations and requirements for natural resource governance.

This imperative percolates through to the legislative level, whereby not only is the country's post-apartheid constitution arguably one of the most tolerant and inclusive in the world, but so are, at least on paper, its regulations related to mining. Certainly much work remains to be done to improve CSR both in South Africa and further afield. As Ololade and Annegarn (2013, 576) contend in their analysis of the Rustenburg platinum-producing region of South Africa, "residents' perceptions [of sustainability] do not match the claims of the mining companies." Thus the challenges of reconciling these divergent perceptions of CSR and constructing more inclusive and responsive CSR policies should serve to spur further research. Nevertheless, despite their imperfections, the legislative and emancipatory potential of the MPRDA, BBBEE, and King III Code illustrate that South Africa's mining legislation and voluntary CSR initiatives render it a leader among emerging markets in the drafting, if not necessarily the enforcement, of provisions to protect communities affected by mining operations.

However, the perceived strength of domestic legislation can have the perverse effect of eliminating opportunities for enhanced accountability vis-à-vis international oversight. Interviews with South African government and industry representatives highlight their contention that the EITI is inapplicable to the South African context. Such views promote the unhelpful belief that incorporating both domestic and international resource governance regulations is not only undesirable, but mutually exclusive. Developing a stronger understanding of whether transnational regimes enhance accountability and transparency in emerging markets would be a valuable endeavour, and could form the basis of further study.

On a more optimistic note, however, the South African example highlights that robust domestic legislation can spur stronger corporate-led norms. The mining sector's embrace of the industry-led and voluntary King III Code suggest that domestic mechanisms can act as a springboard for complementary CSR regulations generated by private actors. King III transports the CSR requisite from compliance to the morally necessary realm, compounding the need for firms to engage in CSR to fulfil their social licence to operate. Moreover the emergence of such private authority has not seen the significant erosion of state sovereignty; rather, the state continues to maintain a central role in the creation and enforcement of legislation for sustainable resource governance and the protection of communities near mining operations. Thus South Africa illustrates that state legislation and corporate-led CSR provisions, spurred by the need to redress apartheid's legacy, can indeed be complementary towards developing stronger CSR policies to benefit communities affected by mining operations.

NOTES

1 In place from 1948 to 1994, South Africa's apartheid regime was predicated on white superiority and racial segregation; non-white South Africans were denied the right to vote and excluded from public areas reserved for white citizens.

2 This chapter adopts the Canadian government's definition of CSR: "the voluntary activities undertaken by a company to operate in an economic, social and environmentally sustainable manner" (Canada 2016).

3 Thirty-four miners were killed at Lonmin's Marikana mine in 2012 during protests over poor CSR provisions, wages, and other grievances.

4 Iron has recently decreased in importance in the face of lower demand from China, with exports of South African iron ore to that country falling 1.6 per cent year over year during the first four months of 2015 (Business Monitor International 2015, 27).

5 Author's interview with executive, Johannesburg Stock Exchange. Johannesburg, 27 January 2016.

6 Author's interview with corporate executive, mining company. Johannesburg, 3 February 2016.

7 "Coloured" is the term given to a distinct minority ethnic group of mixed racial background that primarily speaks Afrikaans. They are the predominant ethnic group in Western Cape province.

8 Author's interview with executive, international financial institution. Johannesburg, 3 February 2016.

9 Author's interview with corporate executive, mining company, Johannesburg, 3 February 2016.

10 Ibid.

11 Inspired by the London Stock Exchange's FTSE4Good Index, the Johannesburg Stock Exchange's Social Responsibility Index ranks listed companies by their social and environmental contributions.

12 Author's interview with executive, international financial institution, Johannesburg, 3 February 2016.

BIBLIOGRAPHY

Ackers, Barry, and Neil Eccles. 2015. "Mandatory Corporate Social Responsibility Assurance Practices: The Case of King III in South Africa." *Accounting, Auditing & Accountability Journal* 28 (4): 515–50. https://doi. org/10.1108/aaaj-12-2013-1554.

Beck, Roger. 2013. *The History of South Africa*. Santa Barbara, CA: ABC-CLIO.

Besada, Hany, and Philip Martin. 2015. "Mining Codes in Africa: Emergence of a 'Fourth' Generation?" *Cambridge Review of International Affairs* 28 (2): 263–82. https://doi.org/10.1080/09557571.2013.84082.

Business Monitor International. 2015. "South Africa Mining Report Q3 2015." London: BMI Research.

Compaoré, W.R. Nadège. 2013. "Towards Understanding South Africa's Differing Attitudes to the Extractive Industries Transparency Initiative and the Open Governance Partnership." Occasional Paper 146. Johannesburg: South African Institute of International Affairs.

Compaoré, W.R. Nadège. 2015. "Re-politicizing State Sovereignty in Global Governance: The Political Economy of Transparency in the Oil Sectors of Gabon and Ghana." PhD diss., Queen's University, Kingston, ON.

Cutler, Claire, Virginia Haufler, and Tony Porter, eds. 1999. *Private Authority and International Affairs.* Albany, NY: SUNY Press.

Dashwood, Hevina S. 2012. *The Rise of Global Corporate Social Responsibility: Mining and the Spread of Global Norms.* Cambridge: Cambridge University Press.

EITI (Extractive Industry Industries Transparency Initiative). 2017. "Countries." Available online at https://eiti.org/countries, accessed 27 February 2017.

Elbra, Ainsley. 2014. "Gold Mining in Sub-Saharan Africa: Towards Private Sector Governance." *Extractive Industries and Society* 1 (2): 216–24. https://doi.org/10.1016/j.exis.2014.07.008.

First, Ruth. 1982. "The Gold of Migrant Labour." *Review of African Political Economy* 9 (25): 5–21. https://doi.org/10.1080/03056248208703509.

Freund, Bill. 1998. *The Making of Contemporary Africa: The Development of African Society since 1880.* 2nd ed. London: Palgrave Macmillan.

Canada. 2016. "Responsible Business Conduct Abroad." Ottawa: Global Affairs Canada. Available online at https://www.international.gc.ca/trade-agreements-accords-commerciaux/topics-domaines/other-autre/csr-rse.aspx?lang=eng#CSR, accessed 31 March 2016.

Grant, J. Andrew, and Spencer Hamilton. 2016. "Norm Dynamics and International Organisations: South Africa in the African Union and International Criminal Court." *Commonwealth & Comparative Politics* 54 (2): 161–85. https://doi.org/10.1080/14662043.2016.1151166.

Hamann, Ralph. 2004. "Corporate Social Responsibility, Partnerships, and Institutional Change: The Case of Mining Companies in South Africa." *Natural Resources Forum* 28 (4): 278–90. https://doi.org/10.1111/j.1477-8947.2004.00101.x.

Hinson, Robert, and Tidings Ndhlovu. 2011. "Conceptualising Corporate Social Responsibility (CSR) and Corporate Social Investment (CSI): The

South African Context." *Social Responsibility Journal* 7 (3): 332–46. https://doi.org/10.1108/17471111111154491.

Idemudia, Uwafiokun. 2010. "Rethinking the Role of Corporate Social Responsibility in the Nigerian Oil Conflict: The Limits of CSR." *Journal of International Development* 22 (7): 833–45. https://doi.org/10.1002/jid.1644.

Institute of Directors in Southern Africa. 2009. *King Code of Governance Principles for South Africa 2009.* Available online at http://c.ymcdn.com/sites/www.iodsa.co.za/resource/collection/94445006-4F18-4335-B7FB-7F5A8B23FB3F/King_III_Code_for_Governance_Principles_.pdf, accessed 29 February 2016.

Milanovic, Ana. 2010. "BBBEE Empowerment Meant to Be Sustainable, Not Slow." Available online at www.polity.org.za/article/bbbee-empowerment-meant-to-be-sustainable-not-slow-2010-09-03, accessed 14 January 2016.

Mining Artifacts. 2017. *South African Mines.* Available online at http://www.miningartifacts.org/South-African-Mines.html, accessed 8 April 2017.

Ololade, Olusola, and Harold Annegarn. 2013. "Contrasting Community and Corporate Perceptions of Sustainability: A Case Study within the Platinum Mining Region of South Africa." *Resources Policy* 38 (4): 568–76. https://doi.org/10.1016/j.resourpol.2013.09.005.

Ramlall, Sharlene. 2012. "Corporate Social Responsibility in Post-Apartheid South Africa." *Responsibility Journal* 8 (2): 270–88. https://doi.org/10.1108/17471111211234888.

Rogerson, Christian. 2011. "Mining Enterprise, Regulatory Frameworks and Local Economic Development in South Africa." *African Journal of Business Management* 5 (35): 13373–82. https://doi.org/10.5897/ajbmx11.013.

Shillington, Kevin. 2005. *History of Africa.* 2nd ed. New York: Palgrave Macmillan.

Smalberger, John. 1976. "The Role of the Diamond-Mining Industry in the Development of the Pass-Law System in South Africa." *International Journal of African Historical Studies* 9 (3): 419–34. https://www.africabib.org/htp.php?RID=189056061.

South Africa. 2010. *Amendment of the Broad-Based Socio-Economic Charter for the South African Mining and Minerals Industry.* Available online at www.dmr.gov.za/publications/finish/108-minerals-act-charter-and-score card/128-amendedofbbseecharter/0.html, accessed 27 February 2017.

Sovacool, Benjamin K., Götz Walter, Thijs Van de Graaf and Nathan Andrews. 2016. "Energy Governance, Transnational Rules, and the Resource Curse: Exploring the Effectiveness of the Extractive Industries Transparency Initiative (EITI)." *World Development* 86: 179–92. https://doi.org/10.1016/j.worlddev.2016.01.021.

Wheatcroft, Geoffrey. 1985. *The Randlords: The Men Who Made South Africa.* London: Weidenfeld & Nicolson.

10 A Natural Resource Boon or Impending Doom in East Africa? Political Settlements and Governance Dynamics in Uganda's Oil Sector

SHINGIRAI TAODZERA

Introduction

Extractive natural resources, especially oil and diamonds, are widely believed to induce adverse outcomes in resource-rich countries and give credence to the so-called resource curse theory. Features of the "curse" include authoritarian governance, violent conflict, weak administrative state institutions, undifferentiated economies, and the marginalization of social groups that are not linked to the ruling political elites or those who govern the resource sector (Collier 2003, 2010; Collier and Hoeffler 2004; Mcferson 2010; Ross 1999; Sachs and Warner 2001; Shaxson 2007). Several scholars argue against the existence of a curse, however, instead proposing various alternative approaches for understanding the effects of natural resources in African countries (Alexeev and Conrad 2009); Brunnschweiler 2008; Fearon 2005; Haber and Menaldo 2007; Stijns 2005). These include statistical analyses that show no direct correlation between natural resources and adverse governance regimes, and qualitative, case-based studies that show the complex interaction of various factors that can produce negative outcomes. Nevertheless, oil remains a particularly notorious resource-curse-inducer. Almost all oil-producing sub-Saharan African countries have experienced, or continue to experience, authoritarian rule, weak economies, political violence, or a combination of some or all of these factors; leading examples include Nigeria, Equatorial Guinea, Gabon, and Angola.

As a result, the discoveries of new oil and gas deposits in East Africa since 2006 have led scholars and policy makers to speculate on whether these states will avoid or experience the resource curse. Uganda has the largest quantities of commercial oil deposits discovered in the region, and it has also made the most advanced progress towards setting up export infrastructure (Kiiza, Bategeka, and Ssewanyana 2011). However, given that none of the East African producers has commenced oil exports, it is premature to answer this question. Current scholarship on the emerging oil industry in East African states mainly revolves around the effect of oil on politics, governance, human rights, and security (Patey 2015).

For instance, Anderson and Browne (2011) and Vokes (2012) give detailed overviews of oil discoveries in East Africa and the emerging oil-induced political dynamics in Uganda, suggesting that the fledgling oil industry likely will induce political instability in the country. In addition, the centralization of oil governance, weak local government capacity, and the lack of coherence among civil society organizations and their limited access to communities likely will result in the failure of the oil industry to exert positive effects on development in Uganda (Van Alstine et al. 2014). Collier (2011) also analyses the country's oil sector, and prescribes several options that likely would steer Uganda away from the "Dutch disease" spectrum. Nevertheless, this literature is based on the resource curse theory, which does not deal adequately with the extent to which the country's underlying political dynamics influence institutional, political, and economic outcomes.

This chapter thus proposes using the concept of "political settlements" as a more effective analytical framework through which to understand the socio-political and economic developments that accompany resource wealth in Uganda, the East African frontier states, and resource-rich countries in general. A political settlements perspective would help determine the feasibility and effectiveness of policy prescriptions for managing the oil industry and its revenue, and contribute to a clearer understanding of the extent to which Uganda might attain positive developmental outcomes with resource wealth. Political settlements generally can be defined as agreements, compromises, and alliances made by the most powerful political actors in society, which, in turn, produce the contextual foundation on which institutions and policies are established (Khan 2010). This framework focuses on relationships between the most powerful political actors, the nature and source of their power, and how their interactions produce specific political, economic, and institutional outcomes. Political dynamics determine the way the resource industry is managed and how the wealth is distributed in resource-rich countries.

This chapter is structured as follows. In the first section, I provide an overview of the resource curse debate, showing the main arguments for and against the framework. This leads to an evaluation of the main tenets of the political settlements approach and its efficacy as an analytical tool for understanding the fate of resource-rich states. Next, I discuss the main features of Uganda's oil sector and the policy options available to the government. In the subsequent section, I analyse the country's politics and oil governance framework through the lens of the political settlements approach, and conclude with remarks on the utility of the political settlements framework in studies of natural resource management in Africa.

The Natural Resource Curse Debate

The resource curse concept has served as a dominant metanarrative and framework for understanding the outcomes of resource endowment in sub-Saharan African countries. Although it plausibly identifies the mechanisms through which the paradoxical relationship between natural resources and adverse political and economic outcomes occur, the resource curse approach does not adequately address the underlying political dynamics that result in the unfavourable consequences of resource endowment. The controversies over the validity of the resource curse approach have produced a major divide in the literature between scholars who support and oppose its use as an analytical tool in the discipline. Proponents argue that natural resources, especially oil and diamonds, have inherently adverse political, economic, and social consequences, and that this occurs through various mechanisms (Collier 2003, 2010; Collier and Hoeffler 2004; Mcferson 2010; Ross 1999; Sachs and Warner 2001; Shaxson 2007).

For instance, resources can induce neopatrimonial governance, which results in repressive political regimes and incumbents' unwillingness to transfer power through elections (Ross 1999). Resource revenue also leads to the creation of "rentier states," whereby the externally derived revenue provides a disincentive for the state to strengthen domestic institutions of political and economic governance that facilitate state-society relations, especially tax regimes (Ross 1999). The resulting weak administrative institutions and high levels of poverty contribute to political instability, as marginalized social groups might resort to seizing political power through violence (Collier and Hoeffler 2004).

Resource-induced political instability also might increase the likelihood that political leaders are forcibly expelled from office, leading to predatory rule and short-sighted policy making by incumbents (Goldsmith 2004). Further arguments refer to economic effects of the resource curse, especially the "Dutch disease," which occurs when lucrative resource wealth leads to economic dependence on externally derived revenue that is subject to unstable global commodity price fluctuations and unfavourable terms of trade. A resource boom also results in currency appreciation, which undermines local industries' competitiveness by making imports cheaper (Ebrahim-zadeh 2003). However, when a "bust" – a sharp decline in commodity prices – occurs, the consequent economic decline is grave because non-resource economic sectors are not sufficiently well developed to withstand the sharp loss of revenue (Sachs and Warner 2001).

Other scholars studying the resource curse focus on the types of natural resources and their political and economic effects. For example, Le Billon (2001) argues that alluvial diamonds are the most notorious resource curse inducers because they are "lootable" or easy to access and transport. Diamonds are often associated with protracted armed conflict because of their high value, ease of transport and trade, and relatively high global demand. The civil wars in Sierra Leone and Angola are notable examples, wherein the mineral enabled armed groups to fund rebellions (Grant, MacLean, and Shaw 2003; Grant and Taylor 2004; Silberfein 2004). Comparatively, Le Billon (2001) notes that other natural resources, such as gold, are not easily extracted and do not have the same value as diamonds and oil, reducing their resource-curse-inducing effects. Agricultural products are also less likely to cause the resource curse because they have a longer value chain, with multiple actors that have diverse interests. Auty (2006) also avers that non-resource-rich countries tend to have fewer violent conflicts in comparison, because they are more likely to create stronger public administrative and tax collection systems and broader economic diversification.

On the other hand, oil is regarded as the most notorious resource curse inducer. This is mainly because it is the world's most traded high-value commodity, which allows governments of oil-exporting states to accrue vast revenue (Le Billon 2001). Apart from motivating incumbents to extend their stay in power, Ross (1999) argues that oil also has "anti-modernisation effects," meaning that the limited economic diversification that often accompanies oil wealth limits the growth of a strong middle class that would create the vibrant civil society needed to drive a robust pluralist political system.

Nevertheless, several scholars have argued against the resource curse theory in various ways. For instance, Stinjs (2005) challenges the mechanisms of the theory, especially the argument that natural resource sectors weaken other economic sectors through the Dutch disease mechanism. He notes that such arguments are based on conventional statistical growth regressions that do not sufficiently capture the complex interaction of context-specific factors within the respective resource-rich states. Haber and Menaldo (2007) also contradict arguments that resource wealth automatically undermines democracy or transitions from authoritarian rule to democracy. Similarly, Fearon (2005) conducts an alternative statistical study that challenges Collier and Hoeffler's (2004) popular "greed and grievance" hypothesis, and discovers weak empirical linkages between a country's having a high percentage of national income from primary commodity exports and its being prone to civil war.

In addition, Alexeev and Conrad (2009)'s study finds that, contrary to the assumptions of the resource curse hypothesis, extractive natural resources have had, in fact, a positive effect on pluralist democracy and the development of strong political institutions in several resource-rich countries. As well, Di John (2011) finds insufficient evidence to support the existence of a resource curse, criticizes the predominantly statistical approaches that proponents of the resource curse typically use, and prescribes more in-depth, historical, and comprehensive qualitative analyses that show the interaction of multiple factors, some of which are unique to specific cases. Moreover, some resource-rich African countries, such as Botswana, which has exported kimberlitic diamonds since 1975, have defied the resource curse. This can be explained by the country's underlying political dynamics, which include its colonial history, demographics, and structure of its public institutions, which determine the way Botswana manages the diamond sector and distributes diamond revenue. It is thus imperative to use the political settlements approach to understand these informal political arrangements, and to determine how they shape the establishment and function of formal political and economic institutions.

Political Settlements and Resource Governance

Broadly, a political settlement is a coalition and set of compromises between powerful political actors in society, which, in turn, provide the contextual foundation on which institutions and policies are established (Khan 2010; Whitfield et al. 2015). Political elites form coalitions based on individual and collective interests and imperatives of self-preservation, with the additional consideration of other context-specific factors (Whitfield et al. 2015, 13). The formation of coalitions occurs through formal and informal processes and practices through which political elites and their supporters consolidate political power (Kelsall 2016, 2). When institutions become incompatible with powerful groups' interests, these groups will strive to change them through various strategies, including violence (Khan 2010). Power is thus a foundational concept in understanding political settlements, especially the concept of "holding power": the ability of political actors to engage in and withstand conflicts (Khan 2010). This approach also provides insight into the type of power that each group possesses, which determines its ability to influence institutional changes and prevail in conflicts. Power could include financial or economic status, the ability to mobilize large groups of supporters for a political cause, and perceptions of legitimacy from other political actors (Khan 2010).

As Khan (2010) explains, political settlements also operate at two levels of analysis: the "social order" and "institutional structure." At a higher level, social order refers to the way a society achieves a level of political stability and economic performance necessary for it to operate. Endemic political violence, for instance, is evidence of the absence of a social order. At a lower level, "institutional structure" refers to the formal and informal institutions that create preferred legal, regulatory, or distributional outcomes for different social groups and classes, particularly the economically and politically powerful. These levels of analysis are interconnected, because the establishment and stability of a social order depends on the presence of institutions and power relations that are politically and economically viable to influential groups. Institutions also influence the distribution of power by creating economic benefits that affect the relative holding power of social groups; conversely, the distribution of power influences institutions because powerful groups will guide the creation of formal and informal institutions to achieve desired outcomes.

Effectively, this can be described as a "state-*in*-society" approach, a perspective that views the state as being embedded in, and influenced by, the society in which it is established. This approach is different from conventional "state *and* society" approaches, which assume the neat separation between the state and the social context (Whitfield et al. 2015). In this way, the political settlements logic can be applied to understand African states' various experiences with resource endowment. For example, Botswana is commonly referred to as a developmental state that has had a successful public-private natural resource management model mainly because of strong institutions (Acemoglu, Johnson, and Robinson 2003; Beaulier 2003; Hillbom 2012). However, the country's political, economic, and institutional structures are largely a product of political arrangements established among the country's most powerful political actors. These included the departing British colonial authorities, Botswana's first president, Seretse Khama, and his Botswana Democratic Party (BDP), the powerful traditional chiefs (of which Khama was one), and De Beers, which, until recently, was the world's largest diamond-mining and global marketing company.

On the other hand, Angola and Sierra Leone have had different and adverse outcomes from resource endowment because of the nature of their political coalitions and other proximate factors. In the former Portuguese colony of Angola, oil extraction has played a leading economic role since the 1950s (Frynas and Wood 2001; Malaquias 2007). The civil war that started in 1975 pitted the People's Movement for the Liberation of Angola (MPLA) against the National Union for the Total Independence of Angola (UNITA), and was sustained by natural resource income. The MPLA controlled the government apparatus and oil industry while UNITA controlled diamond mines in the interior (Grant 2002; Le Billon 2001). In the post–civil war era, the MPLA's ruling coalition has maintained exclusive control of the oil industry through Sonangol, an efficiently managed oil enclave that is relatively autonomous from the government (Grant 2003; Soares de Oliveira 2007a, 2007b). The MPLA government has thus maintained its wartime political settlement, whereby the business-state-military elite coalition maintains an exclusionary domestic regime that also functions in tandem with external business partners (Soares de Oliveira 2007a; Wilson and Mwaka 2003).

Sierra Leone's conflict between 1991 and 2002 can be plausibly described as a consequence of the absence of a strong internal political settlement, in addition to other factors. Sierra Leone began extracting diamonds through De Beers's Sierra Leone Selection Trust (SLST) before attaining political independence (Gberie 2005; Grant 2010; Smillie, Gberie, and Hazleton 2000). Unlike in Botswana, however, the SLST did not establish a strong coalition with the government and other powerful local actors before its departure. Post-independence political leaders – particularly Siaka Stevens, who held power from 1967 to 1985 – mismanaged the diamond industry. Stevens established weak neopatrimonial linkages with some traditional chiefs and Lebanese diamond traders, using diamond revenue to sustain the patron-client networks (Grant 2005; Keen 2005; Smillie, Gberie, and Hazleton 2000). His regime marginalized other powerful social groups, particularly poor urban and rural youth, who constituted the bulk of the armies of the Revolutionary United Front (RUF). The civil war that resulted from the RUF invasion can be viewed as a result of the weakly constituted and highly fragmented political settlement within the governing coalition. If the internal political settlement was strong, the government would have had stronger institutions and a security apparatus to repel the RUF intrusion. Therefore, as this brief overview illustrates, it is crucial to analyse resource-rich countries through the lens of a political settlement framework.

Overview of Uganda's Oil Sector

The observations above have crucial implications for understanding resource management in diverse contexts, particularly the new oil producers in East Africa, such as Uganda, which holds the largest oil reserves in the region at 6,5 billion barrels. Uganda's oil discoveries are a result of junior oil companies' accelerated investment in exploratory activities between 2004 and 2008, when global oil prices were at a near-all-time-high of US$147 per barrel (Anderson and Browne 2011; Patey 2015). These companies include Hardman Resources, Tullow Oil, Heritage Oil and Gas, Petrobras, African Oil Corporation, and Anadarko (Anderson and Browne 2011). The companies' combined discoveries in Uganda amount to an estimated 6.5 billion barrels, the largest onshore discovery in Africa since that of Gabon's 900 million barrels in 1985 (Anderson and Browne 2011; Kiiza, Bategeka, and Ssewanyana 2011). However, Uganda's commercial production is estimated to last up to thirty years, which is a relatively short period.

The government and oil companies will also jointly construct a small refinery in Kibaale, in Hoima District, producing 30,000 barrels per day, and a pipeline for export to global markets through Tanzania (Patey 2015). China's National Offshore Oil Corporation (CNOOC), France's Total E&P currently dominate the country's oil industry through "farm out" or licencing contracts with both the government and Tullow Oil (Vokes 2012). The three companies each paid US$1.45 billion for a single oil block and, with production anticipated to begin in 2022, and expected to peak at 100,000 barrels daily, they will generate an estimated US$2 billion annual revenue (Hickey et al. 2015). This amount, however, will depend on oil prices at the time of production, which likely will be depressed due to global oversupply.

Several political actors have coalesced around the Ugandan oil industry since 2006. These include the current president, Yoweri Museveni, the army, government agencies, international oil companies, donor agencies, parliament, civil society organizations, traditional kingdoms, and ordinary citizens (Hickey et al. 2015; Kiiza, Bategeka, and Ssewanyana 2011). President Museveni assumed direct control over the oil sector from the beginning of his administration, infamously describing it as "my oil" (Mwesigwa 2016). The army, which underwrites Museveni's power, also protects the oil installations, thus ensuring relative political stability and a strong state monopoly over violence in the country. Another key actor is the Petroleum Authority of Uganda (PAU), which is responsible for issuing licences and for regulating the oil industry. The PAU falls under the Ministry of Energy and Mineral Development, and works closely with the Ministry of Finance, the Bank of Uganda, and the Uganda Revenue Authority (Hickey et al. 2015). The Bunyoro-Kitara indigenous kingdom is another key political actor involved in the oil sector, since most of Uganda's oil deposits are located there. It has unsuccessfully requested at least 12.5 per cent of the share of oil revenue from the government. Civil society groups have continuously exerted political pressure on the government on issues pertaining to the oil industry; and these include the Advocates Coalition for Development and Environment, the Civil Society Coalition on Oil and Gas, Uganda Oil Watch Network, and the Parliamentary Forum on Oil and Gas (Kiiza, Bategeka, and Ssewanyana 2011).

The formal policy framework through which the Ugandan government currently manages the oil industry is as follows. As Manyak (2015) explains, the 2015 Public Finance Management Act created a framework for managing oil wealth, which grants the Ministry of Energy and Mineral Development power to give out licences and create additional regulations for the oil sector. The framework also distributes 7 per cent of oil revenue to the twenty-five local governments and districts that the oil sector affects directly, but it is silent on the payment of royalties to traditional kingdoms. Critics say that the act does not clearly divide powers and responsibilities between different agencies, such as the parliament and the office of the president. The act also created an investment fund that functions as a separate government account in which oil revenue is deposited. Overall, legislation governing the oil industry – such as the Petroleum Development Act, the Petroleum Exploration, Development and Production Act, and the Petroleum Refining, Gas Processing and Conversion, Transportation and Storage Act, signed in 2013 – vest the management of all minerals and petroleum wealth under the government's effective control, including regulating all aspects of exploration, development, transportation, and marketing of oil and gas products (Manyak 2015).

Several scholars have provided policy prescriptions that supposedly would guarantee developmental outcomes from oil endowment and avert the natural resource curse in Uganda. These prescription are limited, however, by their minimal recognition of political factors in the Ugandan context – they do not consider adequately underlying political dynamics and how these determine their feasibility, success, or failure. For example, Manyak (2015) argues that the government should establish prudent fiscal management of oil royalties through transparency and accountability, compensating traditional kingdoms, local governments, and citizens who are adversely affected by the oil sector – while minimizing the ecological and environmental effects of oil extraction. Shepherd (2013) indicates that the four key guarantors for avoiding the resource curse are developing a broadly shared commitment to stability and growth; having expert and empowered technical advisers and policy specialists; having strong domestic constituents who can inform and moderate political debates around revenue management; and popular buy-in of the government's revenue distribution priorities (Shepherd 2013).

In addition, Collier (2011) notes that Uganda requires savings and investment strategies, mainly because of the relatively short time frame of thirty years for oil production in the country. This includes managing and sequencing consumption in a way that does not result in inflation, and facilitating the growth of both the resource and non-tradable sectors to avoid the "Dutch disease." Collier argues that this would entail having sovereign wealth funds, which manage financial assets; sovereign resilience funds, which focus on price volatilities and thus guard against the "Dutch disease"; and sovereign development funds, which manage the accumulation of foreign financial assets and domestic investments.

Taken together, these policy prescriptions potentially could result in Uganda's managing its oil wealth in a way that improves human livelihoods and avoids political and economic instability. However, the creation, success, and/or failure of these institutions and strategies largely depend on the political and economic interests of the most influential actors in the country. Given that Museveni's style of governance is authoritarian and averse to transparency and institutional checks and balances within both the government and oil sector, it unlikely that such policy and institutional frameworks will function effectively in Uganda.

Political Settlement and Oil in Uganda

The current political settlement in Uganda is based on the de facto control by President Museveni and his National Resistance Movement (NRM) regime over the political system in general, and the oil industry in particular (Golooba-Mutebi and Hickey 2013, 2016). Museveni's power rests on a combination of military power, political patronage, the manipulation of formal legislative procedures, and strategic alliances with foreign actors (Mwenda 2007; Mwenda and Tangri 2005). The country's security sector, especially the army, and intelligence services are largely responsible for securing Museveni's political power since he came into office in 1986. The elite Special Forces Group that Museveni's son, Lieutenant General Muhoozi Kainerugaba, used to command is largely responsible for protecting sensitive infrastructure in Uganda, including oil wells (Patey 2015; Vokes 2012). Private security companies such as Saracen Uganda, of which Museveni's younger brother, Salim Saleh, is a partial owner, also provide security at some of the oil infrastructure and other government properties (Enns, Andrews, and Grant 2018; Patey 2015). Although this pre-empts attacks by armed groups, it also restricts access by stakeholders such as local communities and civil society organizations, thus maintaining secrecy around the oil industry (Hickey et al. 2015; Patey 2015; Vokes 2012).

Museveni also employs patronage at all levels of the state to garner political support and maintain the cohesion of his ruling coalition (Golooba-Mutebi and Hickey 2016). At the level of the state, he appoints close family members and other loyal personal relations largely drawn from his Bahima ethnic group to high-profile positions both in government and in the security sector. He also co-opts political rivals through appointments to positions at all tiers of government. At the substate levels, he provides employment to supporters in local government and the resident district commissioners. He also makes personal donations to various groups and organizations, particularly in the runup to elections. Museveni also used some of the oil revenue to fund patronage, as well as military spending and electoral campaigns. For instance, he controversially funded an arms deal with Russia to strengthen the security sector in 2011 (de Kock and Sturman 2012). He also disbursed US$8,700 to each of the 330 Members of Parliament from his National Resistance Movement (NRM) party in the runup to the 2011 elections, resulting in NRM candidates winning most seats, especially in the rural areas (de Kock and Sturman 2012).

Apart from patronage, Museveni has used violence and suppression of dissent to preserve his political power and undermine the activities of opposition figures, especially during electoral campaigns in 2001, 2006, 2011, and 2016. For instance, Abrahamsen and Bareebe (2016) reveal that the NRM won 70 per cent of the parliamentary seats in the 2016 general elections mainly using repressive tactics that included the arbitrary arrests of opposition leaders and erstwhile allies Kizza Besigye and Amama Mbabazi and denying them access to the media. The "Crime Preventers" vigilante group, coordinated by the then police commissioner Kale Kayihura, routinely attacked opposition activists in the 2016 election (Golooba-Mutebi and Hickey 2016). Similarly, former state security minister Henry Tumukunde coordinated the Kalangala Action Plan paramilitary group, which attacked and tortured opposition supporters throughout the country in the 2001 elections (Canada 2003; Golooba-Mutebi and Hickey 2016). Other irregular electoral practices include Tumukunde's direct appointment of Electoral Commission staff and use of government funds to pay bribes and other campaign-related expenses. Museveni also manipulates legislative processes, using the ruling NRM's parliamentary majority to ratify his extended stay in power. He systematically uses the NRM parliamentary caucus to introduce legislation into parliament, thus undermining the separation of powers, which is one of the foundational principles of a democratic governance system. For example, parliament amended the constitution to remove presidential term limits in 2005, which made it possible for Museveni to run for office multiple times (Mwenda 2007). The NRM also controversially voted to amend article 102 (b) of the 1995 constitution in 2017 – commonly known as the Age Limit clause – which removed the limit of seventy-five on the age of the president, thus allowing Museveni to stay in office indefinitely. He also routinely issues verbal and written directives, or expresses displeasure with certain decisions to individual ministries. This reduces public institutions of the state to tools for discharging Museveni's personalized rule.

The Museveni regime's subversion of Uganda's traditional kingdoms, which have substantial influence in the country's politics, is another case in point. The Bunyoro kingdom, for example, located in western Uganda, claims historical and customary ownership of the land in the Albertine Graben region on which the country's oil deposits are located, and has unsuccessfully lobbied for oil royalties (Anderson and Browne 2011). Museveni undermines the traditional kingdoms as part of a broader policy of weakening all forms of substate organizations to pre-empt the emergence of any formidable political opposition.

Former president Milton Obote had abolished all traditional kingdoms in Uganda following a clash with the Buganda kingdom in 1966, but Museveni reinstated them in 1993 (Oloka-Onyango 1997). The restoration largely emanated from a political alliance struck between the NRM and the Buganda kingdom during the NRM's insurgency against Obote's government from 1981 to 1986. When the government formalized the reinstatement of the kingdoms in the 1995 constitution, it categorized them as cultural institutions only (Rutanga 2010). This, however, would become a source of future political struggles between the kingdoms, especially the Buganda, and Museveni's government. After the reinstatement, Uganda's kingdoms generally supported Museveni's NRM government because it restored the institutions and gave the kings state-funded salaries, vehicles, and other material benefits. The Buganda and Bunyoro kingdoms, however, began lobbying for the return of properties (*ebyaffe*) that they lost when Obote abolished all kingdoms in 1966

(Rutanga 2010). This included administrative buildings, wetlands, lakes, and land, some of which the government had taken over. In 1993 the government enacted the Assets and Properties Act, pledging to restore all the properties, although it has done so only partially.

Most crucially, the traditional kingdoms asked for the re-establishment of federalism (*federo*), which would have granted them increased political influence and a range of powers such as tax collection, management of infrastructure, and oversight of health and education systems (Englebert 2005). Museveni declined, however, saying this was necessary to promote national unity instead of ethnic politics, which had contributed to political violence and social fragmentation since independence (Goodfellow and Lindemann 2013). This resulted in some kingdoms, especially the Buganda, giving tacit support to the political opposition after the reinstatement of multiparty politics in 2005. This development also demonstrates the dynamic nature of political settlements, whereby political actors shift allegiances from one coalition to another to secure their interests.

The political tensions between the state and traditional kingdoms led to several instances of political violence. For instance, in July 2009 the Buganda accused Museveni of conducting a smear campaign against the Buganda king, and demanded that the state move the country's capital city, Kampala, off Buganda land (Goodfellow and Lindemann 2013). In September 2009, riots occurred between Buganda youths and the police when the government prohibited the Kabaka from visiting the Banyala subgroup, which had sought to secede from the kingdom (Goodfellow and Lindemann 2013). The Baganda also protested the Museveni government's support for Buganda subchiefs of the Banyala, Mengo, Kooki, and Baluli tribes, which intended to break away from the Baganda kingdom (Goodfellow and Lindemann 2013; John Paul II Justice and Peace Centre 2013). Buganda youths and the police also clashed following the burning down of Buganda's Kasubi Royal Tombs in March 2010 by suspected government agents (*IRIN News* 2009). The tombs are an ancestral burial place for Buganda kings and a popular tourist attraction that brings in revenue for the kingdom (Goodfellow and Lindemann 2013). The Ruwenzuru kingdom's Royal Guards also clashed with the army in November 2016 after the government accused the king of trying to secede from Uganda (Human Rights Watch 2016). The violence resulted in the deaths of forty-six guards and fourteen police officers and the arrest of the Ruwenzuru king, Charles Mumbere, on murder charges (Human Rights Watch 2016).

The Bunyoro kingdom has been directly involved in the politics of oil in Uganda, since the country's oil resources are mostly located in areas under its customary jurisdiction, especially near the towns of Hoima, Kabaale, Masindi, and Bulissa (Patey 2015). The kingdom requested 12.5 per cent of royalties from pre-production payments that foreign companies made to the government, but received only 1 per cent, to be shared by all traditional chiefdoms in the Lake Albert area (Patey 2015). The government argued that the kingdom had no claim for preferential access to oil revenues, and that since oil exports had yet to begin, the government could not yet pay out any royalties. However, the state has since received revenues, mainly from licensing fees and taxes. For instance, Tullow revealed in September 2015 that it had paid US$250 million in capital gains tax, of which the Bunyoro demanded a share; however, the Minister of Energy and Mineral Development, Irene Muloni, indicated that the government would not be obliged to allocate the Bunyoro a share, since the payments were not derived from oil sales, but taxes (Mugerwa 2017). The basis for the Bunyoro kingdom's demands emanated from its claims of historical occupation and trusteeship over the land, and also for compensation for the direct and indirect effects of the oil sector, such as displacement and loss of land and sources of livelihood, increased population, and pressure on social services (Manyak 2015; Patey 2015). The Bunyoro kingdom continues to press its demands on the government.

Despite the aforementioned centralization of power by Museveni, the current political settlement has resulted in the maintenance of political stability in Uganda, which has a history of armed conflict, including coups and insurgencies, since independence in 1962. Since coming to power through a coup in 1986, Museveni has defeated several insurgencies, which brought relative stability and facilitated economic development. Former army officers and supporters of former leaders Milton Obote and Idi Amin, who belonged to the Lango and Nubian-Kakwa ethnic groups from Uganda's northern region, formed some of the insurgent groups. These include Alice Lakwena's Holy Spirit Mobile Forces (HSMF) and Joseph Kony's Lord's Resistance Army (LRA) (de Kock and Sturman 2012). Lakwena, a spirit medium, led the HSMF, which consisted mostly of ethnic Acholi men, against Museveni's Nyankole-dominated government (Nasong'o 2015). Kony's LRA, which took over from Lakwena after her defeat in 1987, also fought against Museveni's government, and frequently attacked communities in the northern region, which resulted in an internal refugee problem (Nasong'o 2015). Museveni has since successfully pushed the LRA out of Uganda, with substantial military assistance from the United States.

Thus, Museveni's dominance of Uganda's political system, particularly through military power, patronage, and the use of government institutions and processes, defines Uganda's political settlement. This makes it unlikely that the prudent policies and strong state institutions that currently exist, and others that might be established in the future, would produce beneficial and equitable outcomes from Uganda's oil sector. That sector is deeply embedded in the country's complex political conditions, and only a holistic analytical approach would yield clearer insight into the political, economic, institutional, and distributional outcomes that will emerge around Uganda's oil industry.

Conclusion

The application of a political settlements framework to Uganda and other case studies can lead to a better understanding of the political and economic dynamics of resource-rich countries. This is because the analytical reach of this framework goes beyond natural resources alone to identify the historical background, main political actors, the source of their power, their interests, and the extent to which their negotiation of political power and economic interests influence the manifested outcomes. President Museveni and the ruling NRM coalition has had totalitarian political control over Uganda's politics and economics since before the discovery of oil in that country. This forms the foundation for the way the oil industry is managed, how revenue is distributed, and how the country's political actors interact with both the state and foreign oil companies. Instead of speculating whether or not Uganda will experience the resource curse, it is more useful to unpack the country's underlying political dynamics and assess the way state and non-state political actors have responded to the news of an impending oil bonanza.

The political settlement approach can also be used to determine the feasibility and extent to which policies can succeed in Uganda – and resource-rich countries in general. In the case of Uganda, the several policy prescriptions that scholars have made so far are potentially effective, but this depends on the extent to which they are compatible with the interests of the most powerful and influential political actors. Museveni and his allies are unlikely to cede their direct control of the oil industry, since this would create alternative centres of power that could jeopardize the ruling coalition's political control and access to revenue on which it depends to maintain the patron-client political system. The creation of autonomous, quasi-state agencies and other oil governance institutions, for example, would result in significant decentralization of power away from Museveni and his government. Such institutions would function only with limited autonomy, however, since the delegated authorities would be unquestionably loyal to Museveni. This also facilitates the maintenance of secrecy over sensitive details such as contracts between the state and foreign oil companies and financial transactions.

Nevertheless the political settlements approach has several shortcomings that might limit its analytical scope. For instance, the approach does not sufficiently consider the importance of historical factors. In Uganda's case, the country's colonial history and its post-colonial armed insurgencies and coups considerably influence its political system. Although Museveni's style of governance is largely dictatorial, his unchecked control over the oil sector and pervasive militarization of Uganda can be understood as a strategy to forestall armed attacks against both his government and the oil infrastructure, given the history of coups and insurgencies in Uganda and the Great Lakes region. The political settlements approach is also ill equipped to analyse the relationships between internal and external factors. In this case, foreign actors such as oil companies, investors, and the state of global oil markets also interact with Uganda's domestic context and influence the way the oil sector, and the political system at large, is managed. Future research thus would require the combination of the political settlement approach with other theoretical frameworks in order to produce more comprehensive conclusions.

BIBLIOGRAPHY

Abrahamsen, Rita, and Gerald Bareebe. 2016. "Uganda's 2016 Elections: Not Even Faking It Anymore." *African Affairs* 115 (461): 751–65. https://doi.org/10.1093/afraf/adw056.
Acemoglu, Daron, Simon Johnson, and James A. Robinson. 2003. "An African Success Story: Botswana." In *In Search of Prosperity: Analytic Narratives on Economic Growth*, edited by Dani Rodrik, 80–119. Princeton, NJ: Princeton University Press.
Alexeev, Michael, and Robert Conrad. 2009. "The Elusive Curse of Oil." *Review of Economics and Statistics* 91 (3): 586–98. https://doi.org/10.1162/rest.91.3.586.
Anderson, David M., and Adrian J. Browne. 2011. "The Politics of Oil in Eastern Africa." *Journal of Eastern African Studies* 5 (2): 369–410. https://doi.org/10.1080/17531055.2011.573187.
Auty, Richard M. 2006. "Patterns of Rent-Extraction and Deployment in Developing Countries: Implications for Governance, Economic Policy and

Performance." UNU-WIDER Research Paper 2006/16. February. Available online at http://wider.unu.edu/publications/working-papers/research-papers/2006/en_GB/rp2006-16/_files/78091771104134775/default/rp2006-16.pdf.

Beaulier, Scott A. 2003. "Explaining Botswana's Success: The Critical Role of Post-Colonial Policy." *Cato Journal* 23 (2): 227–40. https://heinonline.org/HOL/P?h=hein.journals/catoj23&i=233.

Brunnschweiler, Christa N. 2008. "Cursing the Blessings? Natural Resource Abundance, Institutions, and Economic Growth." *World Development* 36 (3): 399–419. https://doi.org/10.1016/j.worlddev.2007.03.004.

Canada. 2003. Immigration and Refugee Board of Canada. "Uganda: A Group Called the Kalangala Action Plan; Its Activities and Organizational Structure, Whether It Is Affiliated with the Government." Ottawa: Immigration and Refugee Board of Canada, Research Directorate, 7 July.

Collier, Paul. 2003. "The Market for Civil War." *Foreign Policy* 136 (May–June): 38–45. https://doi.org/10.2307/3183621.

Collier, Paul. 2010. "The Political Economy of Natural Resources." *Social Research* 77 (4): 1105–32. https://muse.jhu.edu/article/527756.

Collier, Paul. 2011. "Managing Uganda's Oil Discovery." Oxford University, Centre for the Study of African Economies. Available online at https://www.bou.or.ug/bou/bou-downloads/publications/special_pubs/2011/All/Managing_Ugandas_Oil_Discovery_Prof_Colliers_paper_Oct_21.pdf, accessed 23 April 2019.

Collier, Paul, and Anke Hoeffler. 2004. "Greed and Grievance in Civil War." *Oxford Economic Papers* 56 (4): 563–95. https://doi.org/10.1093/oep/gpf064.

de Kock, Petrus, and Kathryn Sturman. 2012. *The Power of Oil: Charting Uganda's Transition to a Petro-State*. Research Report 10. Johannesburg: South African Institute for African Affairs.

Di John, Jonathan. 2011. "Is There Really a Resource Curse? A Critical Survey of Theory and Evidence." *Global Governance* 17 (2): 167–84. https://doi.org/10.1163/19426720-01702005.

Ebrahim-zadeh, Christine. 2003. "Dutch Disease: Too Much Wealth Managed Unwisely." *Finance and Development* 40 (1): 50–1. https://www.economics.utoronto.ca/gindart/Dutch%20Diseas1%20-%20W2010.pdf.

Edel, May. 1965. "African Tribalism: Some Reflections on Uganda." *Political Science Quarterly* 80 (3): 357–72. https://doi.org/10.2307/2147686.

Englebert, Pierre. 2005. "Back to the Future? Resurgent Indigenous Structures and the Reconfiguration of Power in Africa." In *Tradition and Politics: Indigenous Political Structures in Africa*, edited by Olufemi Vaughan, 33–60. Trenton, NJ: Africa World Press.

Enns, Charis, Nathan Andrews, and J. Andrew Grant. 2018. "Security for Whom? Analysing Hybrid Security Governance in Africa's Extractive

Sectors." Paper presented at the International Studies Association annual conference, San Francisco, 6 April.

Fearon, James D. 2005. "Primary Commodity Exports and Civil War." *Journal of Conflict Resolution* 49 (4): 483–507. https://doi.org /10.1177/0022002705277544.

Frynas, Jedrzej George, and Geoffrey Wood. 2001. "Oil & War in Angola." *Review of African Political Economy* 28 (90): 587–606. https://doi.org /10.1080/03056240108704568.

Gberie, Lansana. 2005. *A Dirty War in West Africa: The RUF and the Destruction of Sierra Leone*, London: Hurst.

Goldsmith, Arthur A. 2004. "Predatory versus Developmental Rule in Africa." *Democratization* 11 (3): 88–110. https://doi.org/10.1080/1351034042000238185.

Goodfellow, Tom, and Stefan Lindemann. 2013. "The Clash of Institutions: Traditional Authority, Conflict and the 'Failure of Hybridity' in Buganda." *Commonwealth & Comparative Politics* 51 (1): 3–26. https://doi.org/10.1080/ 14662043.2013.752175.

Golooba-Mutebi, Frederick, and Sam Hickey. 2013. "Investigating the Links between Political Settlements and Inclusive Development in Uganda: Towards a Research Agenda." ESID Working Paper 20. Manchester: University of Manchester, School of Environment and Development, Effective States and Inclusive Development. August. Available online at http://www.effective-states.org/wp-content/uploads/working_papers/ final-pdfs/esid_wp_20_goloobamutebi-hickey.pdf.

Golooba-Mutebi, Frederick, and Sam Hickey. 2016. "The Master of Institutional Multiplicity? The Shifting Politics of Regime Survival, State-Building and Democratisation in Museveni's Uganda." *Journal of Eastern African Studies* 10 (4): 601–18. https://doi.org/10.1080/17531055.2016.1278322.

Grant, J. Andrew. 2002. "Angola's Ashes: The Legacy of Dirty Oil, Blood Diamonds, and Government Graft." In *Advancing Human Security and Development in Africa: Reflections on NEPAD*, edited by Sandra J. MacLean, H. John Harker, and Timothy M. Shaw, 87–107. Halifax, NS: Centre for Foreign Policy Studies.

Grant, J. Andrew. 2003. "New Regionalism and Micro-Regionalism in South-Western Africa: The Oil-Rich Enclave of Cabinda." In *The New Regionalism in Africa*, edited by J. Andrew Grant and Fredrik Söderbaum, 125–43. Aldershot, UK: Ashgate.

Grant, J. Andrew. 2005. "Diamonds, Foreign Aid, and the Uncertain Prospects for Post-Conflict Reconstruction in Sierra Leone." *Round Table* 94 (381): 443–57. https://doi.org/10.1080/00358530500243690.

Grant, J. Andrew. 2010. "Natural Resources, International Regimes and State-Building: Diamonds in West Africa." *Comparative Social Research* 27 (1): 223–48. https://doi.org/10.1108/s0195-6310(2010)0000027013.

Grant, J. Andrew, Sandra J. MacLean, and Timothy M. Shaw. 2003. "Emerging
Transnational Coalitions around Diamonds and Oil in Civil Conflicts
in Africa." In *Global Turbulence: Social Activists' and State Responses to
Globalization*, edited by Marjorie Griffin Cohen and Stephen McBride, 124–39.
Aldershot, UK: Ashgate.
Grant, J. Andrew, and Ian Taylor. 2004. "Global Governance and Conflict
Diamonds: The Kimberley Process and the Quest for Clean Gems." *Round
Table* 93 (375): 385–401. https://doi.org/10.1080/0035853042000249979.
Haber, Stephen, and Victor Menaldo. 2007. "Do Natural Resources Fuel
Authoritarianism? A Reappraisal of the Resource Curse." *American Political
Science Review* 105 (1): 1–26. https://www.jstor.org/stable/41480824.
Hickey, Sam, Abdul-Gafaru Abdulai, Angelo Izama, and Giles Mohan. 2015.
"The Politics of Governing Oil Effectively: A Comparative Study of Two
New Oil-Rich States in Africa." Effective States and Inclusive Development
(ESID) Working Paper 54. https://doi.org/10.2139/ssrn.2695723.
Hillbom, Ellen. 2012. "Botswana: A Development-Oriented Gate-Keeping
State." *African Affairs* 111 (442): 67–89. https://doi.org/10.1093/afraf/
adr070.
Human Rights Watch. 2016. "Uganda: Investigate Killings in Rwenzori
Region." 28 November. Available online at https://www.hrw.org/
news/2016/11/28/uganda-investigate-killings-rwenzori-region.
IRIN News. 2009. "A Rough Guide to the Country's Kingdoms." 11 September.
Available online at http://www.thenewhumanitarian.org/report/86107/
uganda-rough-guide-countrys-kingdoms.
John Paul II Justice and Peace Centre. 2013. *The State and Cultural Institutions
in Uganda: Buganda and Bunyoro Kingdoms Perspective*. Kampala: John Paul II
Justice and Peace Centre.
Keen, David. 2005. *Conflict and Collusion in Sierra Leone*, Basingstoke, UK:
Palgrave Macmillan.
Kelsall, Tim. 2016. *Thinking and Working with Political Settlements*. London:
Overseas Development Institute.
Khan, Mushtaq. 2010. "Political Settlements and the Governance of Growth-
Enhancing Institutions." University of London, SOAS. https://eprints.soas.
ac.uk/9968/1/Political_Settlements_internet.pdf.
Kiiza, Julius, Lawrence Bategeka, and Sarah Ssewanyana. 2011. "Righting
Resources-Curse Wrongs in Uganda: The Case of Oil Discovery and the
Management of Popular Expectations." Research Series 78. Kampala:
Economic Policy Research Centre. http://makir.mak.ac.ug/bitstream/
handle/10570/2012/series78.pdf?sequence=1&isAllowed=y.
Le Billon, Philippe. 2001. "Angola's Political Economy of War: The Role of Oil
and Diamonds, 1975–2000." *African Affairs* 100 (398): 55–80. https://doi.
org/10.1093/afraf/100.398.55.

Malaquias, Assis. 2007. *Rebels and Robbers: Violence in Post-Colonial Angola.* Uppsala, Sweden: Nordic Africa Institute.

Manyak, Terrell George. 2015. "Oil and Governance in Uganda." *Journal of Public Administration and Governance* 5 (1): 40–58. https://doi.org/10.5296/jpag.v5i1.7170.

Mcferson, Hazel M. 2010. "Extractive Industries and African Democracy: Can the 'Resource Curse' Be Exorcised?" *International Studies Perspectives* 11 (4): 335–53. https://doi.org/10.1111/j.1528-3585.2010.00410.x.

Mugerwa, Francis. 2017. "Bunyoro Demands Share of Pre-Production Oil Cash." *Daily Monitor,* 27 December. Available online at https://www.monitor.co.ug/News/National/Bunyoro-demands-share-of-pre-production-oil-cash/688334-3010746-11sx87wz/index.html, accessed 25 February 2017.

Mwesigwa, Alon. 2016. "Uganda Determined Not to Let Expected Oil Cash Trickle Away." *Guardian,* 13 January. Available online at https://www.theguardian.com/global-development/2016/jan/13/uganda-oil-production-yoweri-museveni-agriculture.

Mwenda, Andrew M. 2007. "Personalizing Power in Uganda." *Journal of Democracy* 18 (3): 23–37. http://dx.doi.org/10.1353/jod.2007.0048.

Mwenda, Andrew M., and Roger Tangri. 2005. "Patronage Politics, Donor Reforms, and Regime Consolidation in Uganda." *African Affairs* 104 (416): 449–67. http://dx.doi.org/10.1093/afraf/adi030.

Nasong'o, Wanjala S. 2015. *The Roots of Ethnic Conflict in Africa: From Grievance to Violence.* London: Palgrave Macmillan.

Oloka-Onyango, Joe. 1997. "The Question of Buganda in Contemporary Ugandan Politics." *Journal of Contemporary African Studies* 15 (2): 173–89. https://doi.org/10.1080/02589009708729610.

Patey, Luke. 2015. *Oil in Uganda – Hard Bargaining and Complex Politics in East Africa.* London: Oxford Institute for Energy Studies.

Ross, Michael L. 1999. "The Political Economy of the Resource Curse." *World Politics* 51 (2): 297–322. https://doi.org/10.1017/s0043887100008200.

Rutanga, Murindwa. 2010. "Traditional/Cultural Institutions in Uganda's Democratic Transition, Political Stability and Nation Development: A Case of Buganda." *Jadavpur Journal of International Relations* 14 (1): 125–66. http://dx.doi.org/10.1177/0973598410110009.

Sachs, Jeffrey D., and Andrew M. Warner. 2001. "The Curse of Natural Resources." *European Economic Review* 45 (4): 827–38. https://doi.org/10.1016/s0014-2921(01)00125-8.

Shaxson, Nicholas. 2007. "Oil, Corruption and the Resource Curse." *International Affairs* 83 (6): 1123–40. https://doi.org/10.1111/j.1468-2346.2007.00677.x.

Shepherd, Ben. 2013. "Oil in Uganda: International Lessons for Success." London: Royal Institute of International Affairs. Available online at https://www.chathamhouse.org/sites/default/files/public/Research/Africa/0113pr_ugandaoil.pdf.

Silberfein, Marilyn. 2004. "The Geopolitics of Conflict and Diamonds in Sierra Leone." *Geopolitics* 9 (1): 213–41. https://doi.org/10.1080/146500404123313 07892.

Smillie, Ian, Lansana Gberie, and Ralph Hazleton. 2000. *The Heart of the Matter: Sierra Leone, Diamonds and Human Security.* Ottawa: Partnership Africa Canada.

Soares de Oliveira, Ricardo. 2007a. "Business Success, Angola-Style: Postcolonial Politics and the Rise and Rise of Sonangol." *Journal of Modern African Studies* 45 (4): 595–619. https://doi.org/10.1017/s0022278x07002893.

Soares de Oliveira, Ricardo. 2007b. *Oil and Politics in the Gulf of Guinea.* London: Hurst.

Stijns, Jean-Philippe C. 2005. "Natural Resource Abundance and Economic Growth Revisited." *Resources Policy* 30 (2): 107–30. https://doi.org/10.1016/j.resourpol.2005.05.001.

Van Alstine, James, Jacob Manyindo, Laura Smith, Jami Dixon, and Ivan AmanigaRuhanga. 2014. "Resource Governance Dynamics: The Challenge of 'New Oil' in Uganda." *Resources Policy* 40: 48–58. https://doi.org/10.1016/j.resourpol.2014.01.002.

Vokes, Richard. 2012. "The Politics of Oil in Uganda." *African Affairs* 111 (443): 303–14. https://doi.org/10.1093/afraf/ads017.

Whitfield, Lindsay, Ole Therkildsen, Lars Buur, and Anne Mette Kjær. 2015. *The Politics of African Industrial Policy: A Comparative Perspective.* Cambridge: Cambridge University Press.

Wilson, J. Zöe, and Arsène Bwenge Mwaka 2003. "Angola after Savimbi: New Hope for the South/Central Region?" In *The New Regionalism in Africa*, edited by J. Andrew Grant and Fredrik Söderbaum, 144–58. Aldershot, UK: Ashgate.

SECTION IV

Concluding Remarks: Reflections on Corporate Social Responsibility, Legitimacy, and Development

11 Corporate Social Responsibility and Issues of Legitimacy and Development: Reflections on the Mining Sector in Africa

BONNIE CAMPBELL

Introduction

If we are to analyse the implications of the ever-growing presence and increasing scope of strategies undertaken in the name of corporate social responsibility (CSR), it is useful to keep in mind the reservations concerning these measures formulated by Marketa Evans (2007, 314–15) over ten years ago:

> CSR is defined in a myriad of ways. It is, in fact, self-defined by each side, and understood by each quite differently. The concept is amorphous and problematic, since the nature of the definition drives the measures of success. If CSR is supposed to be activity that goes "beyond" normal business practice, and into voluntary good works, then "some" is better than "none" and it really cannot be criticized for not going far enough. But if it is supposed to be about achieving "greater degrees of pro-social behaviour" then some is definitely not enough and sometimes not better than none at all since it pre-empts legislated change or lends positive spin to bad corporate behaviour.

In view of the above critique, which, though formulated at times differently, is in fact shared by other analysts (Banerjee 2014; Harvey 2014; Porter and Kramer 2011; Prieto-Carrón et al. 2006; Renouard 2015; Zadek 2006), it is important to start with a brief examination of what is driving the expansion and the extended reach of CSR initiatives (see also Campbell 2012). To this end, and subsequently to be able to consider certain implications of this expansion, this chapter is divided into two subsections. The first examines the origins of CSR strategies, including the different meanings that have been attributed to them and the reasons for their ever-growing presence and evolving scope, particularly in the mining sector over the last few decades in Africa. In order to underline the importance of the particular institutional contexts into which CSR strategies are introduced, the second subsection summarizes the findings of three recently published African case studies of CSR strategies which constitute three chapters of a volume published in French, *La responsabilité sociale des entreprises dans le secteur minier: réponse ou obstacle aux enjeux de légitimité et de développement en Afrique?* (Campbell and Laforce 2016). These chapters include contributions by Dr Abdulai Darimani entitled "Contribution de la responsabilité sociale des entreprises minières au développement des communautés locales au Ghana" (Darimani 2016); by Dr Amadou Keita entitled "Responsabilité sociale des entreprises minières et développement communautaire dans les zones minières au Mali: du volontariat à l'obligation juridique, une perspective du terrain" (Keita 2016); and by Denis Tougas entitled "Responsabilité sociale des entreprises et minerais de conflit: l'Est de la République démocratique du Congo comme laboratoire" (Tougas 2016). The objective of the volume was to evaluate the consequences of current practices, notably with regard to the issue of the legitimacy of mining operations and the increasing reach of the social development approach of CSR strategies. The current analysis seeks to bring out certain implications of CSR strategies for longer-term social and economic development. The conclusion proposes alternatives to current approaches for CSR strategies.

Examining the Context in which CSR Strategies Have Emerged

Over the past ten to fifteen years, research on the reform of regulatory and legal frameworks for mining in a number of mineral-rich African countries, introduced to establish a more favourable environment for foreign investment (Campbell 2004, 2009), has analysed the implications for social and economic development and the protection of the environment in the countries concerned. Findings reveal that the reforms have had the effect of provoking an important redefinition of the role and functions of local states, a new delineation between public and private spheres of authority, as well as a reshaping of institutional arrangements. These transformations have had very far-reaching but often overlooked implications. In fact the political consequences of the process of liberalization were to have important impacts for the operations of the companies themselves that are linked directly to issues of CSR. The conceptual challenges these political dimensions of the liberalization process raise have yet to be fully explored.

An interesting contribution in this regard is that of Uwafiokun Ide-mudia and colleagues (Chapter 2, in this volume), who propose that it might be more appropriate to use the notion of "network space," rather than retain the concept of the state that refers to state forms which emerged from radically different historical processes to those considered here. This notion seeks to draw attention to the role that a national state such as Canada plays in a process of self-limitation and extension of co-responsibilities that involve not only the government but also other actors and companies. Similarly, setting the boundary of how risk is managed is not only a corporate responsibility, but also a political one. The notion of "network space" underlines the dynamic trends at play in which states participate in a gradual shift of the demarcation of responsibilities based on economic rationale and business case law; this allows companies to define and domesticate areas of critical importance, notably areas concerning development and ethics.

The extent of the political consequences of the manner in which regulatory frameworks were liberalized in the mining sector in Africa beginning in the 1980s and over the following thirty years can be explained by several factors. First, the strong retrenchment of the state from the sector has been accompanied by parallel processes: the redefinition of the role and functions of the state has led to a reduction of state sovereignty. Second, the process of redefining the role of the state in the mining sector has been accompanied by the reduced autonomy and authority of states, as well as their reduced capacity to influence the evolution of their own structures. Finally, the narrowing of the margin of manoeuvre of mineral-rich states and of their policy space as a result of having to respond to an externally driven reform process has, in certain circumstances, been accompanied by the institutionalizing of particular modes of reproducing domestic power relations. In some cases, and notably in very mineral-rich countries such as Guinea and the Democratic Republic of Congo (DRC), this has led to the institutionalization of a *politics of mining* involving powerful foreign actors and national interests in processes severely lacking in transparency and accountability.

One important consequence of the liberalization of the African mining sector has been the way in which past functions of the state have been increasingly delegated over time to private operators. These include service delivery and also rule setting and implementation. The tendency has been for "an increased (and often reluctant) assumption of state-like responsibilities by transnational mining enterprises at the discreet behest of weak governments" (Szablowski 2007, 59). Such strategies, also described by Strange (1996) as illustrative of a process of the "retreat of the state," are presented by Szablowski (2007, 28) with reference to the way states deal with new mining regimes as strategies of "selective absence" in which the state "absented itself from substantial parts" of the legal regimes intended to help "mediate between investors and community interests" (Szablowski 2007, 45). The resulting blurring of responsibilities and ambiguities that such situations at times produce explains why companies might find themselves dealing *directly* with the demands and expectations of communities, with the risk of potential degeneration into conflicts and a growing concern over the security of mining activities and the employment of private security companies.

The issue of weakened institutional and political capacity and, consequently, the regulatory capacity of host governments is therefore particularly salient. As legitimacy and regulation are interdependent products of legal processes, absence of attention to such issues can only detract from the establishment of regulatory terms that are deemed legitimate (Szablowski 2007). There is therefore a historical, institutional, and political context that explains current problems with legitimacy, the risk of confrontation, and the tendency for mining companies to have to deal increasingly with security issues. As Idemudia (2014) suggests, these ongoing processes also invite us to revisit the manner in which risk is conceptualized and managed and to recognize that, given the particular historical context in which CSR strategies are deployed, issues run deeper than what might sometimes be suggested as corporate responsibility.

In the context of the reduced autonomy, authority, and policy space of mineral-rich states, mining companies are presented as agents of development, and communities increasingly are invited to turn to them for the provision of social services. In such situations, CSR strategies might be seen as an attempt to manage risk and to respond to the very real challenges of the legitimacy of companies' activities. These challenges, however, are linked at a deeper structural level to the perpetuation of particular and often very asymmetrical relations of power between companies and communities and between companies and governments that go far beyond the control of any single enterprise.

It follows that issues concerning *human security and CSR* need to be resituated within a much broader institutional and political perspective that takes into account the origins of the problems of the legitimacy of the operations of mining companies. If not, one most likely will end up responding to security issues by attempting to reinforce and bolster investment and growth strategies that are incompatible with more equitable, sustainable, and intergenerational social and economic development and the broadening of democratic political space.

Similarly, with regard to the issue of *governance frameworks and CSR*, in an attempt to explain the disappointing effects of mining, an important current of thought has tended to draw attention to the dysfunctional administrative and political processes that are internal to the governments of the countries in which the activities take place. Such perspectives point to what are identified as "governance gaps" that need to be remedied by the introduction of better administrative processes in order for the sector to contribute to development and poverty reduction. Consequently, given the weakened capacity of the institutions in many countries where mining companies operate, a vast and growing body of literature has sought to explore how the CSR strategies of these companies could contribute to improving results. Here again, although in no way discounting the existence of such dysfunctional processes, there is obviously need for caution.

Moreover, current trends involving the assumption of state-like responsibilities by transnational mining enterprises through the adoption of CSR strategies have potentially far-reaching implications for the democratic nature of the political processes in which they are implemented that merit far more attention than they have been accorded. As Mitchell (2014) notes:

> Worst still, CSR may actually undermine the formation of a fully functioning democracy with appropriate taxation mechanisms in place. As Ellen Morgan argues, CSR can displace accountability for the provision of social services or environmental protection – responsibilities that are at the heart of the state-citizen social contract. Rather than rely upon CSR to deliver an illusion of sustainable development, host governments must surely focus upon rebalancing the often-inequitable resource extraction taxation regimes in place in most developing countries, and use the taxation revenue to provide adequate social services and to regulate [multinational extractive firms'] behaviour more effectively.

At least part of the reason such implications tend to be overlooked can be explained by the tendency to formulate governance issues in essentially procedural and administrative terms – that is, to "technicize" and depoliticize these processes. Governance, however, concerns the regulation of the conditions of access, control, and the terms on which the resource is exploited, issues which are not only technical but imminently political.[1] In this perspective, matters of governance and governance frameworks would appear most usefully addressed as a component of the broader set of issues concerning constitutive development agendas and strategies. Here again, an invitation to renew approaches in this area is proposed by Idemudia and colleagues (Chapter 2, in this volume), whose recommendation to revisit the state and to favour the concept of "network space," noted above, leads to the call for insights from the perspective of relational governance.

If one takes a longer-term perspective, the central issue is not only to determine how mining activities can be developed in a sustainable manner, but, above all, how mines, minerals, and metals can contribute to the economic and social development of the regions and countries concerned in a more sustainable and equitable manner. Such a perspective involves not only adopting an intergenerational time frame, but also multisectoral approaches in which the resource is seen as a catalyst that can be used while it still exists to spur more lasting development. It implies ensuring a central place is given to issues regarding the responsibility and accountability for such strategies, as well as clarifying the delineation of responsibilities between public and private actors.

An additional aspect of the current situation that needs to be taken into account is the fact that CSR strategies not only are increasingly present, but the areas they cover are becoming more and more extensive. This can be illustrated by the positions adopted at the international level, whether by professional organizations such as the International Council on Mining and Metals (ICMM) or financial ones such as the World Bank. With regard to the former, ICMM's position clearly in favour of broadening the reach of CSR is illustrated in the organization's "Sustainable Development Framework," where the ninth principle advises that mining companies should "[c]ontribute to the social, economic and institutional development of host countries and communities" and "[e]nhance social and economic development by seeking opportunities to address poverty" (ICMM 2015). Concerning multilateral financial institutions, the World Bank's 2009 document "Value Chain Approach for the Extractive Industries" includes six stages leading to the introduction of sustainable development in the countries concerned: 1) optimizing the award of contracts and licences; 2) regulating and monitoring operations; 3) improving the collection of taxes and royalties; 4) enforcing environmental protection and social mitigation requirements; 5) managing revenue distribution and public investment; and 6) implementing sustainable development policies (Mayorga 2009, 3).

To sum up, the concept of CSR clearly has evolved in recent years to include strategies of ever-increasing scope with regard to their objectives, notably with a view to promoting community development, economic, and social development of host communities and contributing to reducing poverty.[2]

Three African Case Studies of CSR Strategies

As we shall see with reference to three recent African case studies that analyse the effect of the introduction of CSR strategies, such measures are introduced into contexts characterized by a particular heritage that has generated a legacy of institutional arrangements and structural relations of power among the actors concerned that at times have tended to provoke quite different consequences than those intended.

The Social and Economic Development Effects of CSR Strategies in Ghana

The originality of Dr Abdulai Darimani's (2016) contribution resides in the fact that it is informed by interviews that highlight the perspectives of communities affected by mining activities alongside interviews of staff at Newmont Ghana Gold Limited and Ghana Bauxite Company. Darimani's research also includes interviews with members of the communities and public officials concerned by the operations of Goldfields Ghana Limited and AngloGold Ashanti. The study examines the effect of CSR initiatives in light of the objectives of "sustainable development," looking at what these measures mean in practice for rural communities affected by mining in Ghana. To do this, Darimani's approach was to break down the concept of "sustainable development" to examine five interrelated aspects that compose it: 1) ownership; 2) locus; 3) improved livelihood; 4) continuity; and 5) accountability.

More specifically, Darimani (2016) defines these five dimensions as follows. Ownership means that local people must value the resource: (i) they must possess some property rights to the resource; and (ii) they must construct local-level institutions that control the use of the resource. Locus means that beneficiary communities have control over the design, location, costs, award of contract, and decisions of CSR projects in their localities. Improved livelihood means that CSR projects constitute adequate replacement and socially recognized resources. Continuity means that CSR projects have been mainstreamed into the normative framework of the community and can continue after the life of the mine or without support from the mining company. Accountability means the absence of any forms of restrictions on beneficiaries of CSR to hold the company responsible for its actions or inactions.

Ensuring the sustainability of CSR projects and mining projects raises challenges that imply having access to economic, political, and technical capacities and power. This, in turn, entails the existence of complex and dynamic institutional arrangements that are most often developed in spaces rural communities have difficulty accessing because the latter are most often politically and economically marginalized.

The findings of Darimani (2016) may be summarized briefly as follows. The fieldwork documents how, at first glance, CSR initiatives in Ghana clearly have improved over the past few years. Mining companies now deliberately adapt their CSR strategies and programs to the areas in which they operate and, indeed, provide specific CSR projects to local communities. Infrastructure such as schools, clinics, and community centres represents a key area where the investments made by the four companies studied were the most visible. The analysis also uncovered that the CSR strategies and the types of activities introduced by the four companies were characterized more by similarities than by differences. Each of the four companies also created its own foundation with a view to collecting funds to finance their CSR projects, and these foundations had become an integral part of the companies' structure.

The analysis also reveals, however, that the areas of CSR investment are not necessarily those that might have been privileged by the people displaced or affected by the mining activities during the period studied. For example, the study reveals that access to new agricultural land was the biggest priority of the majority of farmers, while access to employment was most valued by youth displaced by mining activities in the concerned areas. Moreover, responding to the constantly growing expectations of communities is not necessarily compatible with the introduction of a consistent CSR strategy. In the case of Newmont Ghana Gold, the evident success of the company's CSR strategy created a constant demand on the part of communities and the public for additional CSR projects. Thus, a company's adoption of a global and coherent CSR strategy does not necessarily permit responding to all and to the ever-growing needs and grievances of locally affected communities.

Darimani (2016) also demonstrates that the conceptualization of CSR projects increasingly has taken into account the needs of the local communities in the mining regions and that, in general, the projects correspond somewhat more to national development priorities than in the past. The decrease in the number of violent conflicts between communities and mining companies in the area of study is an example of the effect of mining companies' CSR strategies. However, when the five dimensions of sustainable development noted above were applied to the results of the empirical research, it became apparent that serious drawbacks remained concerning the effect of CSR strategies on the ground, with some of the major concerns relating to the marginalization of the most vulnerable groups in the communities as well as the issue of non-existent or poor accountability. The study observes that, within the framework of the mining companies' CSR strategies, the right of individuals and communities to formulate dissident opinions could be limited. It also notes that mining companies retained the liberty to pursue their activities without being subjected to conditions that would oblige them to be held accountable should this become necessary. This aspect comes out clearly in the agreements between communities and the mining companies, which tend to suggest that the implementation of CSR projects depends on the guarantee of a degree of "social peace" around mining activities.

The procedures leading to the local approbation of the four companies' CSR projects were usually formulated within the framework of partnerships with local communities and local governments. These types of partnerships, however, tend to confer power and authority from the top down, rather than the opposite. Moreover, while emphasis is put on partnerships that are "mutually advantageous" or that are presented as resulting in what is called a "win-win" situation, they often ignore the dynamics of power inherent in the implementation of CSR projects in the communities. Such partnerships also tend to cloud over the demarcations of responsibility between mining companies and the state with regard to the supply of basic social services for affected communities, a situation that necessarily affects the structure of the relations of power among actors on the ground. As another study on Ghana notes, "as much as mining companies respond to failures of central government in delivering public goods (and in extreme cases, in enforcing collectively binding rules), they play a role in directly influencing the governance context in which they operate ... this influence can be supporting or damaging" (Dashwood and Puplampu 2015, 135).

Despite the fact that the participation of local communities in the implementation and management of CSR projects is clearly important, Darimani (2016) finds that the role assigned to local committees often appeared narrow and circumscribed. The role and the responsibilities of a local committee is based on a hypothesis that ignores the dynamics of power, and might result in the prioritization and selection of only projects that are desired by elites and local opinion leaders. For example, the study notes that chiefs and local political leaders exercised considerable influence over CSR projects due to their links with the institutions and the structures of power of local and central governments.

Even if the inclusion of local political actors in CSR initiatives is a potential sign of a certain evolution in corporate practices, the participation and mobilization of local political representatives as "agents of development" via roles in the management of CSR projects through various structures established by the companies (e.g., foundations, committees, etc.), tends to contribute to a minimization of their roles at the various levels of government in the formulation and implementation of endogenous socio-economic development strategies. Hence, they cannot be seen as a solution to broader local governance challenges. Indeed, in the face of the challenges of longer term broadly based local governance, the CSR strategies of mining companies in themselves obviously cannot offer a satisfactory solution. Moreover, under certain circumstances, the inclusion of representatives of different levels of government in the implementation of company CSR initiatives in fact might deter attention from needed debates concerning the overall contribution to the region and the country of the mining activities themselves, rather than the socially derived activities of CSR strategies.

Although CSR initiatives in Ghana have seen considerable improvements over the past years and their costs are by no means negligible for the companies involved, it is nonetheless true that these initiatives contribute to reinforcing the control mining companies exercise over the conditions of livelihood and, therefore, over the lives of the recipient communities. In other words, such strategies are based above all on the premise of positive economic repercussions from mining activities, and do not lead one to look more closely at the social and political conditions that might permit the maximization of the development effect of mining activities. Moreover, although the companies' strategies clearly have contributed to reinforcing their own legitimacy, as shown by the reduction of conflicts, the asymmetrical relations of power and authority that are perpetuated by existing regulatory frameworks at the national level remain very much the same. This critically important factor – notably, ongoing asymmetrical relations of power and authority – might well explain the shortcomings inherent in the implementations of CSR initiatives analysed in Darimani (2016).

In the longer term, these shortcomings (e.g., power imbalances and social exclusion) might well risk undermining the positive "results" presented as improvements over the past few years – notably, with regard to the legitimacy that companies have attempted to gain in their relations with communities. It will be important to pay close attention, in the context of the process of decentralization in Ghana, to the fact that the division of responsibilities between the mining companies and the state regarding the provision of public services and goods to residents of rural communities affected by mining remains quite unclear.

From Voluntarism to Legal Obligations and Regulating CSR in Mali

The second case study to be summarized was undertaken by Dr Amadou Keita (2016), who directs the Groupe d'Etudes et de Recherche en Sociologie et Droit Appliqué in Mali. As a result of pressure from civil society and regional organizations, the 2012 Malian Mining Code introduced for the first time legal obligations for mining companies concerning community development in that country. This innovative measure took place, however, in a context already characterized by several years of voluntary CSR initiatives and a particular culture of decision making. Moreover, as elsewhere, mining activities in Mali have important implications for local communities in terms of property rights, which are not always dealt with adequately by existing legal instruments.

The research undertaken by Keita (2016) on the Malian experience with regard to CSR from the perspective of legal studies and socio-economic implications brings out several interesting findings. The introduction of voluntary measures by companies has allowed them to operate in contexts that are more or less calm, to obtain a certain degree of legitimacy, and to meet their financial objectives. This type of strategy, which is a reflection of the Malian government's policy to attract investors, does not appear capable, however, of ensuring the sustainable development of local communities affected by these activities. Although the introduction of binding norms regarding the responsibilities of companies has the potential to increase their accountability and the advantages that accrue to communities, these processes entail certain drawbacks that are likely to call into question the possibilities of community development.

Keita (2016) begins by examining the issue of CSR in the policies and legislation in Mali so as to trace the evolution from soft law to binding norms. Then, based on extensive fieldwork, the study analyses the realities and effects of CSR strategies in Mali's mining zones in light of the mining companies' different strategies. The study then looks at the implications of the binding nature of provisions for local community development. To this end, it examines the challenges and drawbacks these might present for communities, as well as the opportunities they create and their limits, considering that these innovative measures have been introduced into an unchanged political, institutional, and economic landscape. This synthesis of Keita (2016) emphasizes the third and last aspect, and highlights several points to underline some of the main conclusions.

First, although companies have been invited to participate in community development as a CSR strategy, in the absence of locally determined normative and regulatory frameworks their interventions have taken many different forms. The study reveals that the initiatives companies adopt and define themselves remain relatively short term in scope, while community expectations are often of quite another nature, and entail a different perspective and longer time horizon. Second, and more basically, it is the nature of the country's mining strategy more generally that encourages an ever-increasing amount of investment in the sector. As in the past, this contributes to the present in making more precarious – and even threatening – the livelihoods of communities, above all because the issue of access to land has not been addressed. Third, people who have lost their land and can no longer farm look to mining activities for employment, but are often unsuccessful, resulting in increasing poverty in mining zones. Fourth, it was as a result of the efforts of civil society organizations that the steps from voluntarism to legal obligation of CSR initiatives took place.

This process, however, has moved forwards rapidly without local communities necessarily being in a position to draw up community plans or to exercise a leadership role. To the extent that this is true, the process as it is presently unfolding could lead, paradoxically, to the danger of a certain "de-responsibilization" of communities. In the absence of bottom-up community presence, engagement, and leadership, many of the issues raised are then taken up by members of the local elite. Discussions often become formulated in technical terms around, for example, standards and norms, and consequently are taken out of the hands of local communities. This point echoes the emphasis placed on norm proliferation in the extractive sector by Compaoré (2018) to underline the important distinction between focusing on a micro-level perspective, as in CSR strategies, or on a more macro-level one, which necessarily entails home-state responsibility.

The Malian case study also underlines the danger that the issue of community development becomes a political football between the communities and the public authorities responsible for local territorial governments in a struggle to capture more of the revenue derived from mining activities. Essentially, there is a tension between, on the one hand, the country's "mining model" based on attracting ever-increasing amounts of investment and, on the other, reconciling these strategies of openness with the country's regional obligations to the Economic Community of West African States. These obligations concern, among other issues, the rights of communities affected by mining, including the rights of communities to their land; free, prior, and informed consent; and the adoption of international standards concerning the displacement of affected populations.

Although potentially innovative, the move towards regulating CSR is introduced into a context that raises important technical and political difficulties confronting community representatives, particularly with regard to the definition of the plans to be introduced and the resulting tendency for companies to fail to align their CSR strategies on such plans. Keita (2016) concludes by expressing the hope that the changes in the 2012 Malian Mining Code represent only a first step towards greater consideration for the interests and needs of communities living in mining areas.

These two case studies present both contrasts and similarities. In the Ghanaian experience, there appears to be an important tradition of community development and, notably, of community participation. The Malian situation is innovative in view of the fact that legal measures have been introduced to formalize CSR strategies. What comes out of both case studies is a recognition that, although mining companies tend to place increasing emphasis on CSR strategies to improve the situation of communities affected by mining projects, both countries' political and social contexts remain characterized by tensions caused by mining companies' tendency to perpetuate fiscal, employment, and production strategies that proved disappointing in the past in terms of promoting social and economic development. The current tendency appears to be to combine these past corporate strategies with CSR initiatives, resulting in the risk of perpetuating the same issues of legitimacy to ongoing operations that were at the origin of the CSR strategies themselves.

CSR in Situations of Conflict Minerals: Lessons from the Democratic Republic of Congo

The importance of taking account of the political dimensions of issues surrounding CSR brought out in the Ghana and Mali case studies is all the more striking in situations such as that which prevails in the DRC. In some regards, the situation there might be considered extreme, but, as Tougas (2016) suggests, this special case of CSR serves in certain ways as a "laboratory" for the problems of legitimacy of the actors involved in the extraction of minerals (or other resources) defined as "conflict resources." The weakness of the DRC's regulatory capacity and the absence of political will on the part of the government must be set in the context of a heritage of prolonged years of war and illicit trafficking of minerals. These factors, among others, explain why the initiatives that have attempted to respond to problems of the legitimacy of companies that source their minerals in this region have, for the most part, emanated from the international arena.

Tougas (2016) describes the working conditions of artisanal miners who live in situations of extreme vulnerability due to many factors, including relations between armed groups. He also details the nature and positioning of the organizations involved in formulating recommendations to respond to the challenges of transparency and accountability facing large mining companies, which seek, often with the best intentions, to address the resulting problems that affect the working and living conditions of the artisanal miners. In situations of considerable asymmetry in the relations of power, there is a need to think through the "solutions" to the problems conflict minerals raise in such a way as to articulate them in a dynamic manner with the real needs of the populations concerned at the local level.

The perverse on-the-ground effects of several traceability initiatives presented in the study, introduced in good faith by external initiators and in keeping with the logic of CSR, suggest very eloquently the critical need for a careful articulation that takes into account on-the-ground realities and international initiatives that seek to promote greater transparency and better accountability. This type of articulation appears as a precondition, so that what are proposed as solutions might in fact respond to the problems they are intended to resolve; what is at issue here is conflict and the violation of human rights associated with it – not merely the problems of legitimacy of the companies involved in the sale of the minerals extracted from the region.

According to Global Witness (2014), the problem of "conflict resources" is not unique to the DRC, and conflict-prone natural resources more than likely will continue to be part of the international security agenda. The Congolese "laboratory" is extremely useful as it underlines the need to adopt a much more global approach to the problem and at the same time introduce measures in this area that are informed by the realities of specific local situations, and consequently far more precise, as well as binding.

Conclusion

The case studies summarized here lead to several concluding remarks. A first conclusion is the need to recognize the importance of local appropriation of proposed solutions and strategies and, more generally, to heed local perspectives and initiatives to promote development in mining areas.

As well, CSR strategies that are initiated externally raise very real risks regarding the sustainability of projects, particularly in terms of the equity of the distribution of benefits and of their possible effects on local political and democratic processes. In this regard, there is a real danger that promises associated with CSR initiatives might deter attention from the legitimate right and responsibility of public sector actors to provide social services to their populations – the very condition that allows governments to be held accountable (see Compaoré 2015).

The findings summarized in this chapter concur with Bruce Harvey's (2014, abstract 7) observation that the adoption of objectives to spur social and economic development through CSR strategies "encourages company priorities and behaviours which blur appropriate boundaries between firms, governments and communities; and may lead to unintended consequences which ultimately result in poorer community outcomes, and thence dilution of the 'social licence' eagerly sought." Harvey also concurs with the arguments presented in this chapter concerning issues of legitimacy and accountability with regard to CSR strategies:

Regrettably, some publications assert there is equal development value to be gained by stand-alone "social and environmental initiatives" (ICMM 2013) and government rents. Alas, it has to be observed that the impact of "initiatives" disconnected to business have a long history of negatives outweighing positives (Frynas 2005; Ite 2005; Slack 2012), and without concerted locally-driven accountability (which is unfortunately rare), government rents have a tendency to end up elsewhere. Furthermore, development initiatives and penalty payments both lead to "trade off" thinking, rather than a desirable preference for avoiding impacts in the first place through design and operational adjustments. (Harvey 2014, 8)

This observation takes on particular significance in view of the increasingly recognized possibility that well-managed mining revenue indeed might finance access to social services such as health services, rather than mineral-rich countries having to rely on continuing outlays of development assistance to cover expenditures in this area. Such possibilities have been documented in ongoing research – see, for example, Ridde, Campbell, and Martel (2015); Tax Justice Network-Africa and ActionAid (2015).

More scholarly attention clearly needs to be given to the potential role of well-managed mining revenues, appropriately designed public policies, including effective and efficient tax systems, the elimination of corporate income tax holidays and incentives, and addressing tax evasion through practices such as transfer mispricing (see Tax Justice Network-Africa and ActionAid 2015). Similarly, on the subject of revenue transparency, it is important that countries that are home to mining companies make mandatory the publication of disaggregated information, country-by-country and project-by-project, for all taxes paid outside their own jurisdiction, and ensure that policies of transparency concerning contracts are in place.

Again, with regard to possible new directions for needed changes, notably the need to clarify the roles and responsibilities of public and private actors in the area of CSR, a report by the United Nations Economic Commission for Africa and the African Union Commission, entitled *Minerals and Africa's Development: The International Study Group Report on Africa's Mineral Regimes*, is instructive: "From a policy perspective, CSR initiatives should not be considered a substitute for government responsibility towards its citizens in providing basic infrastructure and other public goods. Indeed, CSR initiatives should complement government efforts through local government institutions and local authorities. The framework that a government chooses to entrench CSR should be clear about the responsibilities of mining companies and which responsibilities should be matched with and communicated to mining communities" (UNECA and AUC 2011, 89). This position echoes the renewed recognition of the importance of public policies, as illustrated in the following contribution by Dashwood and Puplampu (2014, 131), who refer to a "national development strategy that interconnects with policies at the local community level to produce lasting economic value." The recognition of the role of public policies, as suggested in the emphasis placed on home-state responsibility, comes as a very direct answer to the observations Keita (2016) makes in his study on Mali, which draws attention to the ambiguities and problems concerning the sustainability of CSR initiatives in a context characterized by the weakened intervention of both the state and the authorities responsible for local government. This heritage explains why mining companies have come to appear as the actors that should take on the role and responsibility of compensating for the weaknesses and insufficiencies of national and decentralized authorities.

The complexity of this heritage, which is well documented in the case studies, the particular social and political contexts in which the broadening of CSR strategies is taking place, and the problems such situations raise, give particular force to the caveat put forward by Bruce Harvey that "[e]xtractive companies are not development NGOs and should not attempt to emulate them by placing too much emphasis on stand-alone 'outreach' programmes. Instead, to enhance relationships with and contributions to host communities, what is more appropriate and what can and has worked is a single-minded behavioural shift in internal business and workforce practices" (Wand and Harvey 2012, quoted in Harvey 2014, 9). Further, as Harvey (2014, 9–10) argues:

To improve their "social licence," extractive companies should prioritise "in-reach," not "outreach." What does this mean in practice? It means working to change the behaviours and thence attitudes of its own employees across the full spectrum of the workforce. It means very consciously minimising the belief that "outreach" programmes can substitute for the implacably difficult task of working with local people on a face to face basis on issues which are important to them, not agendas set by the developers and their national or international "development" partners. "Outreach" programmes and "development" may have a role, but they should not be central. At a fundamental level, the focus should be on business-connected "activities," not business-disconnected programmes.

On the basis of the above synthesis, there is good reason to question whether the current emphasis on the enlargement of the scope of CSR strategies with a view to promoting sustainable social and economic development is appropriate. Indeed, under the present conditions, there is ample evidence to suggest that the adoption of strategies that continue to blur the boundaries delineating the roles and responsibilities of firms, governments, and communities might well be taking companies in a direction increasingly distant from one that would allow them to address the origins of the problems of legitimacy they face.

NOTES

1 To the extent that the regulatory frameworks which resulted from the liberalization reform process might be seen both as the expression of existing power relations and as an instrument that contributes to their reproduction, one can conceive of mining regimes as part of a larger power structure that orients and conditions the relations among the actors involved, and that helps to shape the negotiating spaces among them, the results of negotiations, and the capacity of stakeholders to formulate and introduce alternative policies (Laforce, Campbell, and Sarrasin 2012). It is the regulatory and institutional heritage that resulted from these reforms which continues to condition the context in which CSR strategies are proposed.

2 This position has been called into question, however, by certain industry observers. As Harvey (2014, abstract) observes: "A growing number of industry-sponsored, consultancy and academic publications describe how the sector can contribute to the economic and social development of host communities. However, despite its good intentions and frequent focus on confronting issues, the social development approach is fundamentally flawed. It frequently fails to communicate to intended audiences and it asks extractive companies to adopt policies, such as 'contributing to reducing poverty,' which do not sit comfortably with the remit, capabilities and business imperatives of the extractive sector."

BIBLIOGRAPHY

Banerjee, Subhabrata Bobby. 2014. "A Critical Perspective on Corporate Social Responsibility: Towards a Global Governance Framework." *Critical Perspectives on International Business* 10 (1-2): 84–95. https://doi.org/ 10.1108/cpoib-06-2013-0021.

Campbell, Bonnie, ed. 2004. *Regulating Mining in Africa: For Whose Benefit?* Discussion Paper 26. Uppsala, Sweden: Nordic Africa Institute.

Campbell, Bonnie, ed. 2009. *Mining in Africa: Regulation and Development.* London: Pluto Press; Ottawa: International Development Research Centre; Uppsala, Sweden: Nordic Africa Institute.

Campbell, Bonnie. 2012. "CSR and Development in Africa: Redefining Roles and Responsibilities of Public and Private Actors in the Mining Sector." *Resources Policy* 37 (2): 138–43. https://doi.org/10.1016/j. resourpol.2011.05.002.

Campbell, Bonnie, and Myriam Laforce, eds. 2016. *La responsabilité sociale des entreprises dans le secteur minier: réponse ou obstacle aux enjeux de légitimité et de développement en Afrique?* Quebec City: Presses de l'Université du Québec.

Compaoré, W.R. Nadège. 2015. "Re-politicizing State Sovereignty in Global Governance: The Political Economy of Transparency in the Oil Sectors of Gabon and Ghana." PhD diss., Queen's University, Kingston, ON.

Compaoré, W.R. Nadège. 2018. "Escaping the 'Resource Curse' by Localizing Transparency Norms." In *African Actors in International Security: Shaping Contemporary Norms,* edited by Katharina P. Coleman and Thomas K. Tieku, 137–52. Boulder, CO: Lynne Rienner.

Darimani, Abdulai. 2016. "Contribution de la responsabilité sociale des entreprises minières au développement des communautés locales au Ghana." In *La responsabilité sociale des entreprises dans le secteur minier: réponse ou obstacle aux enjeux de légitimité et de développement en Afrique?* edited by Bonnie Campbell and Myriam Laforce, 91–162. Quebec City: Presses de l'Université du Québec.

Dashwood, Hevina S., and Buenar B. Puplampu. 2015. "Multi-Stakeholder Partnerships in Mining: From Engagement to Development in Ghana." In *New Approaches to the Governance of Natural Resources: Insights from Africa,* edited by J. Andrew Grant, W.R. Nadège Compaoré, and Matthew I. Mitchell, 131–53. London: Palgrave Macmillan.

Evans, Marketa D. 2007. "New Collaborations for International Development. Corporate Social Responsibility and Beyond." *International Journal* 62 (2): 311–25. https://doi.org/10.1177/002070200706200207.

Frynas, Jedrzej G. 2005. "The False Developmental Promise of Corporate Social Responsibility: Evidence from Multinational Oil Companies." *International Affairs* 81 (3): 581–98. https://doi.org/10.1111/j.1468-2346. 2005.00470.x.

Global Witness. 2014. "Country Focus: The Extent of the Conflict Resources Problem." [London]. Available online at http://www.globalwitness.org/documents/17872/casestudies.pdf, accessed 21 December 2015.

Harvey, Bruce. 2014. "Social Development Will Not Deliver Social Licence to Operate for the Extractive Sector." *Extractive Industries and Society* 1 (1): 7–11. https://doi.org/10.1016/j.exis.2013.11.001.

Idemudia, Uwafiokun. 2014. "Corporate-Community Engagement Strategies in the Niger Delta: Some Critical Reflections." *Extractive Industries and Society* 1 (2): 154–62. https://doi.org/10.1016/j.exis.2014.07.005.

ICMM (International Council on Mining and Metals). 2015. *ICCM 10 Principles*. London: ICMM. Available online at https://www.icmm.com/website/publications/pdfs/commitments/revised-2015_icmm-principles.pdf, accessed 27 July 2019.

Ite, Uwen E. 2005. "Poverty Reduction in Resource-Rich Developing Countries: What Have Multinational Corporations Got to Do with It?" *Journal of International Development* 17 (7): 913–29. https://doi.org/10.1002/jid.1177.

Keita, Amadou. 2016. "Responsabilité sociale des entreprises minières et développement communautaire dans les zones minières au Mali: du volontariat à l'obligation juridique, une perspective du terrain." In *La responsabilité sociale des entreprises dans le secteur minier: réponse ou obstacle aux enjeux de légitimité et de développement en Afrique?* edited by Bonnie Campbell and Myriam Laforce, 53–89. Quebec City: Presses de l'Université du Québec.

Laforce, Myriam, Bonnie Campbell, and Bruno Sarrasin. 2012. *Pouvoir et régulation dans le secteur minier: leçons à partir de l'expérience canadienne*. Quebec City: Presses de l'Université du Québec.

Mayorga, Eleodoro Alba. 2009. "Extractive Industries Value Chain: A Comprehensive Integrated Approach to Developing Extractive Industries." Extractive Industries and Development Series 3; Africa Working Paper Series 125. Washington, DC: World Bank, Oil, Gas and Mining Policy Division and the Africa Poverty Reduction and Economic Management Department. Available online at http://documents.worldbank.org/curated/en/282401468339611763/pdf/484240NWP0Box31ei1for1development13.pdf, accessed 3 April 2016.

Mitchell, James. 2014. "The Resource Curse of Corporate Social Responsibility: The Case of Rio Tinto." Available online at http://jamesmitchellmining.wordpress.com/2014/05/08/the-resource-curse-of-corporate-social-responsibility-the-case-of-rio-tinto/, accessed 15 December 2015.

Porter, Michael E., and Mark Kramer. 2011. "Creating Shared Value." Harvard Business Review (January–February): 2–17. Available online at https://hbr.org/2011/01/the-big-idea-creating-shared-value, accessed 4 May 2017.

Prieto-Carrón, Marina, Peter Lund-Thomsen, Anita Chan, Ana Muro, and Chandra Bhushan. 2006. "Critical Perspectives on CSR and Development: What We Know, What We Don't Know, and What We Need to Know."

International Affairs 82 (5): 977–87. https://doi.org/10.1111/j.1468-2346.2006.00581.x.

Renouard, Cécile. 2015. *Éthique et entreprise.* Ivry-sur Seine, France: Les Éditions de l'Atelier/Les Éditions Ouvrières.

Ridde, Valéry, Bonnie Campbell, and Andréanne Martel. 2015. "Mining Revenue and Access to Health Care in Africa: Could the Revenue Drawn from Well-Managed Mining Sectors Finance Exemption from Payment for Health?" *Development in Practice* 25 (6): 909–18. https://doi.org/10.1080/09614524.2015.1062470.

Slack, Keith. 2012. "Mission Impossible? Adopting a CSR-Based Business Model for Extractive Industries in Developing Countries." *Resources Policy* 37 (2): 179–84. https://doi.org/10.1016/j.resourpol.2011.02.003.

Strange, Susan. 1996. *The Retreat of the State. The Diffusion of Power in the World Economy.* Cambridge: Cambridge University Press.

Szablowski, David. 2007. *Transnational Law and Local Struggles: Mining, Communities and the World Bank.* Oxford; Portland, OR: Hart Publishing.

Tax Justice Network-Africa and ActionAid. 2015. *The West African Giveaway: Use and Abuse of Corporate Tax Incentives in ECOWAS.* Nairobi; Johannesburg: Tax Justice Network-Africa and ActionAid. Available online at https://www.globaltaxjustice.org/sites/default/files/the_west_african_giveaway_2.pdf, accessed 4 May 2017.

Tougas, Denis. 2016. "Responsabilité et imputabilité dans le trafic des 'minerais de conflit' à l'Est de la République démocratique du Congo." In *La responsabilité sociale des entreprises dans le secteur minier: réponse ou obstacle aux enjeux de légitimité et de développement en Afrique?* edited by Bonnie Campbell and Myriam Laforce, 163–229. Quebec City: Presses de l'Université du Québec.

UNECA and AUC (United Nations Economic Commission for Africa and African Union Commission). 2011. *Minerals and Africa's Development: The International Study Group Report on Africa's Mineral Regimes.* Addis Ababa: UNECA and AUC. Available online at https://repository.uneca.org/bitstream/handle/10855/21569/Bib-69220.pdf?sequence=1.

Wand, Paul, and Bruce Harvey. 2012. "The Sky Did Not Fall In! Rio Tinto after Mabo." In *The Limits of Change: Mabo and Native Title 20 Years On,* edited by Toni Bauman and Lydia Glick, 289–309. Canberra: Australian Institute of Aboriginal and Torres Strait Islander Studies.

Zadek, Simon. 2006. *The Civil Corporation.* London: Routledge.

12 Reflections on Africa-Canada Relations in Natural Resource Sectors in the 2020s

J. ANDREW GRANT AND NATHAN ANDREWS

Introduction

As the decade of the 2010s comes to a close, some of Africa's leading producers of natural resources have witnessed their long-serving presidents finally step down (e.g., José Eduardo dos Santos in Angola) or be forced out (e.g., Robert Mugabe by the military in Zimbabwe). Although he served as president for just under nine years, Jacob Zuma was forced to resign by the ruling party, African National Congress, in South Africa. And before the current decade is out, we have also seen a change of president in the Democratic Republic of Congo (DRC), as Joseph Kabila's delaying tactics to prevent leaving office have been exhausted. All four regimes have been criticized for exhibiting a governance that not only permits corruption (especially in natural resource sectors), but also restricts the ability of opposition parties, media, and individuals to criticize the government. These four leaders have been intimately involved in overseeing the various contracts, partnerships, and arrangements governing the way in which natural resources have been extracted and exported from their countries.

Although new leaders in these countries will apply their own stamp on such governance arrangements, we caution against declaring the dawn of a "new era of natural resource governance" across the continent in the 2020s. We are somewhat optimistic that natural resource governance will experience modest improvement in the coming decade, although we expect that will be due not to presidential turnover, but largely to a combination of internal factors, such as African state and non-state actors exerting agency as norm leaders (especially of forms of "resource nationalism"); regional governance initiatives such as the Africa Mining Vision (AMV); and, to some extent, external factors such as global governance initiatives, including the Voluntary Principles on Security and Human

Rights (VPs), the Extractive Industries Transparency Initiative (EITI), the United Nations Global Compact, and the UN Guiding Principles on Business and Human Rights. New presidents, however, will still have certain "select" constituencies to serve and patronage networks to sustain, and repackaging resource nationalism for domestic political gain is always a facile tactic when a political diversion is needed.

Natural resource governance is also a reflection not only of how legislation is written, but of how it is applied to stakeholders such as transnational extractive sector firms, domestic wholesalers, buyers, "middlemen," local traders, and artisanal and small-scale mining participants. When Sierra Leone overhauled its mining legislation in the late 2000s, civil society was provided only a modicum of veritable input, while industry quietly yet effectively lobbied for more favourable terms. The DRC is in the midst of a similar exercise, and one wonders how large transnational extractive companies, such as Swiss-based Glencore,[1] will approach the announced increases in royalties and various taxes on the extraction of the country's minerals. The DRC features prominently in various discussions of natural resource sector governance challenges, which is no great surprise given its notoriety as a source of conflict-prone minerals as well as rampant cases of exploitative working conditions, including child labour and environmental degradation owing to lax enforcement of labour laws, environmental protection, and rehabilitation regulations, respectively. These challenges will continue in the coming decade in concert with resurgent world prices for minerals as well as increased demand for key mineral components – such as cobalt – in the production of rechargeable batteries for electric vehicles.

While Glencore has a significant – albeit at times controversial[2] – presence in the DRC's mining sectors, so too do a couple of Canadian mining firms. Although considered a Canadian mining firm owing to its listing on the Toronto Stock Exchange, Katanga Mining – owned primarily by Glencore through an 86 per cent stake – has been mining cobalt in the DRC for several years, and has been ensnared in disputes with the Congolese government concerning interest payment differentials between its parent company and its joint-venture partner, state-owned Gécamines, which claims it has been forced to pay higher rates than Glencore (York 2018). Given the capital-intensive nature of mining, interest payments are a key cost for firms in the sector. Adding to Katanga Mining's governance woes is an ongoing investigation, launched in 2017 by the Ontario Securities Commission, into the firm's accounting practices (York 2018). Another Canadian mining company prominent in the region is ninety-year-old Sherritt International, which "has operating mines in Cuba and Madagascar, as well as a refinery in Fort Saskatchewan, Alta. The company mainly produces nickel, but in 2017 it also produced just under 3,000 tonnes of cobalt ... [and] as one of the world's Top 10 producers, Sherritt will benefit from any future surge in cobalt pricing" (Cain 2018). Sherritt International has cultivated a good reputation by implementing the VPs as part of its business practices in Madagascar's extractive sector since 2009 and further expanding these practices to its Cuban and Canadian mines in recent years. As this book goes to press, cobalt is trading at record highs, with no signs of receding as we move towards the 2020s. Cobalt prices are also buoyed by efforts by large information and communications technology companies such as Apple to find ways to source cobalt and other minerals directly from large producers to help avoid child labour and other deleterious practices in the production pipelines of their products. Although Canada and China compete for second place among cobalt producers, the DRC is by far the largest producer, accounting for roughly two-thirds of global production, amounting to some 100,000 tonnes per annum.

Although scholars often conclude that norms, such as those that have produced corporate social responsibility (CSR), are to some extent influencing – or at least meant to inform monitoring of – the behaviour of state and non-state actors, it is important to apply such assertions in policy-relevant and theoretical context (see Andrews 2019b). To that end, we offer an assessment of CSR policy frameworks and how these have shaped Canada's role in Africa's natural resource sectors. Implicitly or explicitly, the contributors to this volume also draw much-needed attention to the norm dynamics of CSR, "good" governance, "best" practices, and global and regional governance initiatives in the context of extractive resource sectors. The norm dynamics of CSR also have important ramifications for socio-economic development (Andrews 2016, 2019a; Grant 2018; Idemudia 2014). Hence, in the next section, we also delve into the legitimacy dynamics that influence natural resource governance by analysing some of the ways in which stakeholder perceptions of legitimacy have been applied in the scholarly literature on CSR.

Aiming for Balanced Reflections on Canada's Role in Africa's Natural Resource Sectors

Despite one's particular ontological, epistemological, or political position, most will agree on at least a couple of broad observations, which we noted in the introductory chapter: first, Canada has had – and will continue to have – a significant presence in Africa's natural resource sectors; second, Canada's presence has not often translated into demonstrable and sustained development outcomes for recipient countries and host communities. Ultimately, these observations have served as good starting points of discussion for the contributions in this volume. In a similar vein, the cases of Katanga Mining and Sherritt International also speak to the challenges that remain despite the recent efforts of two different Canadian governments – one Conservative and the other Liberal – to compel Canadian firms to respect sustainable development objectives and CSR goals in their dealings with local communities. Policy frameworks such as "Building the Canadian Advantage: A Corporate Social Responsibility (CSR) Strategy for the Canadian International Extractive Sector" (Canada 2009) and "Doing Business the Canadian Way: A Strategy to Advance Corporate Social Responsibility in Canada's Extractive Sector Abroad" (Canada 2014) were important initial steps. But, as contributors to this book point out (see, for example, Chapters 1–3), these are still preliminary in many ways. Although expectations perhaps were high for these policy frameworks, this should not be taken as an excuse for their limited effect on the ground. Since Canada is home to some 75 per cent of the world's corporate headquarters for mining firms, the expectations should be high – especially given the strong potential for setting the tone for CSR across the globe.

One of our main contributions – indeed, main challenges – has been to provide a balanced assessment of the role of Canadian policies and companies in Africa's natural resource sectors. For every Bonte Gold Mines that departs without rehabilitating its mine after closure, there is a Golden Star Resources that has built some two hundred clean-water pipe-borne systems for local communities in and around their Prestea and Wassa concessions in Ghana, funds a breast cancer awareness program in that country, and has been recognized by the Ghanaian government as a firm that relies on local content when procuring mining supplies and related support services (PDAC 2018, 9). Importantly, however, the latter case does not absolve the former in Ghana or elsewhere across the continent where Canadian firms (or mining firms with significant Canadian ownership stakes) operate. Furthermore, as we and our contributors emphasize, Canada's track record in generating development outcomes via Africa's natural resource sector is mixed. Employment, investment, and local procurement numbers can be offered and linked to economic growth in host countries, but does this make up for reports of deforestation, tailing pond spills, and human rights abuses? In a similar vein, even if 99 per cent of Toronto-based Golden Star Resources' some 2,500 employees are Ghanaian, does this obviate the negative activities of other Canadian mining companies in Ghana in the past? Does this Canadian firm's investment in *local human resources* respond to the wider trend of promoting *local content* as regards extractive sector suppliers of goods and services as an emerging best practice?

There are no easy answers to these complex questions, and observers have been watching how the Liberal government under Prime Minister Justin Trudeau approaches the governance challenges posed by these questions. During the 2015 Canadian federal election, one of the Trudeau Liberals' campaign promises was to establish an ombudsperson office that would be responsible for hearing complaints against Canadian extractive sector companies operating internationally. This campaign promise actually repeated a pledge the Liberals made under then party leader Michael Ignatieff in the 2011 federal election campaign to establish "an independent ombudsman office to advise Canadian [extractive sector] companies, consider complaints made against them, and investigate those complaints where it is deemed warranted" (Liberal Party of Canada 2011, 87). This ombudsperson would have replaced the Office of the Extractive Sector CSR Counsellor, which was established in 2009 by the Harper Conservative government in response to a series of government-initiated roundtables with industry, civil society, and academics in the latter half of 2006 and an attendant report that appeared in March 2007 (National Roundtables on Corporate Social Responsibility (CSR) and the Canadian Extractive Industry in Developing Countries 2007). The roundtables that led to the report were themselves a reflection of growing media interest and civil society pressure in holding Canadian extractive sector firms to account when reports of environmental or human rights abuses arise.

It is common for political parties, when in opposition, to criticize the various policies and agencies of the government in power. It also did not help that the Office of the Extractive Sector CSR Counsellor, which was abolished in 2018, suffered from a limited mandate and relatively low profile. For instance, it did not help that the post was left vacant for nearly a year and a half after Marketa Evans resigned in October 2014. The office was later given a more explicit mandate, however, following the release of "Doing Business the Canadian Way" (Canada 2014), and reinvigorated once Jeffrey Davidson took on the post in early 2015. Davidson travelled across Canada and abroad, meeting with mining firms, professional associations, academics, students, government officials, and various mining sector stakeholders in order to advance the CSR themes and objectives of his office as well as establish important networks and linkages among stakeholders.

In January 2018 the Minister of International Trade, François-Philippe Champagne, issued the following statement: "Canada's leadership in *strengthening responsible business conduct abroad* reflects the values supported by Canada's progressive trade agenda where *all parties should benefit from economic development*, and contributes to Canada's reputation as an international business partner of choice" (Canada 2018, emphasis added). This ambitious claim was supported by an announcement that the Canadian government was in the midst of establishing a Canadian Ombudsperson for Responsible Enterprise (CORE) office to promote Canadian leadership on improving CSR in extractive sectors, which is expected to begin operations by mid-2019. The establishment of the CORE seems to align with the 2016 iteration of Canada's CSR policy document entitled "Canada's Enhanced Corporate Social Responsibility Strategy to Strengthen Canada's Extractive Sector Abroad" (Canada 2016). The CORE office is meant to replace the Office of the Extractive Sector CSR Counsellor, but at present it is too early in its development to assess whether this new office is a more effective governance instrument. That said, observers from civil society, government, industry, local communities, and academia – including this volume's contributors – will be monitoring the activities of the CORE office very closely over the coming years.

Legitimacy Dynamics in Extractive Resource Sectors

A fundamental element of governance is *legitimacy*, which our contributors examine either explicitly or implicitly in this volume and in turn shed light on the following type of questions. Who is a legitimate stakeholder? Who is a legitimate representative of a particular group or community? Are government representatives always considered legitimate, even if office holders obtained their positions via rigged elections or repressive means or engaged subsequently in corrupt behaviour? Is the governance arrangement concerning a particular issue-area legitimate? Are the constitutive norms of CSR legitimate? How does legitimacy apply to global governance frameworks and institutions that focus on CSR more broadly?

There is no need to rehash the arguments of our contributors in this concluding chapter. It is useful, however, to delve into the concept of *legitimacy*, which underpins the constitutive norms of CSR and influences stakeholders' perceptions and behaviours. Legitimacy dynamics in extractive resource sectors is a fertile area of enquiry, and its study takes on different forms ranging from African state behaviour to firm-local community relations in conflict-prone areas of Africa to the burgeoning African oil sector (see, for example, Compaoré 2018b; Enns, Andrews, and Grant 2018; Mayanja 2018; Winn, Jennings, and

Mitchell 2015; Yates 2015). Legitimacy concerns also reflect on whether regional governance initiatives (e.g., the AMV) are more "legitimate" than global governance initiatives (e.g., the EITI). Although these concerns regarding legitimacy are important, it is facile to assume that the AMV was devised by African technocrats and that the EITI was devised by their "Western" counterparts. Yet such assumptions are erroneous because Western consultants played a role in the drafting of the AMV, and African actors have greatly influenced the development of the EITI – not to mention the role that African state and non-state actors have performed as norm shapers of the latter (see Andrews 2018; Compaoré 2018a). Liberal norms are also infused in the AMV, questioning the assumption that liberal norms are by definition Western norms.

It is useful to begin by offering a definition of the contested concept of legitimacy. Legitimacy, like many other social science concepts, is difficult to define with precision. Opinion polls can shed light on the *degree of* legitimacy of a certain government or organized group (e.g., political parties, rebels, secessionists movements, etc.), but such insights are often transient, and depend on the logistical ability and interest to conduct such polls. Although many scholars offer definitions of legitimacy, Franck (1992, 50) advances a definition that is applicable to this volume's focus on stakeholders and compliance by firms: "the quality of a rule, or a system of rules, or a process for making or interpreting rules that pulls both the rule makers and those addressed by the rules towards voluntary compliance." Adding to Franck's rule-based definition of legitimacy, we suggest that *perception* plays a significant role in terms of ascribing legitimacy. Even if perceptions can be more ephemeral and less tangible than rules, procedures, and processes, it is the *interpretation* of these considerations by stakeholders that is important. Like groups and individuals, firms not only seek to exhibit legitimacy, but also to assess the legitimacy of international institutions, domestic institutions, and other stakeholders on a regular basis. The dialectical interplay of interpreting rules, procedures, and processes continues until legitimacy ebbs. Once this latter stage occurs, actors will follow such rules only when compelled to do so.

Observing the importance of legitimacy, groups and individuals can also seek to exhibit their possession of it based on certain claims on the following grounds: legal (a country's constitution and laws confer legitimacy); electoral (via elections, democratic or otherwise); traditional authority (i.e., chiefs as hereditary custodians of, for example, the land); temporal (the length of time involved in a particular issue-area or residing in a particular area or region); or moral (high ethical or principled behaviour). As the contributors to this volume reveal, these perceptions and assessments concerning legitimacy are in constant flux. Although we can extrapolate some trends from "snapshot" analyses of primary and secondary scholarly sources, the legitimacy of stakeholders and the relationships among them are perpetually changing.

Our conception of legitimacy diverges somewhat from the works of some scholars, such as Mitchell, Agle, and Wood (1997), who advance a typology that attempts to portray how one stakeholder group might perceive other stakeholder groups based on qualitative, binary assessments of legitimacy, power, and urgency. Mitchell and colleagues apply this typology to how a firm perceives other stakeholder groups regardless of issue-area, the category of "firm" could be replaced by a state or even a non-governmental organization (NGO). Although appealing at first glance, assigning a binary "yes/no" to the legitimacy, power, and urgency of each stakeholder group is fraught with drawbacks, illustrated by the following cases, which are composites inspired by realistic examples. For example, if a researcher is unable to meet with a civil society stakeholder group owing to scheduling difficulties, the former might deem the latter to be lacking in urgency concerning the issue-area. A small grassroots NGO might have outsize power because its executive director is the sister-in-law of the deputy minister whose ministry is one of the stakeholder groups. A large transnational NGO might have invested several years in outreach and sensitization efforts and drawn much international attention to a particular issue-area – but other stakeholders might view the NGO as lacking in legitimacy owing to its lack of prior engagement with previous issue-areas affecting the country. Although it is helpful to incorporate considerations pertaining to the legitimacy, power, and urgency of stakeholder groups, these concepts lose their explanative ability when placed in binary schemas.

In the more than twenty years since the work of Mitchell and colleagues (1997) appeared, the concept of "social licence to operate" has gained much traction in scholarly circles (see, for example, Gehrman, Lefsrud, and Fast 2017; Mercer-Mapstone et al. 2017; Parsons, Lacey, and Moffat 2014; Wilburn and Wilburn 2011). Although the legitimacy of stakeholders is central to the social licence to operate in natural resource sectors, how do stakeholders *build trust*? Bowen, Newenham-Kahindi, and Herremans (2010) and Mercer-Mapstone and colleagues (2017) are correct in their assertions that trust building among stakeholders is best achieved via a "transformational" set of strategies that promote frequent, two-way communications that cultivate co-generation of information and knowledge. Through iteration, this dialogue breaks down misperceptions among stakeholders and produces governance insights. Bowen and colleagues (2010) also advocate for adding other "transformational" strategies – such as joint project management, joint decision making, and co-ownership between firms and local communities – as a means of building trust. Although these strategies certainly are appealing, it is highly unlikely that natural resource sector firms would relinquish influence and capital to local communities. Indeed Bowen and colleagues (2010) concede that such strategies are the least-implemented form of firm-local community engagement – for good reason. There are grounds for modest optimism, however, concerning these strategies, as holding frequent meetings to promote two-way communications between firms and local communities has some utility and could build trust – so long as the industry partner truly integrates the views of local communities and produces a veritable form of collaborative knowledge that is applied to governance and decision making. Furthermore, the focus of the above scholars on firm-local community forms of interaction is helpful, but it excludes the role of state and civil society representatives – vital actors who influence the "trust equation" in fundamental ways – not to mention the importance of governance networks among this trio of stakeholder types in natural resource sectors (see Djomo et al. 2018; Grant et al. 2015; Grant, Balraj, and Mavropoulos-Vagelis 2013; Grant, Djomo, and Krause 2016; Teye 2013). These stakeholders must be included in the communication and meeting structures of the co-generation of knowledge as well, for they possess expertise and an intimate knowledge of extractive resource sector governance challenges.

Conclusion

Mirroring CSR considerations and their attendant global governance frameworks, natural resource sector global supply chains are also quickly evolving at the dawn of the 2020s. To this end, the introduction of blockchain technologies is starting to generate responses from state and non-state actors alike. From the former, the response is one of suspicion, which is understandable. Global supply chains have long resisted the intrusion of the state, with the traditional view being that too much regulation, oversight, taxes, and the like restrict the speed and profitability of these chains. States respond that sovereignty grants them such rights – even if those "rights" are based on norms. States also rely on the norms and widely recognized informal rules that constitute sovereignty to carry out fiscal and monetary policy within their borders. Running budgetary surpluses or deficits, increasing or decreasing the supply of currency, and influencing interest rates via central banks are all based on the assumption that the state is the legitimate instigator of such actions. Cryptocurrencies and other blockchain technologies, some of which might transform the way in which natural resource sectors operate, are making inroads in Africa, especially among entrepreneurs.

Although some might have doubts concerning the *legitimacy* of cryptocurrencies – and many governments see the rise of cryptocurrencies as a threat – the blockchain is a way of *increasing trust* via a transparent series of "promises" set in a "ledger" that is readily verifiable through digital means. These promises are wide ranging, but for entrepreneurs they are a way to ensure that they gain access to (and repay) loans or a way to track a particular mineral or resource throughout the supply chain. Trial uses of blockchain technologies are providing African farmers with access to low-interest loans in order to secure fertilizer, equipment, and other inputs. In turn the loans are repaid via the same blockchain technology once the crops are harvested and sold. IMPACT, a transnational NGO formerly known as Partnership Africa Canada, is working with several partners to enable artisanal and small-scale miners to have their output included in a supply chain that is transparent and that guarantees a fair price. The digital "ledger" is transparent for users, and computers within the blockchain can verify the "promises" underpinning the transactions. If blockchain technologies increase *trust* among users – which is one of their aims and something that advocates expect as blockchains proliferate – their *legitimacy* will grow proportionately.

As Africa continues to draw foreign investment from across the globe, the continent's natural resource sector will be buoyed by such inflows. For instance, from the mid-2000s to the mid-2010s, the amount of foreign investment from the United Kingdom to Africa nearly doubled. As Brexit proceeds and the United Kingdom continues to seek new trade partners and develop existing ones, the annual value of its trade with Africa – currently well into the £30 billion range – is expected to continue to grow as the decade of the 2020s unfolds. Since this increase in UK investment will carry over to extant and emerging parts of Africa's natural resource sectors, Canadian firms will encounter greater competition from firms that espouse a similar set of CSR values and norms. If Canadian natural resource sector firms choose to "rest on the laurels" of the "Canadian way" and do not engage in veritable CSR, they might well face limited access to Africa's vital global supply chains. Africa's natural resource sector will become increasingly crowded, and the legitimacy dynamics of rules, procedures, and processes will intensify rather than abate. Instead of seeking a "social licence to operate," the credo of transnational mining firms in the 2020s might be to secure the "privilege to operate" – especially considering ongoing contestation around how and when an often non-contractual "social licence" can be attained.

With the objective of taking advantage of competing economic interests on the continent, including those from Global South counterparts such as China, Brazil, and India, there is an ongoing quest by several governments to make natural resource exploitation particularly beneficial to domestic populations in ways consistent with broad-based developmental goals. This trend was consolidated in the establishment of the AMV in 2009, and is expected to intensify in the 2020s with more "ownership" over beneficial legislation in the extractive sectors. As Nwapi and Andrews (2017) discuss, the burgeoning trend towards different forms of resource nationalism – or what Ovadia (2016) refers to as "petro-developmentalism" – via local-content-procurement policies reflects African leaders' realization of their competitive advantage in the international commodity market for high-value natural resources such as diamonds, gold, copper, tungsten, oil, and gas.

Also, these internally driven reforms could reverse the erosion of state *legitimacy* and capacity that occurred under such externally driven reforms as structural adjustment programs. Evidence suggests that there is some political will in various African countries to apply local-content policies to all firms, including Canadian companies, operating in the natural resource sectors (Andrews and Nwapi 2018; Nwapi and Andrews 2017; Ovadia 2016). Perhaps these policies will serve as a way to salvage the developmental deficits of CSR activities on the continent or, in some cases, the non-payment of requisite taxes and royalties due host governments. As we postulate for the decade of the 2020s, it remains to be seen if these efforts will be sustained over time and if the local beneficiaries of such developmental policies actually will experience significant improvement in their livelihood or well-being.

NOTES

1 In February 2018, Glencore's chief executive officer expressed the hope that "there would be a consultation with the mining industry before the revised [mining] code is signed into law" (Hume 2018, 15). In recent years, Glencore's relationship with the government of the DRC has been acrimonious over unpaid mining sector royalties totalling approximately US$200 million.
2 See Global Witness (2014) and Resource Matters (2017) for critical assessments of Glencore's operations in the DRC.

BIBLIOGRAPHY

Andrews, Nathan. 2016. "The Challenges of Corporate Social Responsibility (CSR) in Domestic Settings: An Exploration of Mining Regulation vis-à-vis CSR in Ghana." *Resources Policy* 47: 9–17. https://doi.org/10.1016/j.resourpol.2015.11.001.

Andrews, Nathan. 2018. "How Global Norms Matter: The Forward and Backward Linkages of Transparency Norm Diffusion in the Extractive Industry." Paper presented at the International Studies Association annual conference, San Francisco, 5 April.

Andrews, Nathan. 2019a. *Gold Mining and the Discourses of Corporate Social Responsibility in Ghana*. New York: Palgrave Macmillan.

Andrews, Nathan. 2019b. "Normative Spaces and the UN Global Compact for Transnational Corporations: The Norm Diffusion Paradox." *Journal of International Relations and Development* 22 (1): 77–106. https://doi.org/10.1057/s41268-017-0103-3.

Andrews, Nathan, and Chilenye Nwapi. 2018. "Bringing the State Back In Again? The Emerging Developmental State in Africa's Energy Sector." *Energy Research & Social Science* 41 (July): 48–58. https://doi.org/10.1016/j.erss.2018.04.004.

Bowen, Frances, Aloysius Newenham-Kahindi, and Irene Herremans. 2010. "When Suits Meet Roots: The Antecedents and Consequences of Community Engagement Strategy." *Journal of Business Ethics* 95 (2): 297–318. https://doi.org/10.1007/s10551-009-0360-1.

Cain, Terry. 2018. "Scarce, Expensive Cobalt Essential for Electric Cars." *Globe and Mail*, 3 March.

Canada. 2009. "Building the Canadian Advantage: A Corporate Social Responsibility (CSR) Strategy for the Canadian International Extractive Sector." Ottawa. Available online at https://www.international.gc.ca/trade-agreements-accords-commerciaux/topics-domaines/other-autre/csr-strat-rse-2009.aspx?lang=eng.

Canada. 2014. "Doing Business the Canadian Way: A Strategy to Advance Corporate Social Responsibility in Canada's Extractive Sector Abroad." Ottawa. Available online at https://www.international.gc.ca/trade-agreements-accords-commerciaux/topics-domaines/other-autre/csr-strat-rse.aspx?lang=eng.

Canada. 2016. "Canada's Enhanced Corporate Social Responsibility Strategy to Strengthen Canada's Extractive Sector Abroad." Ottawa: Global Affairs Canada. Available online at https://www.international.gc.ca/trade-agreements-accords-commerciaux/topics-domaines/other-autre/csr-strat-rse.aspx?lang=eng.

Canada. 2018. "The Government of Canada Brings Leadership to Responsible Business Conduct Abroad." News Release, 17 January. Ottawa: Global Affairs Canada. Available online at https://www.canada.ca/en/global-affairs/news/2018/01/the_government_ofcanadabringsleadershiptoresponsiblebusinesscond.html.

Compaoré, W.R. Nadège. 2018a. "Escaping the 'Resource Curse' by Localizing Transparency Norms." In *African Actors in International Security: Shaping Contemporary Norms*, edited by Katharina P. Coleman and Thomas K. Tieku, 137–52. Boulder, CO: Lynne Rienner.

Compaoré, W.R. Nadège. 2018b. "Rise of the (Other) Rest? Exploring Small State Agency and Collective Power in International Relations." *International Studies Review* 20 (2): 264–71. https://doi.org/10.1093/isr/viy036.

Djomo, Adrien N., J. Andrew Grant, L. Celestine Fonyikeh-Bomboh, Julie G. Tchoko, Noël H. Fonton, Neal A. Scott, and Denis J. Sonwa. 2018. "Forest Governance and REDD+ in Central Africa: Towards a Participatory Model to Increase Stakeholder Involvement in Carbon Markets." *International Journal of Environmental Studies* 75 (2): 251–66. https://doi.org/10.1080/00207233.2017.1347358.

Enns, Charis, Nathan Andrews, and J. Andrew Grant. 2018. "Security for Whom? Analysing Hybrid Security Governance in Africa's Extractive Sectors." Paper presented at the International Studies Association annual conference, San Francisco, 6 April.

Franck, Thomas. 1992. "The Emerging Right to Democratic Governance." *American Journal of International Law* 86 (1): 46–91. https://doi.org/10.2307/2203138.

Gehrman, Joel, Lianne M. Lefsrud, and Stewart Fast. 2017. "Social License to Operate: Legitimacy by Another Name?" *Canadian Public Administration* 60 (2): 293–317. https://doi.org/10.1111/capa.12218.

Global Witness. 2014. *Glencore and the Gatekeeper: How the World's Largest Commodities Trader Made a Friend of Congo's President $67 Million Richer.* London: Global Witness.

Grant, J. Andrew. 2018. "Agential Constructivism and Change in World Politics." *International Studies Review* 20 (2): 255–63. https://doi.org/10.1093/isr/viy021.

Grant, J. Andrew. Dianne Balraj, and Georgia Mavropoulos-Vagelis. 2013. "Reflections on Network Governance in Africa's Forestry Sector." *Natural Resources Forum* 37 (4): 269–79. https://doi.org/10.1111/1477-8947.12028.

Grant, J. Andrew, Adrien N. Djomo, and Maria G. Krause. 2016. "Afro-Optimism Re-Invigorated? Reflections on the Glocal Networks of Sexual Identity, Health, and Natural Resources in Africa." *Global Change, Peace & Security* 28 (3): 317–28. https://doi.org/10.1080/14781158.2016.1193847.

Grant, J. Andrew, Dianne Balraj, Jeremy Davison, and Georgia Mavropoulos-Vagelis. 2015. "Network Governance and the African Timber Organization: Prospects for Regional Forestry Governance in Africa." In *New Approaches to the Governance of Natural Resources: Insights from Africa*, edited by J. Andrew Grant, W.R. Nadège Compaoré, and Matthew I. Mitchell, 154–80. London: Palgrave Macmillan.

Hume, Neil. 2018. "Glencore Sets $2.9bn Payout As Earnings Soar." *Financial Times*, 22 February.

Idemudia, Uwafiokun. 2014. "Corporate Social Responsibility and Development in Africa: Issues and Possibilities." *Geography Compass* 8 (7): 421–35. https://doi.org/10.1111/gec3.12143.

Liberal Party of Canada. 2011. *Your Family. Your Future. Your Canada*. Ottawa: Liberal Party of Canada.

Mayanja, Evelyn Namakula Birabwa. 2018. "People's Experiences and Perceptions of War and Peace in South Kivu Province, Eastern Democratic Republic of Congo." PhD diss., University of Manitoba.

Mercer-Mapstone, Lucy, Will Rifkin, Kieren Moffat, and Winnifred Louis. 2017. "Conceptualising the Role of Dialogue in Social Licence to Operate." *Resources Policy* 54: 137–46. https://doi.org/10.1016/j.resourpol.2017.09.007.

Mitchell, Ronald K., Bradley R. Agle, and Donna J. Wood. 1997. "Toward a Theory of Stakeholder Identification and Salience: Defining the Principle of Who and What Really Counts." *Academy of Management Review* 22 (4): 853–86. https://doi.org/10.5465/amr.1997.9711022105.

National Roundtables on Corporate Social Responsibility (CSR) and the Canadian Extractive Industry in Developing Countries, Advisory Group Report. 2007. Ottawa: Advisory Group to the Roundtable Process and Government of Canada.

Nwapi, Chilenye, and Nathan Andrews. 2017. "A New Developmental State in Africa: Evaluating Recent State Interventions vis-à-vis Resource Extraction in Kenya, Tanzania, and Rwanda." *McGill Journal of Sustainable Development Law* 13: 223–67.

Ovadia, Jesse Salah. 2016. "Local Content Policies and Petro-Development in Sub-Saharan Africa: A Comparative Analysis." *Resources Policy* 49: 20–30. https://doi.org/10.1016/j.resourpol.2016.04.003.

Parsons, Richard, Justine Lacey, and Kieren Moffat. 2014. "Maintaining Legitimacy of a Contested Practice: How the Minerals Industry Understands Its 'Social Licence to Operate'." *Resources Policy* 41 (September): 83–90. https://doi.org/10.1016/j.resourpol.2014.04.002.

PDAC (Prospectors & Developers Association of Canada). 2018. "Environmental & Social Responsibility Award." *CORE: The Voice of Mineral Exploration* (Winter): 9.

Resource Matters. 2017. "Deciphering the $440 Million Discount for Glencore's DR Congo Mines." November. Available online at https://resourcematters. org/deciphering-440-million-discount-glencore-congo-mines.

Teye, Joseph K. 2013. "Analysing Forest Resource Governance in Africa: Proposition for an Integrated Policy Network Model." *Forest Policy and Economics* 26: 63–70. https://doi.org/10.1016/j.forpol.2012.08.012.

Wilburn, Kathleen M., and Ralph Wilburn. 2011. "Achieving Social License to Operate Using Stakeholder Theory." *Journal of International Business Ethics* 4 (2): 3–16. Available online at https://www.researchgate.net/ publication/284663470_Achieving_social_license_to_operate_using_ stakeholder_theory.

Winn, Conrad, Melissa Jennings, and Matthew I. Mitchell. 2015. "Bridging the Governance Gap in South Sudan: Connecting Policy-Makers to Populations in Africa's Newest Oil-Producing Country." In *New Approaches to the Governance of Natural Resources: Insights from Africa*, edited by J. Andrew Grant, W.R. Nadège Compaoré, and Matthew I. Mitchell, 113–28. London: Palgrave Macmillan.

Yates, Douglas A. 2015. "The Rise and Fall of Oil-Rentier States in Africa." In *New Approaches to the Governance of Natural Resources: Insights from Africa*, edited by J. Andrew Grant, W.R. Nadège Compaoré, and Matthew I. Mitchell, 45–64. London: Palgrave Macmillan.

York, Geoffrey. 2018. "Katanga Mining Faces Threat from Congo Company." *Global and Mail*, 24 April. Available online at https://www.theglobeandmail. com/business/article-katanga-mining-faces-threat-from-congo-company/.

Contributors

Raynold Wonder Alorse is a Joseph-Armand Bombardier Canada Graduate Scholar (CGS) and doctoral candidate in the Department of Political Studies at Queen's University, Kingston. He is one of the few recipients of a special Social Sciences and Humanities Research Council of Canada (SSHRC) award in honour of Nelson Mandela, which celebrates Mandela's legacy, leadership, and tireless pursuit of peace, democracy, justice, and freedom through learning, understanding, and education. Alorse's academic credentials and leadership qualities were recognized via the receipt of the Nelson Mandela award and Nepean's Canada 150 Anniversary Medal of Excellence for outstanding community service. His research on corporate social responsibility (CSR), natural resources, and mining policy has been published in *Contemporary Politics* and *Encyclopedia of Mineral and Energy Policy*. Alorse was a Graduate Research Fellow with the Queen's University SSHRC-funded Partnership Development Project entitled *Global Actors and Community-Level Security: Developing Best Practices*, which examines the CSR aspects of security in mining areas. Alorse also serves as Director of Policy and Research for Public Governance International (PGI) in Ottawa, where he has completed policy case studies focusing on Canadian defence and environmental sustainability, Canada's smart-city approach, and boosting civic pride through environmental citizenship and community self-organization.

Nathan Andrews is an assistant professor of Global and International Studies at the University of Northern British Columbia (UNBC). Dr Andrews was a 2018 Faculty of Arts and Science Visiting Scholar at Queen's University, and his scholarly output has been recognized by awards from the Trudeau Foundation, SSHRC, and the Banting Postdoctoral Fellowship Program, among others. He was selected as a

Finalist for a 2017 SSHRC Talent Award. He recently received the University Excellence Award in Research (May 2019) at the UNBC. Dr Andrews has authored or co-authored several journal articles and book chapters on topics ranging from foreign aid policy to international relations theory to corporate social responsibility and natural resource governance to economic development. His findings have been published in scholarly journals such as *World Development, Resources Policy, International Journal, Energy Research and Social Science, Business and Society Review*, and *Africa Today*, among others. The present book is his fourth co-edited volume, and Dr Andrews has authored two monographs, including *Gold Mining and the Discourses of Corporate Social Responsibility in Ghana* (Palgrave Macmillan, 2019).

Timothy Adivilah Balag'kutu is a doctoral candidate in Global Governance and Human Security in the John W. McCormack Graduate School of Policy and Global Studies at the University of Massachusetts, Boston. His doctoral research straddles natural resource governance, focusing on artisanal and small-scale mining, and environmental politics/governance. His research interests also include electoral politics, democratization, governance, and sustainable development in Africa. His research has been published in *The Routledge Handbook of Environmental Conflict and Peacebuilding* (2018), *A Research Agenda for Global Environmental Politics* (Edward Elgar, 2018), United Nations University Institute for Natural Resources in Africa (UNU-INRA) Working Papers and Policy Briefs, and *Extractive Industries and Society*. Balag'kutu has obtained two MA degrees, in Political Science and International Affairs (African Studies), from Ohio University. He holds a BA degree in Political Science and Swahili from the University of Ghana. He also studied at the University of Dar es Salaam in Tanzania on a Ghana Government Language Proficiency Fellowship. Balag'kutu is also an Adjunct Lecturer in the Department of History and Society at Babson College, Massachusetts, where he teaches Global Environmental Activism with a focus on the extractive sector, Political Economy of Africa, and Introduction to Contemporary Africa.

Paula Butler is a former CUSO-Nigeria teacher, and worked for over a decade in the international civil society sector focused on economic justice and human rights. In that capacity she travelled extensively across the African continent, including the leading mining countries of Tanzania, Zambia, South Africa, and the DRC. In 2001 she participated in an international team that travelled to Tanzania to investigate allegations of deaths at the Bulyanhulu gold mine. Following doctoral studies at University of Toronto in critical race theory and anti-racism education, she has taught courses on human rights, social movements, critical race theory, and sustainable development. She currently teaches graduate courses in the Balsillie School of International Affairs and the Institute for Globalization and the Human Condition at McMaster University, and undergraduate courses in the Department of Global Studies at Wilfrid Laurier University. Dr Butler is the author of *Colonial Extractions: Race and Canadian Mining in Contemporary Africa* (University of Toronto Press, 2015). She has published scholarly articles on community-corporate tensions at the North Mara gold mine in Tanzania and on the Plan Canada-IAMGOLD corporate social responsibility project in Burkina Faso. She is currently researching corporate tax evasion involving Canadian companies in Tanzania.

Bonnie Campbell is professor emeritus in the Department of Political Science at l'Université du Québec à Montréal. Dr Campbell is a long-time scholar of the political economy of natural resources in Africa. She has published in numerous scholarly journals and has authored, edited, or co-edited sixteen volumes – many of which examine mining and regulation in Africa. Her most recent edited books include: *La responsabilité sociale des entreprises dans le secteur minier: réponse ou obstacle aux enjeux de légitimité et de développement en Afrique?* (with Myriam Laforce; Presses de l'Université du Québec, 2016); *Les transformations des politiques de cooperation: secteurs agricoles et miniers au Canada et en France* (with Jean-Jacques Gabas, Denis Pesche, and Vincent Ribier; Presses de l'Université du Québec, 2016); *Modes of Governance and Revenue Flows in African Mining* (Palgrave Macmillan, 2013), and *Pouvoir et régulation dans le secteur minier: leçons à partir de l'expérience canadienne* (with Myriam Laforce and Bruno Sarrasin; Presses de l'Université du Québec, 2012). Dr Campbell was a member of the Advisory Group to the National Round Tables on Social Responsibility and the Canadian Extractive Industry in Developing Countries appointed by the Canadian federal government (2006–07). From 2007 to 2011 she was a member of the International Study Group on the review of mining regimes in Africa of the United Nations Economic Commission for Africa. Dr Campbell has been a Fellow of the Royal Society of Canada since 2012.

W.R. Nadège Compaoré is a Provost Postdoctoral Fellow at the University of Toronto. Prior to this, she was a Postdoctoral Fellow at the Balsillie School of International Affairs with the University of Waterloo, a Research Analyst at the Canadian Institute for Advanced Research, and a SSHRC Postdoctoral Fellow in the Department of Social Science at York University. Her research interests are anchored within International Relations theory and explore two interconnected areas. First, she examines discourses and dynamics of sovereignty, legitimacy, and agency in natural resource governance and global environmental politics, with an empirical focus on both mineral-rich and oil-rich African countries. Second, she critically examines knowledge production in IR, by locating gender and race in international politics. Nadège's research draws from extensive fieldwork in Gabon, Ghana, and South Africa, and has been funded by SSHRC, the Centre for International Governance Innovation, and the Canadian International Development Agency. Her work has been published in journals such as *International Studies Review, Études internationales, Millennium: Journal of International Studies,* and *Contemporary Politics.* She is co-editor of *New Approaches to the Governance of Natural Resources: Insights from Africa* (Palgrave, 2015). Nadège holds a PhD in Political Studies from Queen's University.

Jeffrey Davidson left Queen's University in May 2015, where he was professor of Applied Mineral Economics and Mining Sustainability, to serve as Canada's Extractive Sector CSR Counsellor. He was tasked to implement the government's enhanced 2014 CSR strategy, "Doing Business the Canadian Way," with Canadian oil, gas, and mining companies operating abroad. During his three-year tenure as Canada's CSR counsellor, his office published two substantial country-company studies (Honduras and Panama) and the *CSR Standards Navigation Tool.* Prior to his time at Queen's, he spent seventeen years in the field working on peace-making and relationship-building initiatives with Placer Dome Latin America in Venezuela (e.g., with community-based artisanal miners) and Chile, and Rio Tinto in Australia (e.g., with traditional land owners in Jabiru) and the United States (e.g., co-authored a resource guide for integrating gender considerations, *Why Gender Matters*). Davidson also taught mineral economics at McGill University (1984–95), spent four years at the World Bank, and was the principal architect of Nigeria's mining sector reform project, *Sustainable Management of Mineral Resources* (2005). He was mining advisor to the Northern Quebec Inuit in their negotiation of the Raglan Agreement (1994) with Falconbridge Corporation. This agreement rapidly became the benchmark for negotiating impact and benefits agreements between mining companies and First Nations in Canada. Davidson contributed to the writing of *Mining Contracts: How to Read and Understand Them* (Columbia University, 2013).

Charis Enns is a lecturer in International Development in the Department of Geography at the University of Sheffield. She is also an Affiliate Researcher with the East African Institute at the Aga Khan University in Kenya. Prior to her arrival at Sheffield, Dr Enns was a SSHRC Postdoctoral Fellow in the Department of Political Science and International Development Studies at the University of Guelph. Her research interests include corporate social responsibility and corporate-community engagement practices around sites of large-scale investment. Her recent academic research has been published in *Journal of Peasant Studies*, *Geoforum*, and *Extractive Industries and Society*. Dr Enns has served on the board of the Canadian Association for the Study of International Development, and conducted consultancies and policy research for the Centre for International Governance Innovation, the Overseas Development Institute, and Global Affairs Canada, as well as for civil society groups in East Africa, related to resource extraction, human rights, and rural livelihoods.

J. Andrew Grant is undergraduate chair and associate professor of Political Studies at Queen's University. He is the recipient of an Early Researcher Award from the government of Ontario's Ministry of Research and Innovation for analyses of governance dynamics in natural resource sectors. His findings on natural resources and regional security based on fieldwork conducted across Africa have appeared in *International Studies Review*, *Natural Resources Forum*, *Extractive Industries and Society*, *Resources Policy*, *Journal of Cleaner Production*, *International Journal of Environmental Studies*, *Contemporary Politics*, *Commonwealth & Comparative Politics*, *Global Change, Peace & Security*, *Social Science Quarterly*, and *Land Use Policy*. He also co-edited *New Approaches to the Governance of Natural Resources: Insights from Africa* (Palgrave Macmillan, 2015). He is a Faculty Fellow with the Queen's Centre for International and Defence Policy, the Southern African Research Centre, the Centre for the Study of Democracy and Diversity, and a Research Fellow with the Centre for the Study of Security and Development at Dalhousie University. Dr Grant has advised Canadian, US, British, and German policy makers, and he served as program chair for the 2017 International Studies Association annual conference.

Uwafiokun Idemudia is an associate professor in the Department of Social Science at York University and program coordinator for the African Studies and International Development Studies Programs. His research interests are in the areas of critical development studies, political economy, and political ecology approaches to natural resource extraction in developing countries, business and development, and issues of governance, transparency, and accountability in resource-rich African countries. Dr Idemudia is also interested in the relationship between development and conflict, as well as environmental security. He has published works in a number of journals, including *Journal of Business Ethics, Organization and Environment, Business Strategy and Environment,* and *African Security.* He has recently published two books: *Africapitalism: Rethinking the Role of Business in Africa* (Cambridge University Press) and *Africapitalism: Sustainable Business and Development* (Routledge).

Nketti Johnston-Taylor is an instructor at the University of Calgary in the Department of Political Science and Social Work. She is also an adjunct assistant professor at Saint Mary's University in Calgary, with a focus on economics and economic development. In Calgary, she has taken senior and executive roles at The United Way and the Coalition for Equal Access to Education as the executive director. Her research interests include Africa, its natural resources, the continent's developmental challenges, and human development. Dr Johnston-Taylor is a member of the Canadian Political Science Association, and was a lead researcher for a SSHRC Knowledge Synthesis Grant at the University of Calgary's Department of Political Science in 2016. The project explored the role of Canada's extractive companies in developing countries. Her recent scholarly article in *Resources Policy* focuses on environmental governance challenges in Sierra Leone's mining sector. Dr Johnston-Taylor is passionate about international and local development, and has had considerable research, strategic planning, project management, and leadership experience. Dr Johnston-Taylor holds a PhD from the University of Leeds, and her doctoral research analysed the effectiveness of natural resource governance initiatives in addressing developmental challenges in Africa, with a focus on environmental governance in Sierra Leone.

Cynthia Kwakyewah is a PhD student at the University of Oxford (UK) with academic interests in business and human rights, corporate social responsibility, sustainable development, management of natural resources in the Global South, governance and politics in Sub-Saharan Africa and issues of social justice. Her doctoral study seeks to better understand the drivers and inhibitors of companies' (non)implementation of human rights principles. Prior to her doctoral studies, Cynthia completed a bachelor's degree in International

Development Studies and a Master of Arts in Interdisciplinary Studies with a specialization in Business and International Human Rights Law from York University (Canada). In 2019, Cynthia received the Governor General's Gold Medal, Canada's most prestigious academic award for students. Her work has been published in peer-reviewed academic journals such as *Corporate Social Responsibility and Environmental Management, Citizenship Education Research Journal*, and *The Transnational Human Rights Review*.

Jason J. McSparren has a PhD from the Global Governance and Human Security program at the McCormack Graduate School, University of Massachusetts, Boston. He was a pre-doctoral fellow (2017–18) for the West African Research Association, and a research assistant for a multiyear project funded by the Qatar National Research Foundation entitled "Natural Resource Governance in Africa, Promoting a Qatari Perspective and Economic Diversification." His doctoral research investigates the political-institutional norms of governance at the national and subnational levels of natural resource governance in Mali. McSparren's findings have been published in scholarly journals such as *African Solutions Journal* and *Palgrave Communications* and by research centres such as the London School of Economics Middle East Centre. His broader research interests include the political economy of natural resources, multistakeholder governance mechanisms, migration, peace, and conflict in relation to natural resource extraction and security dynamics in the Sahara-Sahel region.

David W. Orr is an international development consultant with Mott MacDonald in London. His work focuses on promoting inclusive private sector and trade growth in the Middle East and South Asia. Having recently completed his MPhil at the University of Cambridge with Distinction, Orr is continuing to research natural resource governance in East Africa – in particular, the implications of political devolution to strengthen peripheral voices in natural resource governance processes. He holds a BA (Hons) from Queen's University, where he received the Arts and Science Undergraduate Society's highest award for academic and extracurricular contributions. Orr has conducted field research in Southern Africa and East Africa, and his findings have been published in *Extractive Industries and Society, BMJ Global Health*, and Harvard University's *Africa Policy Journal*. He is also the co-founder of the State of Things, a multiplatform initiative to spur youth engagement in politics.

Shingirai Taodzera is a doctoral candidate in International Development at the University of Ottawa, and the inaugural dissertation fellow (2017–19) at Wellesley College, Massachusetts. Shingirai is also the Associate Director for the Freedom Project at Wellesley College for the 2019–20 academic year. He has an MA in Comparative Political Science from Dalhousie University, where he held a Southern African Student Education Programme scholarship. He also earned an MA in International Relations (Political Economy) from the University of the Witwatersrand, Johannesburg, where he was a Canon Collins scholar. His doctoral dissertation investigates the political effects of the nascent oil industry in Uganda, and his research interests broadly revolve around post-colonial state building and the political economy of extractive natural resources in sub-Saharan Africa. The Ontario Trillium Scholarship (University of Ottawa), Andrew W. Mellon Foundation (United States), Woodrow Wilson National Fellowship Foundation (United States), Freedom Project (Wellesley College), Social Sciences Research Council (United States), and International Human Rights Exchange (Bard College) have supported his scholarly work. Taodzera also writes monthly country monitoring reports for business audiences, on behalf of a UK-based international consulting company, and provides analyses for media organizations, including the *Wall Street Journal*.

Index